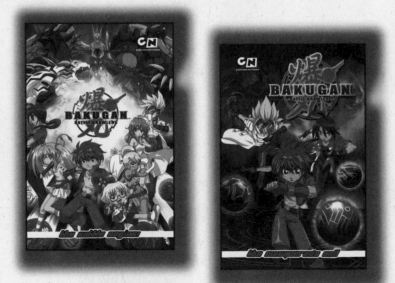
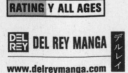

TOMARE!

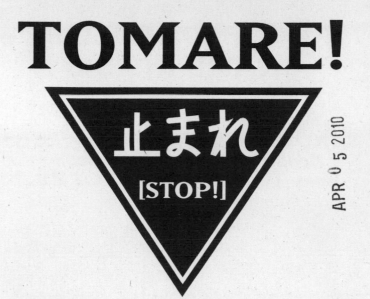

止まれ

[STOP!]

APR 05 2010

You're going the wrong way!

Manga is a completely different
type of reading experience.

To start at the *beginning*,
go to the *end*!

That's right! Authentic manga is read the traditional Japanese way—
from right to left, exactly the opposite of how American books are
read. It's easy to follow: Just go to the other end of the book and read
each page—and each panel—from right side to left side, starting at
the top right. Now you're experiencing manga as it was meant to be!

FAIRY TAIL

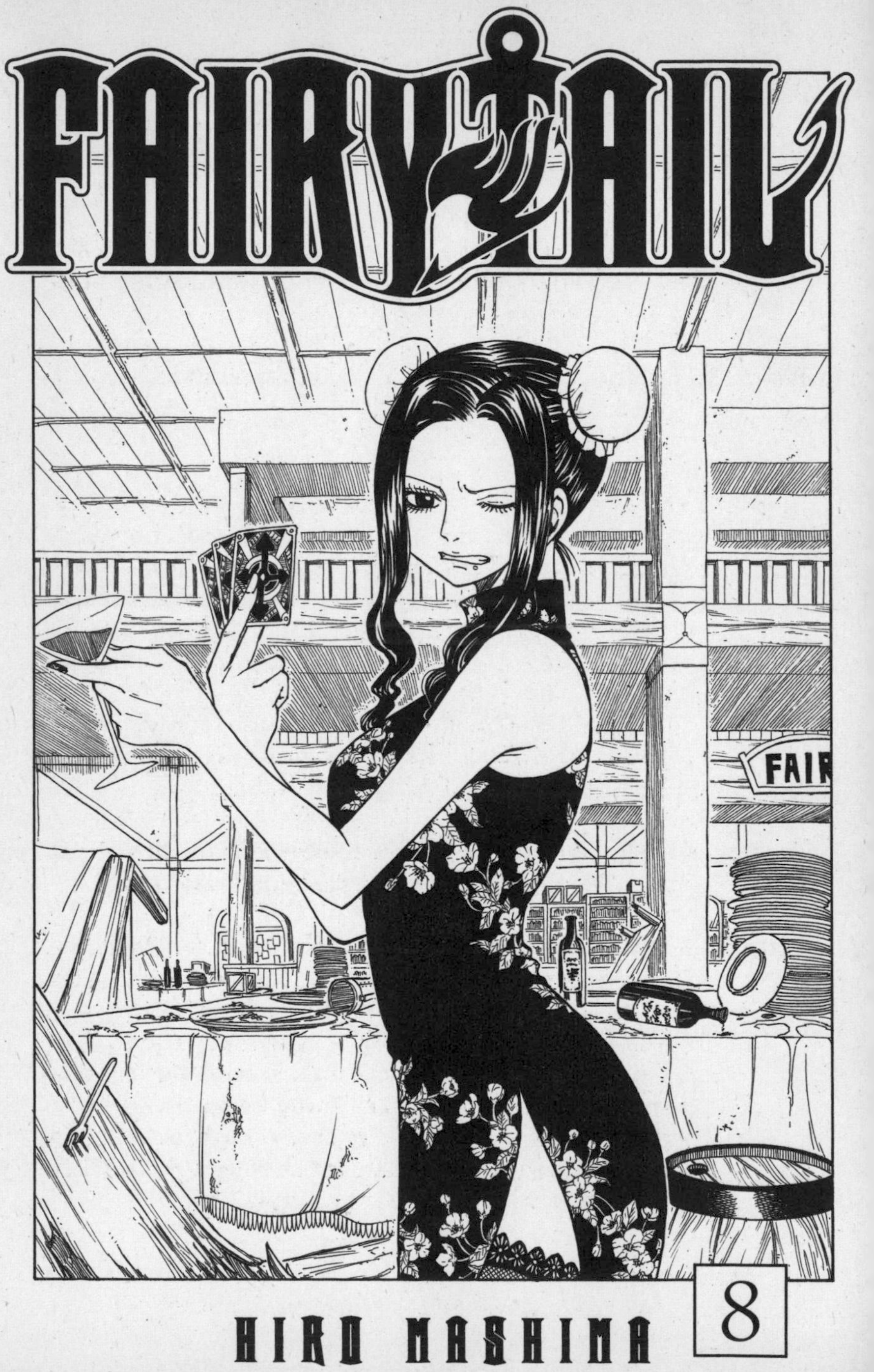
FAIR

8

HIRO MASHIMA

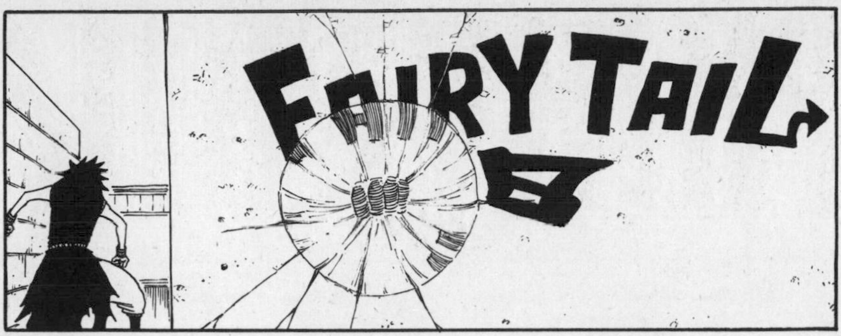
FAIRY TAIL
8

FAIRY TAIL

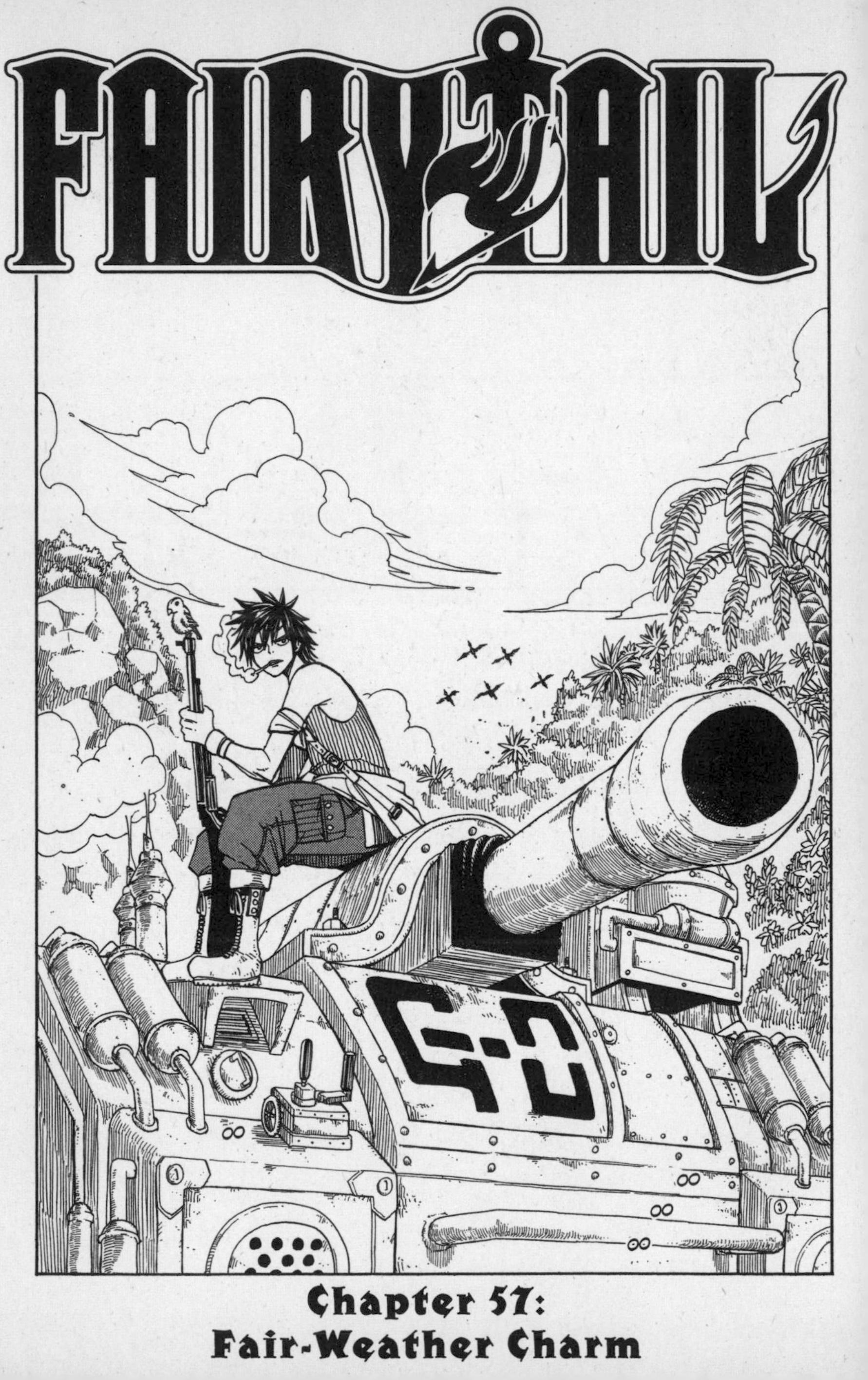

Chapter 57: Fair-Weather Charm

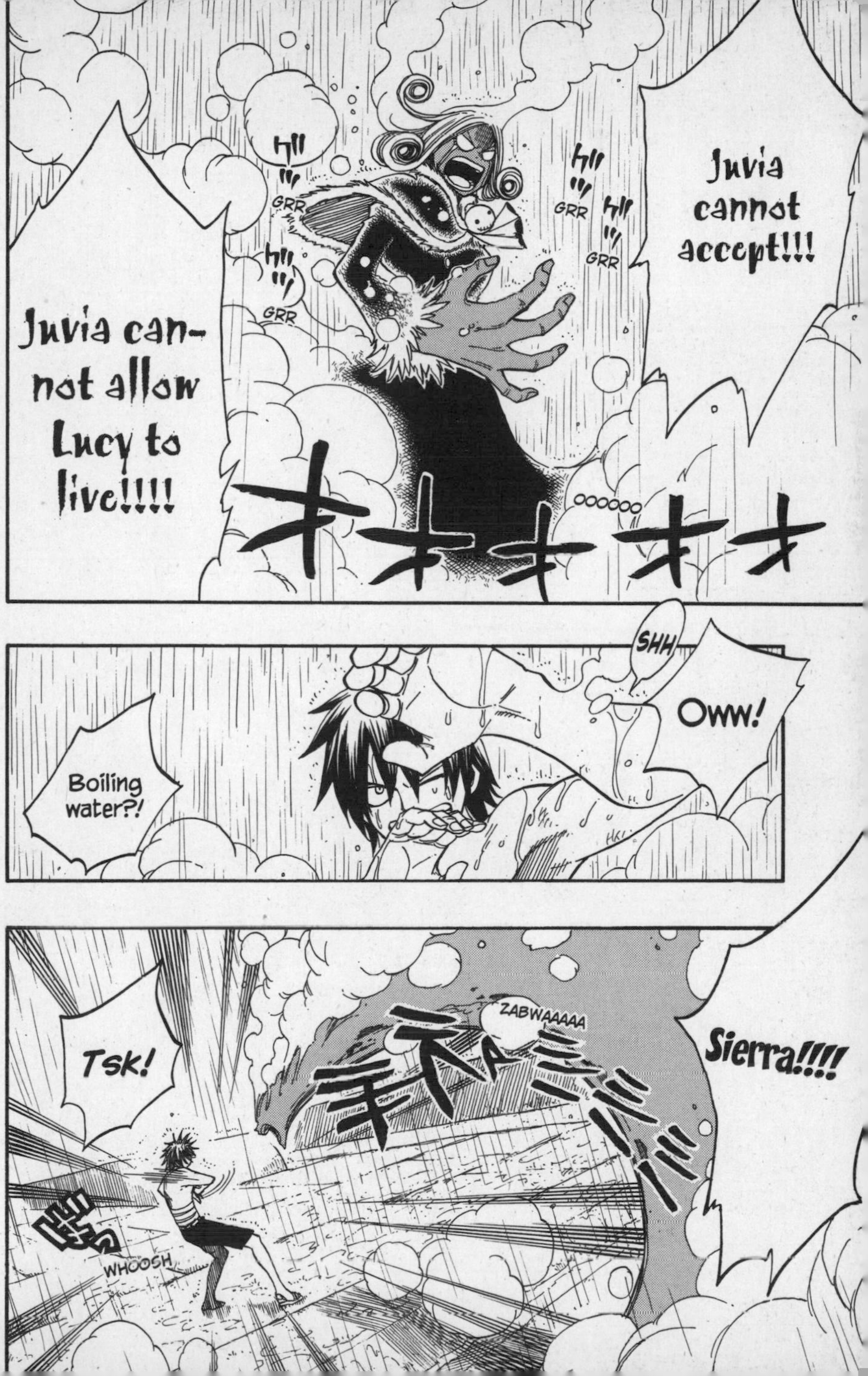
Juvia cannot accept!!!
GRR
GRR
GRR
GRR
Juvia cannot allow Lucy to live!!!!
OOOOOO
SHH
Oww!
Boiling water?!
Sierra!!!!
ZABWAAAAA
Tsk!
WHOOSH

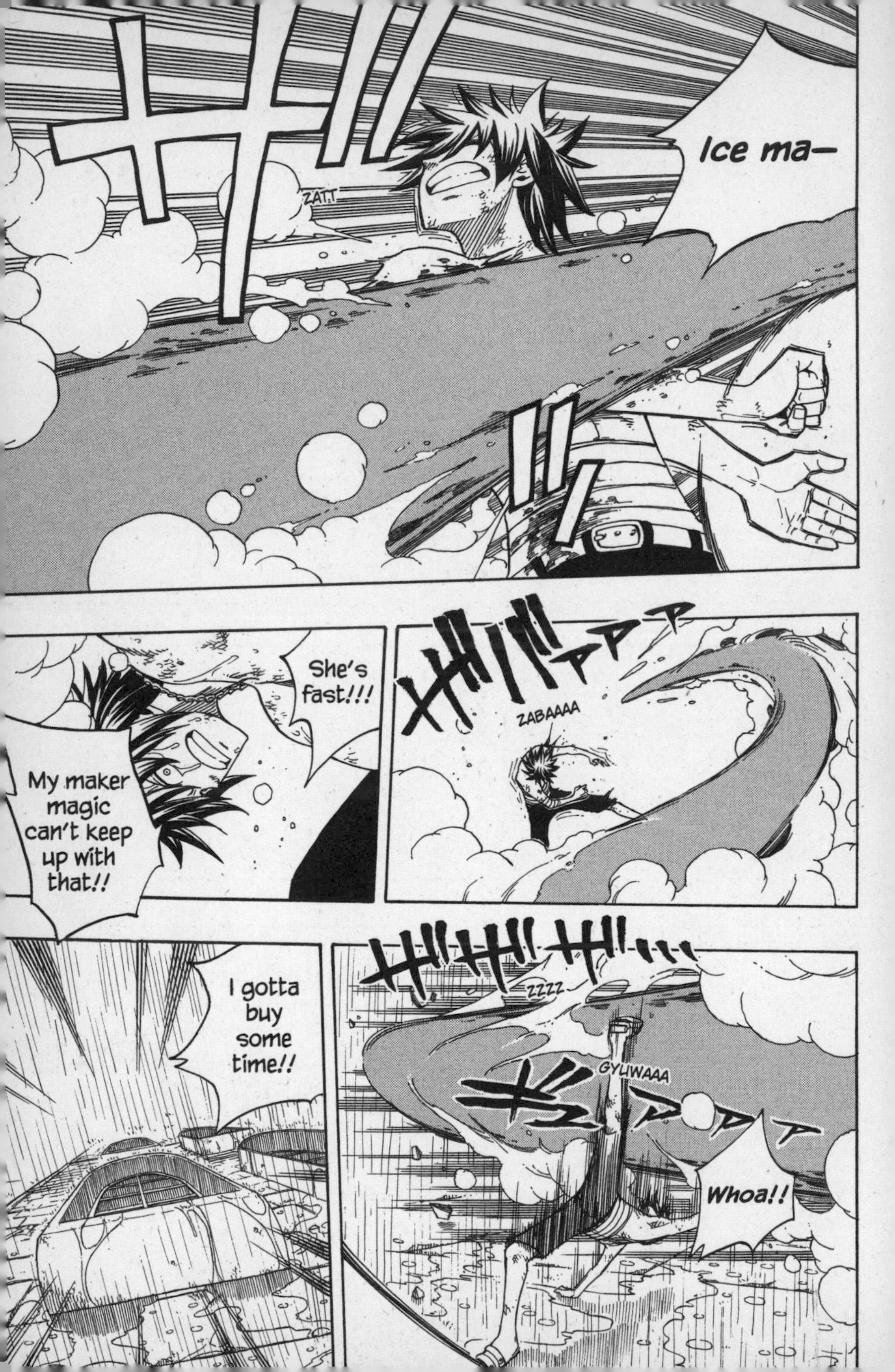
ZATT
Ice ma—
ZABAAAA
She's fast!!!
My maker magic can't keep up with that!!
ZZZZ
GYUWAAA
Whoa!!
I gotta buy some time!!

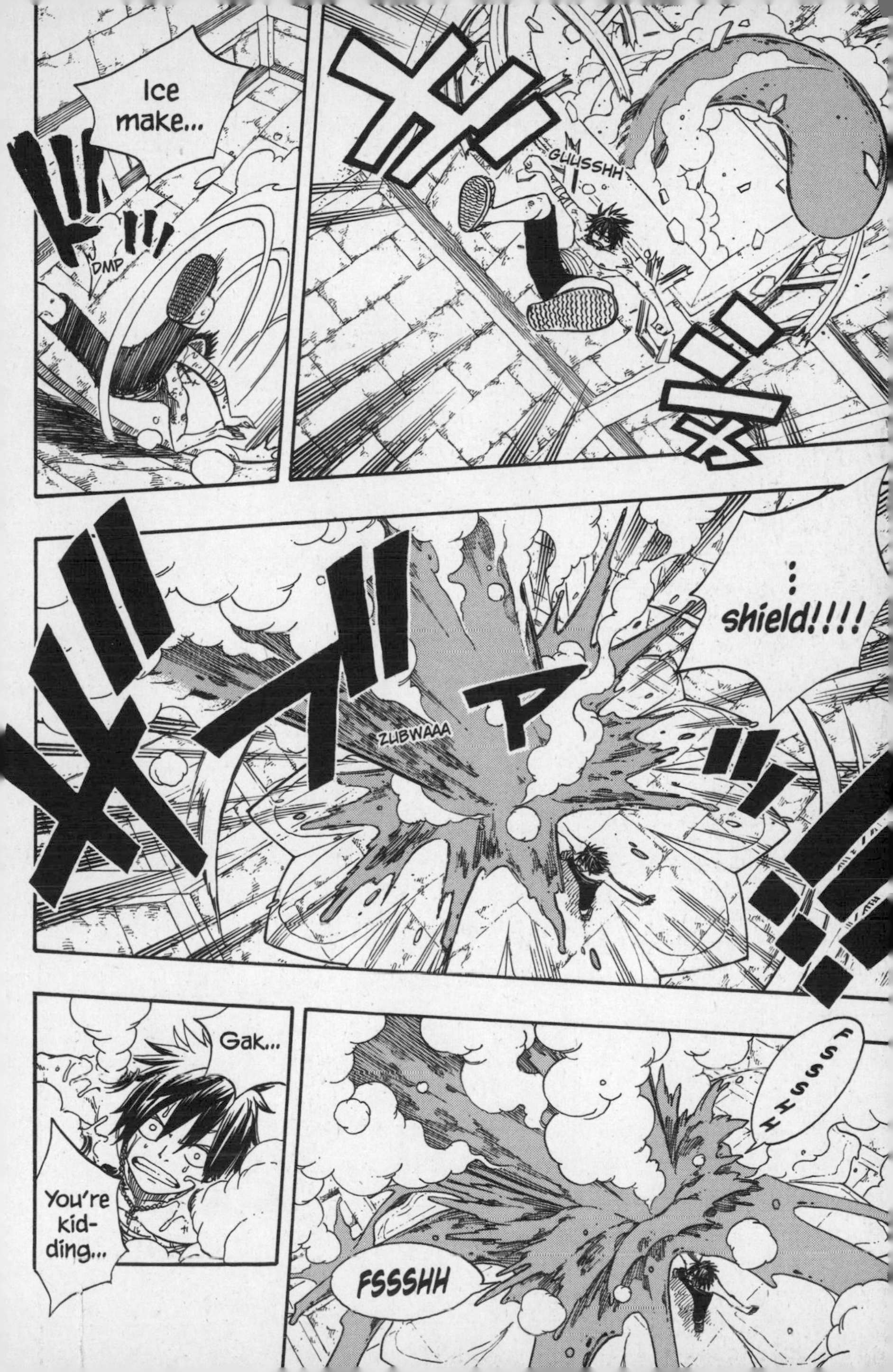
GUUSSHH
Ice make...
DMP
...shield!!!!
ZUBWAAA
FSSSHH
FSSSHH
Gak...
You're kidding...

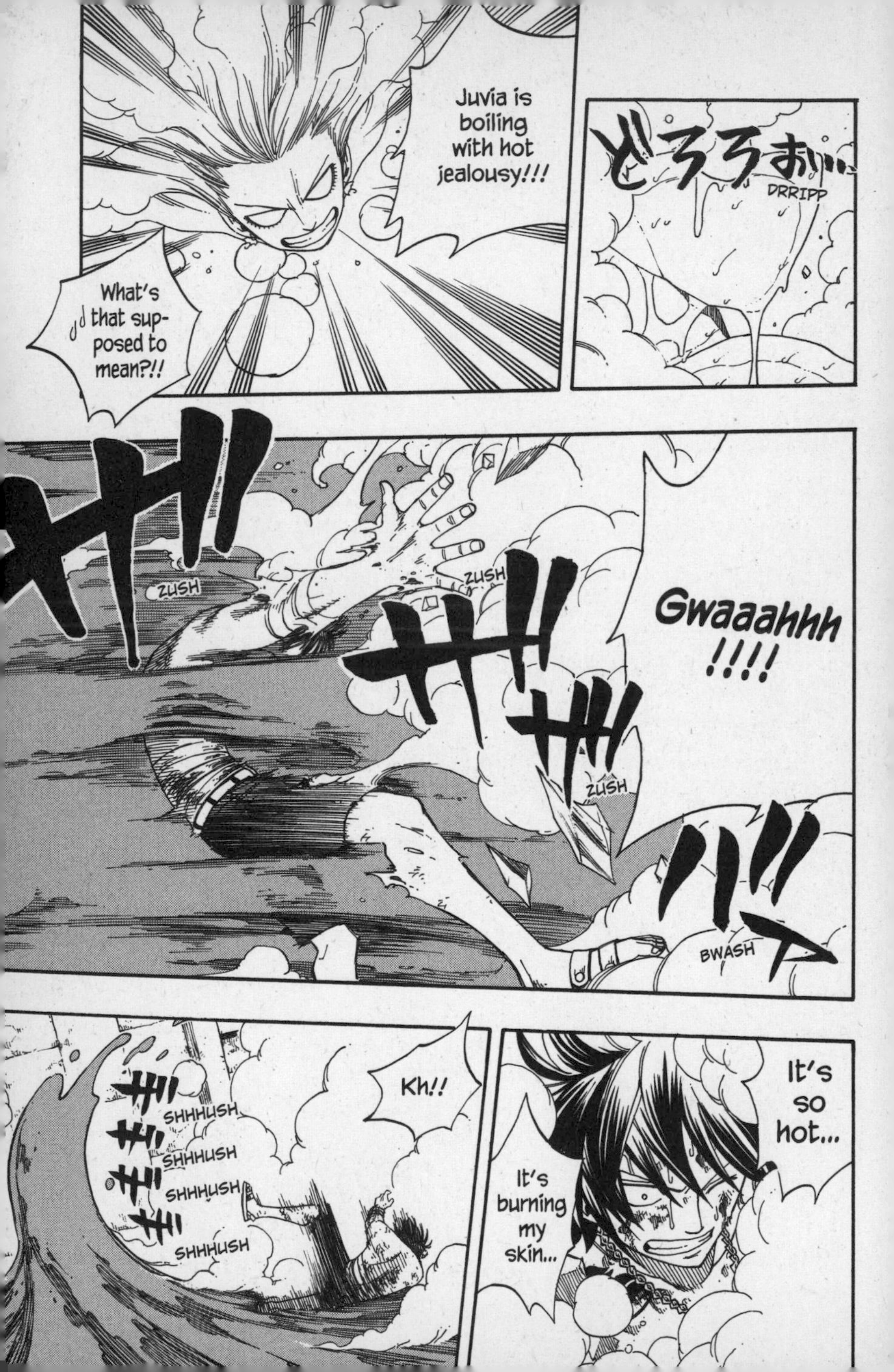
DRRIPP
Juvia is boiling with hot jealousy!!!
What's that supposed to mean?!!
Gwaaahhh!!!!
ZUSH
ZUSH
ZUSH
BWASH
It's so hot...
It's burning my skin...
Kh!!
SHHHUSH
SHHHUSH
SHHHUSH
SHHHUSH

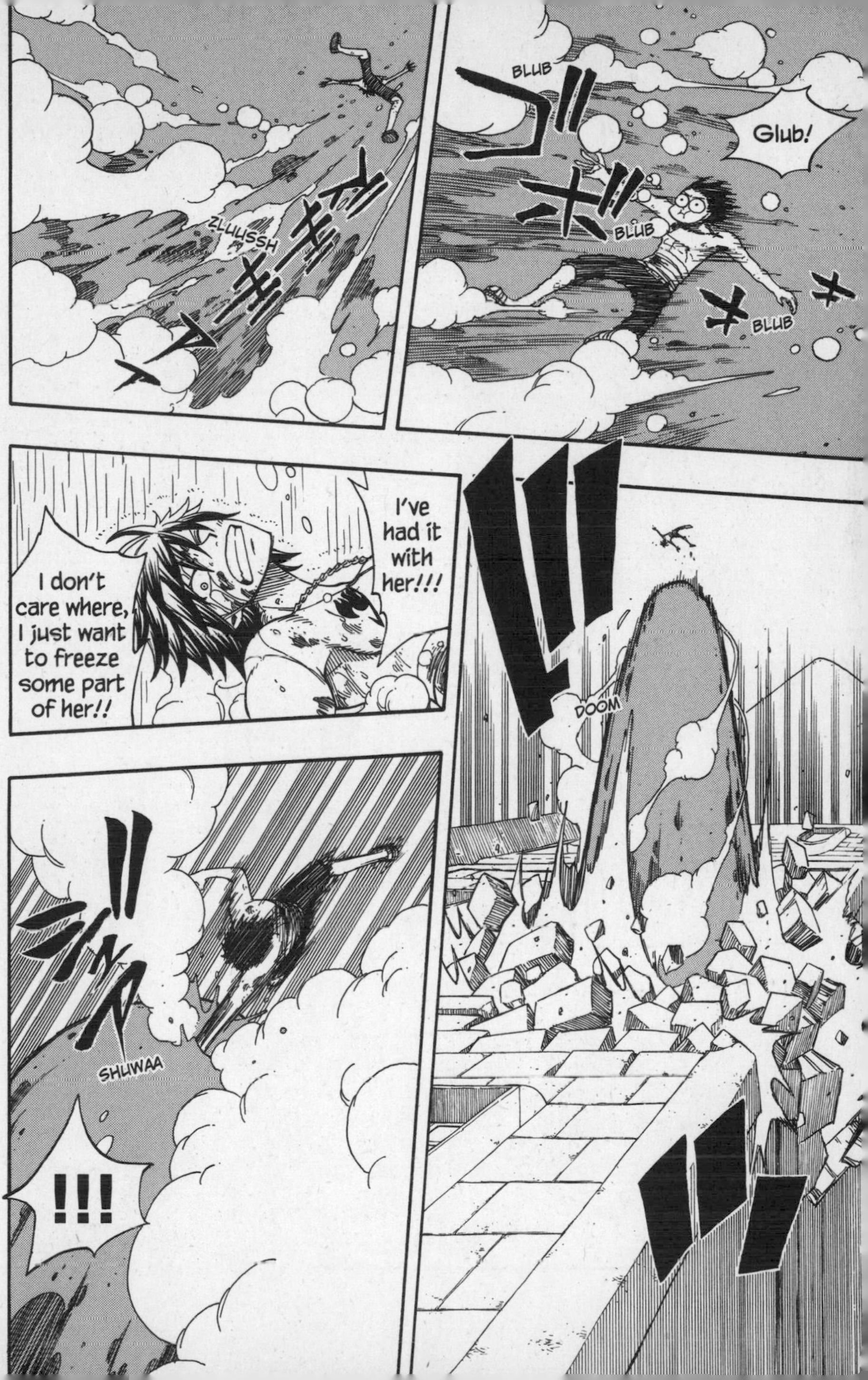
BLUB
Glub!
BLUB
BLUB
ZLUUSSH
DOOM
I've had it with her!!!
I don't care where, I just want to freeze some part of her!!
SHUWAA
!!!

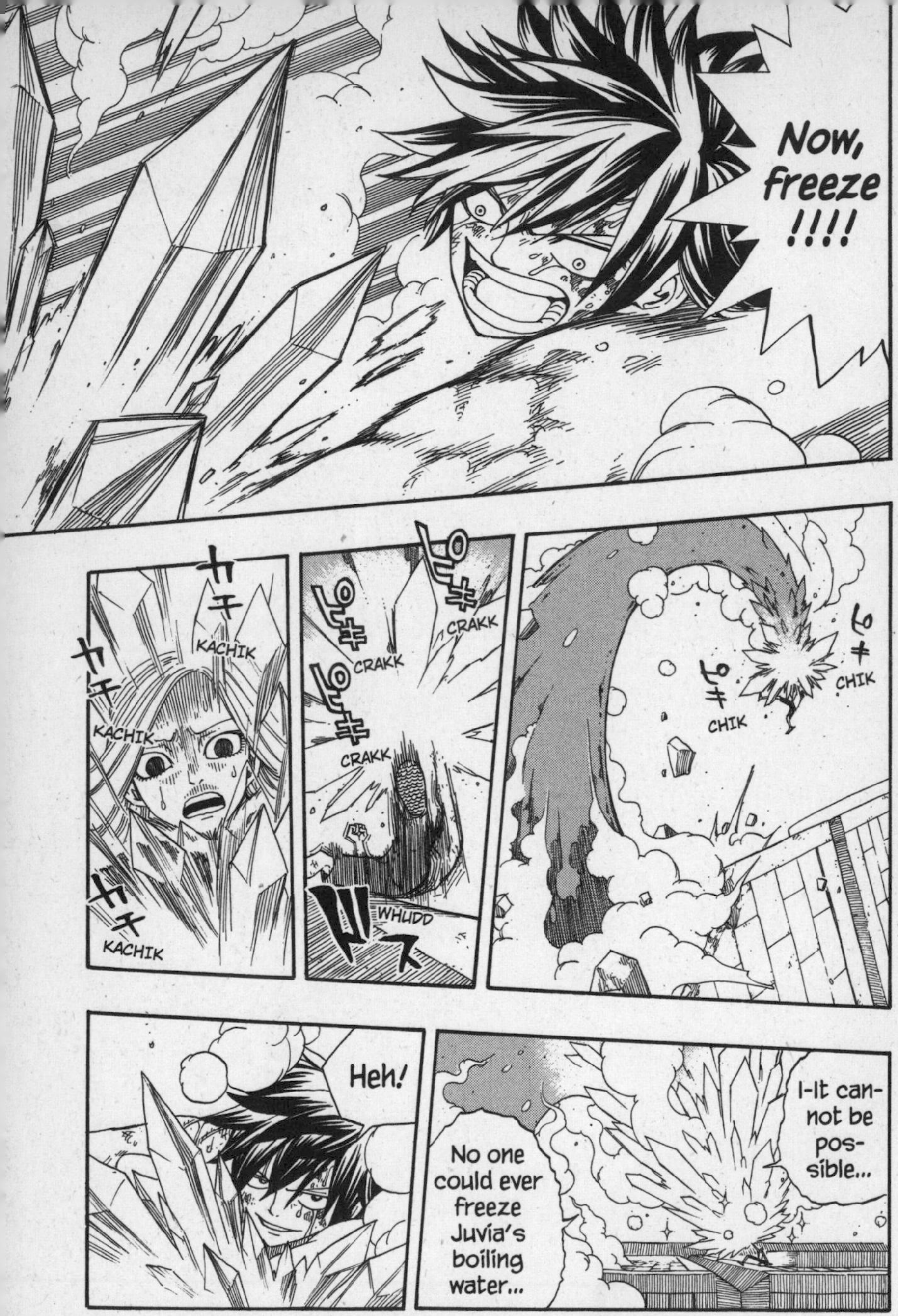
Now, freeze !!!!
CHIK
CHIK
CRAKK
CRAKK
CRAKK
WHUDD
KACHIK
KACHIK
KACHIK
I-It cannot be possible...
No one could ever freeze Juvia's boiling water...
Heh!

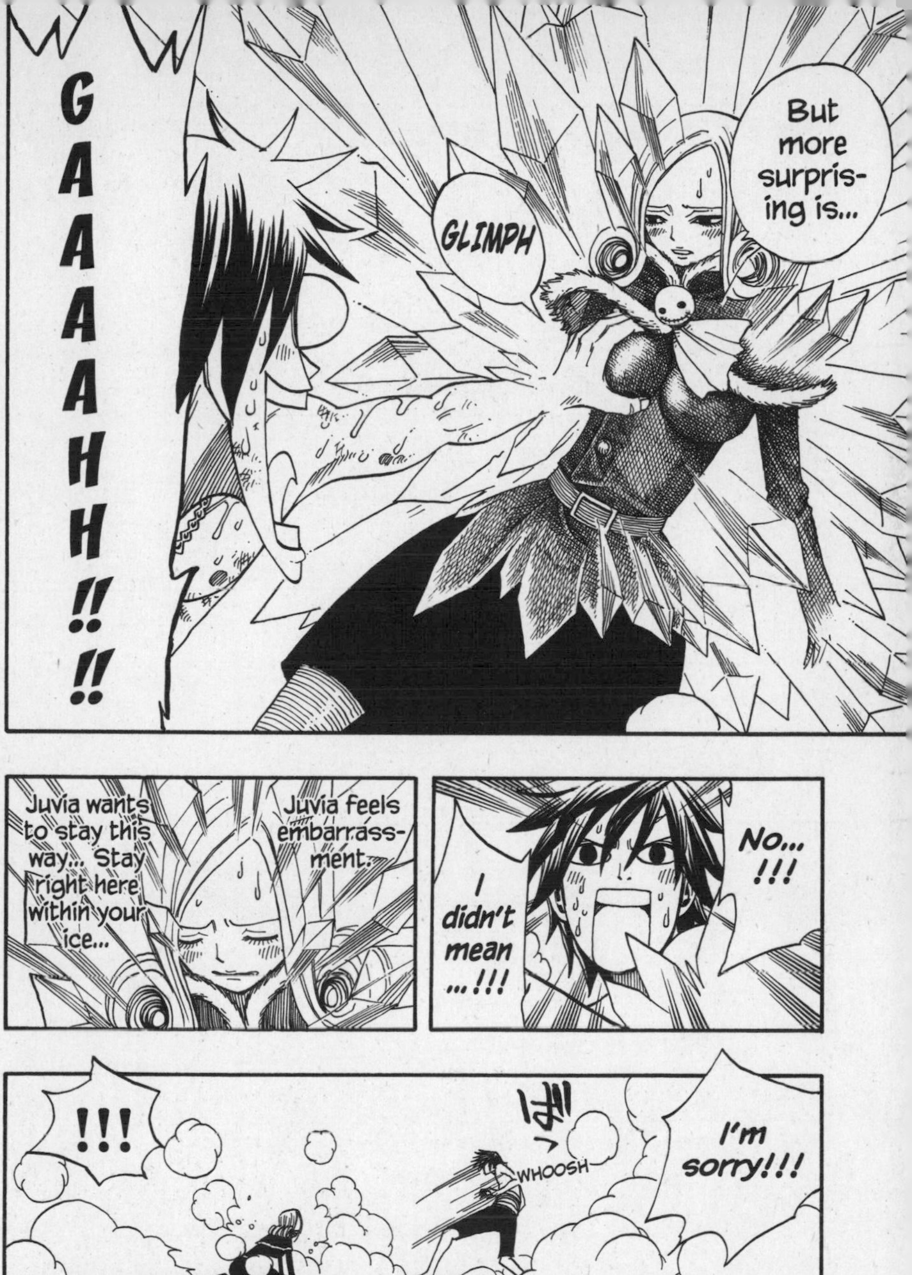
But more surprising is...
GLIMPH
GAAAAHH!!!!
No...!!!
I didn't mean ...!!!
Juvia feels embarrassment.
Juvia wants to stay this way... Stay right here within your ice...
I'm sorry!!!
WHOOSH
!!!

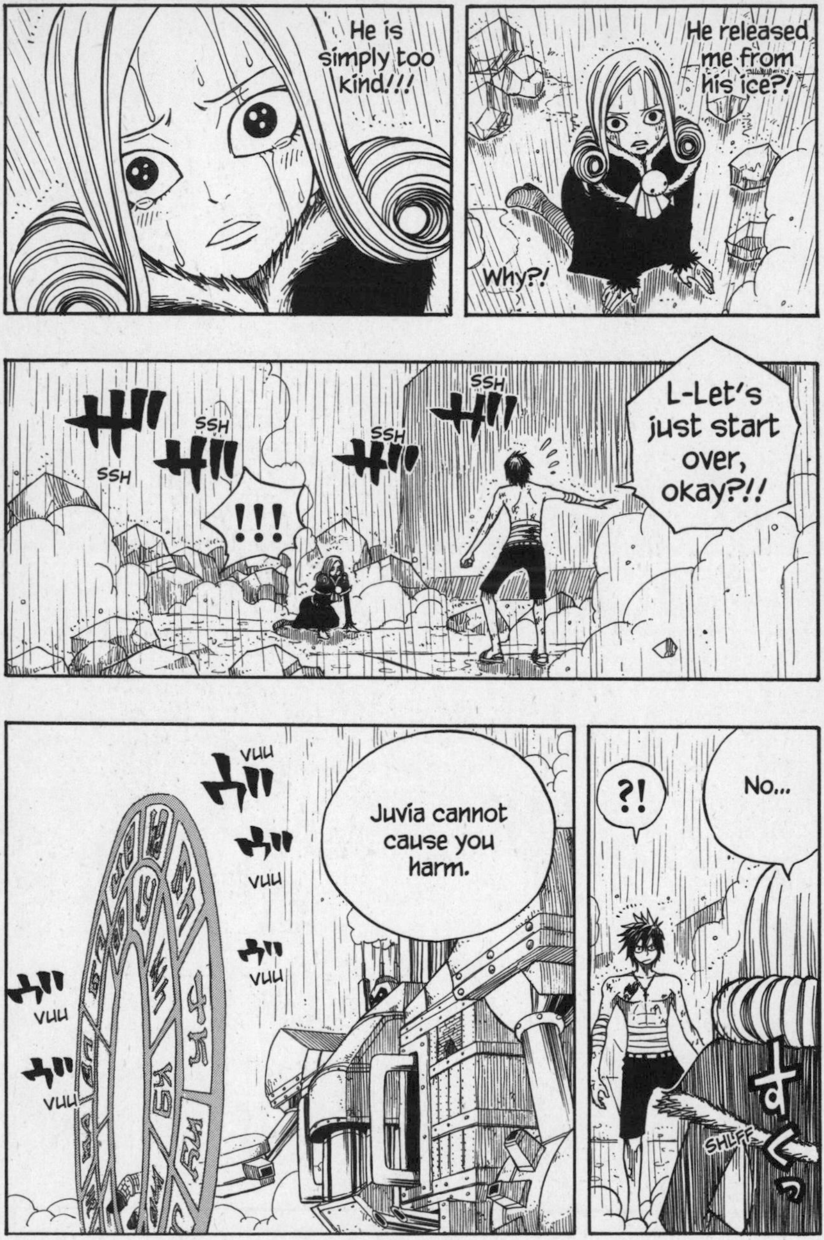

He released me from his ice?!
Why?!
He is simply too kind!!!
L-Let's just start over, okay?!!
SSH
SSH
!!!
SSH
SSH
No...
?!
SHLFF
Juvia cannot cause you harm.
VUU
VUU
VUU
VUU
VUU

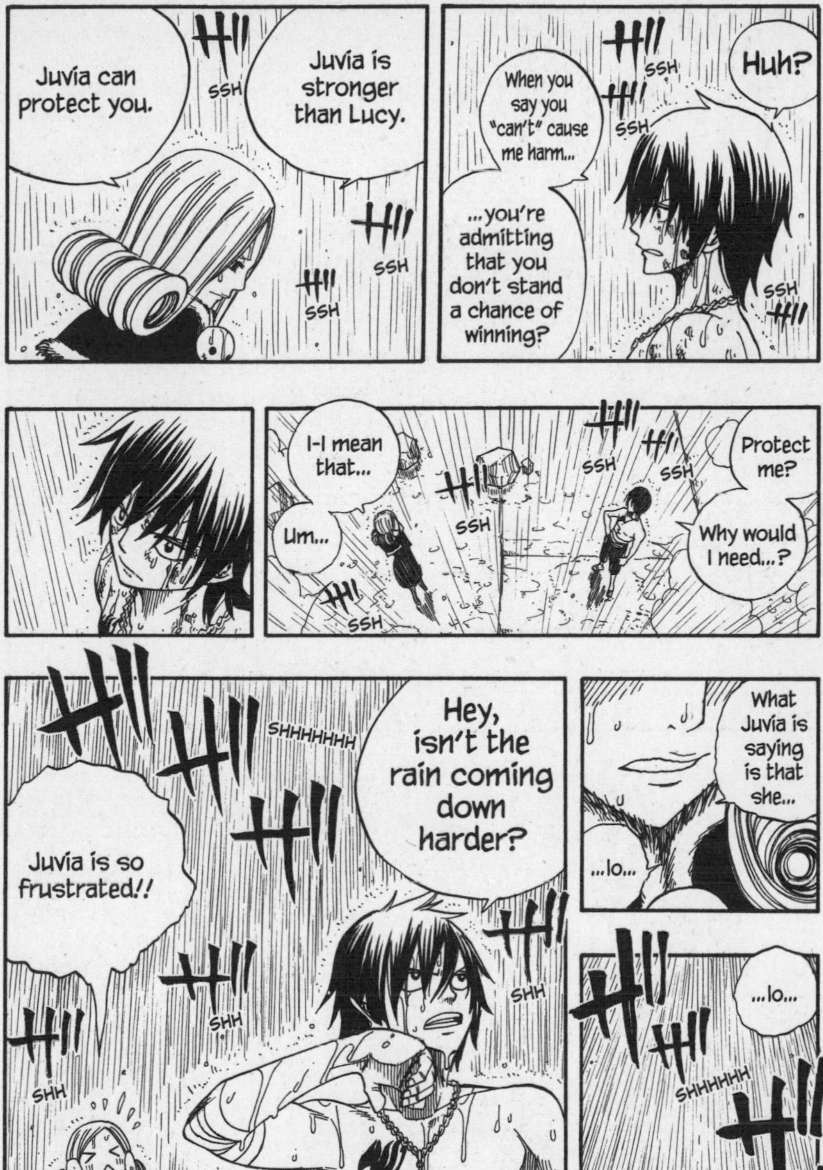
Huh?
When you say you "can't" cause me harm...
...you're admitting that you don't stand a chance of winning?
SSH
SSH
SSH
Juvia is stronger than Lucy.
Juvia can protect you.
SSH
SSH
SSH
Protect me?
Why would I need...?
SSH
SSH
I-I mean that...
Um...
SSH
SSH
What Juvia is saying is that she...
...lo...
...lo...
SHHHHHH
Hey, isn't the rain coming down harder?
SHHHHHHH
Juvia is so frustrated!!
SHH
SHH
SHH

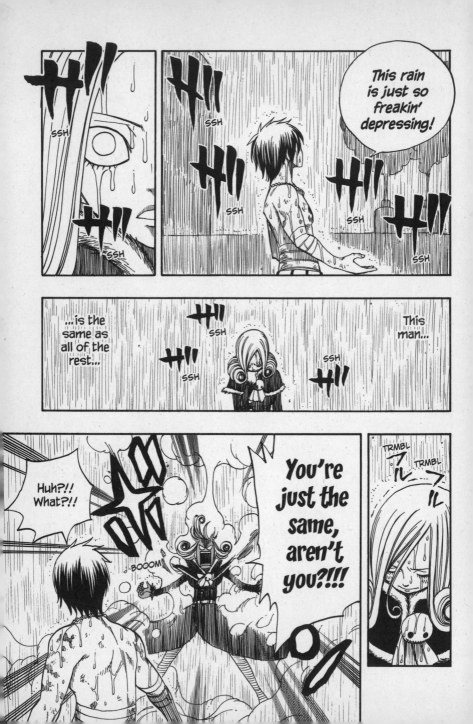

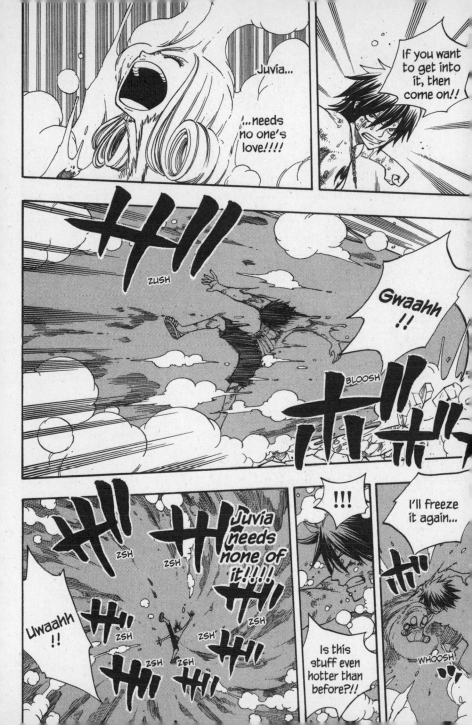

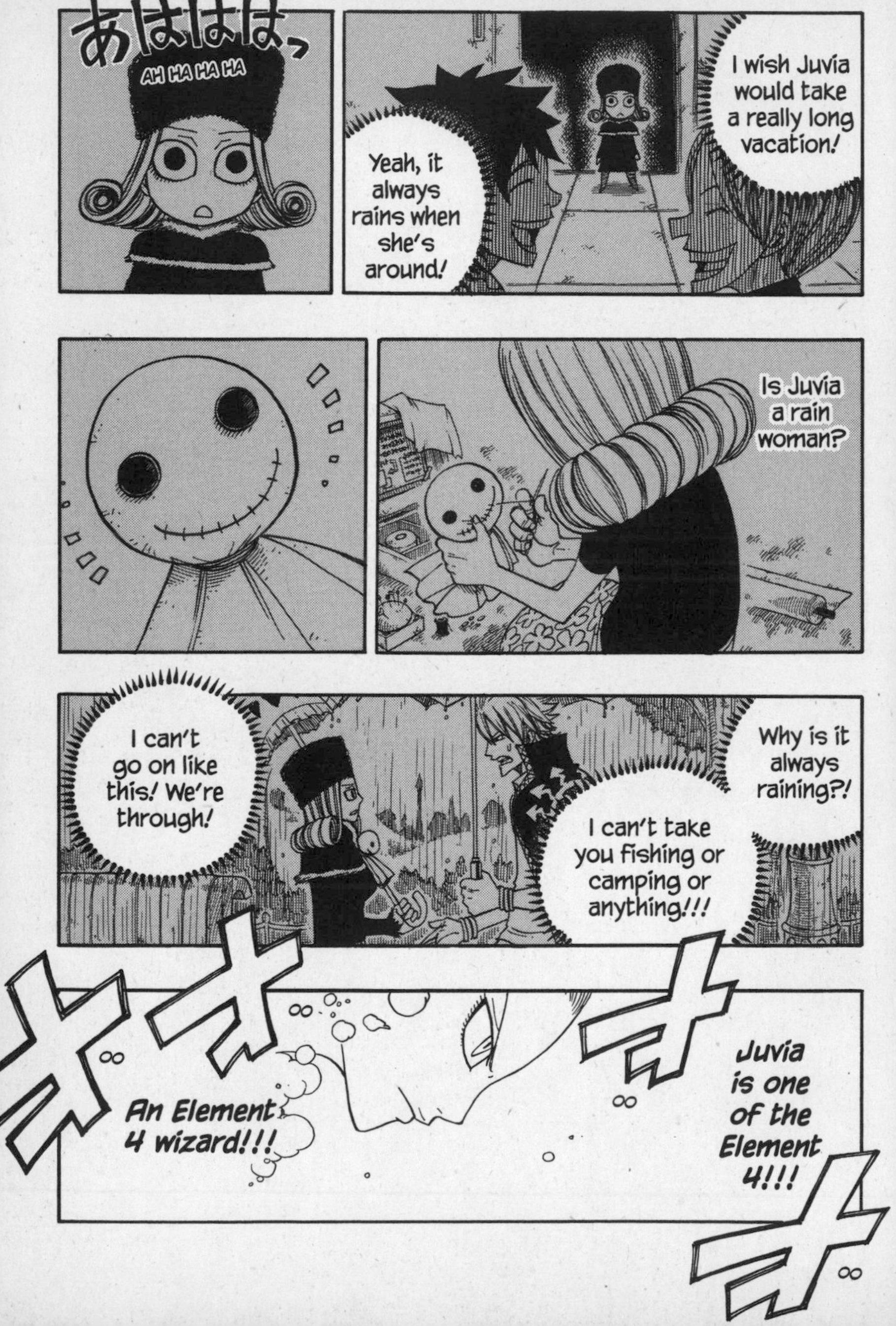
I wish Juvia would take a really long vacation!
Yeah, it always rains when she's around!
あははは
AH HA HA HA
Is Juvia a rain woman?
Why is it always raining?!
I can't take you fishing or camping or anything!!!
I can't go on like this! We're through!
Juvia is one of the Element 4!!!
An Element 4 wizard!!!

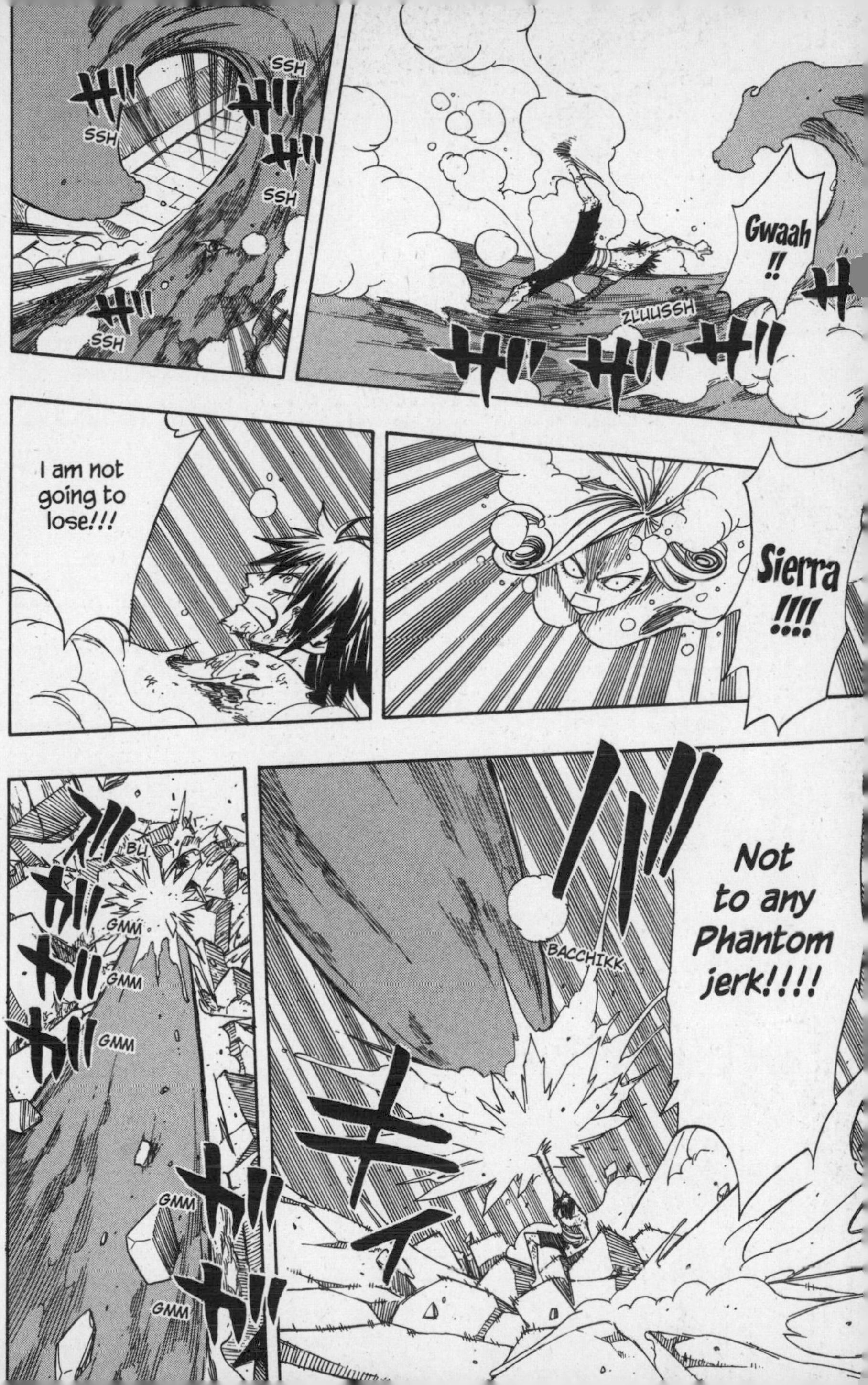
Gwaah!!
ZLUUSSH
SSH
SSH
SSH
SSH
Sierra!!!!
I am not going to lose!!!
Not to any Phantom jerk!!!!
BACCHIKK
BU
GMM
GMM
GMM
GMM
GMM

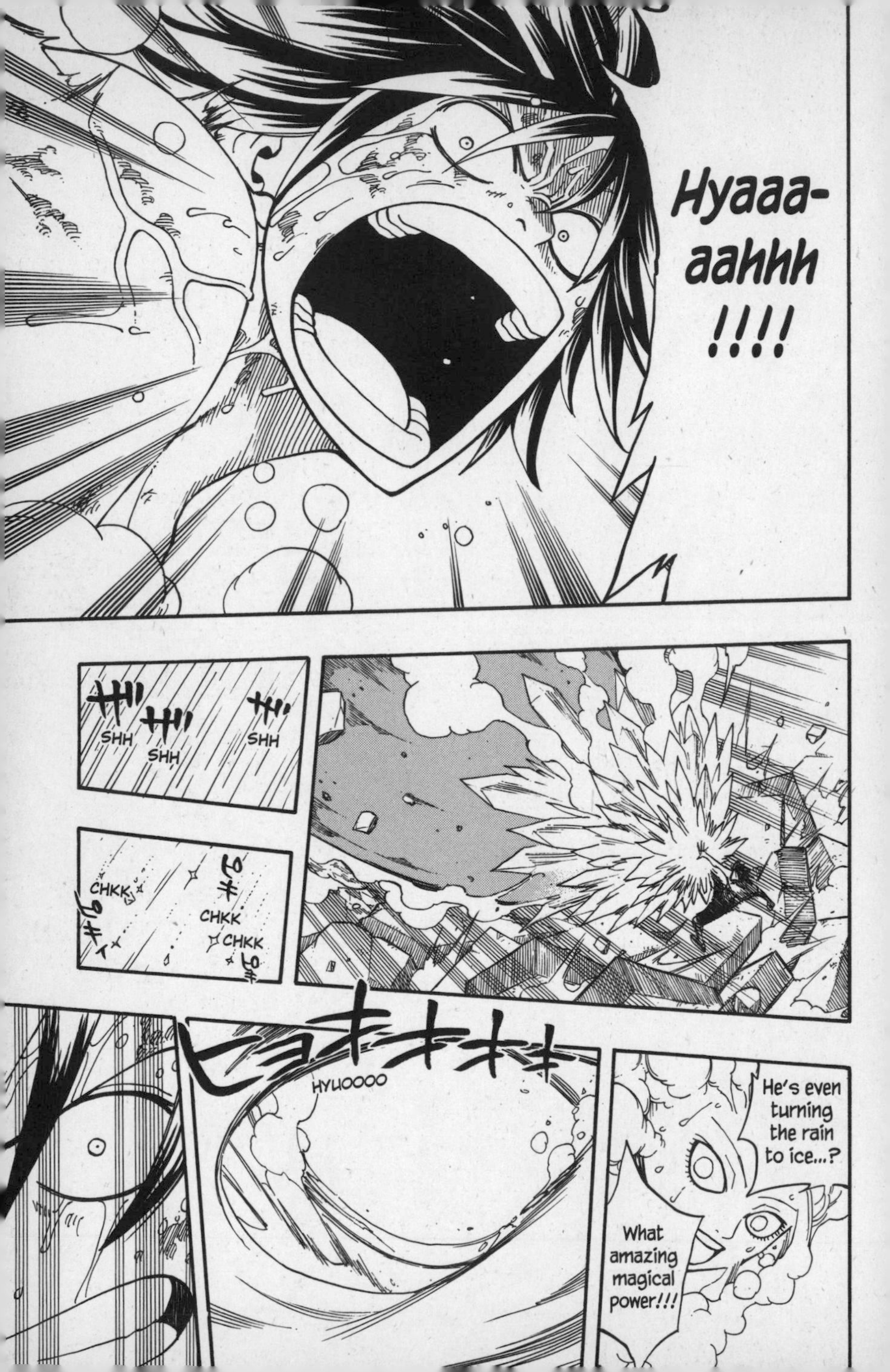
Hyaaa-aahhh!!!!
SHH
SHH
SHH
CHKK
CHKK
CHKK
He's even turning the rain to ice...?
What amazing magical power!!!
HYUOOOO

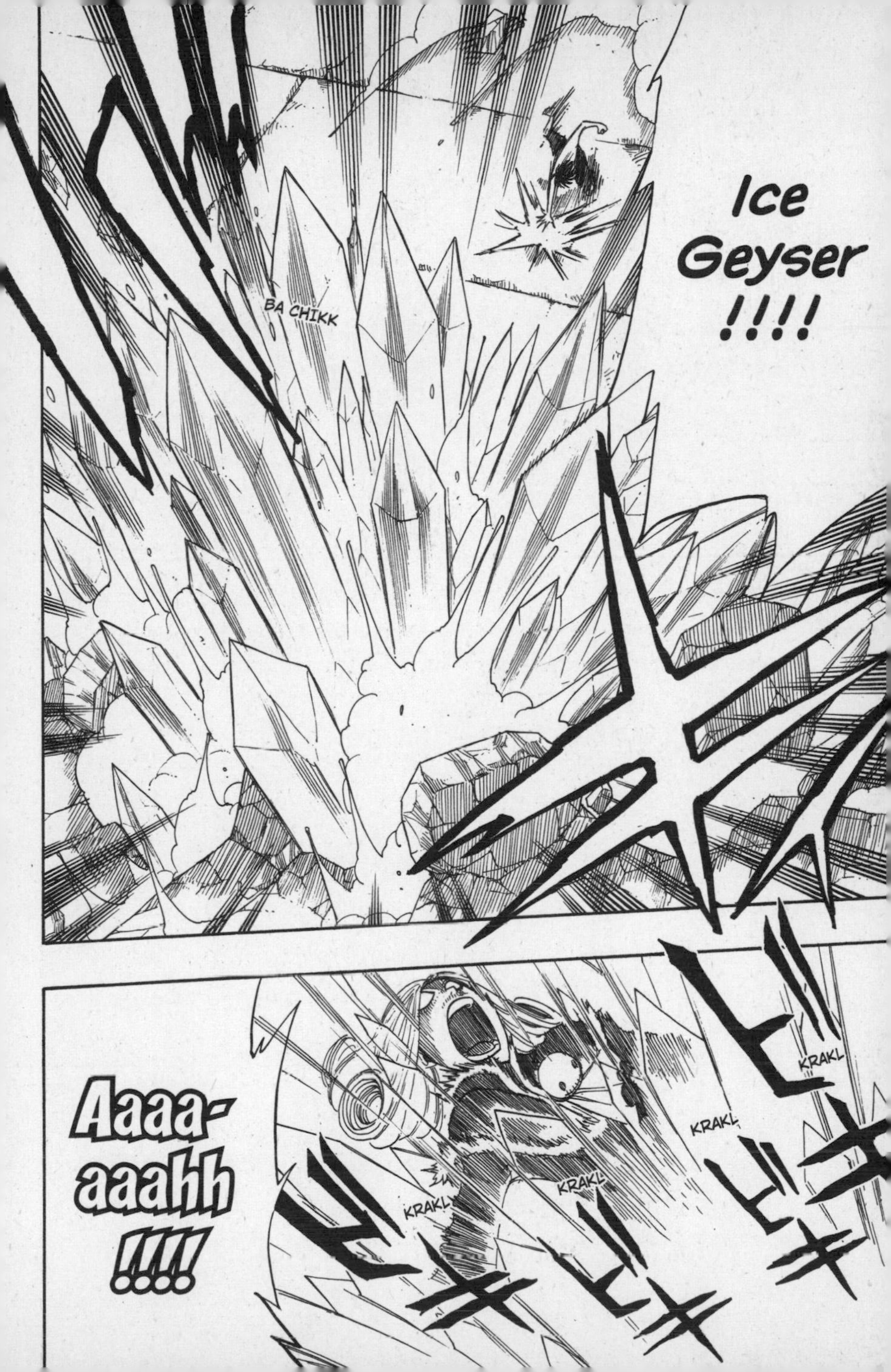
Ice Geyser !!!!
BA CHIKK
KRAKL
KRAKL
KRAKL
KRAKL
Aaaa-aaahh !!!!

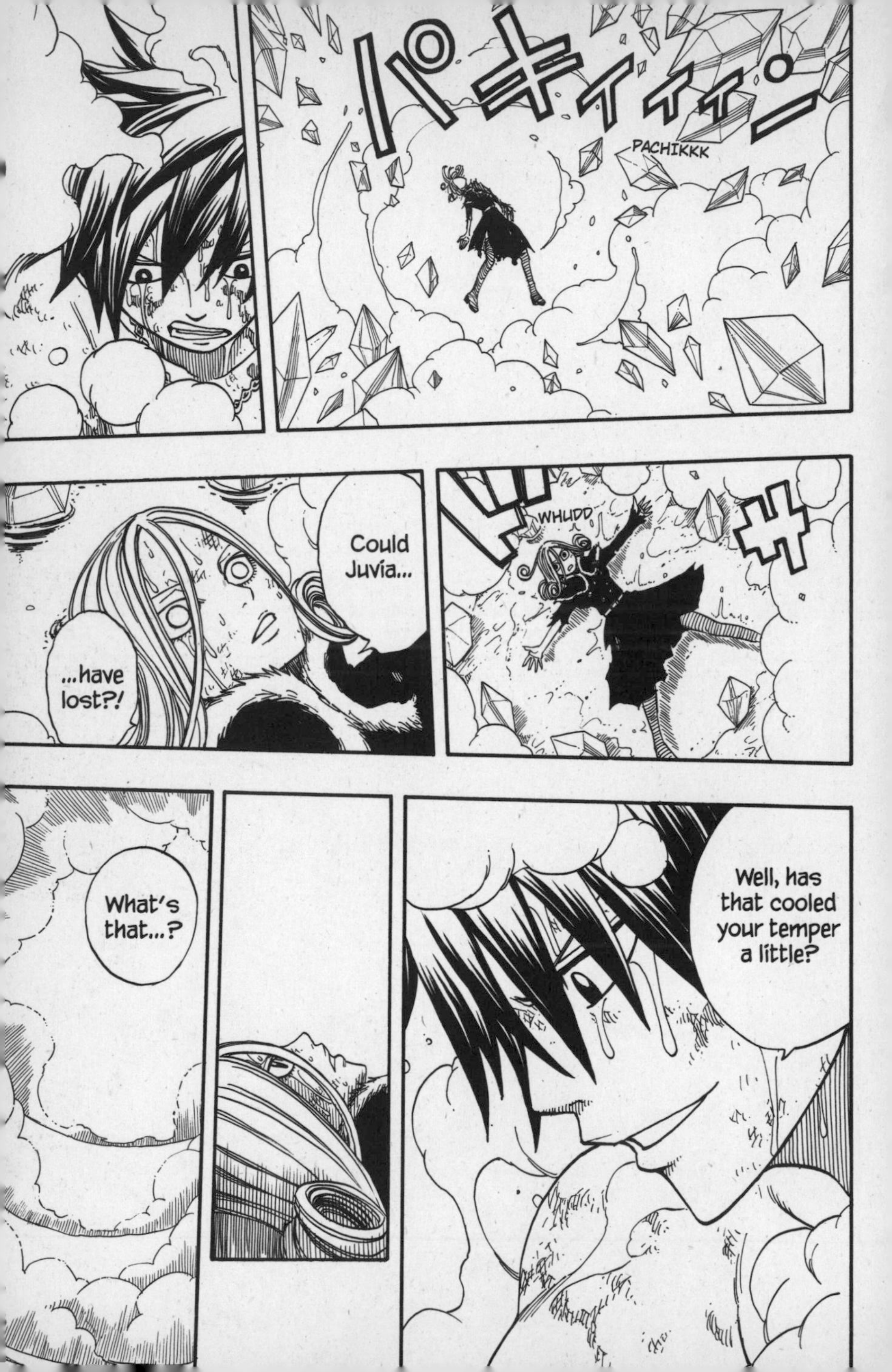

PACHIKKK
WHUDD
Could Juvia...
...have lost?!
Well, has that cooled your temper a little?
What's that...?

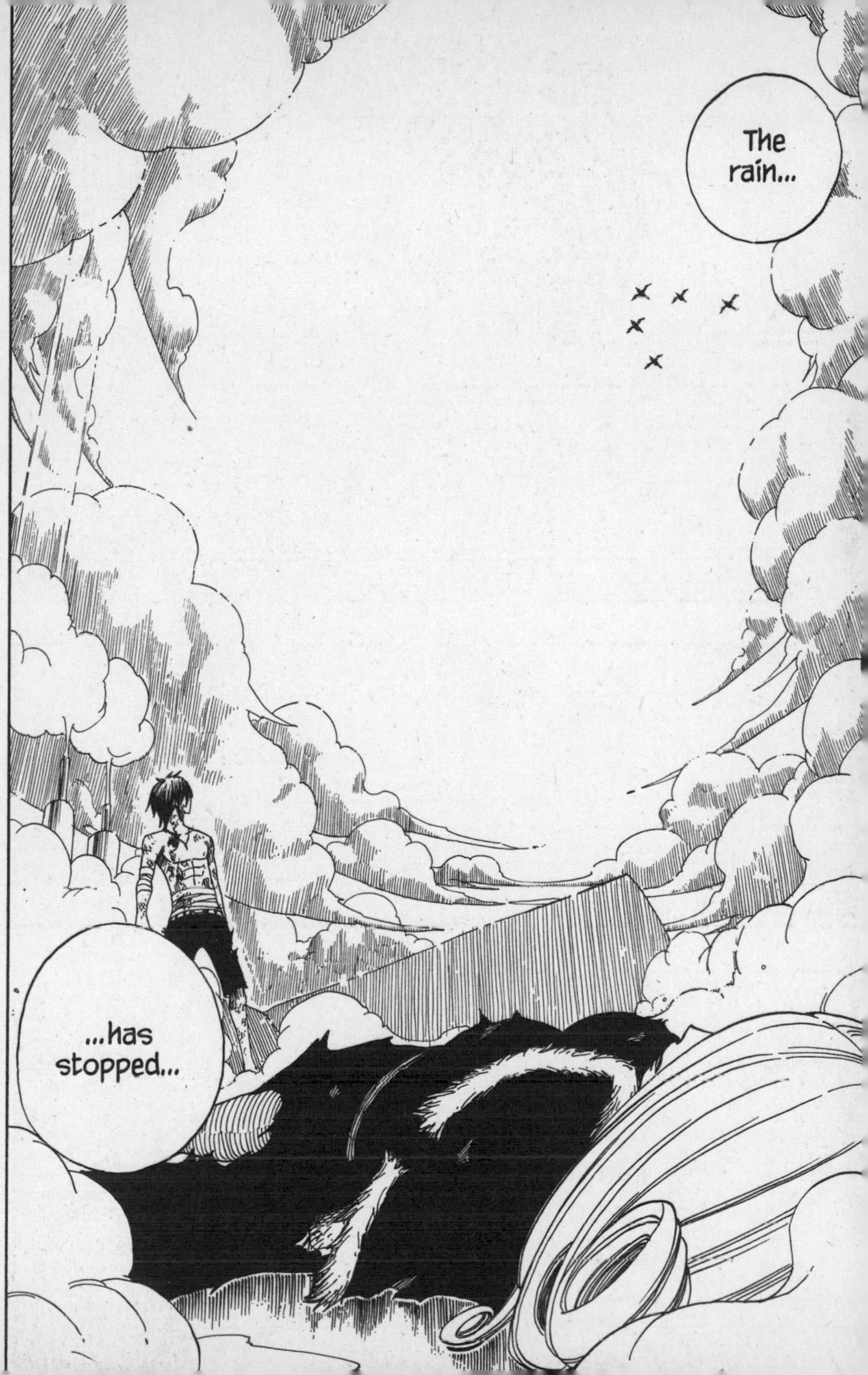
The rain...
...has stopped...

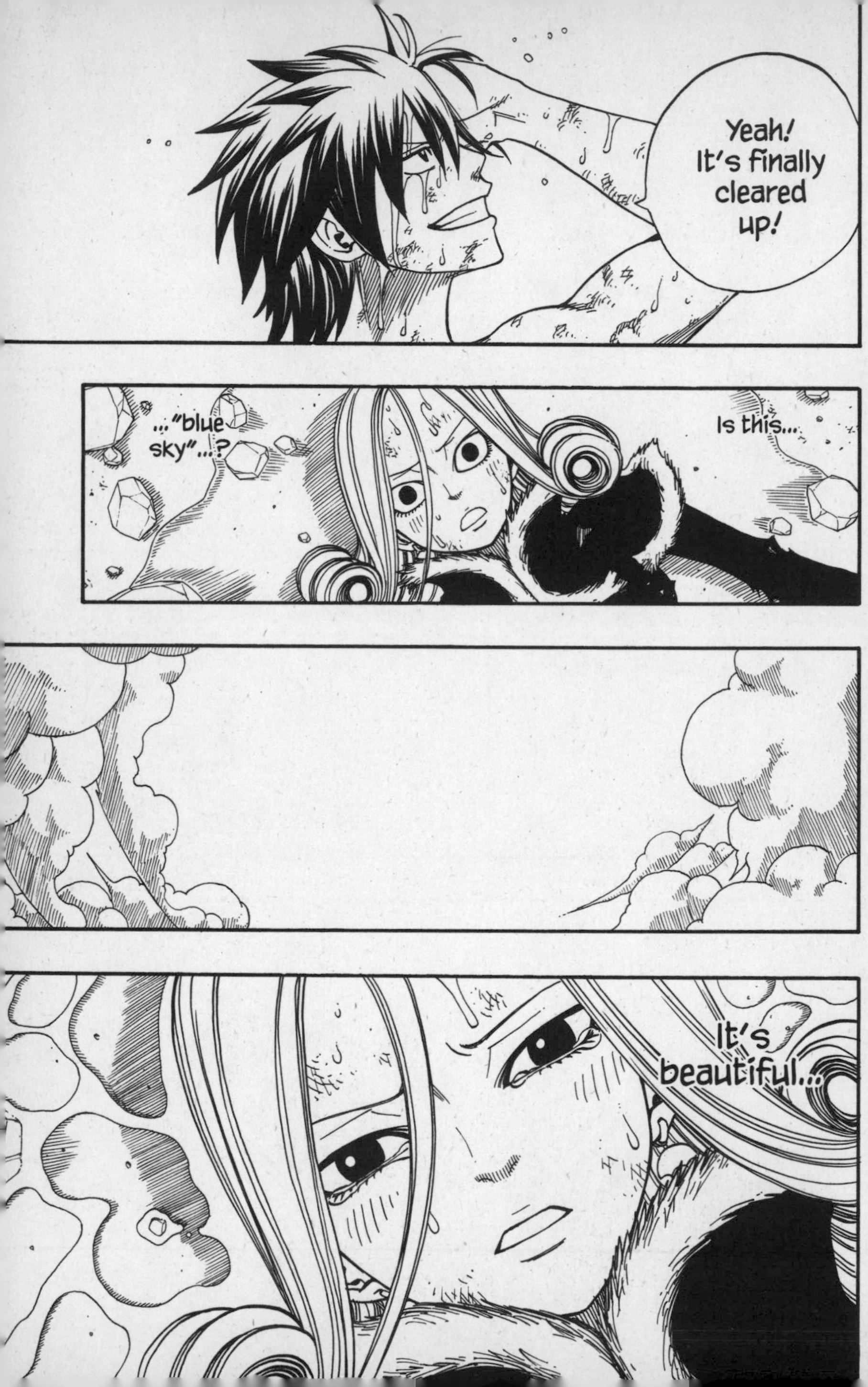
Yeah! It's finally cleared up!
Is this...
..."blue sky"...?
It's beautiful...

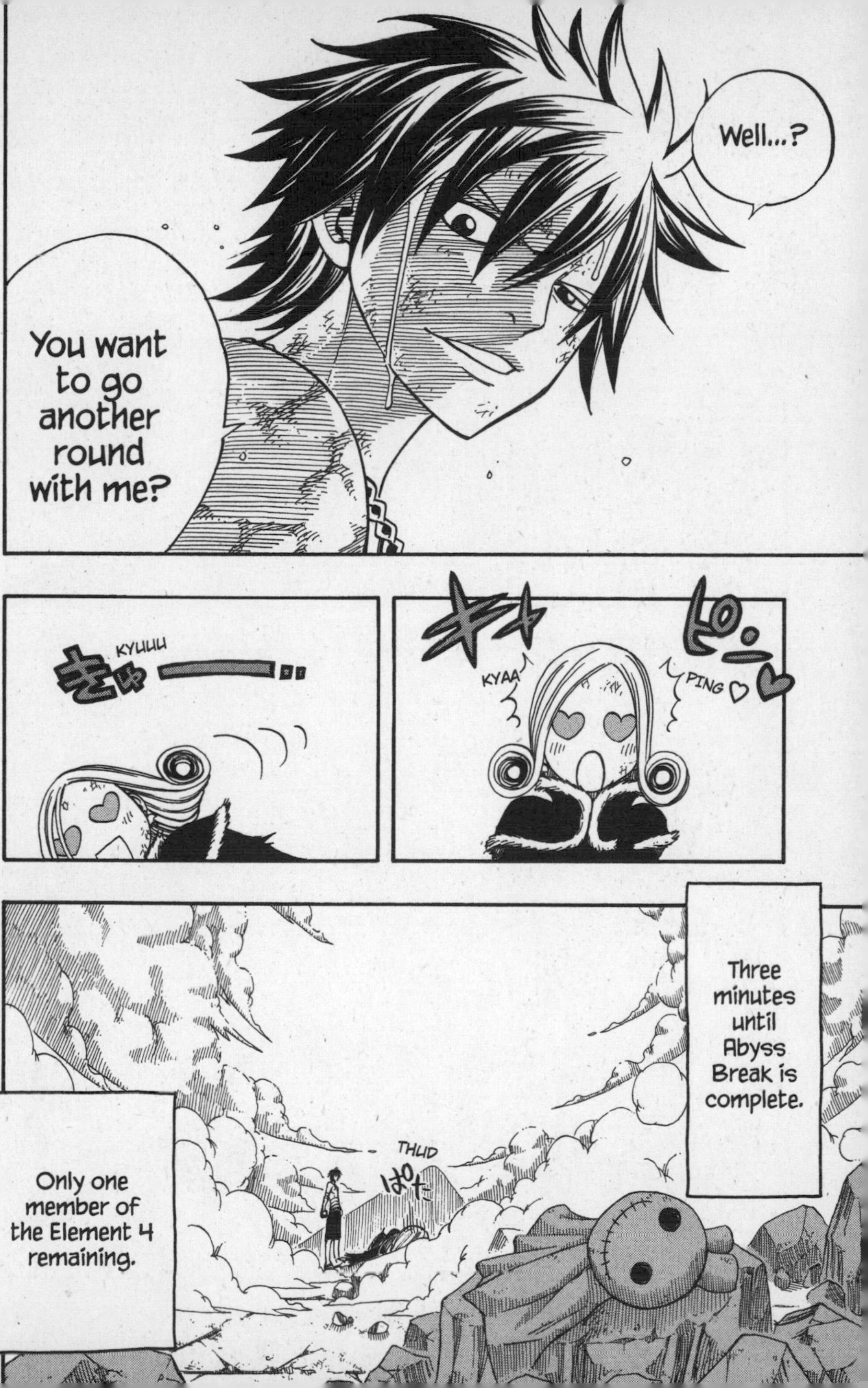
Well...?
You want to go another round with me?
KYAA
PING
KYUUU
Three minutes until Abyss Break is complete.
THUD
Only one member of the Element 4 remaining.

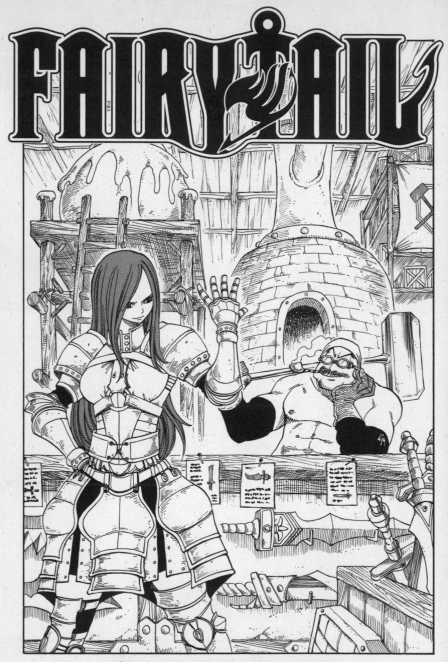

Chapter 58: There Is Always Someone Better

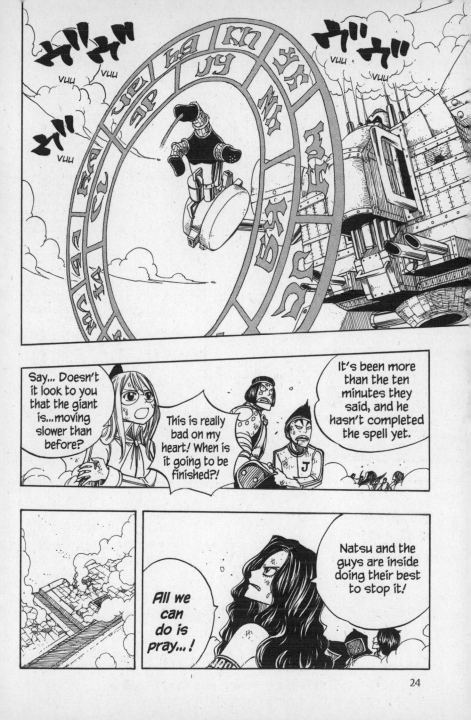

Say... Doesn't it look to you that the giant is...moving slower than before?

This is really bad on my heart! When is it going to be finished?!

It's been more than the ten minutes they said, and he hasn't completed the spell yet.

All we can do is pray...!

Natsu and the guys are inside doing their best to stop it!

24

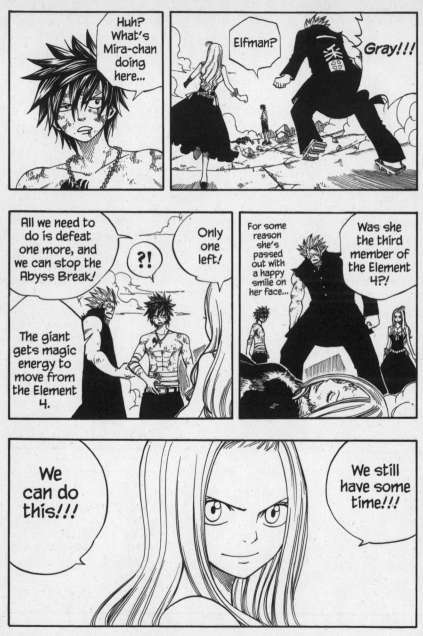

Huh? What's Mira-chan doing here...

Elfman?

Gray!!!

All we need to do is defeat one more, and we can stop the Abyss Break!

?!

Only one left!

The giant gets magic energy to move from the Element 4.

For some reason she's passed out with a happy smile on her face...

Was she the third member of the Element 4?!

We can do this!!!

We still have some time!!!

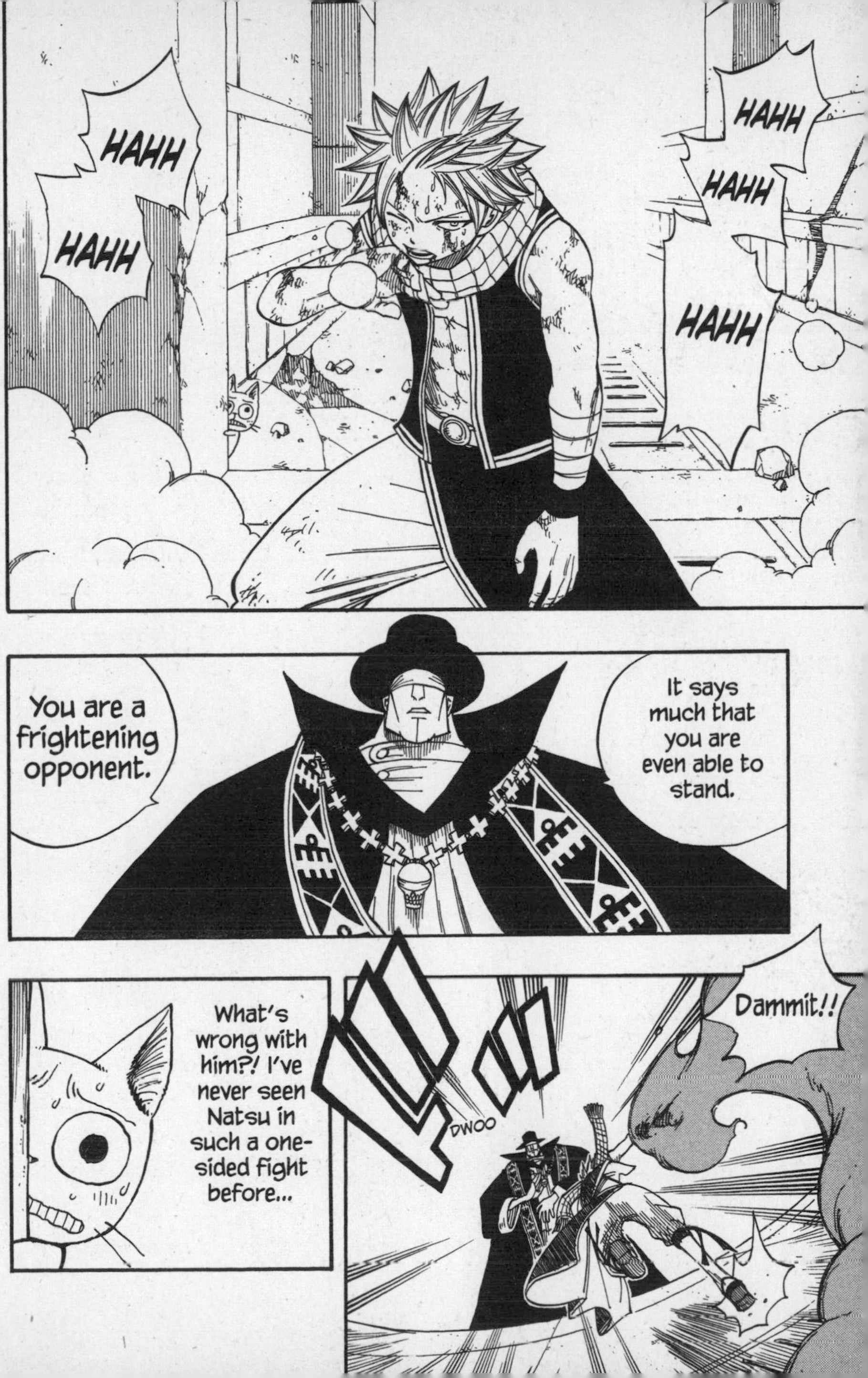
HAHH
HAHH
HAHH
HAHH
HAHH
It says much that you are even able to stand.
You are a frightening opponent.
Dammit!!
DWOO
What's wrong with him?! I've never seen Natsu in such a one-sided fight before...

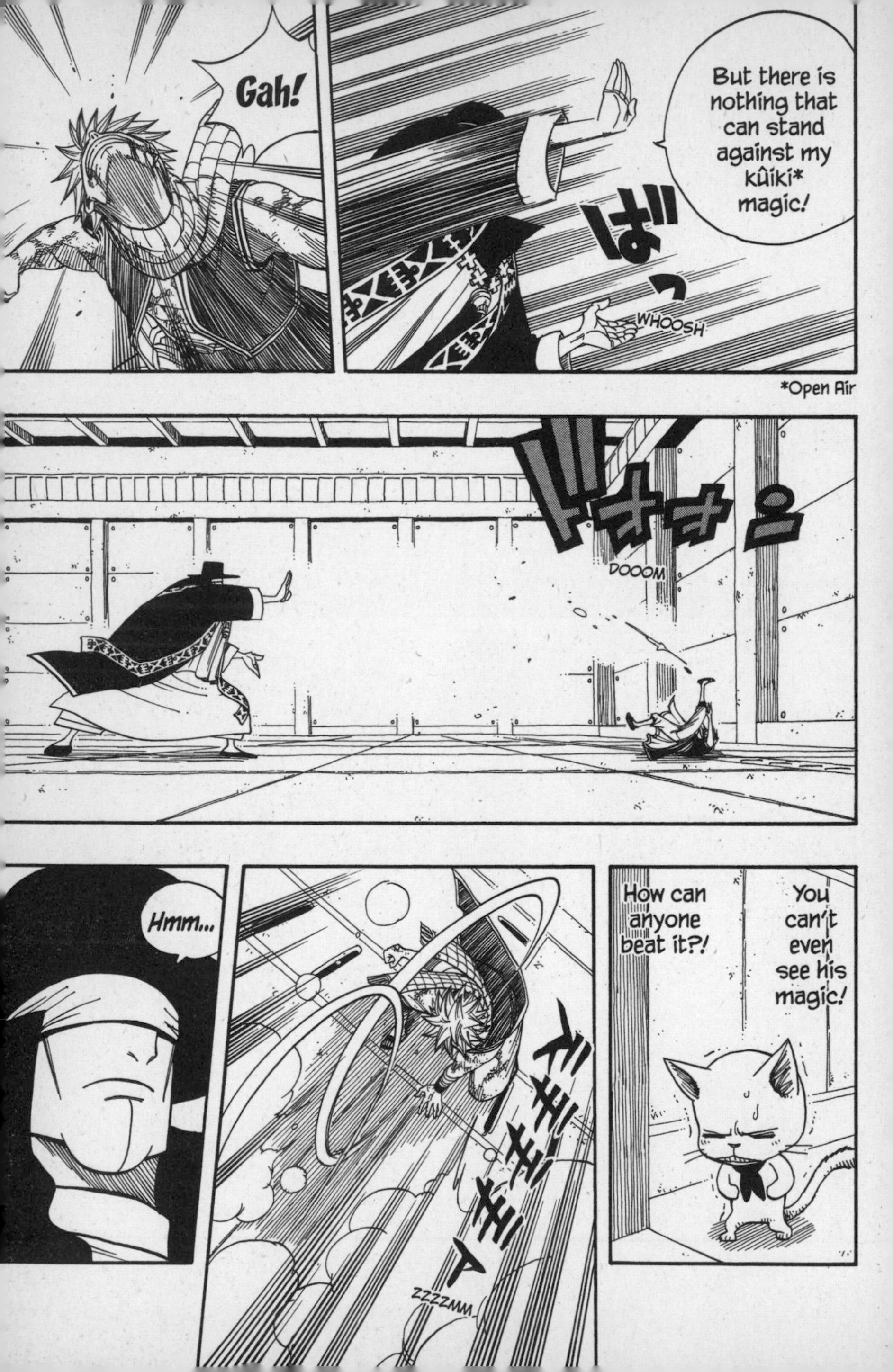
But there is nothing that can stand against my kûiki* magic!
ばっ
WHOOSH
Gah!
DOOOM
You can't even see his magic!
How can anyone beat it?!
ZZZZMM
Hmm...

*Open Air

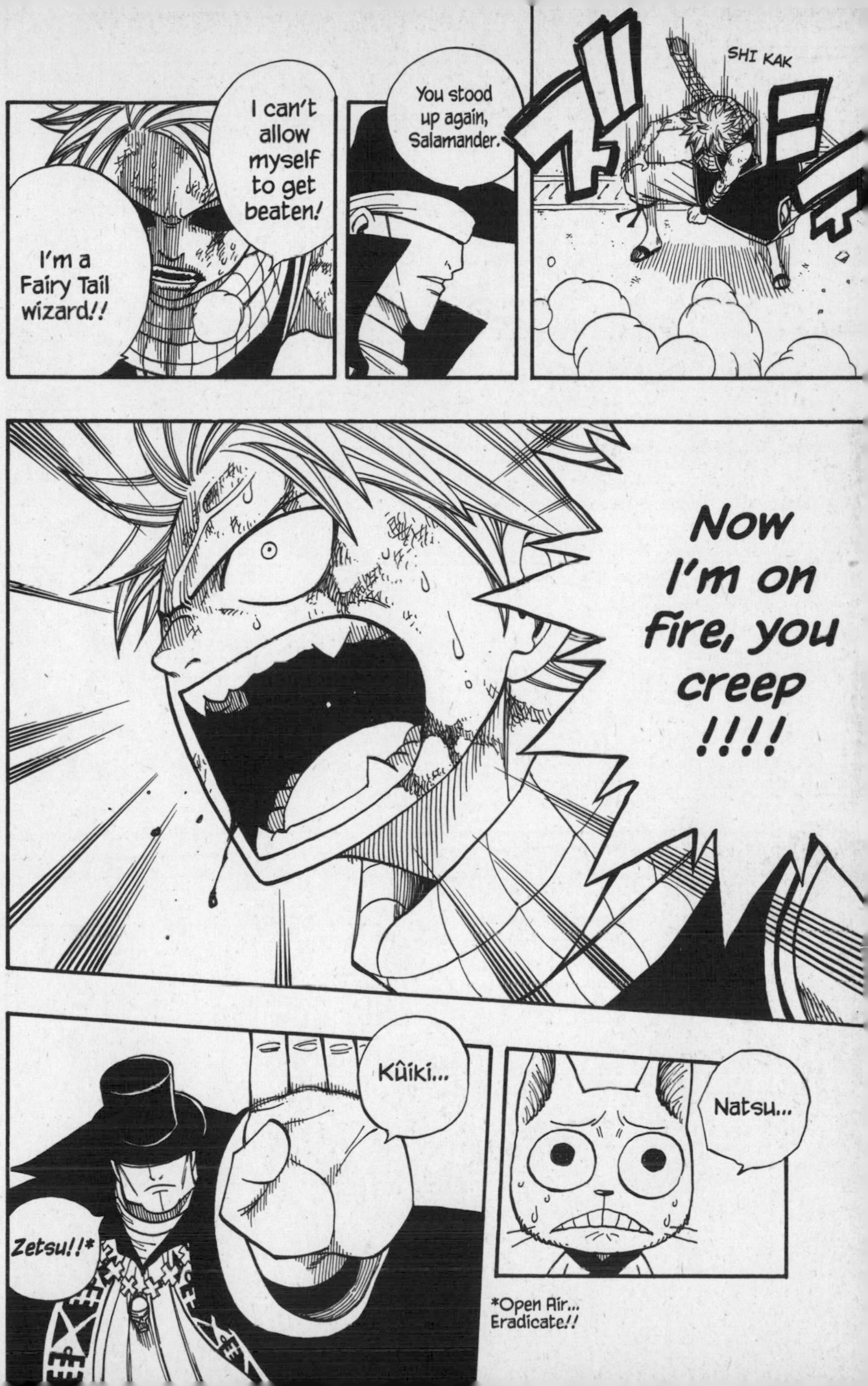
SHI KAK
You stood up again, Salamander.
I can't allow myself to get beaten!
I'm a Fairy Tail wizard!!
Now I'm on fire, you creep !!!!
Natsu...
Kûiki...
Zetsu!!*
*Open Air... Eradicate!!

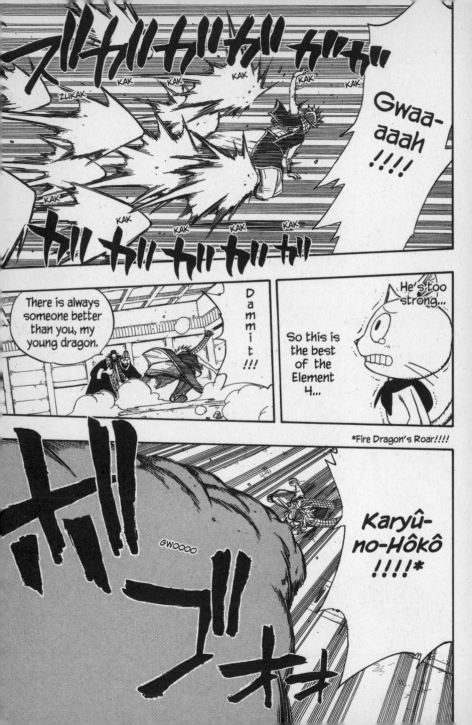

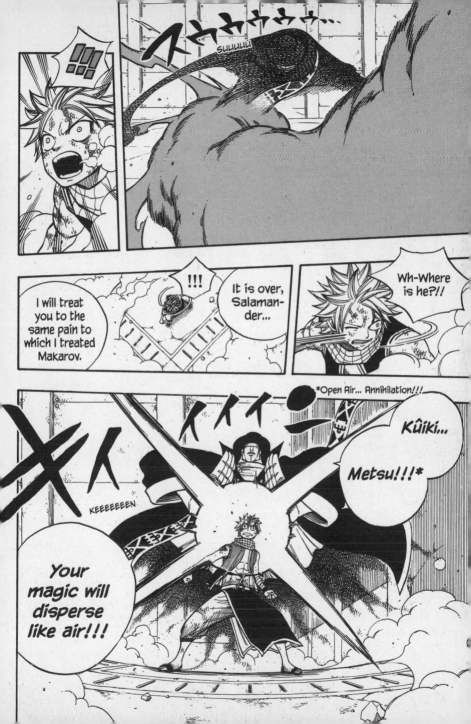

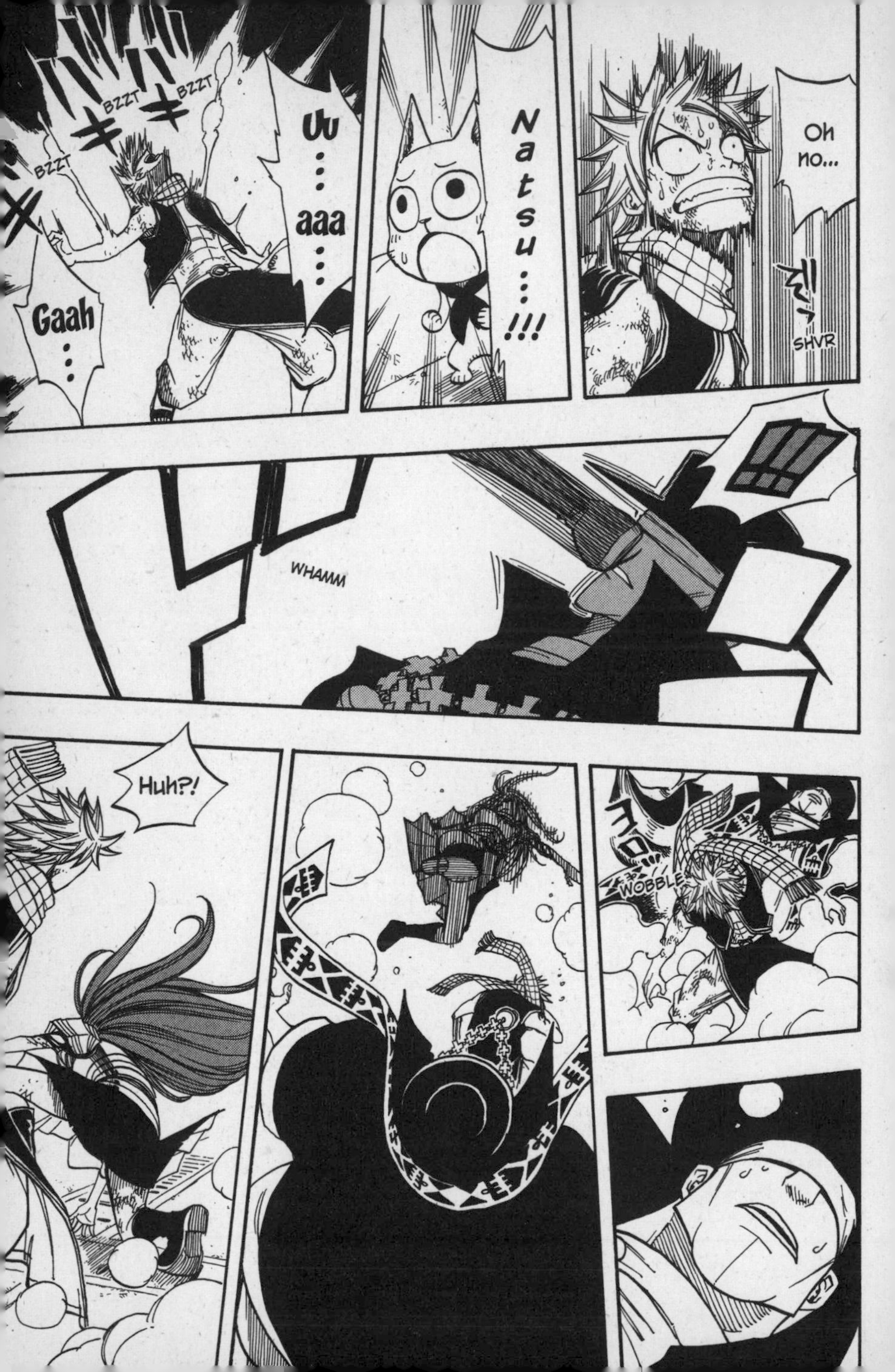
Oh no...
SHVR
Natsu...!!!
Uu... aaa...
BZZT
BZZT
BZZT
Gaah...
WHAMM
WOBBLE
Huh?!

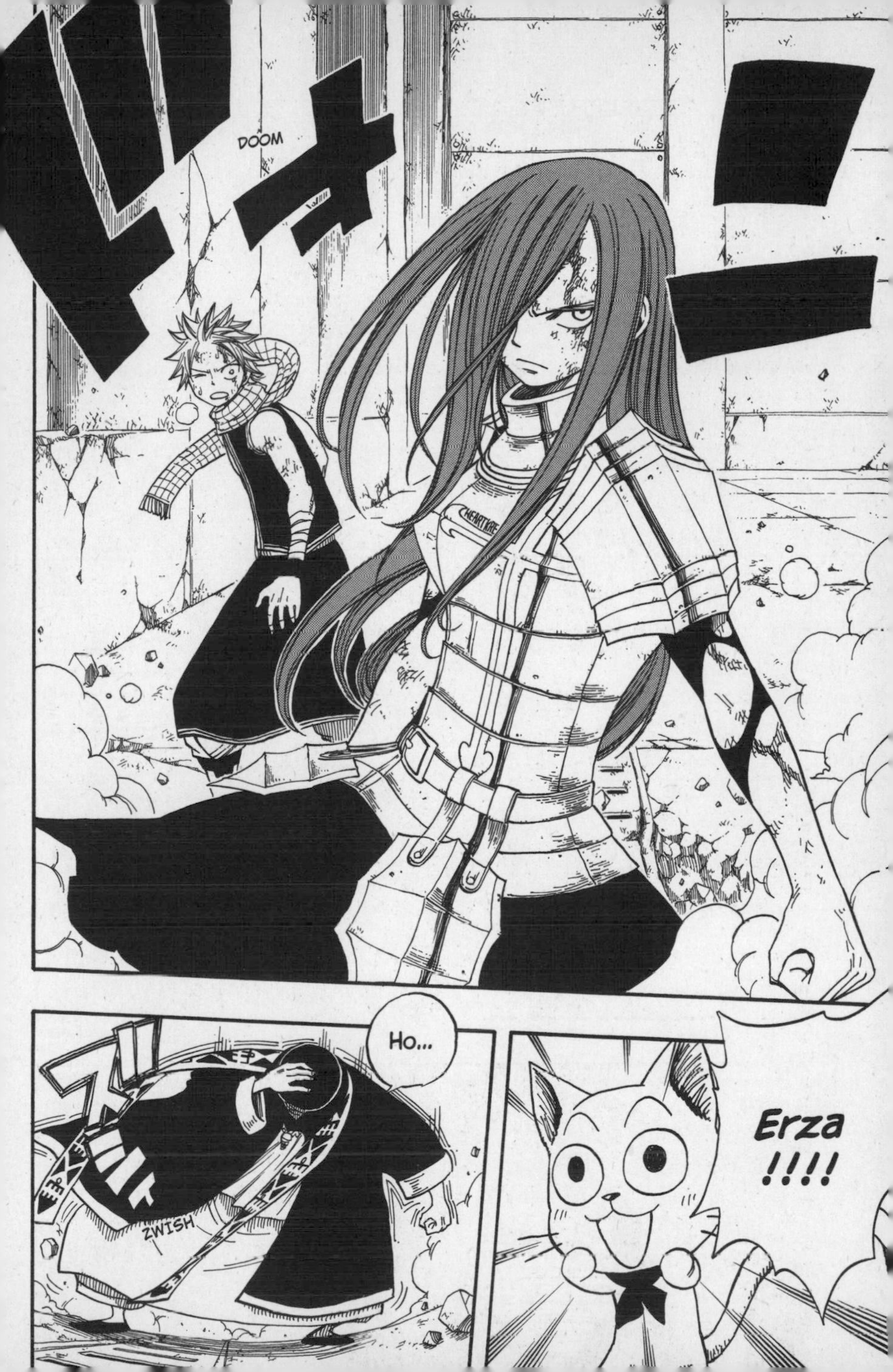
DOOM
Erza
!!!!
Ho...
ZWISH

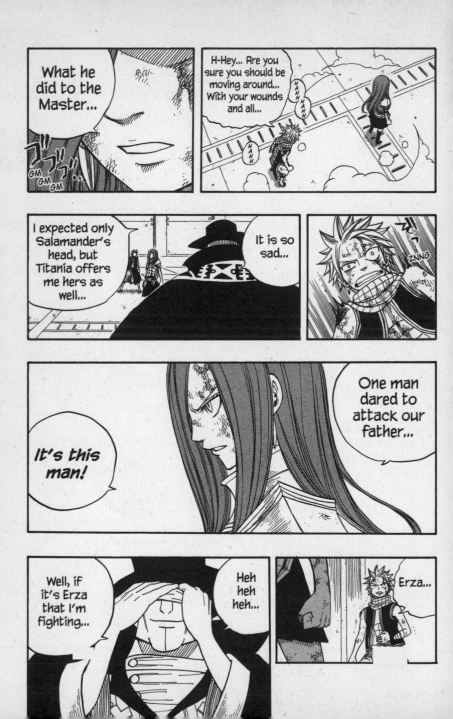

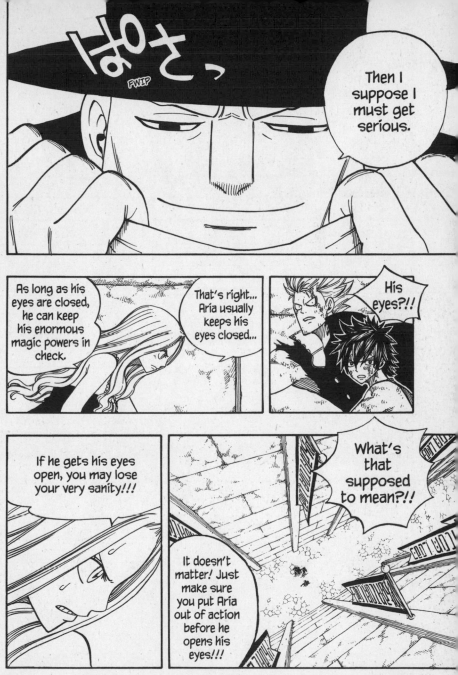

FWIP

Then I suppose I must get serious.

As long as his eyes are closed, he can keep his enormous magic powers in check.

That's right... Aria usually keeps his eyes closed...

His eyes?!!

If he gets his eyes open, you may lose your very sanity!!!

What's that supposed to mean?!!

It doesn't matter! Just make sure you put Aria out of action before he opens his eyes!!!

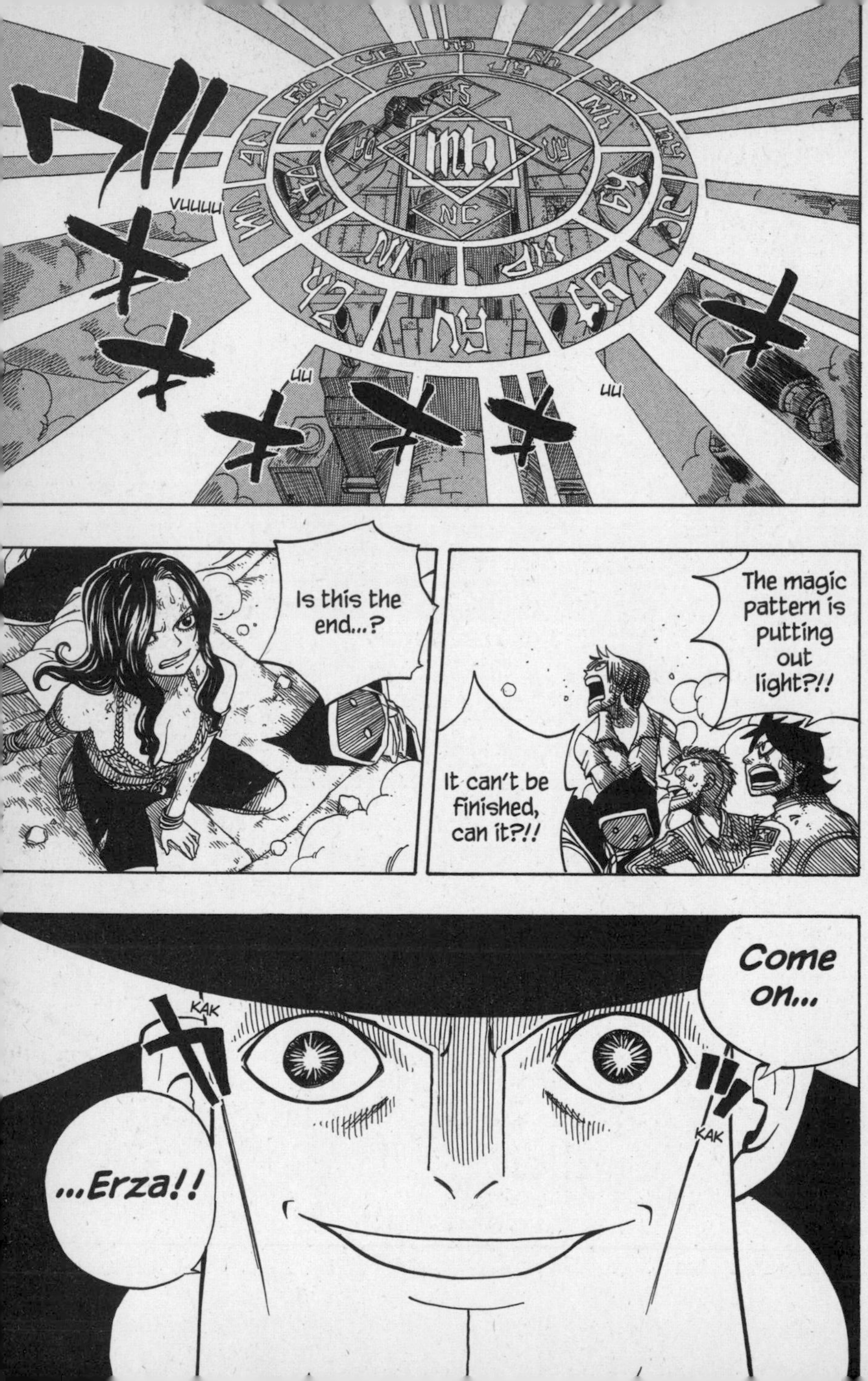
VUUUU
UU
UU
The magic pattern is putting out light?!!
It can't be finished, can it?!!
Is this the end...?
Come on...
KAK
KAK
...Erza!!

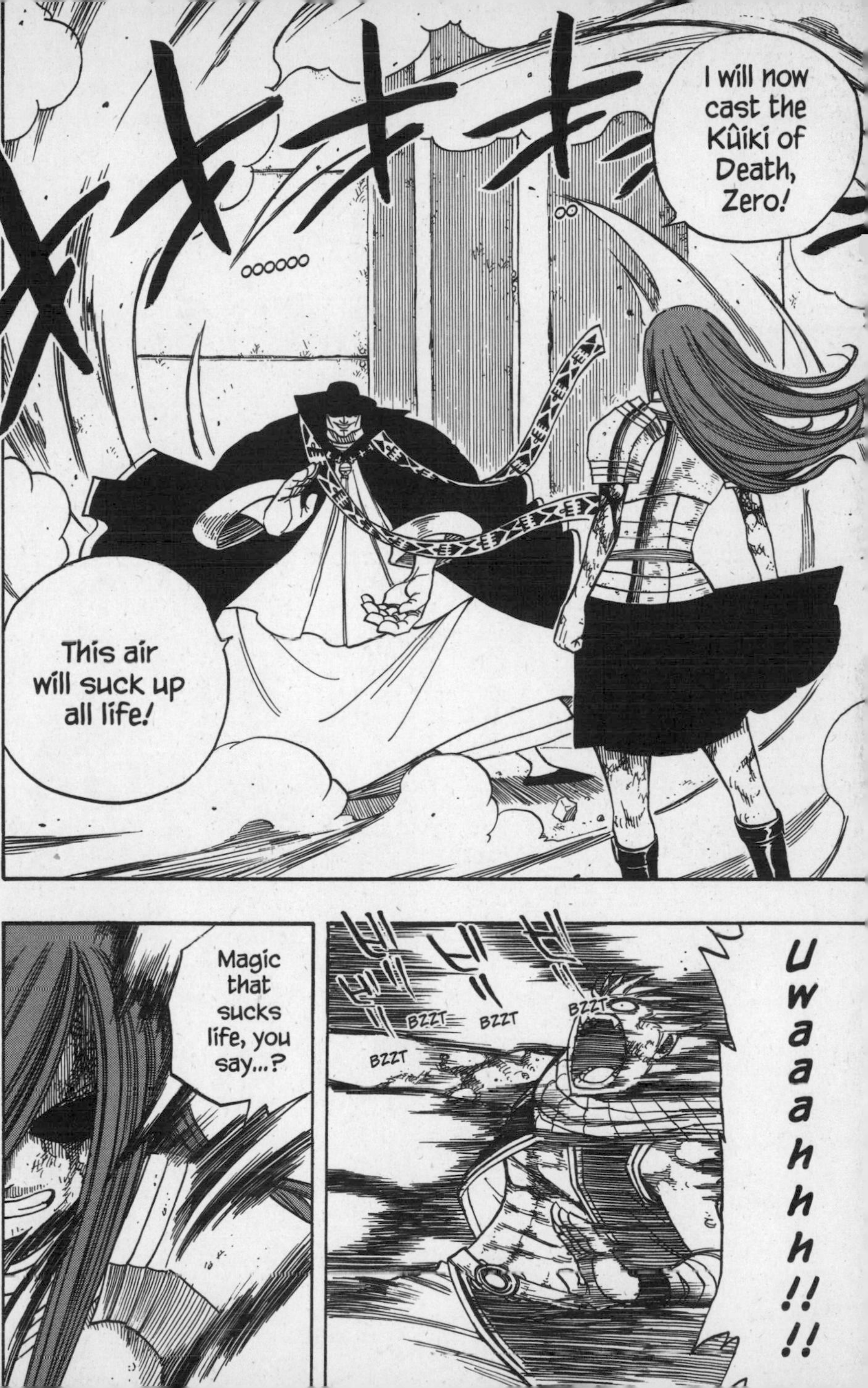
I will now cast the Kûiki of Death, Zero!
oooooo
This air will suck up all life!
Uwaaahhhh!!!!
BZZT
BZZT
BZZT
BZZT
Magic that sucks life, you say...?

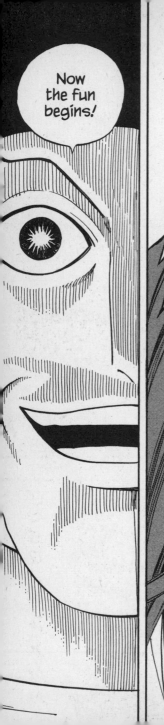

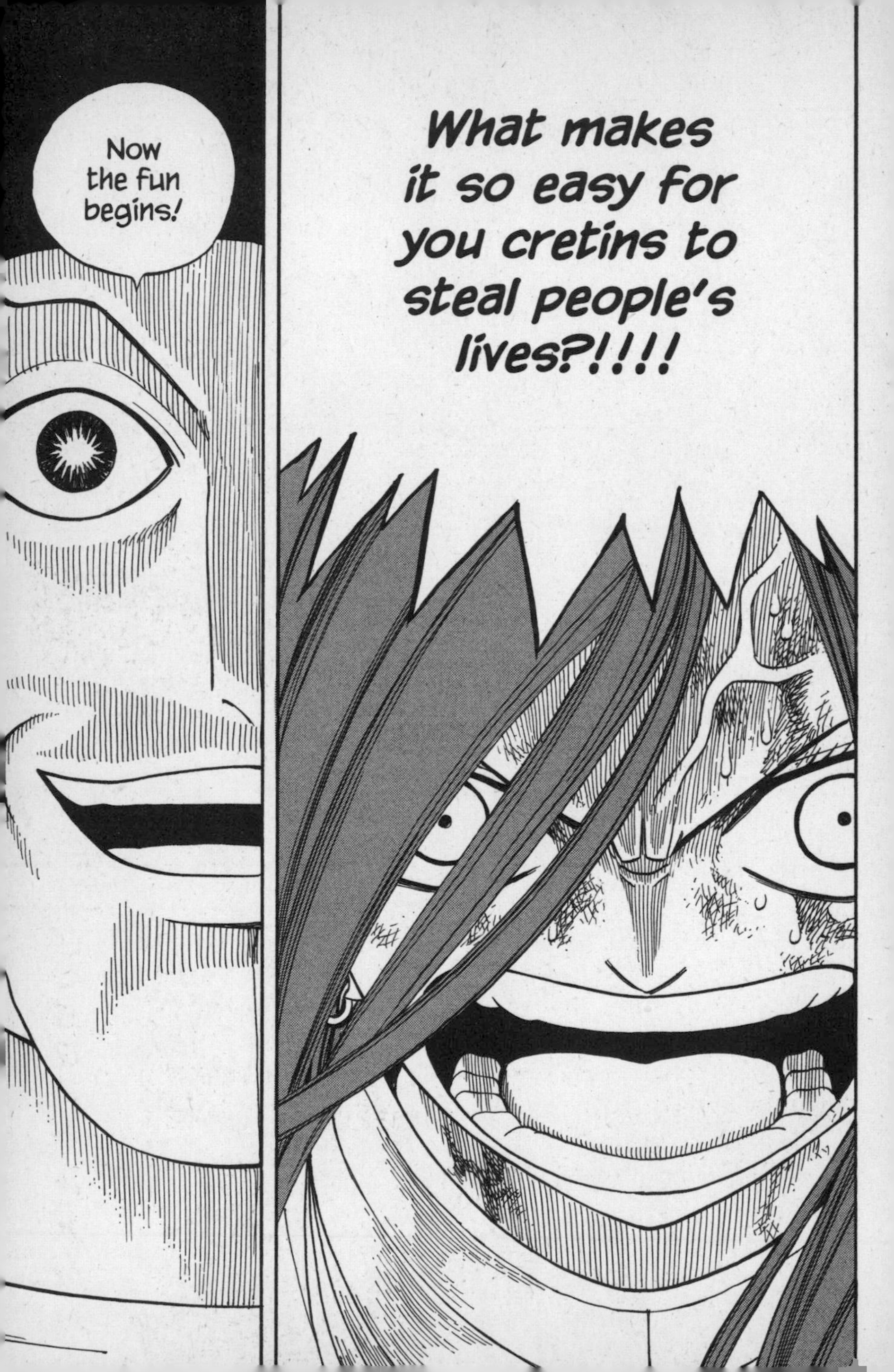
What makes it so easy for you cretins to steal people's lives?!!!!
Now the fun begins!

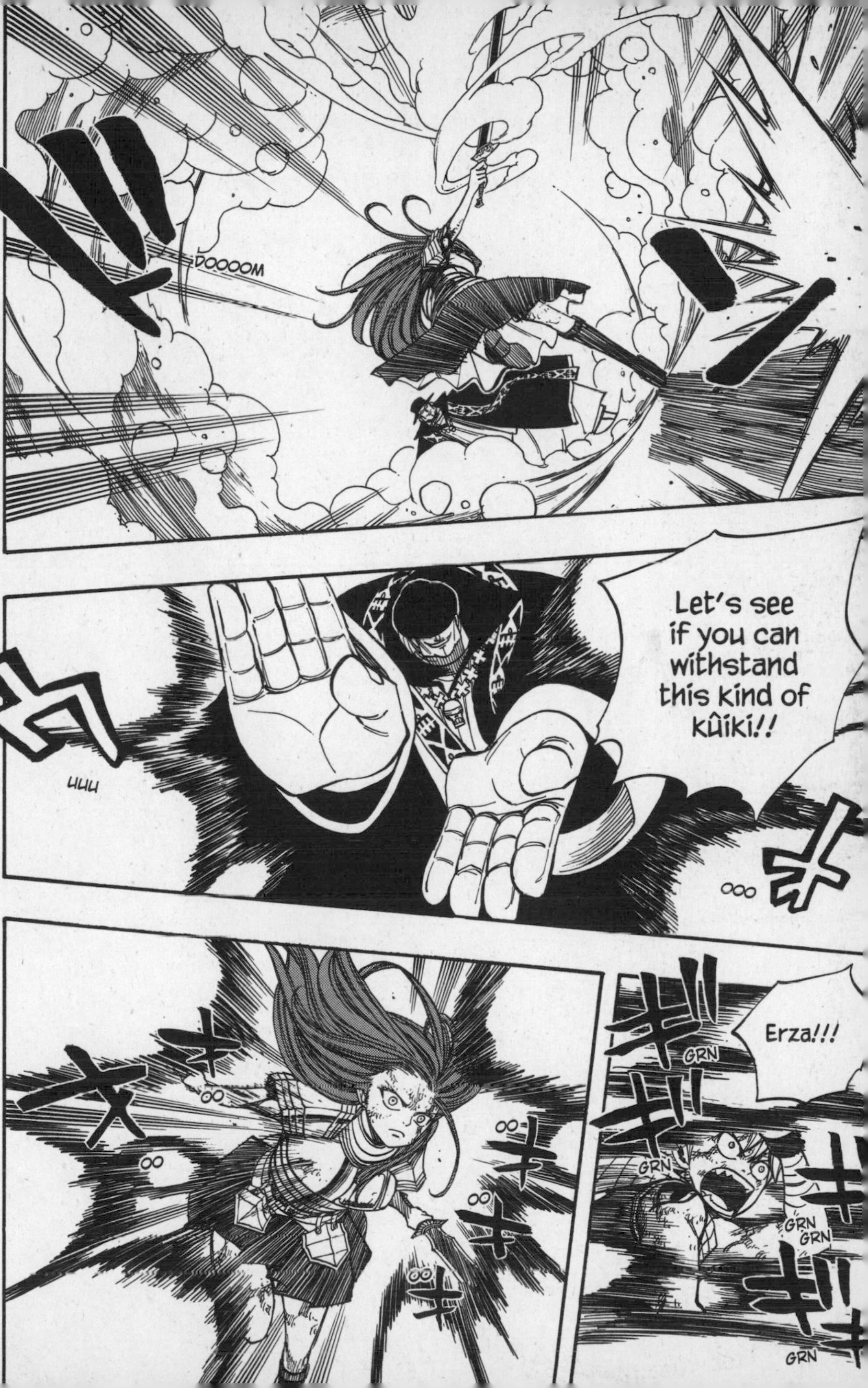
DOOOOM
Let's see if you can withstand this kind of kûiki!!
uuu
ooo
Erza!!!
GRN
GRN
GRN
GRN
GRN

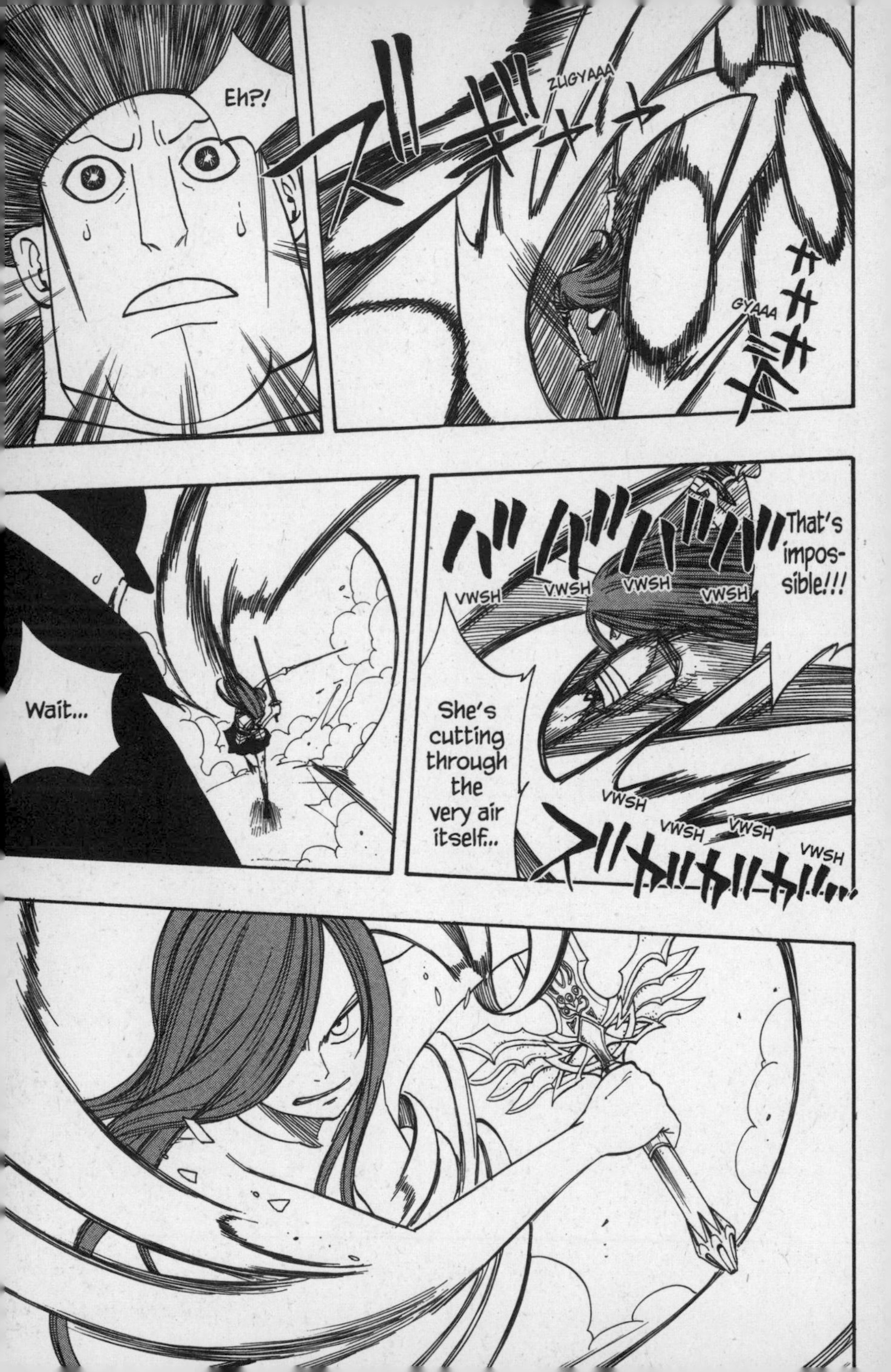
ZUGYAAA
GYAAA
Eh?!
VWSH
VWSH
VWSH
VWSH
That's impos-sible!!!
She's cutting through the very air itself...
VWSH
VWSH
VWSH
VWSH
Wait...

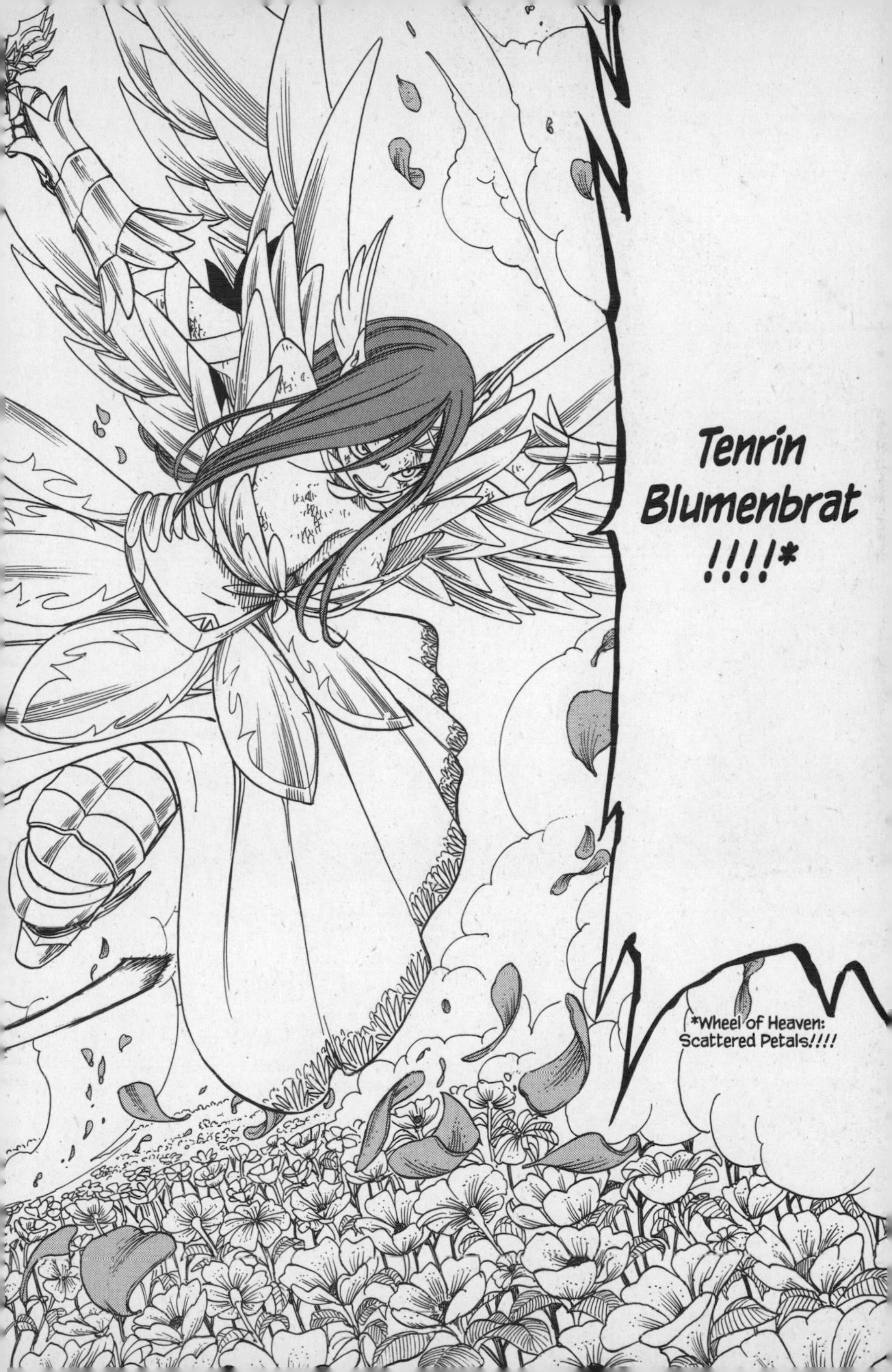
Tenrin Blumenbrat !!!!*
*Wheel of Heaven: Scattered Petals!!!!

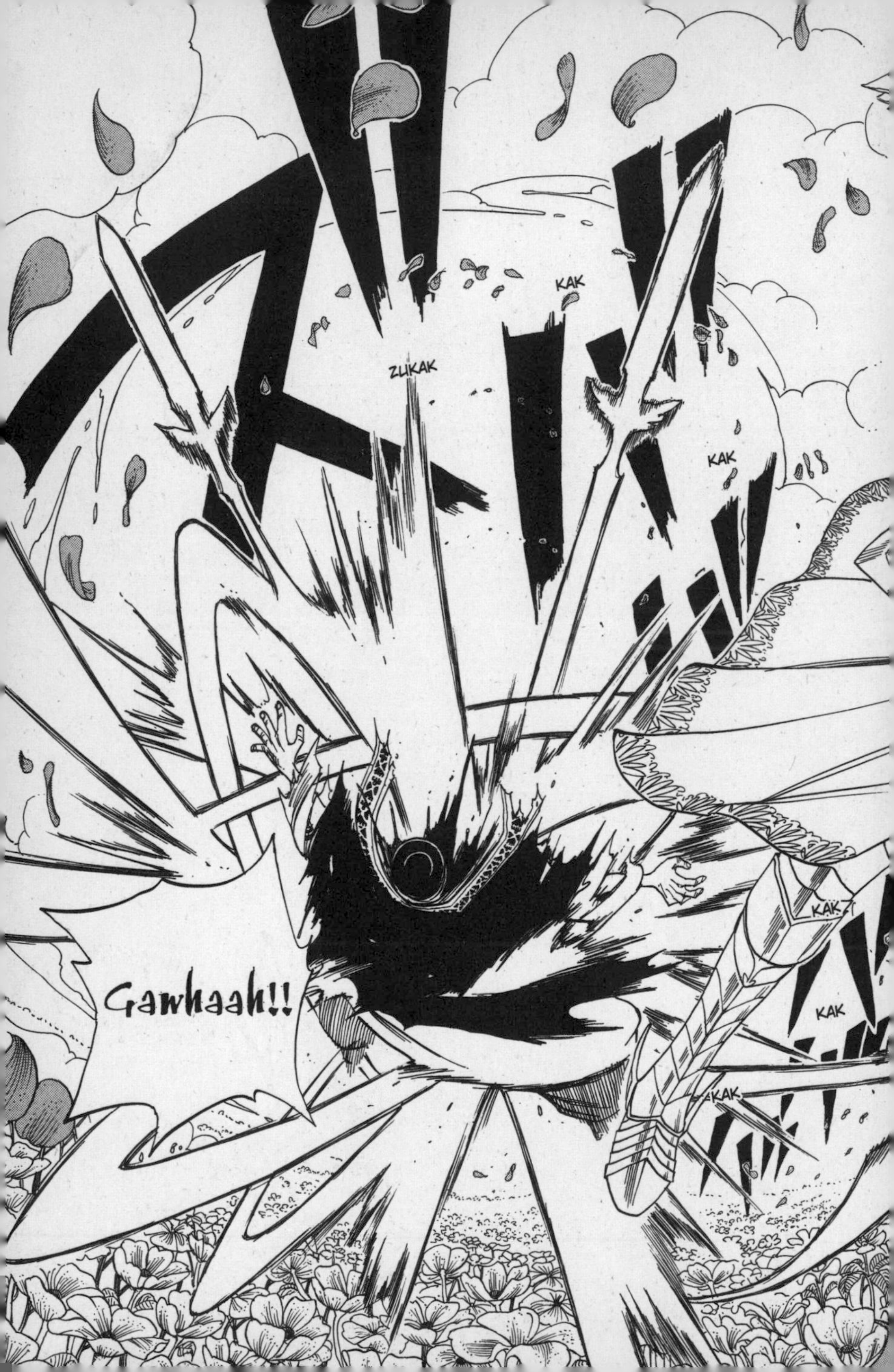
KAK
ZUKAK
KAK
KAK
KAK
KAK
Gawhaah!!

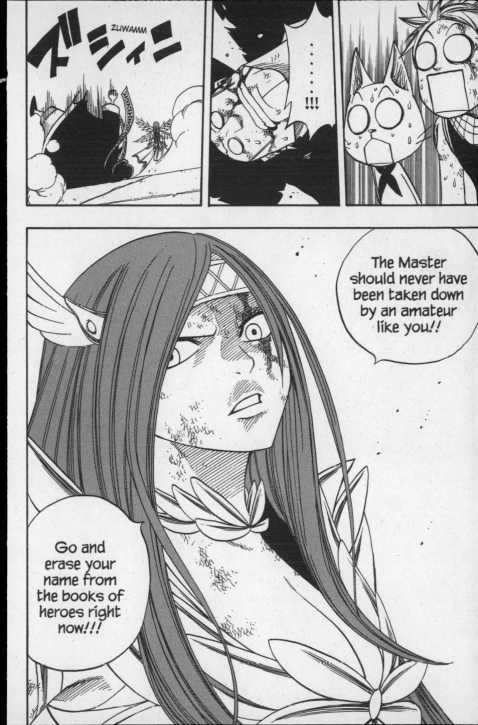

FAIRY TAIL

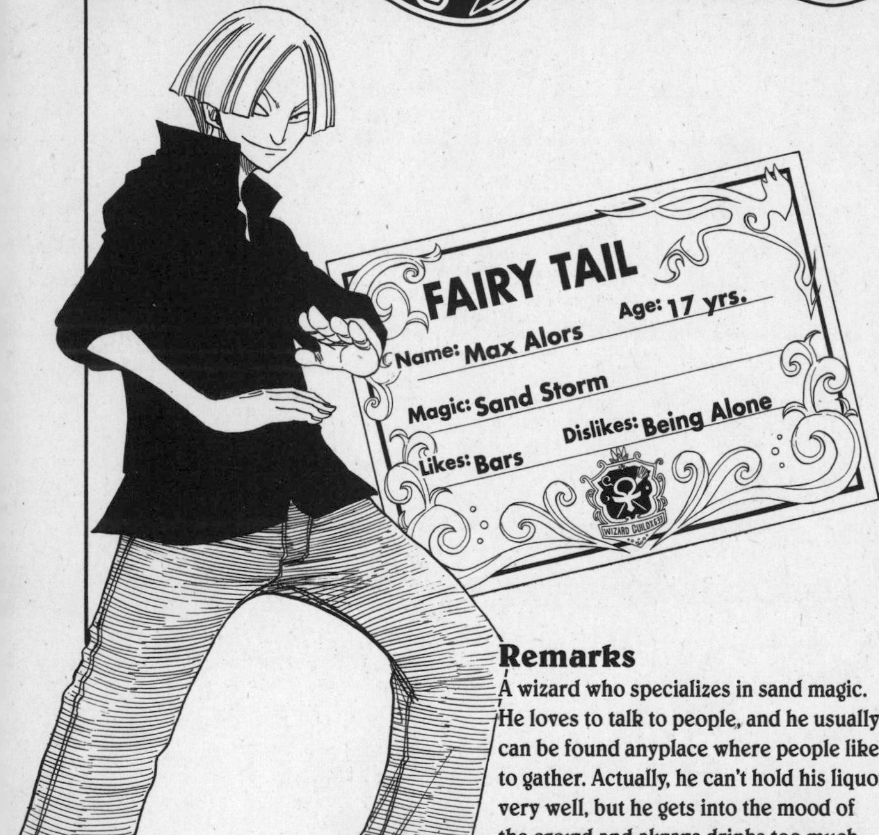
FAIRY TAIL
Name: Max Alors
Age: 17 yrs.
Magic: Sand Storm
Likes: Bars
Dislikes: Being Alone
WIZARD GUILD X633

Remarks

A wizard who specializes in sand magic. He loves to talk to people, and he usually can be found anyplace where people like to gather. Actually, he can't hold his liquor very well, but he gets into the mood of the crowd and always drinks too much. Every time, he regrets it the next day. As a reaction to his generally friendless childhood, he spends as much time as he can in conversation, but nobody knows of his past.

Chapter 59: Inspire

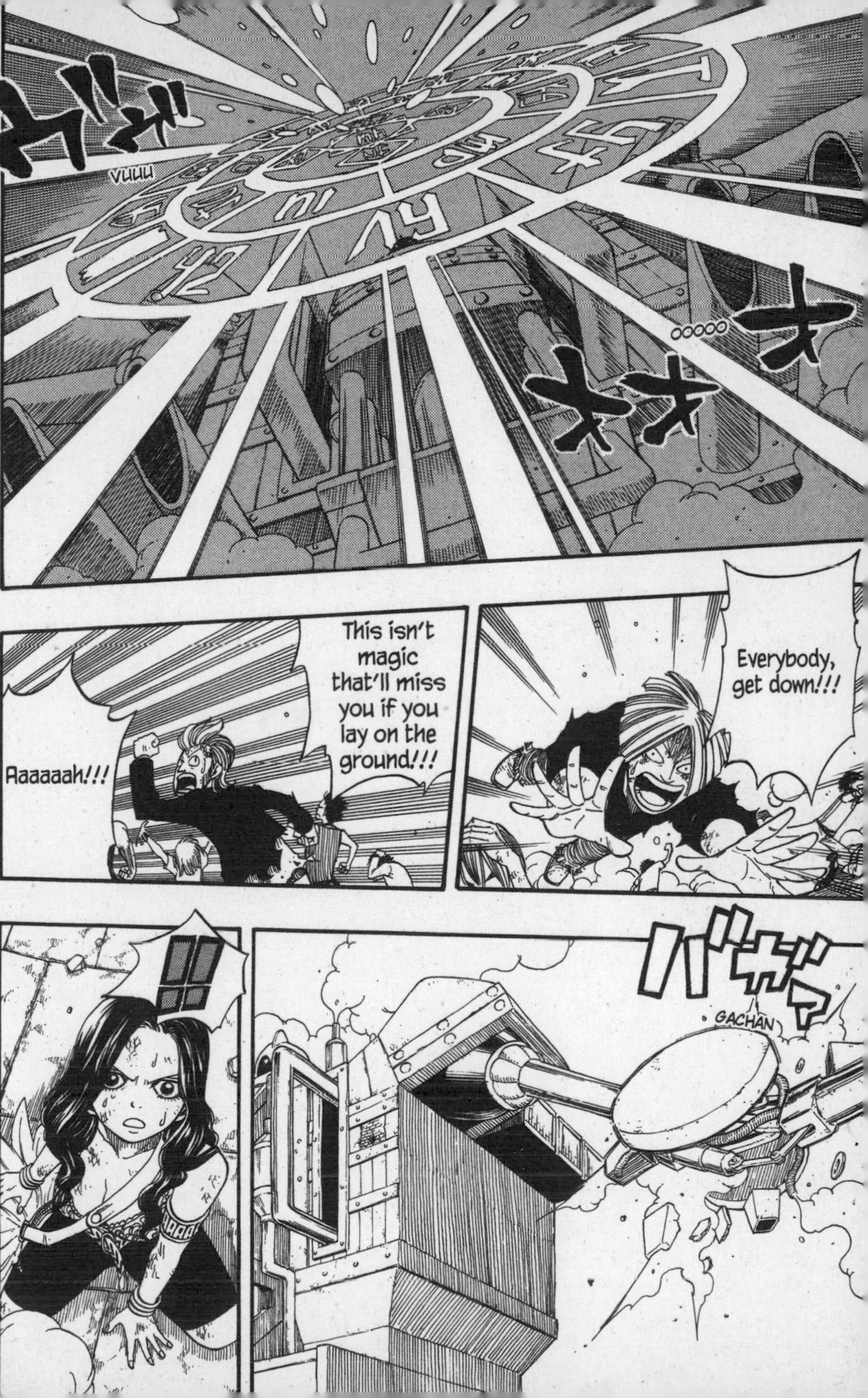
VUUU
Everybody, get down!!!
This isn't magic that'll miss you if you lay on the ground!!!
Aaaaaah!!!
GACHAN

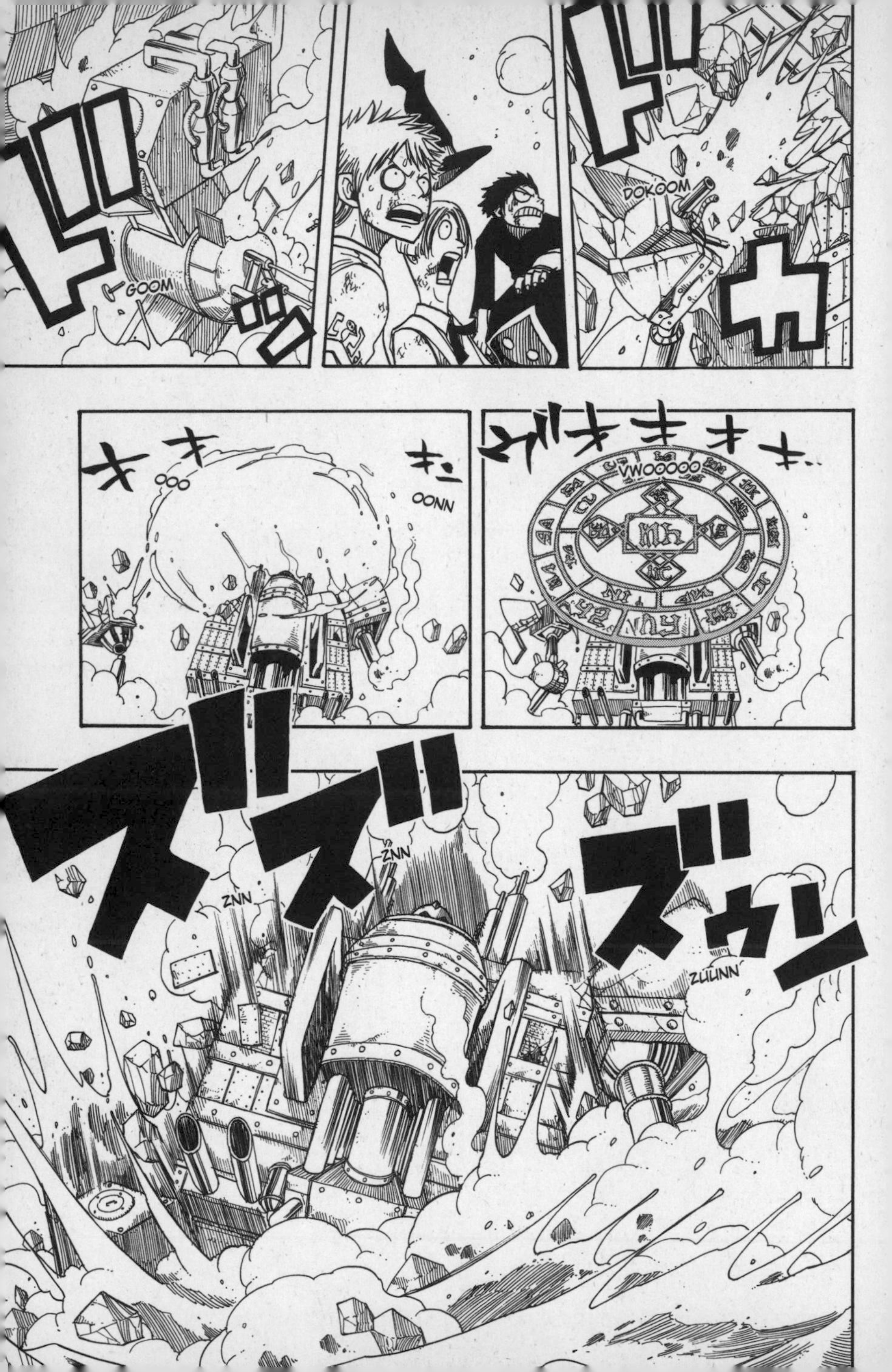
DOKOOM
GOOM
VWOOOOO
OONN
ZUUNN
ZNN
ZNN

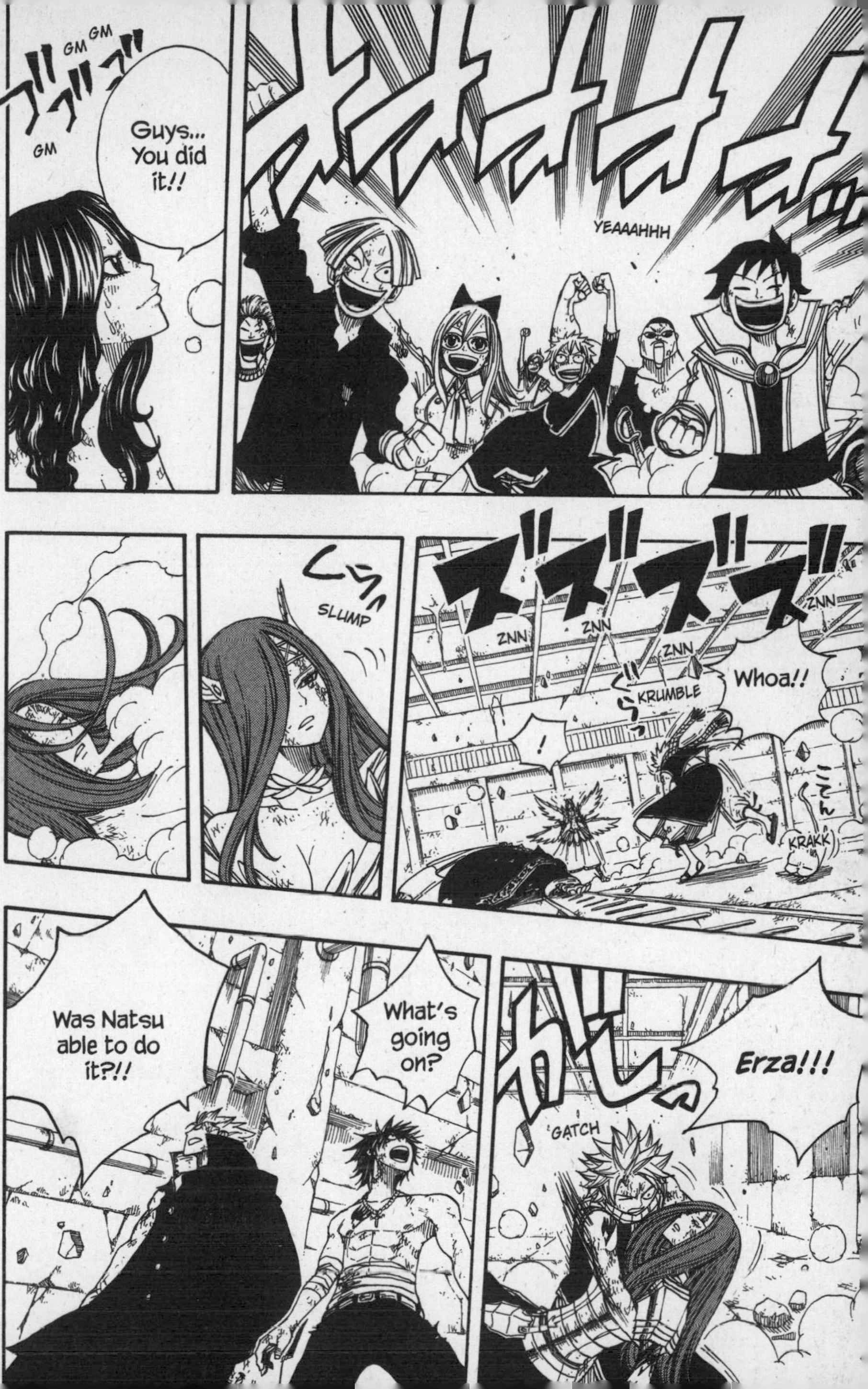

YEAAAHHH
GM GM
GM
Guys... You did it!!
ZNN
ZNN
ZNN
ZNN
KRUMBLE
Whoa!!
!
KRAKK
SLUMP
Erza!!!
GATCH
What's going on?
Was Natsu able to do it?!!

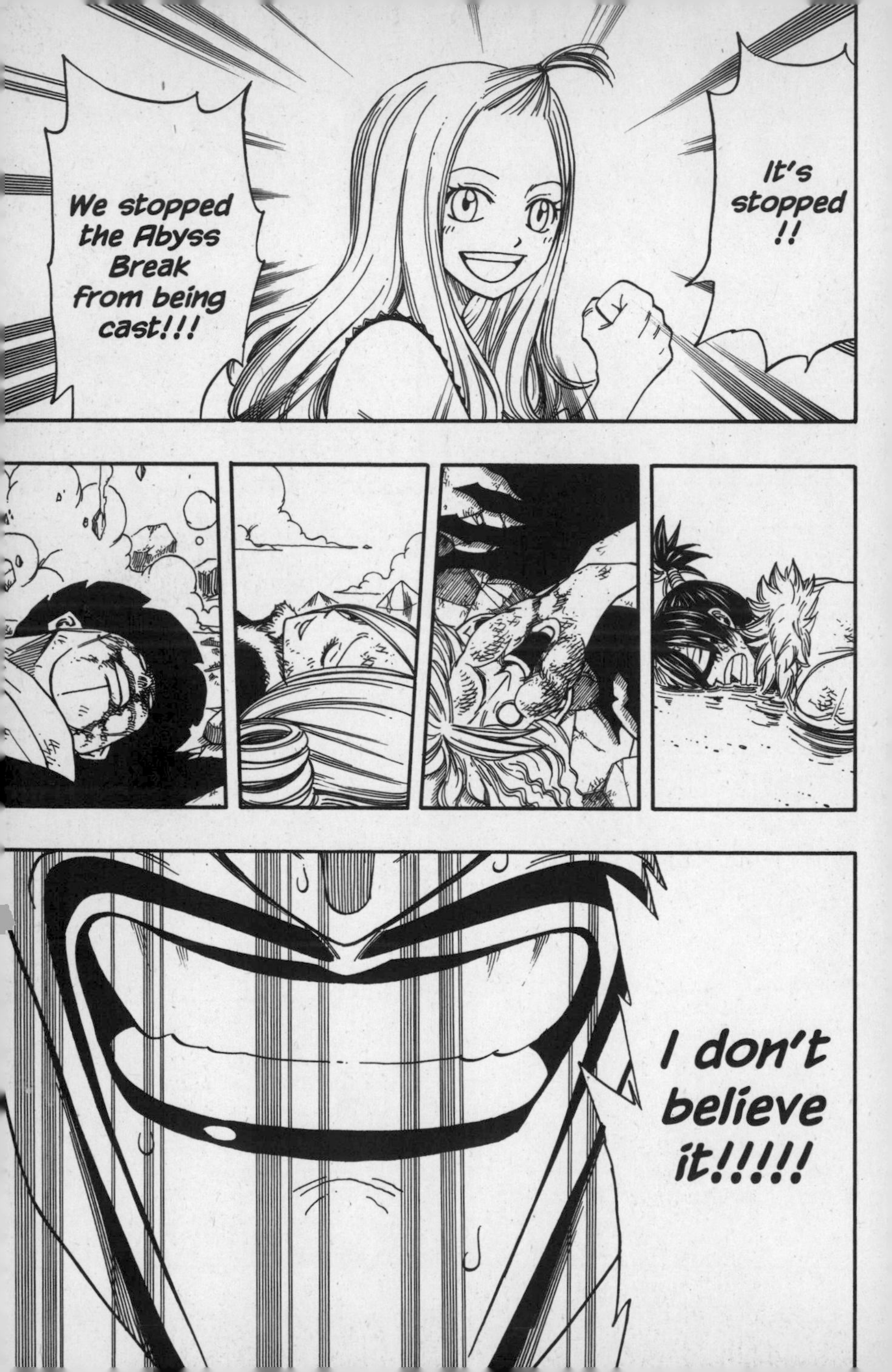
It's stopped!!
We stopped the Abyss Break from being cast!!!
I don't believe it!!!!!

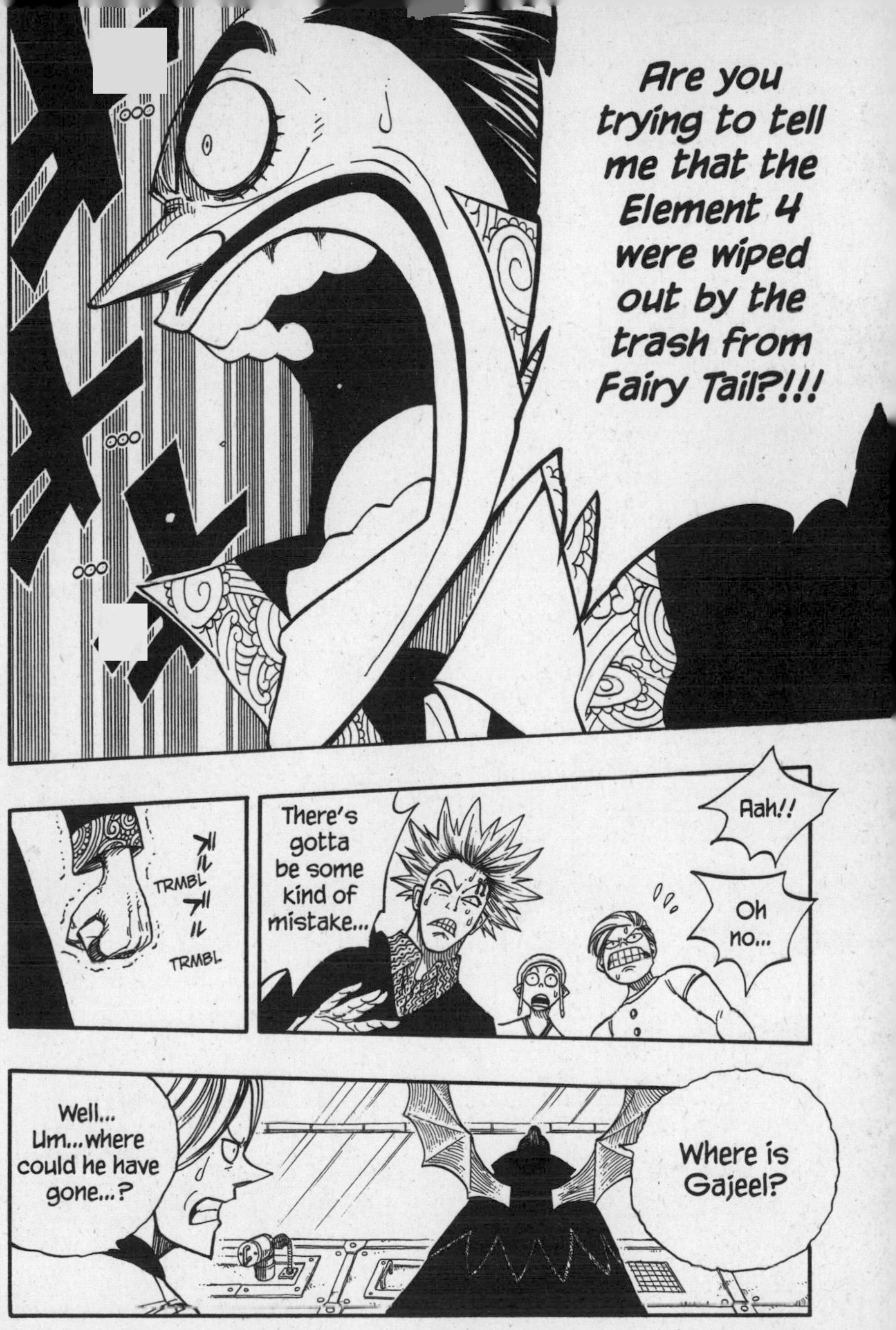
Are you trying to tell me that the Element 4 were wiped out by the trash from Fairy Tail?!!!
Aah!!
Oh no...
There's gotta be some kind of mistake...
TRMBL
TRMBL
Where is Gajeel?
Well... Um...where could he have gone...?

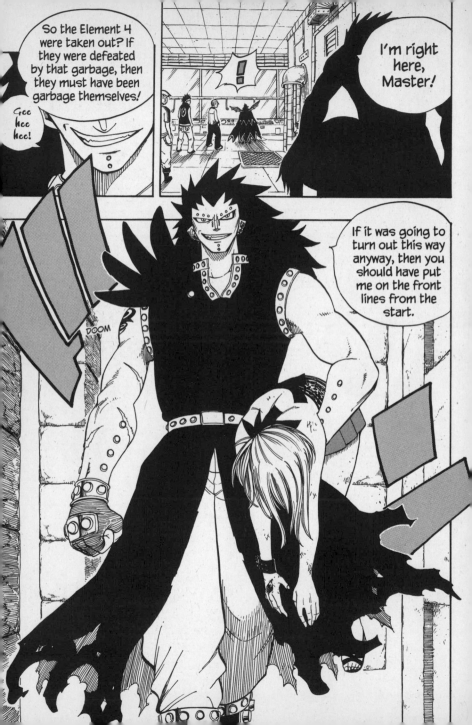

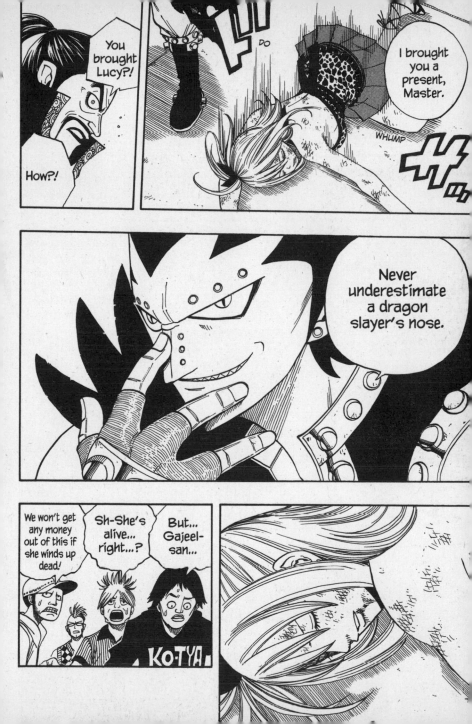

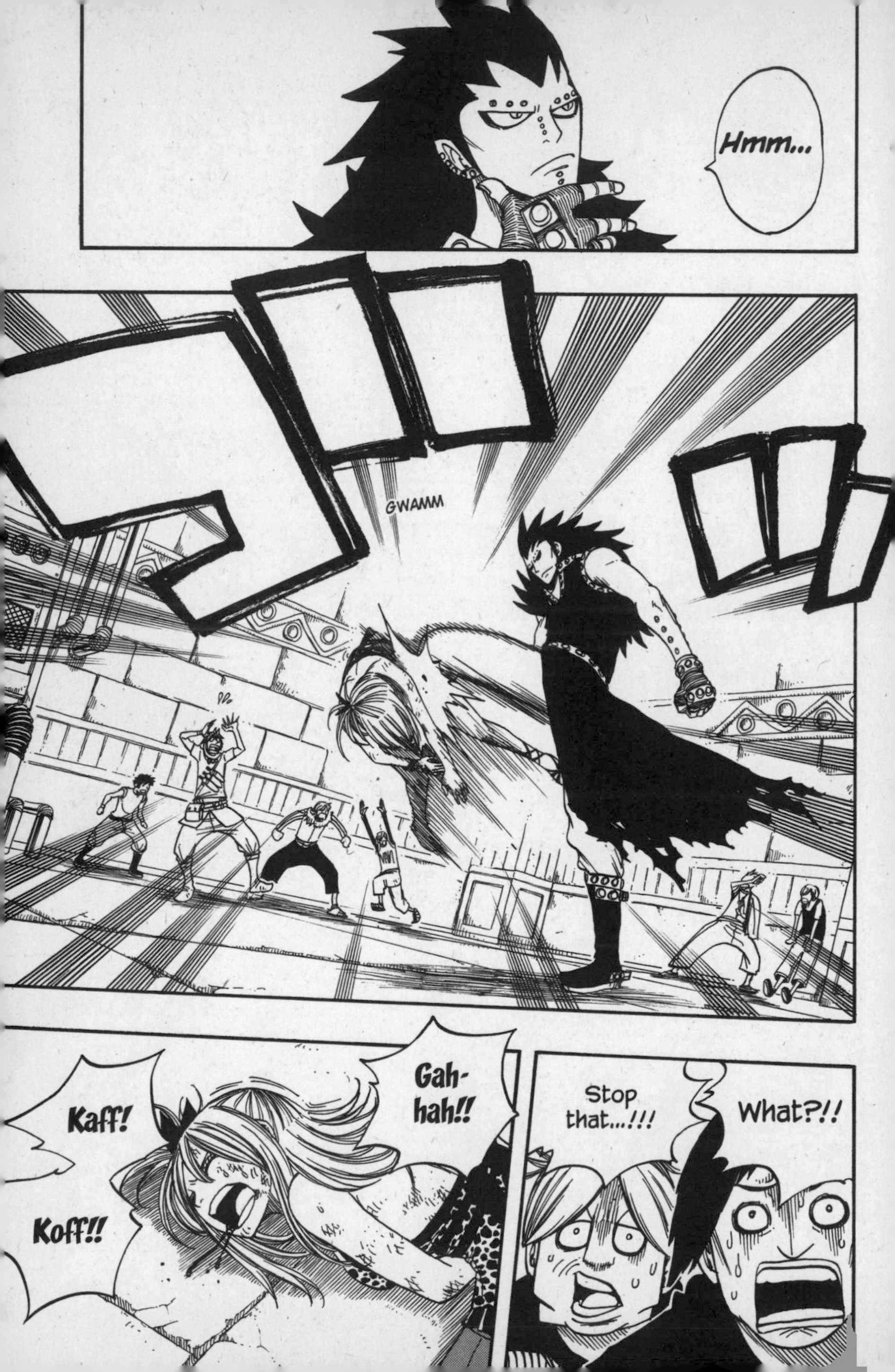
Hmm...
GWAMM
What?!!
Stop that...!!!
Gah-hah!!
Kaff!
Koff!!

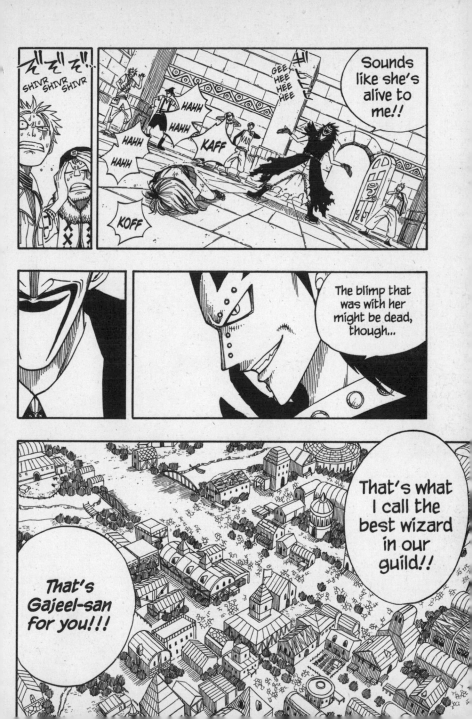

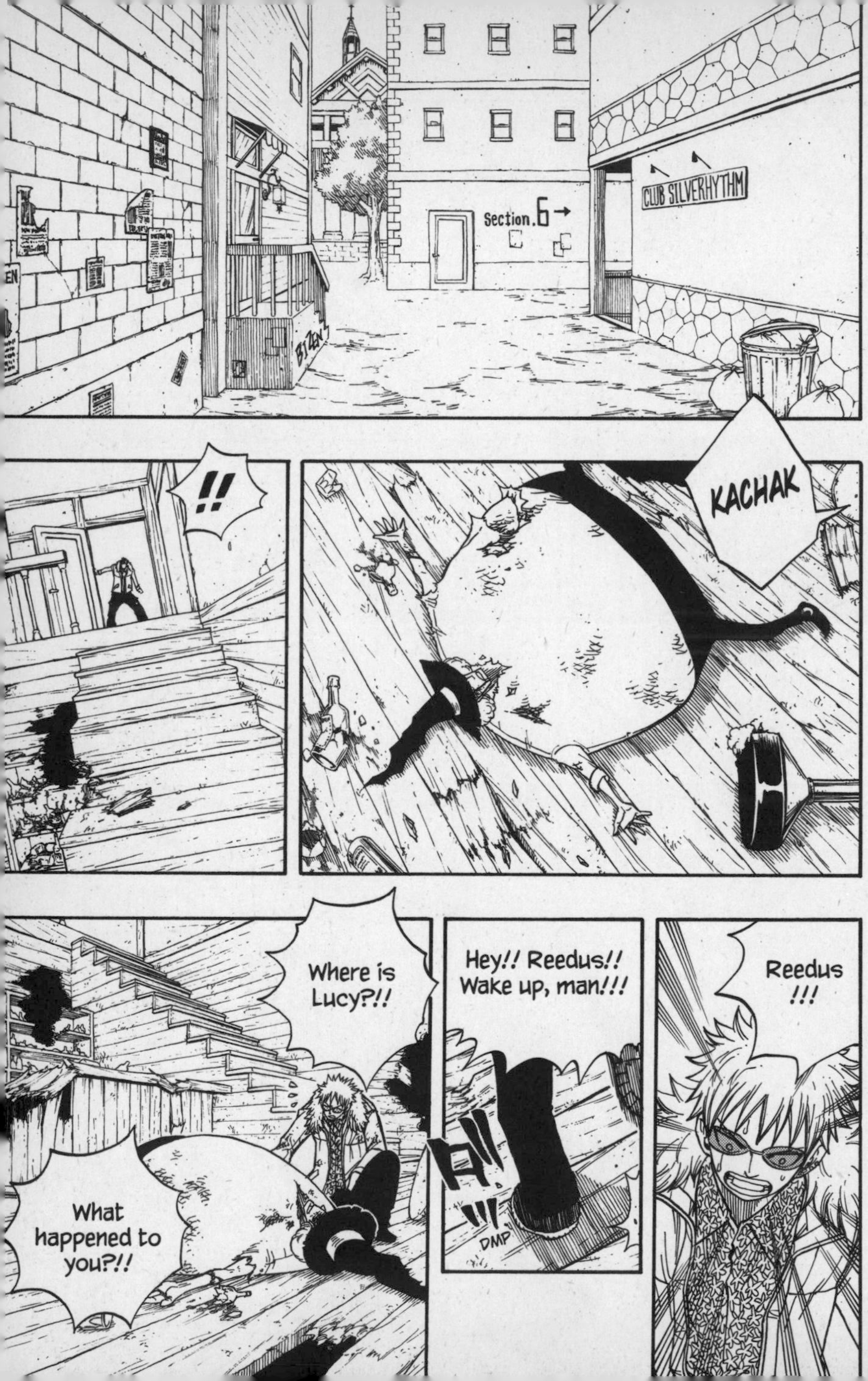
CLUB SILVERHYTHM
Section.6 →
KACHAK
!!
Reedus !!!
Hey!! Reedus!! Wake up, man!!!
DMP
Where is Lucy?!!
What happened to you?!!

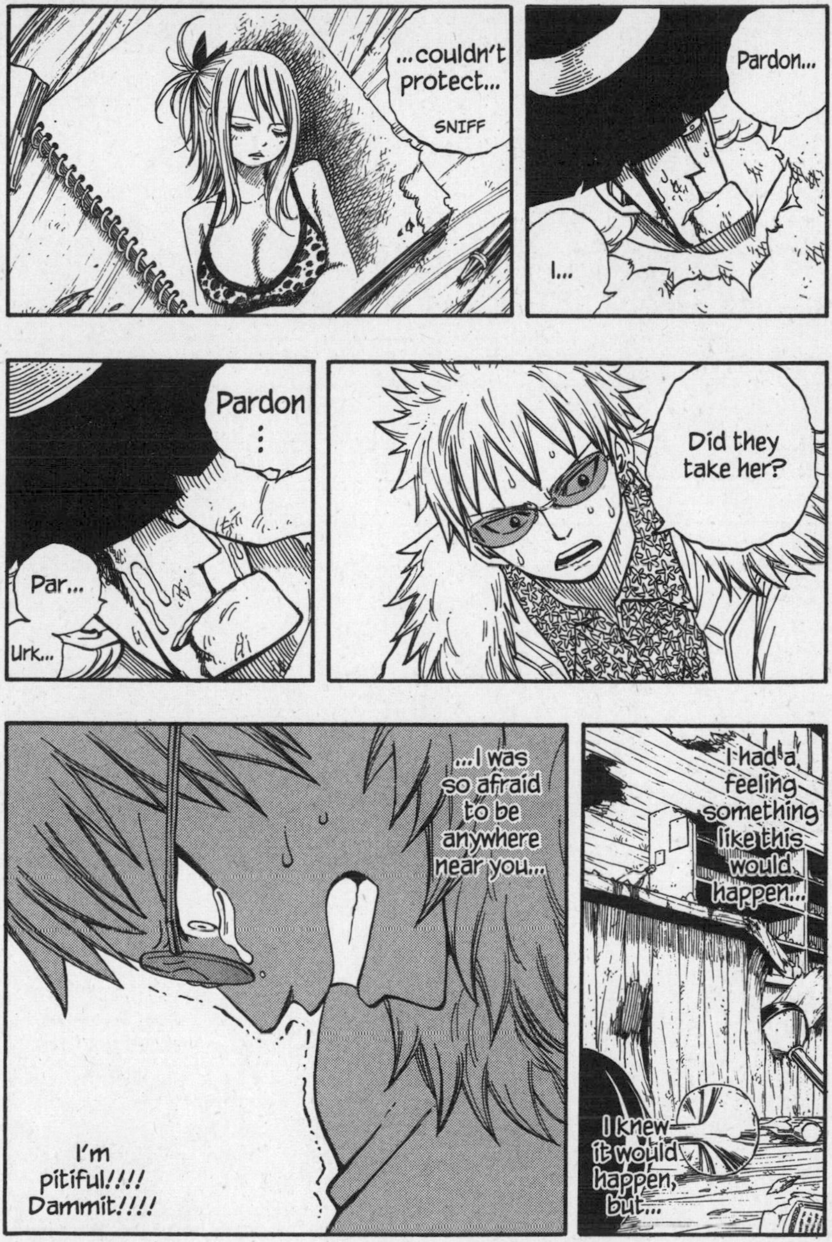
Pardon...
I...
...couldn't protect...
SNIFF
Did they take her?
Pardon ...
Par...
Urk...
I had a feeling something like this would happen...
I knew it would happen, but...
...I was so afraid to be anywhere near you...
I'm pitiful!!!! Dammit!!!!

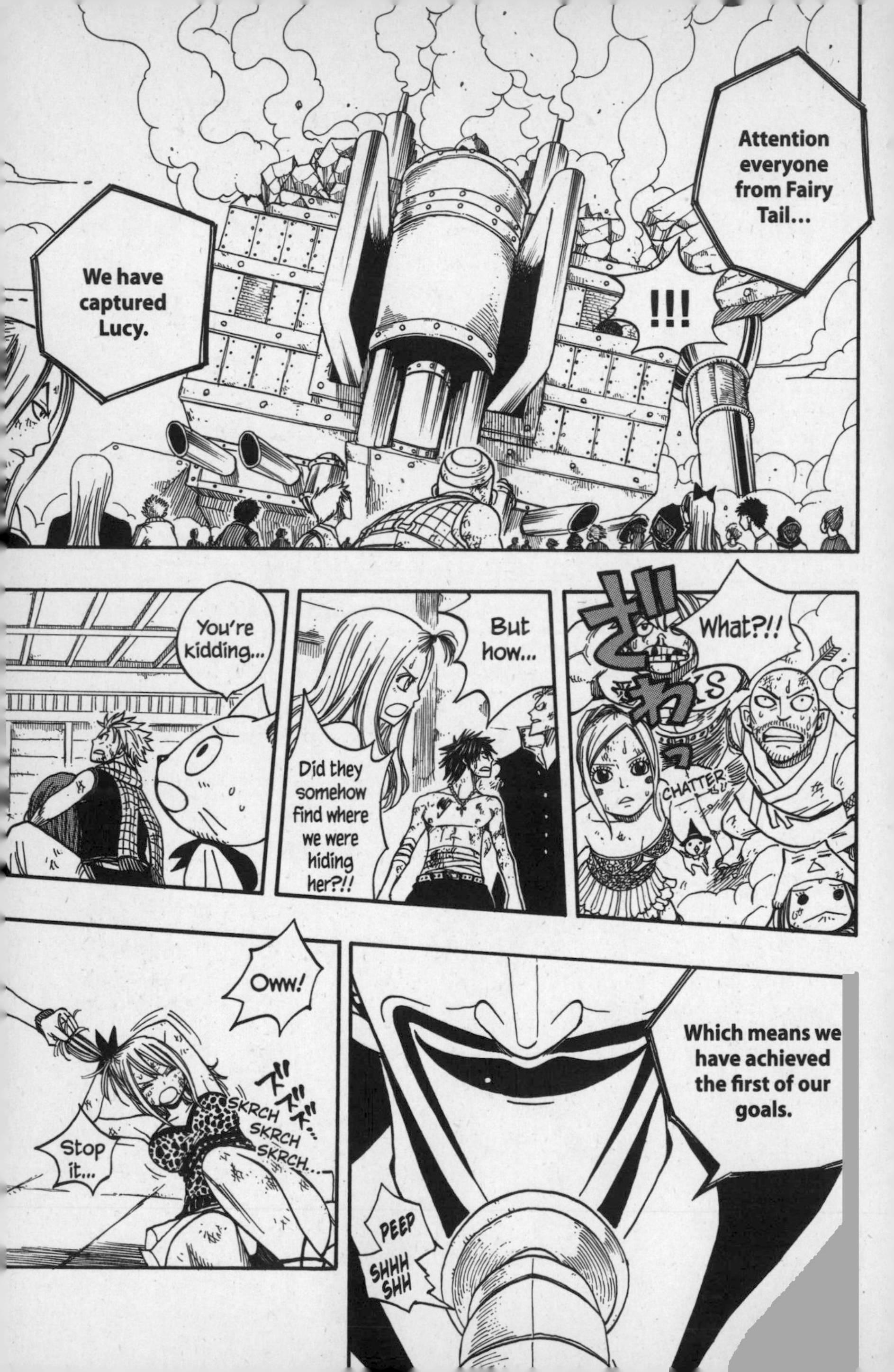
Attention everyone from Fairy Tail...
!!!
We have captured Lucy.
ざわっ
CHATTER
What?!!
But how...
Did they somehow find where we were hiding her?!!
You're kidding...
Which means we have achieved the first of our goals.
PEEP
SHHH SHH
Oww!
ズズズ...
SKRCH SKRCH SKRCH...
Stop it...

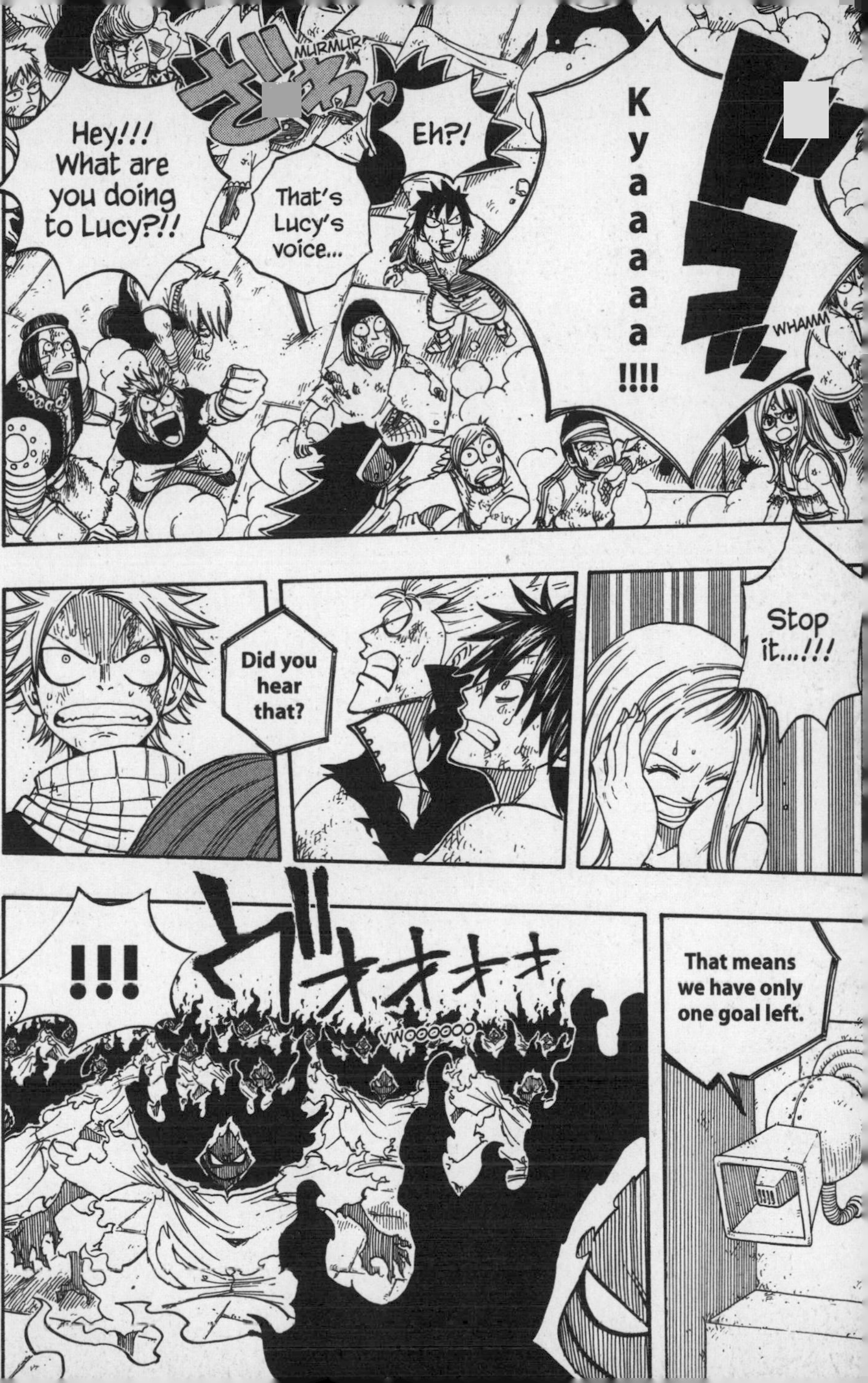
Kyaaaaa!!!!
WHAMM
Eh?!
That's Lucy's voice...
MURMUR
Hey!!! What are you doing to Lucy?!!
Stop it...!!!
Did you hear that?
That means we have only one goal left.
!!!
VWOOOOOO

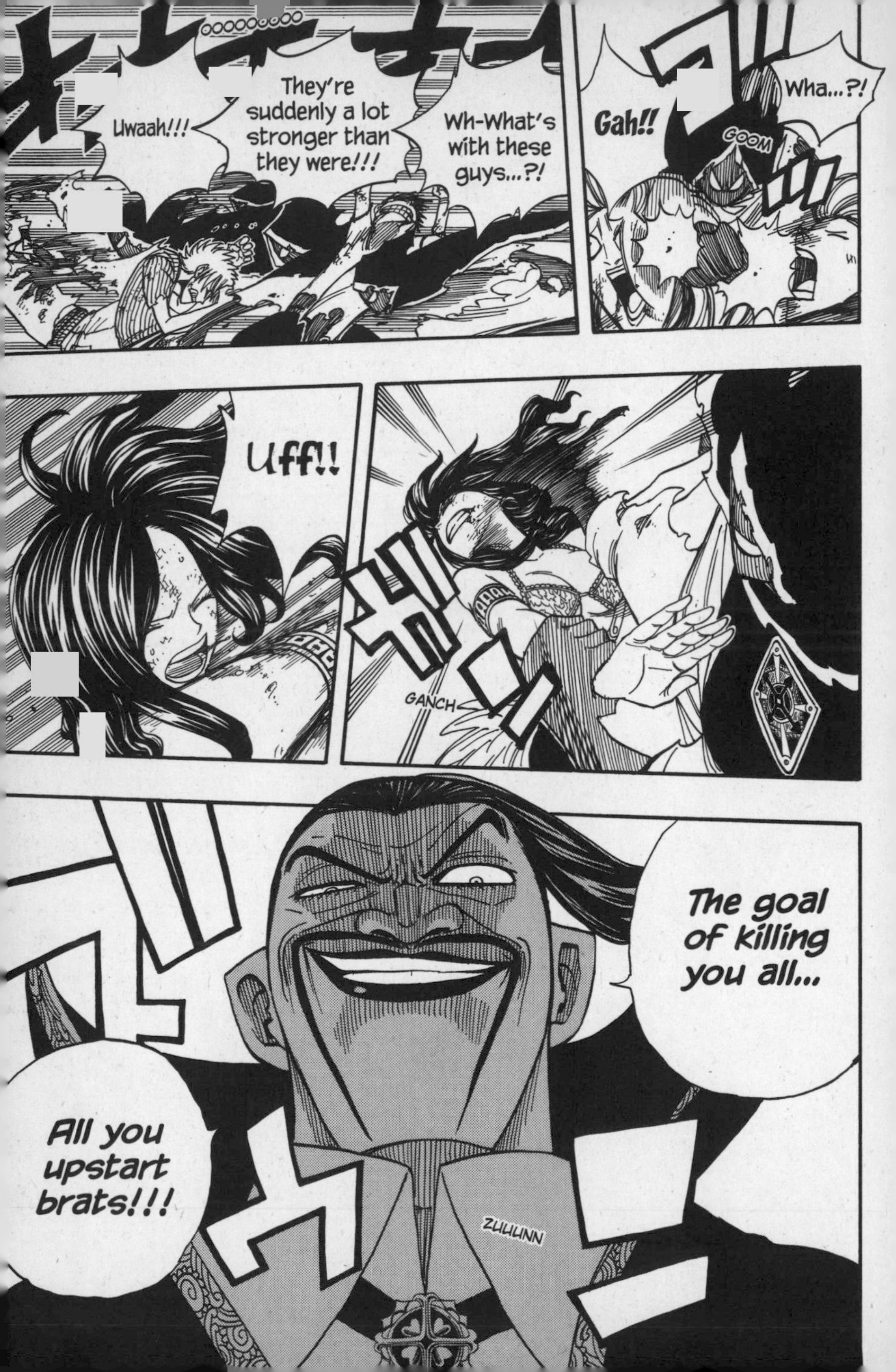
Wha...?!
Gah!!
GOOM
Wh-What's with these guys...?!
They're suddenly a lot stronger than they were!!!
Uwaah!!!
GANCH
Uff!!
The goal of killing you all...
All you upstart brats!!!
ZUUUNN

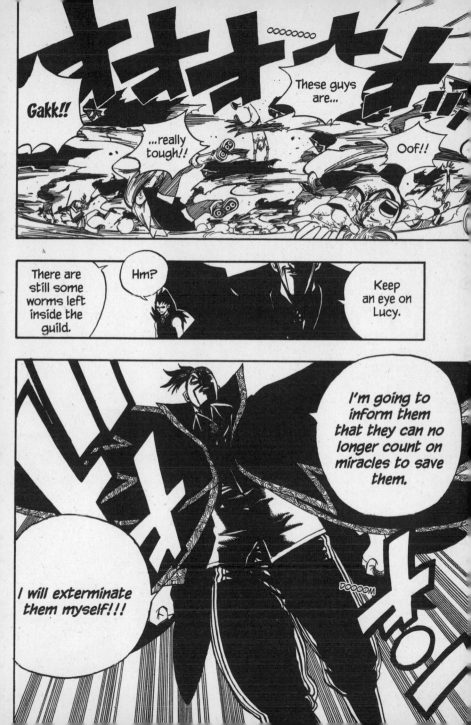

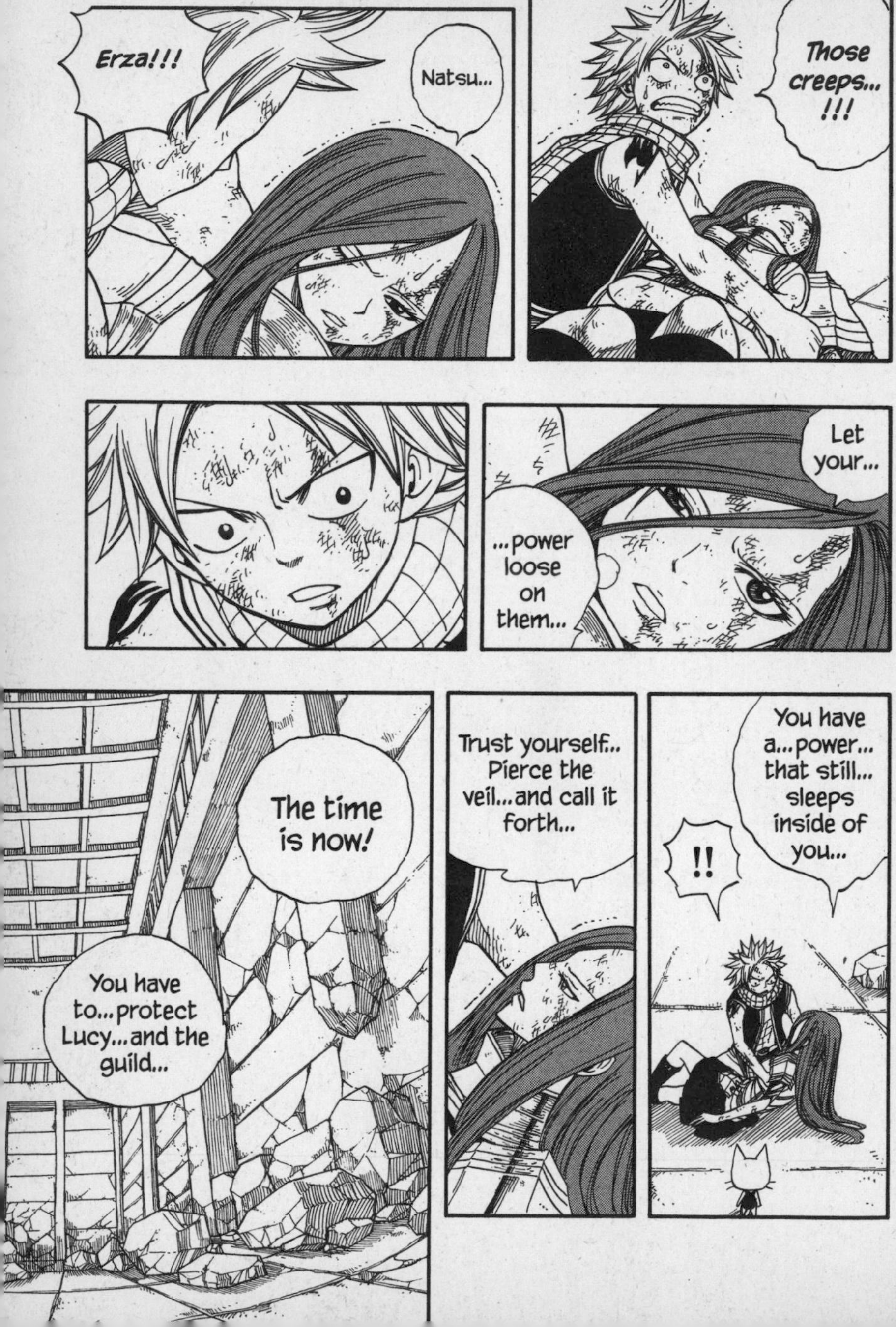
Those creeps... !!!
Natsu...
Erza!!!
Let your...
...power loose on them...
You have a...power... that still... sleeps inside of you...
!!
Trust yourself... Pierce the veil...and call it forth...
The time is now!
You have to...protect Lucy...and the guild...

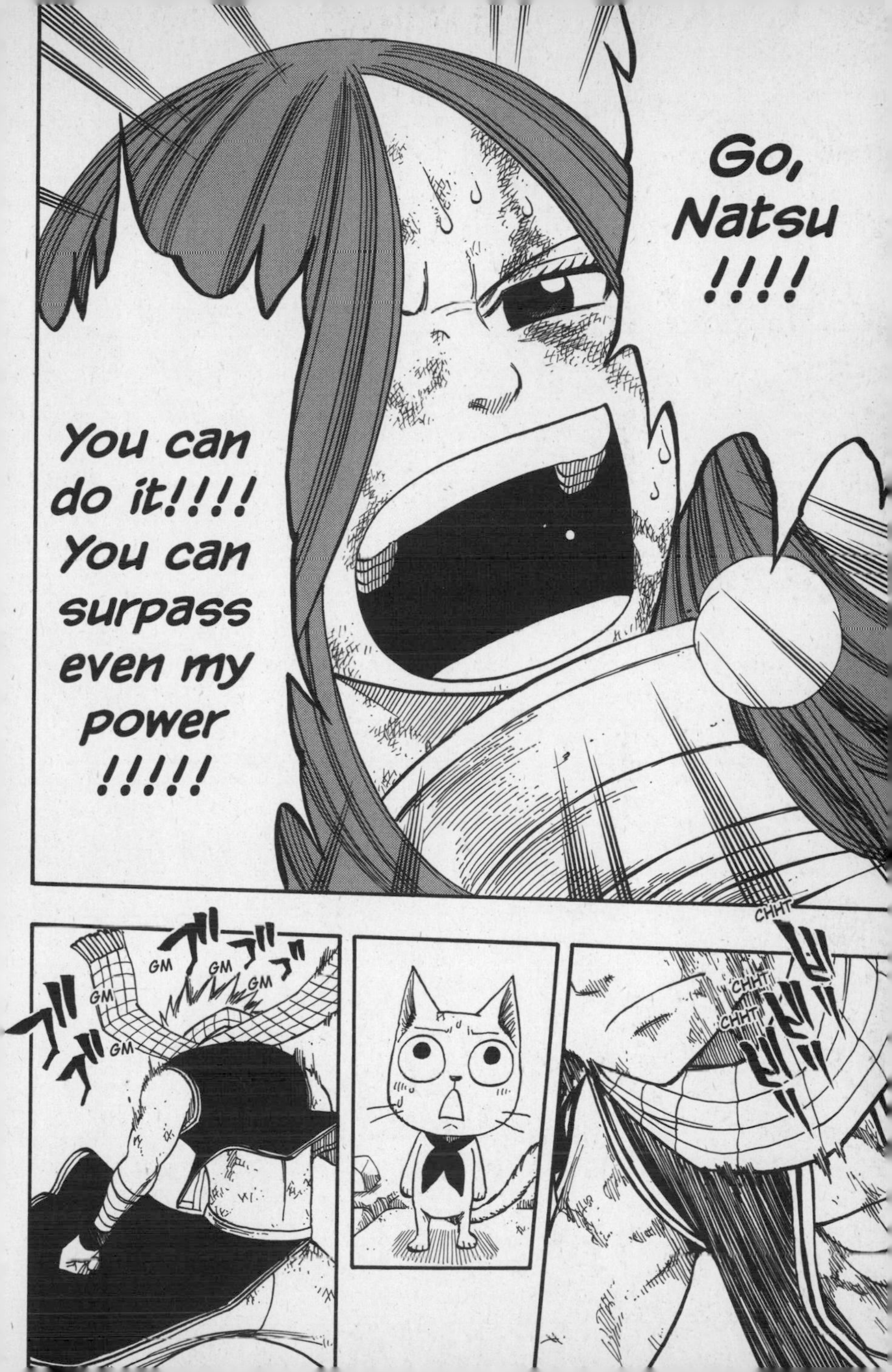
Go, Natsu !!!!
You can do it!!!! You can surpass even my power !!!!!
CHHT
CHHT
CHHT
GM
GM
GM
GM
GM

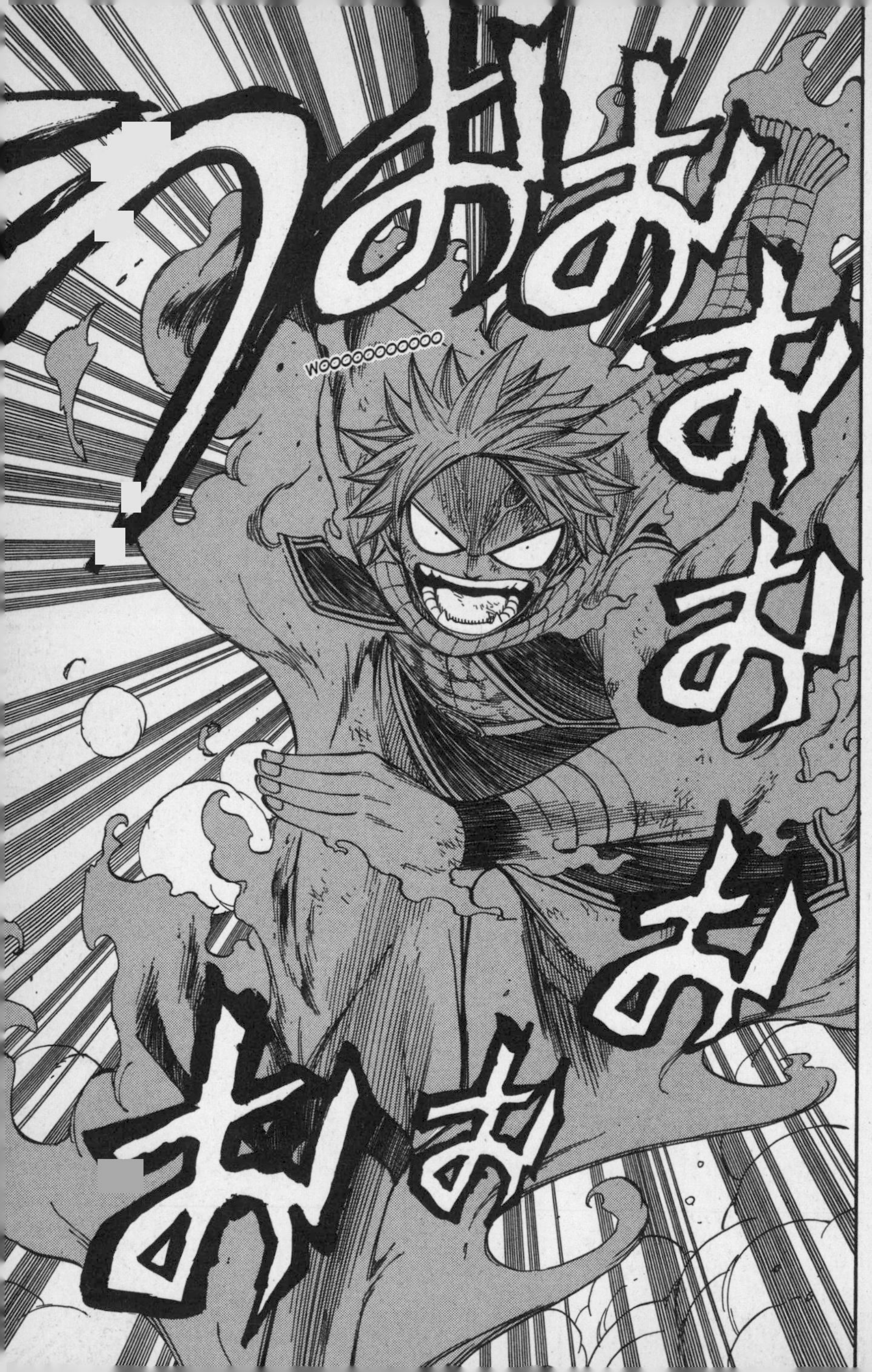
WOOOOOOOOOOO

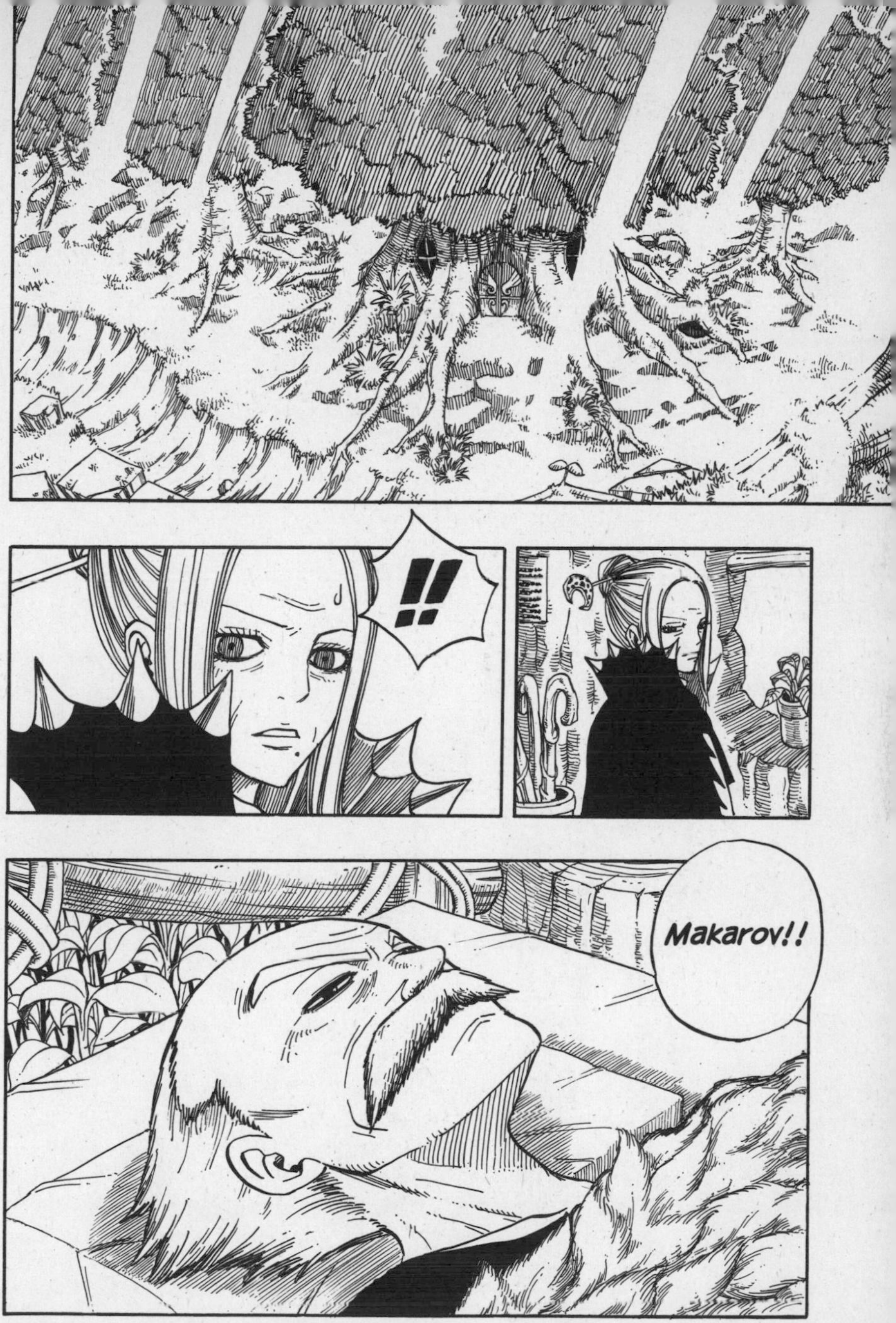
!!
Makarov!!

FAIRY TAIL

Chapter 60: Wings of Fire

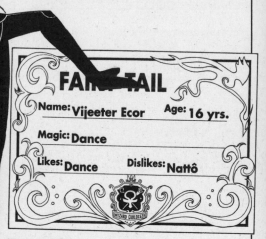

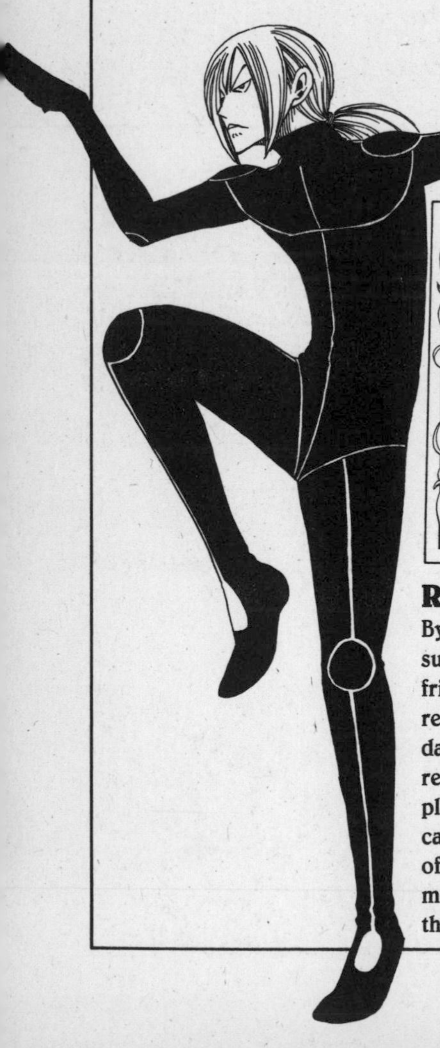

FAIRY TAIL

Name: Vijeeter Ecor   Age: 16 yrs.

Magic: Dance

Likes: Dance   Dislikes: Nattô

Remarks

By dancing particular dances, he can do things such as boost the fighting power of all of his friends within a ten meter radius or, similarly, reduce the fighting power of enemies with his dance magic. He's always loved dance, and can regularly be seen dancing within the guild. His plan for the future seems to be to save up his cash and go study at Minstrel, the cultural capital of dance. But he never can seem to save any money. As a side note, he has a hundred suits that all look alike.

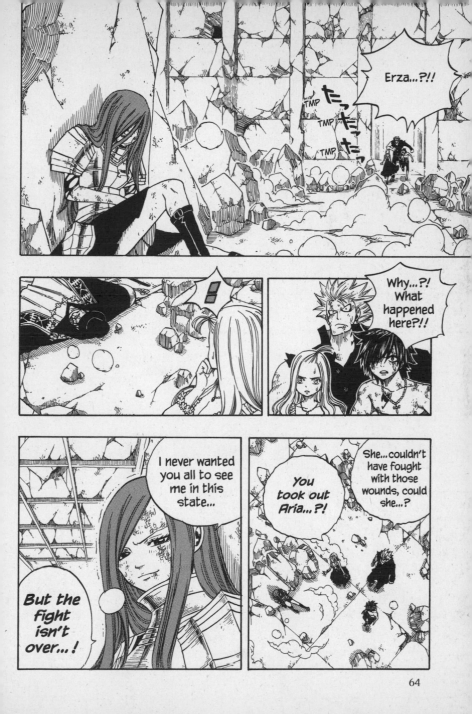

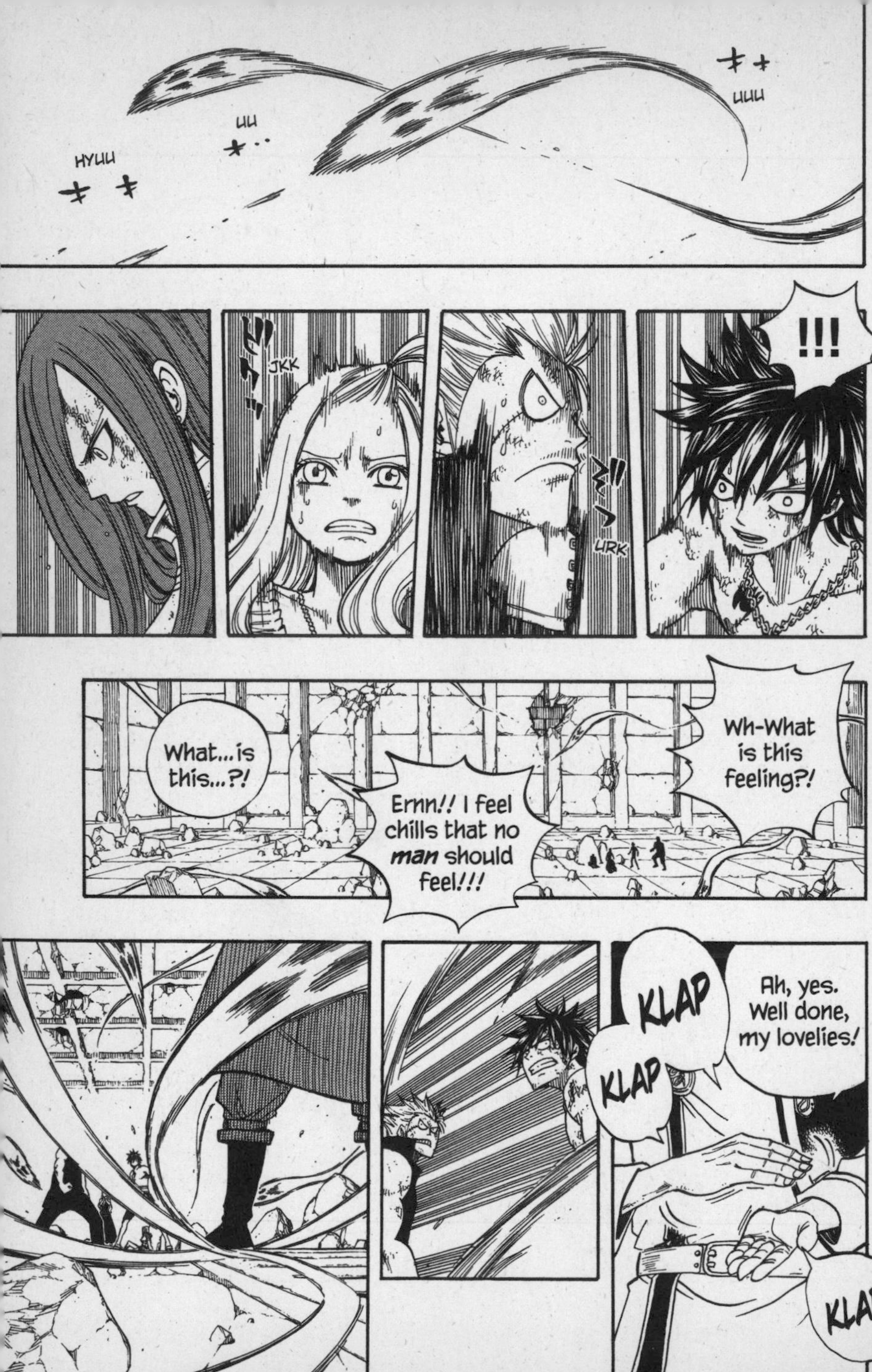
UUU
UU
HYUU
!!!
URK
JKK
Wh-What is this feeling?!
Ernn!! I feel chills that no *man* should feel!!!
What...is this...?!
Ah, yes. Well done, my lovelies!
KLAP
KLAP
KLAP

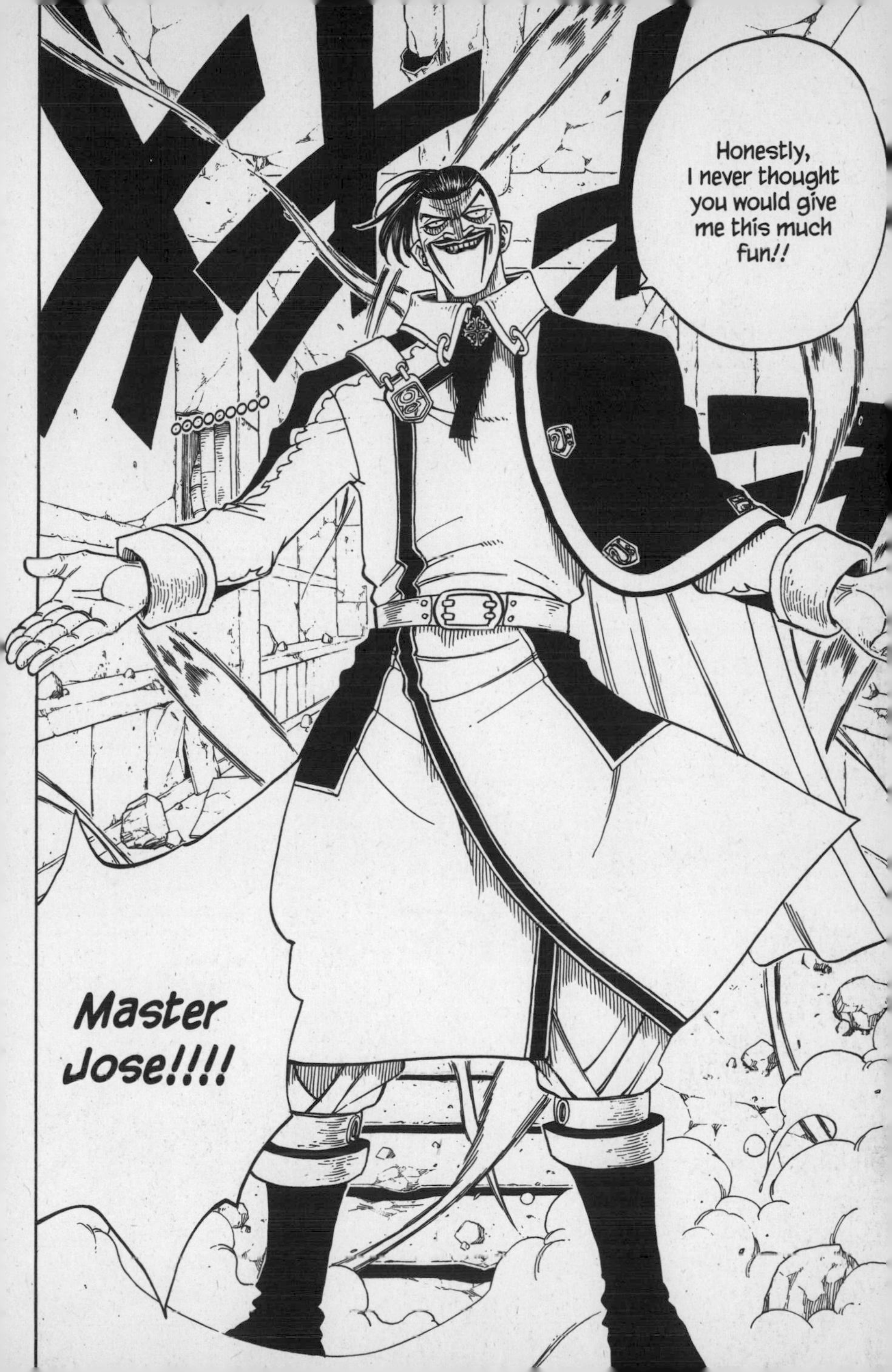
Honestly, I never thought you would give me this much fun!!
Master Jose!!!!

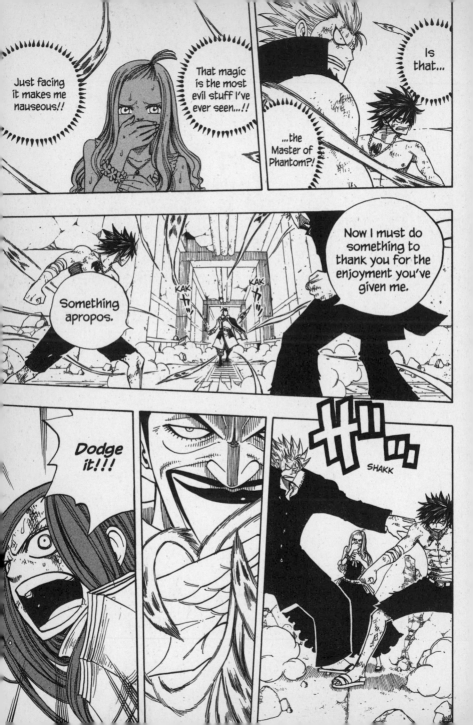

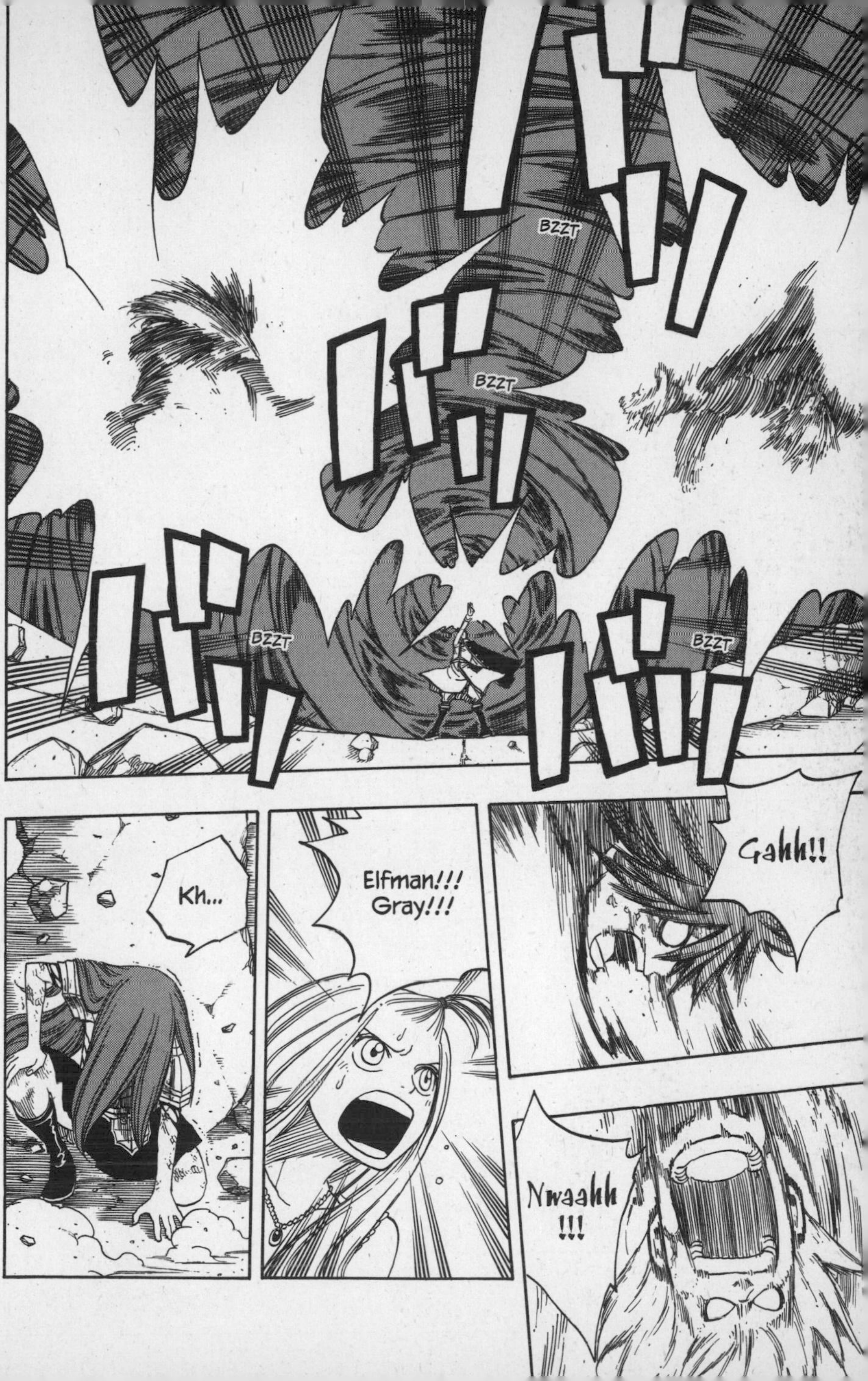
BZZT
BZZT
BZZT
BZZT
Gahh!!
Nwaahh !!!
Elfman!!! Gray!!!
Kh...

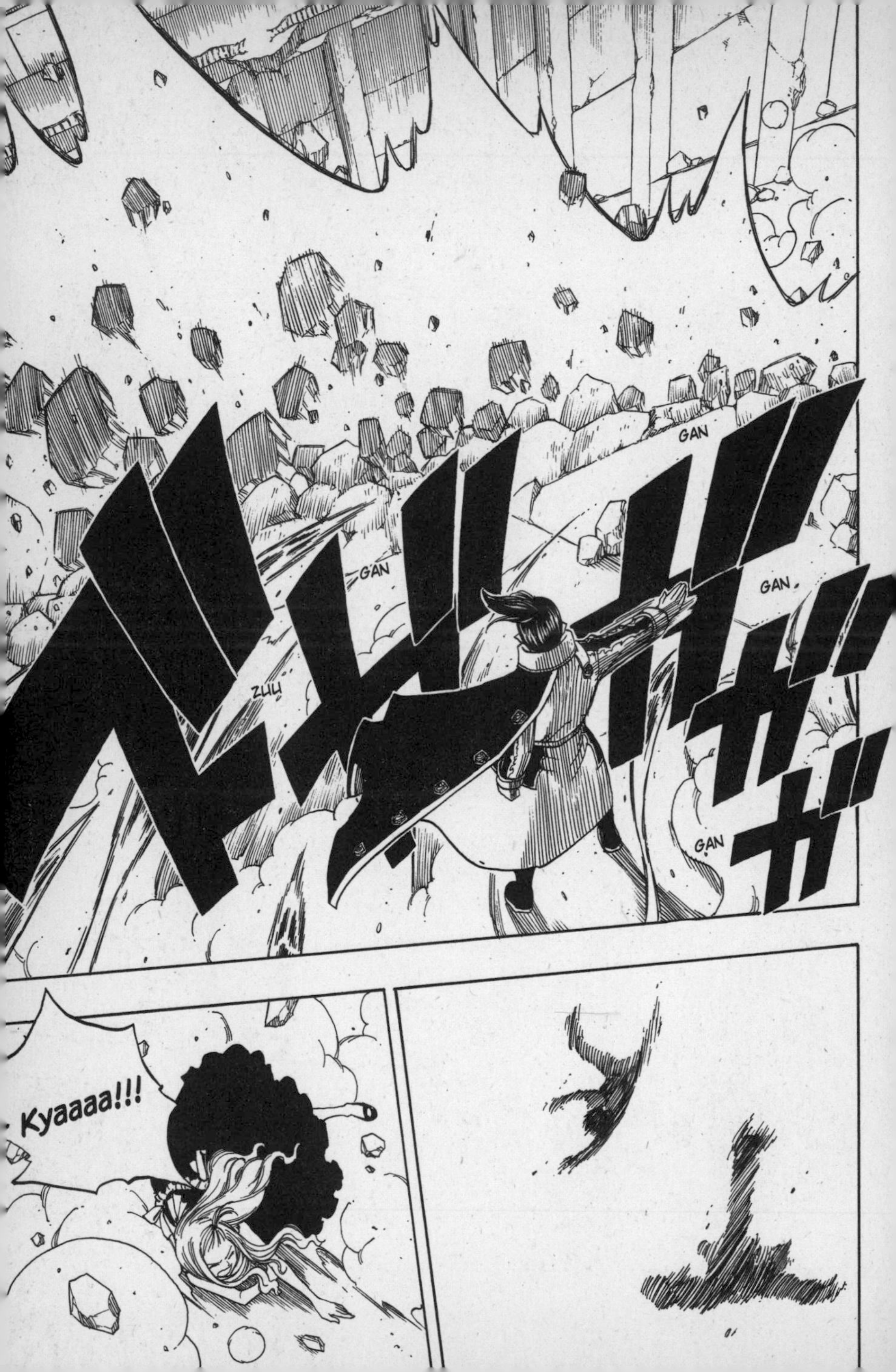
GAN
GAN
GAN
GAN
ZUU
Kyaaaa!!!

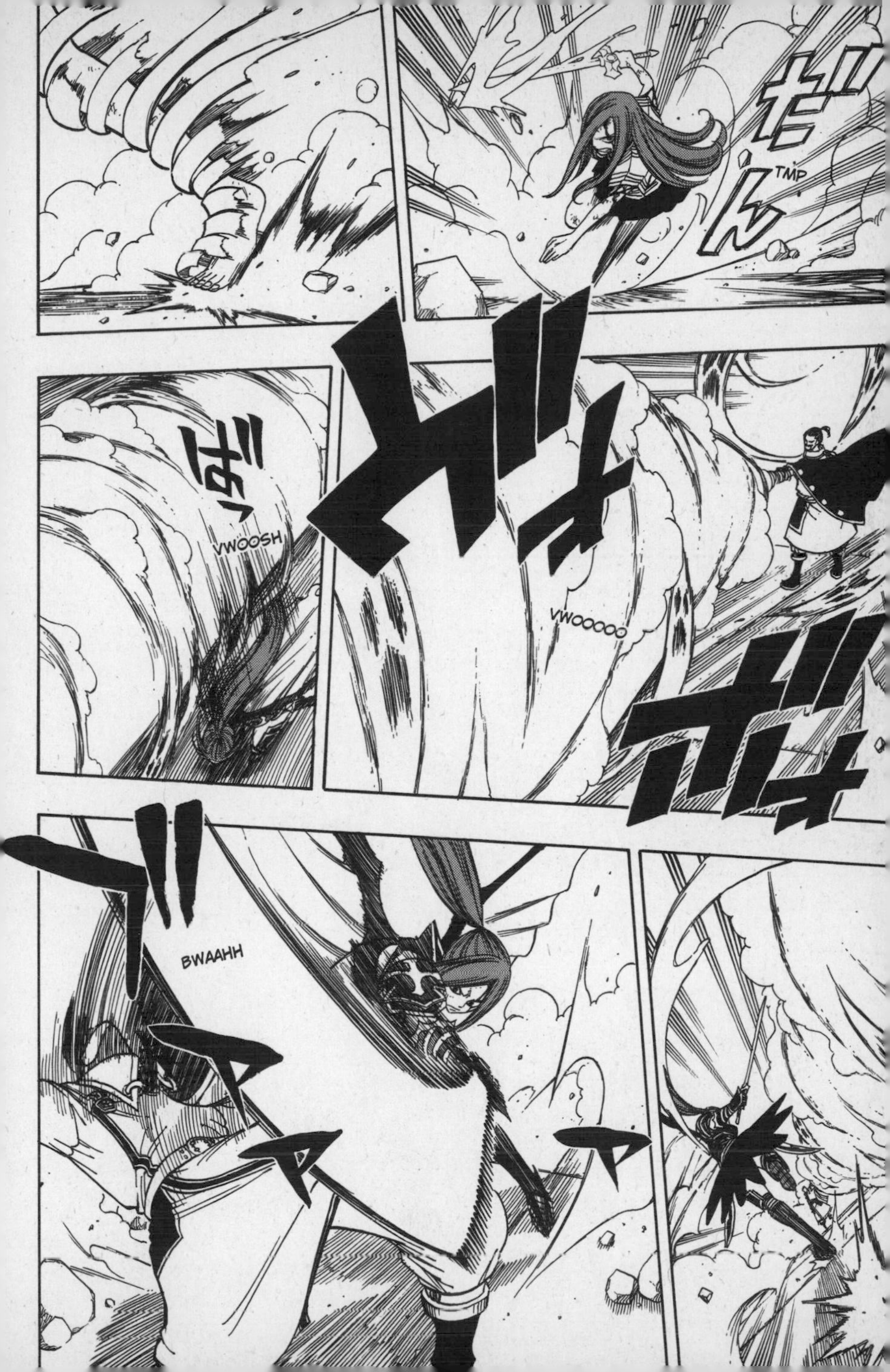
だん
TMP
VWOOOOO
ばっ
VWOOSH
BWAAHH

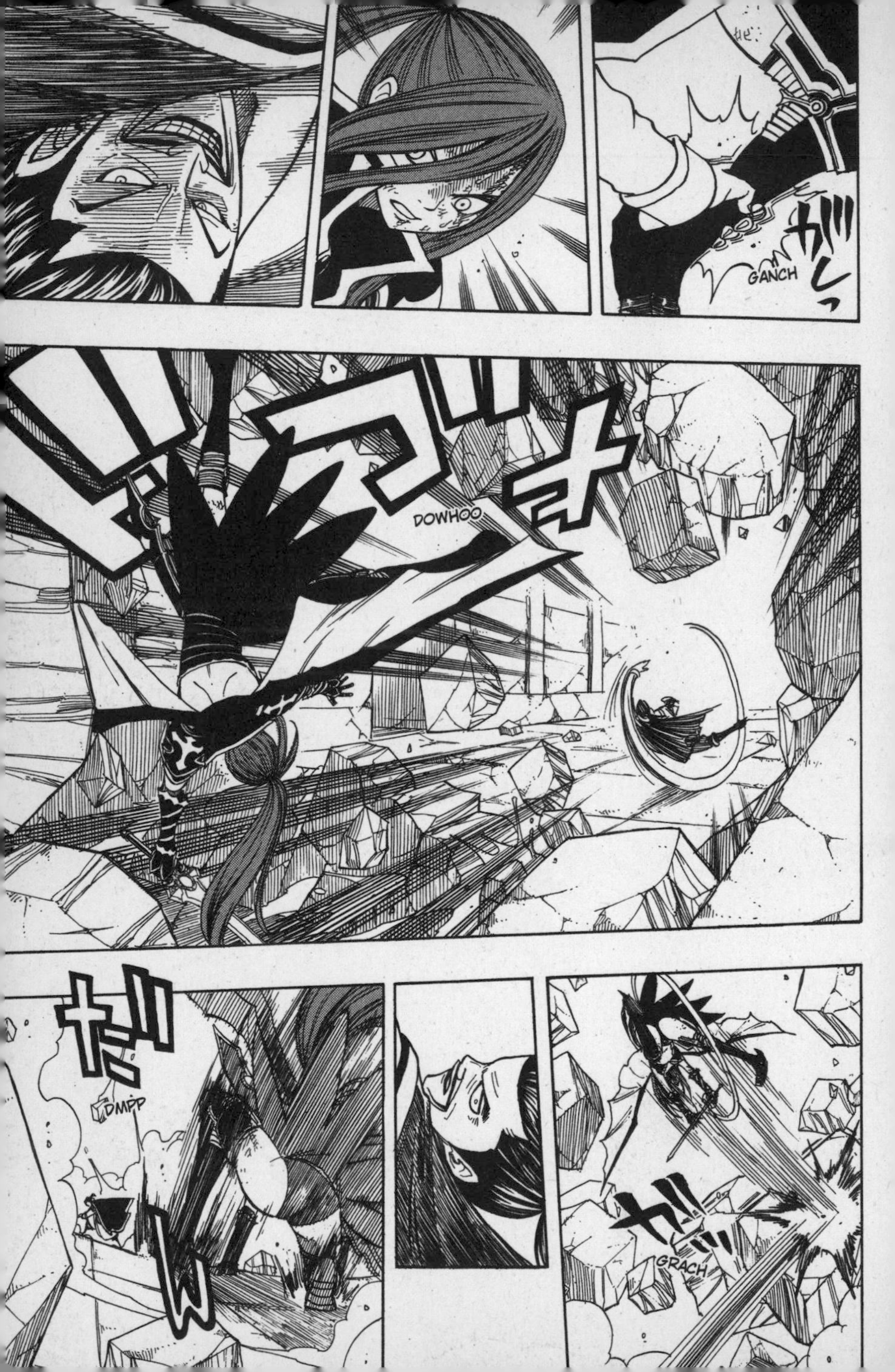
GANCH
DOWHOO
GRACH
DMPP

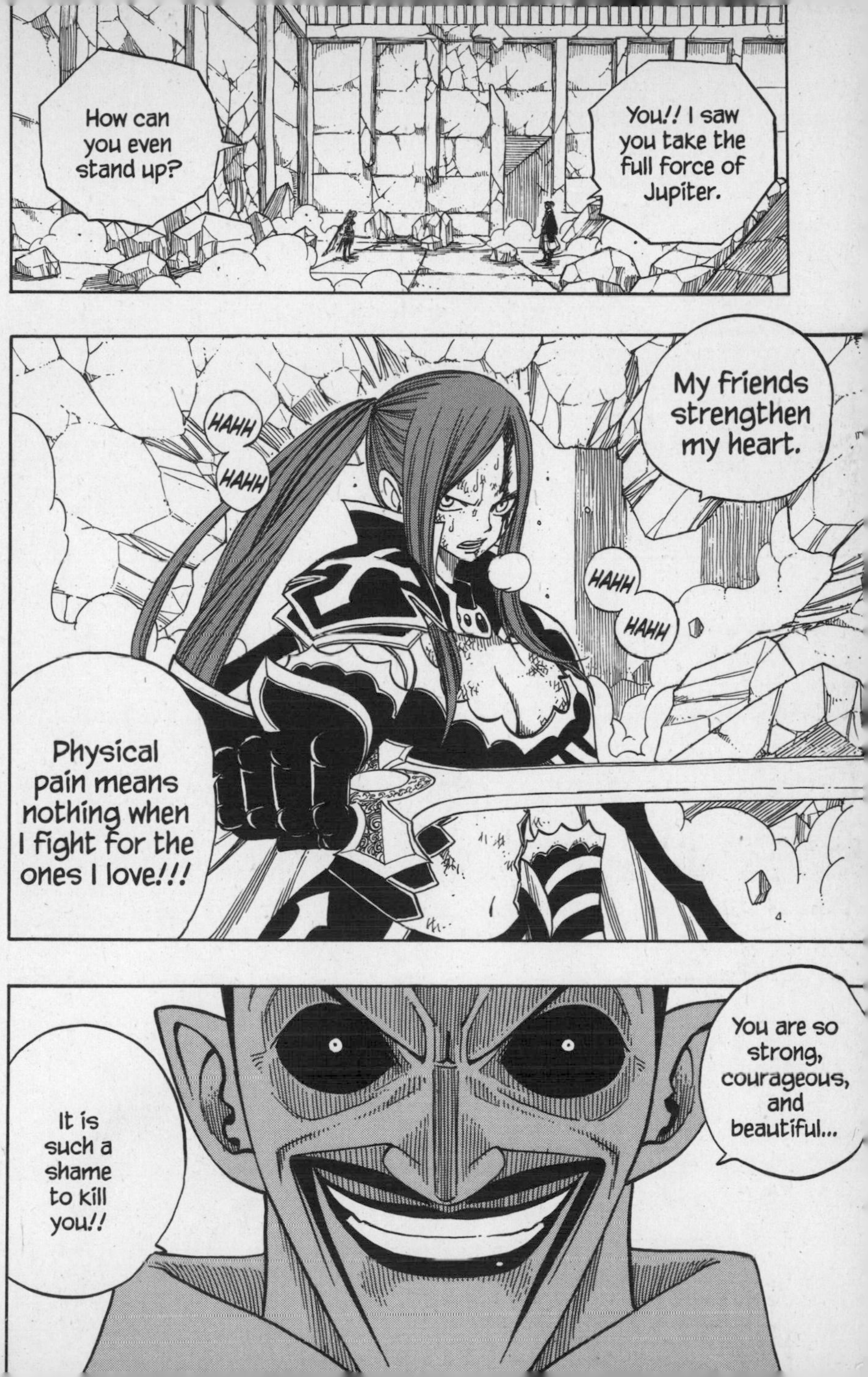
You!! I saw you take the full force of Jupiter.
How can you even stand up?
My friends strengthen my heart.
HAHH HAHH
HAHH HAHH
Physical pain means nothing when I fight for the ones I love!!!
You are so strong, courageous, and beautiful...
It is such a shame to kill you!!

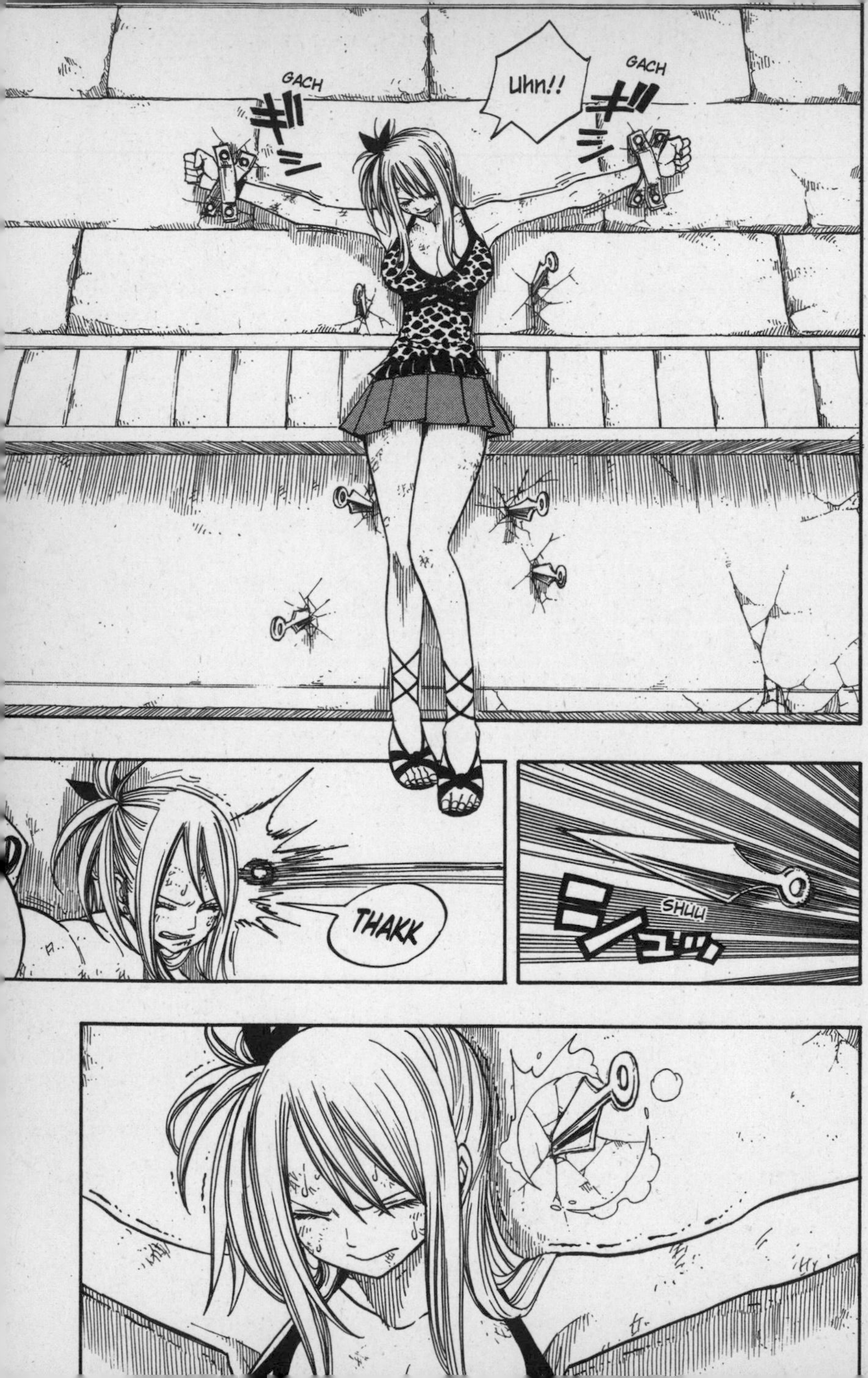
GACH
Uhn!!
GACH
SHUU
THAKK

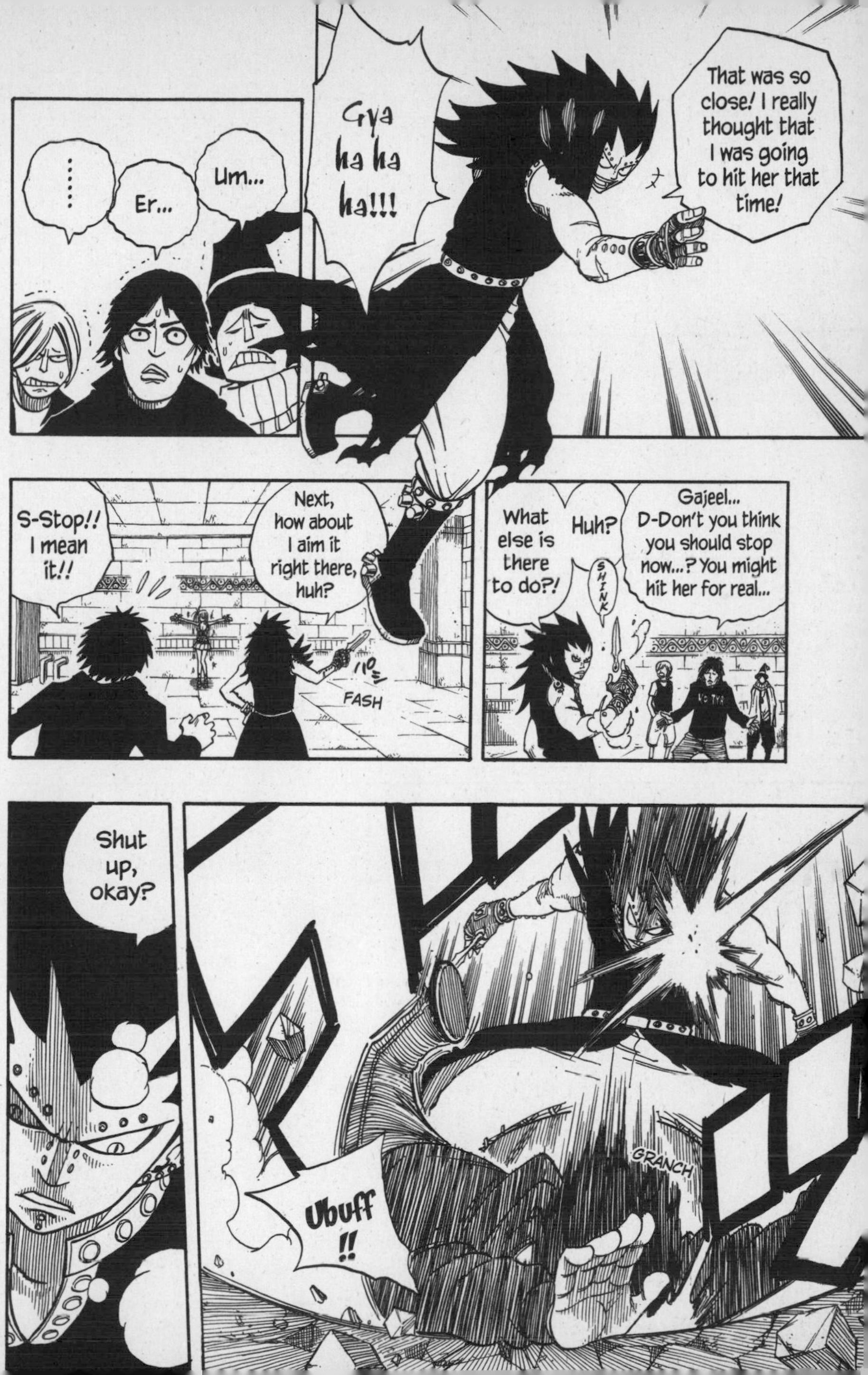
That was so close! I really thought that I was going to hit her that time!
Gya ha ha ha!!!
Um...
Er...
......
Gajeel... D-Don't you think you should stop now...? You might hit her for real...
Huh?
SHINK
What else is there to do?!
Next, how about I aim it right there, huh?
S-Stop!! I mean it!!
FASH
GRANCH
Ubuff!!
Shut up, okay?

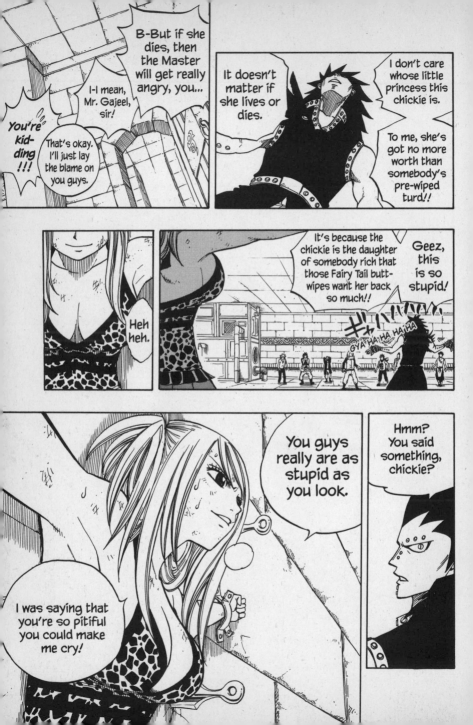

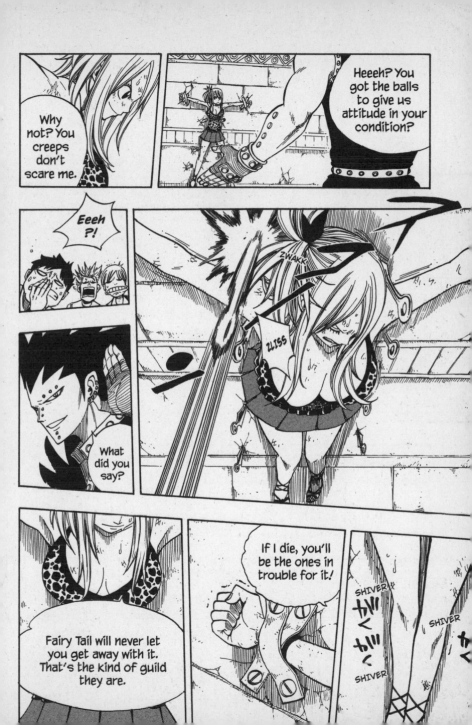

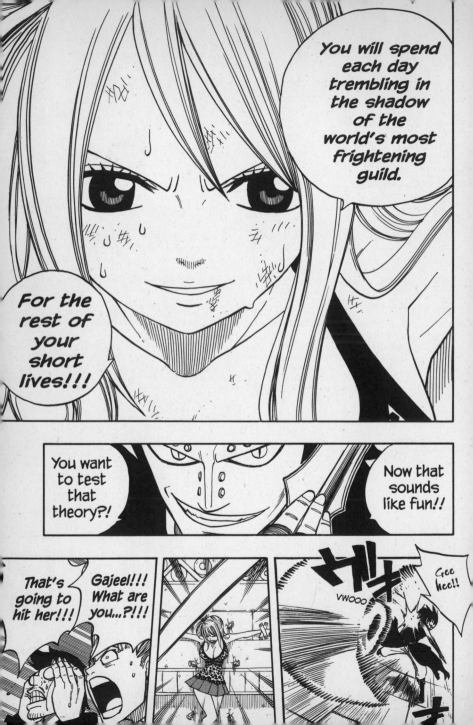

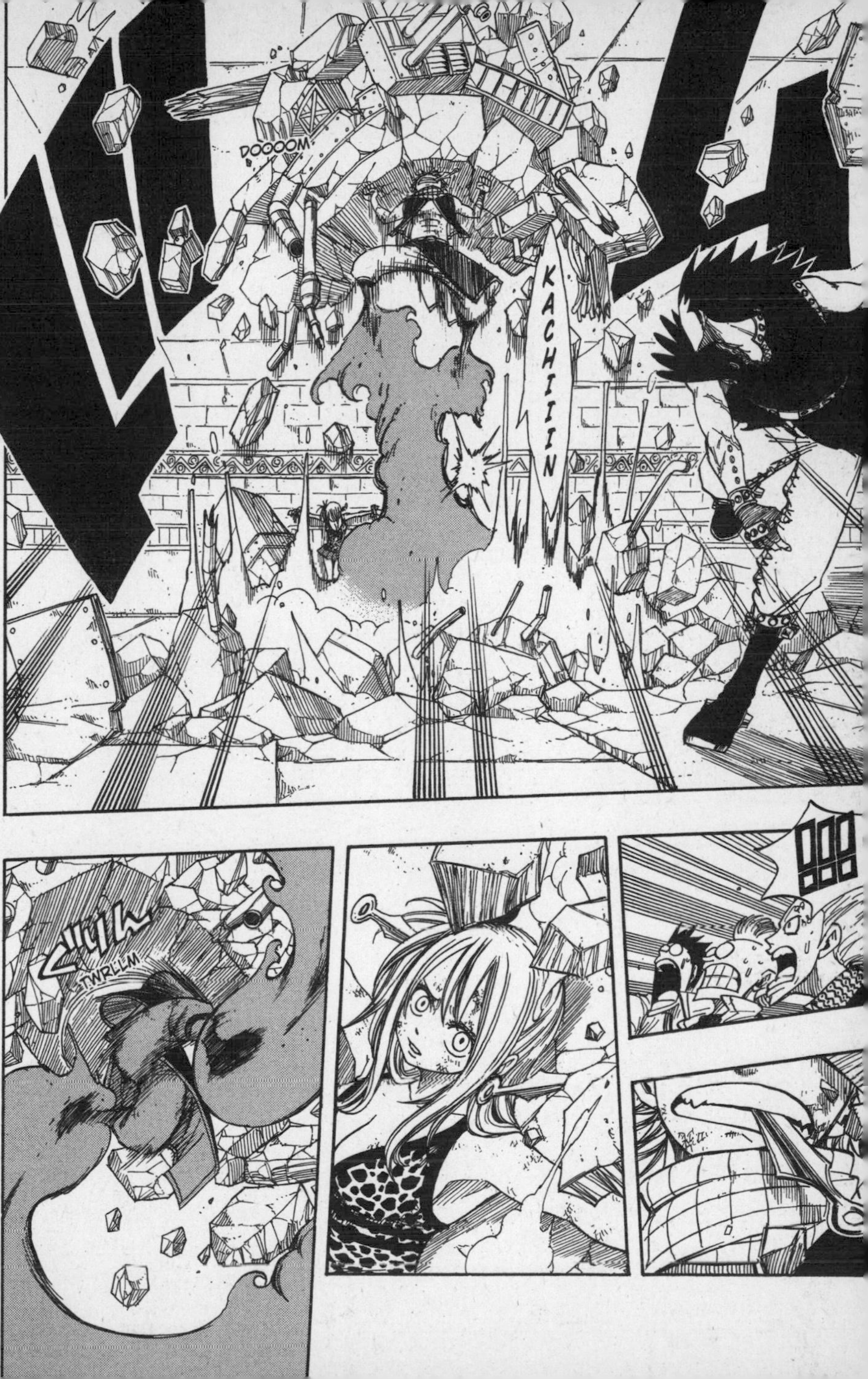
DOOOOM
KACHIIIN
!!!
TWRLLM

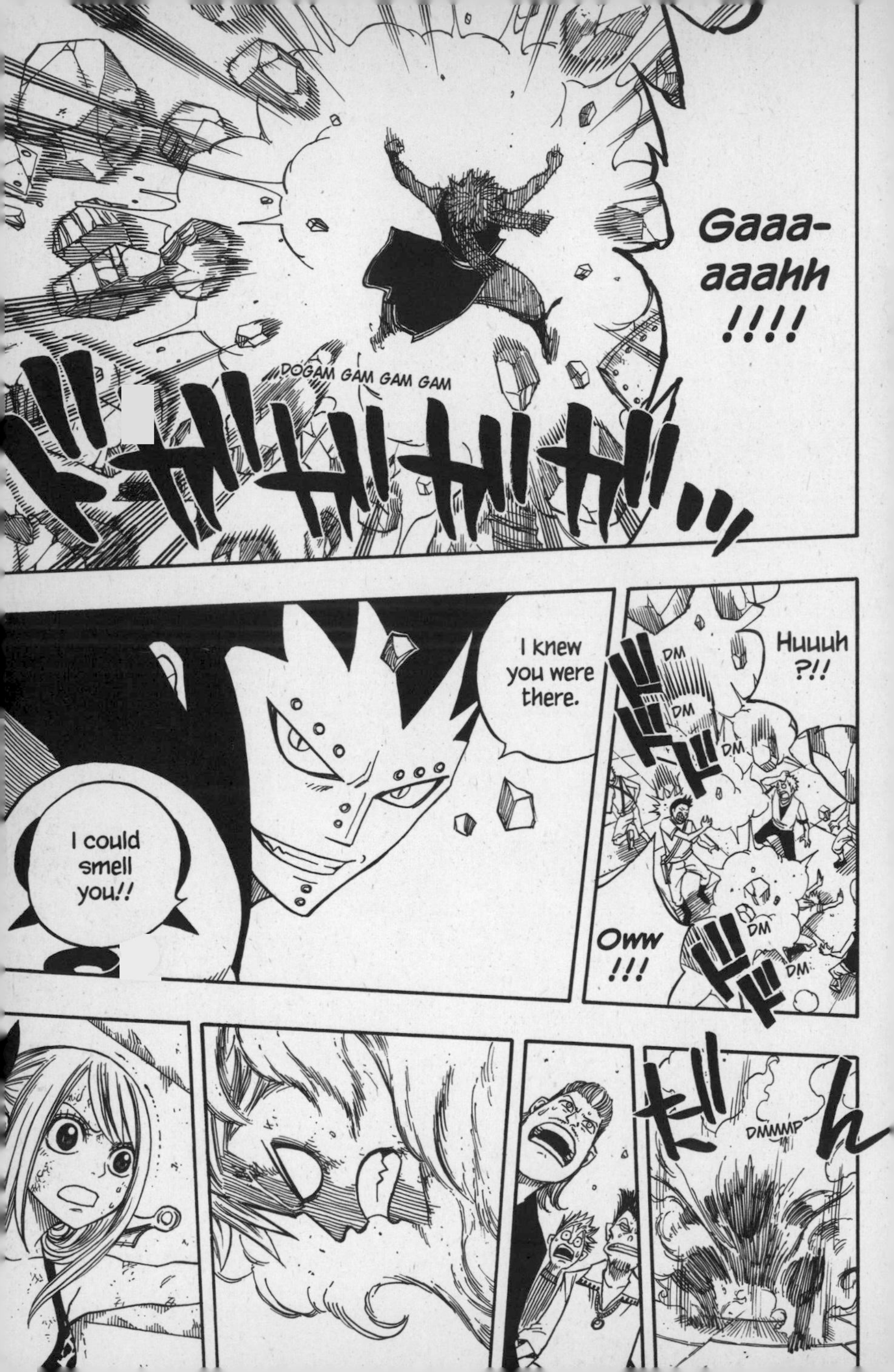
Gaaa-aaahh!!!!
DOGAM GAM GAM GAM
Huuuh?!!
DM
DM
DM
DM
DM
Oww!!!
I knew you were there.
I could smell you!!
DMMMP

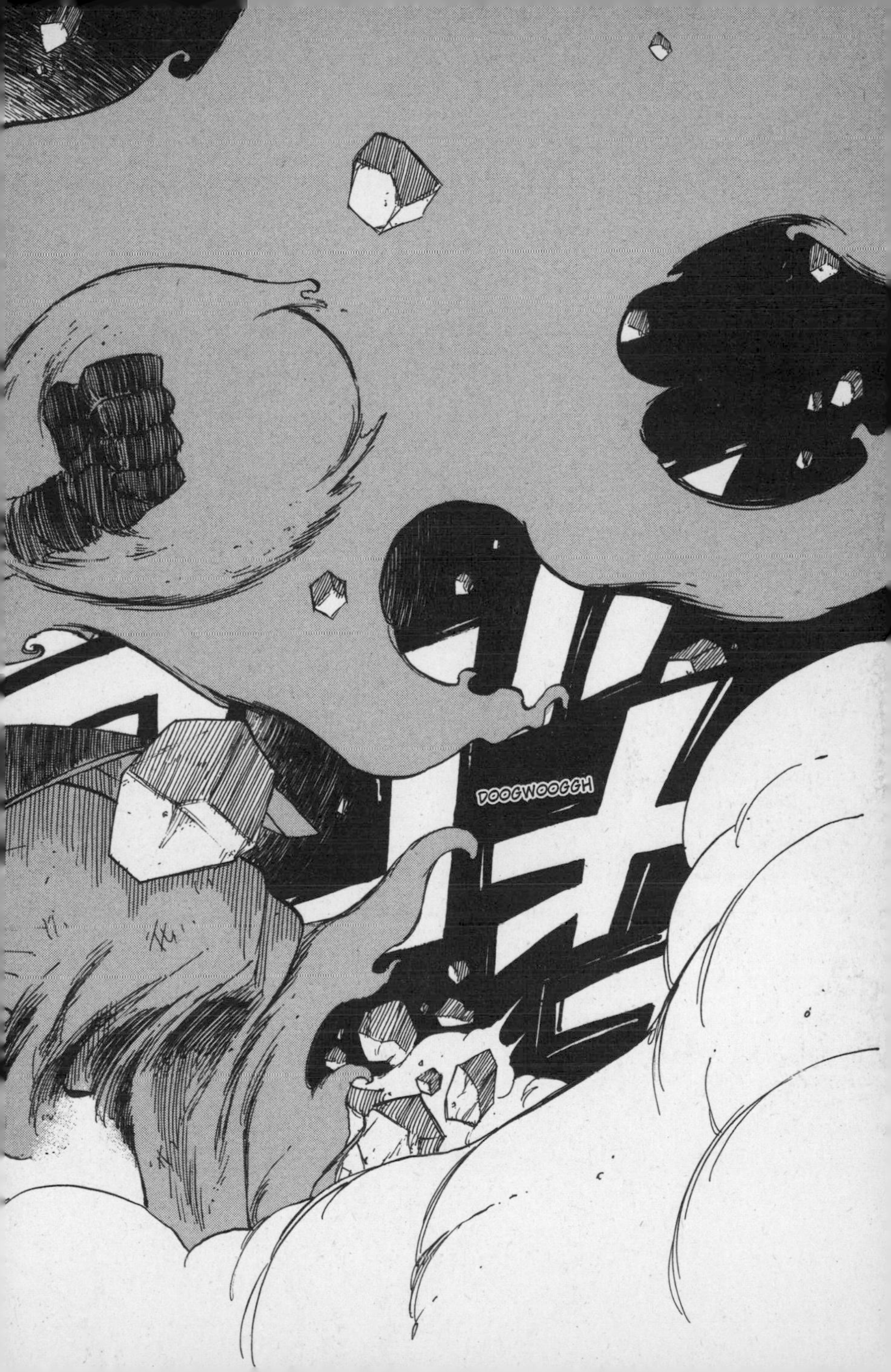
DOOGWOOGGH

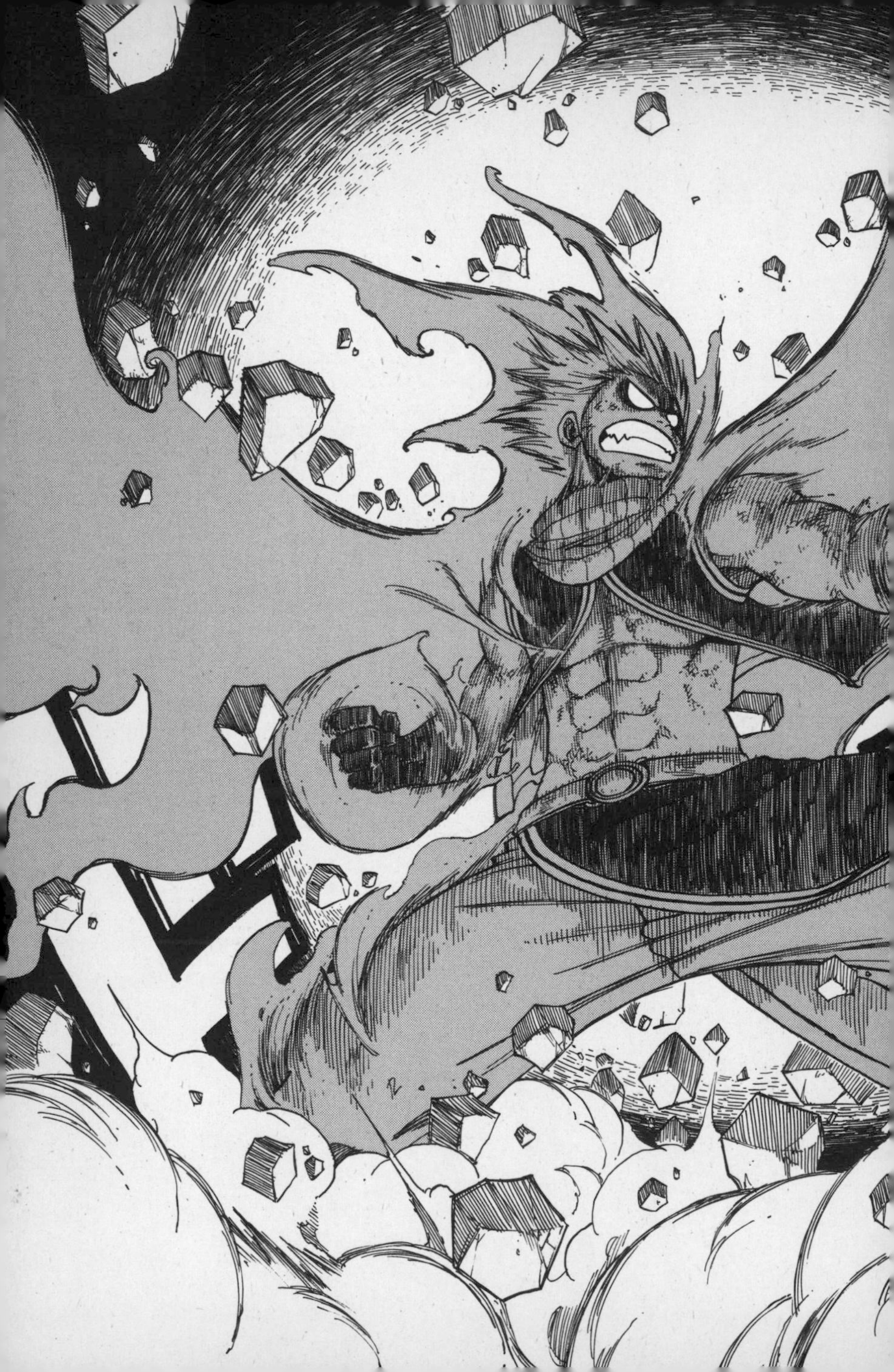

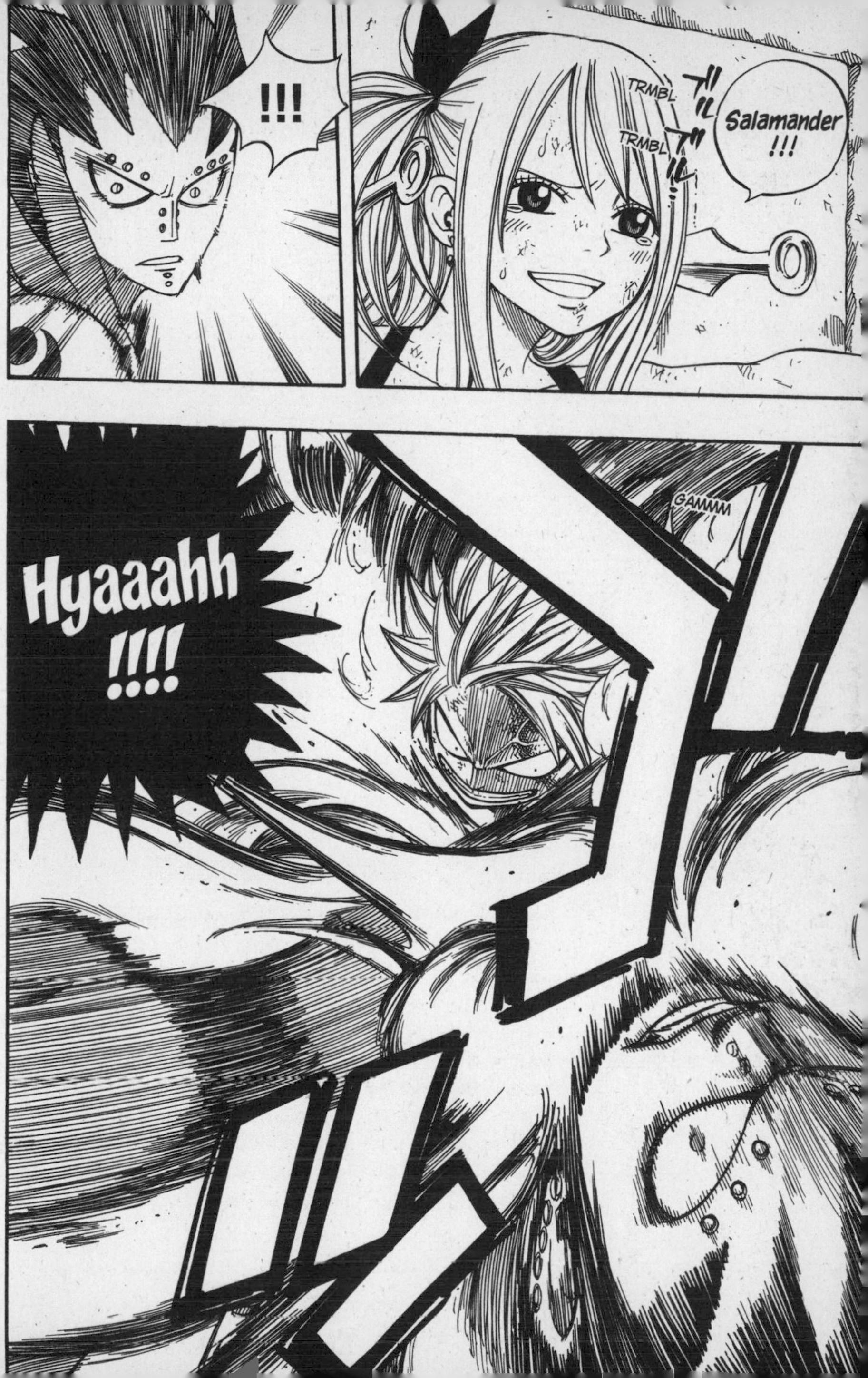
TRMBL
TRMBL
Salamander
!!!
!!!
GAMMM
Hyaaahh
!!!!

FAIRY TAIL

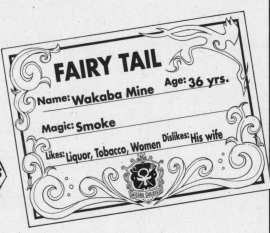

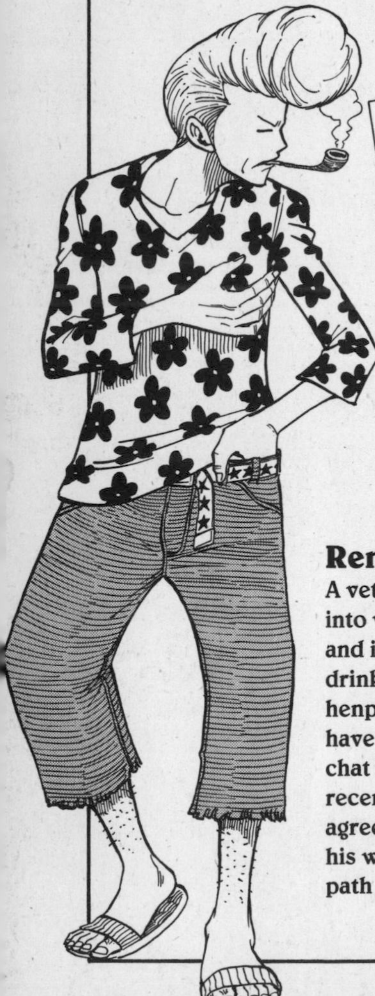

FAIRY TAIL

Name: Wakaba Mine Age: 36 yrs.

Magic: Smoke

Likes: Liquor, Tobacco, Women Dislikes: His wife

WIZARD GUILD×637

Remarks

A veteran wizard who can fight by shaping smoke into various forms. He has much the same history and is the same age as Macao, so at times they are drinking buddies, and at other times, rivals. He is henpecked by his wife, so even when he doesn't have work, you can find him at the guild trying to chat up the pretty young guild employees. His most recent target was Mirajane, saying that if she would agree to go out with him, he would break it off with his wife. She turned him down flat. He's well on the path to mastering the art of being a creepy old guy.

Chapter 61: The Two Dragon Slayers

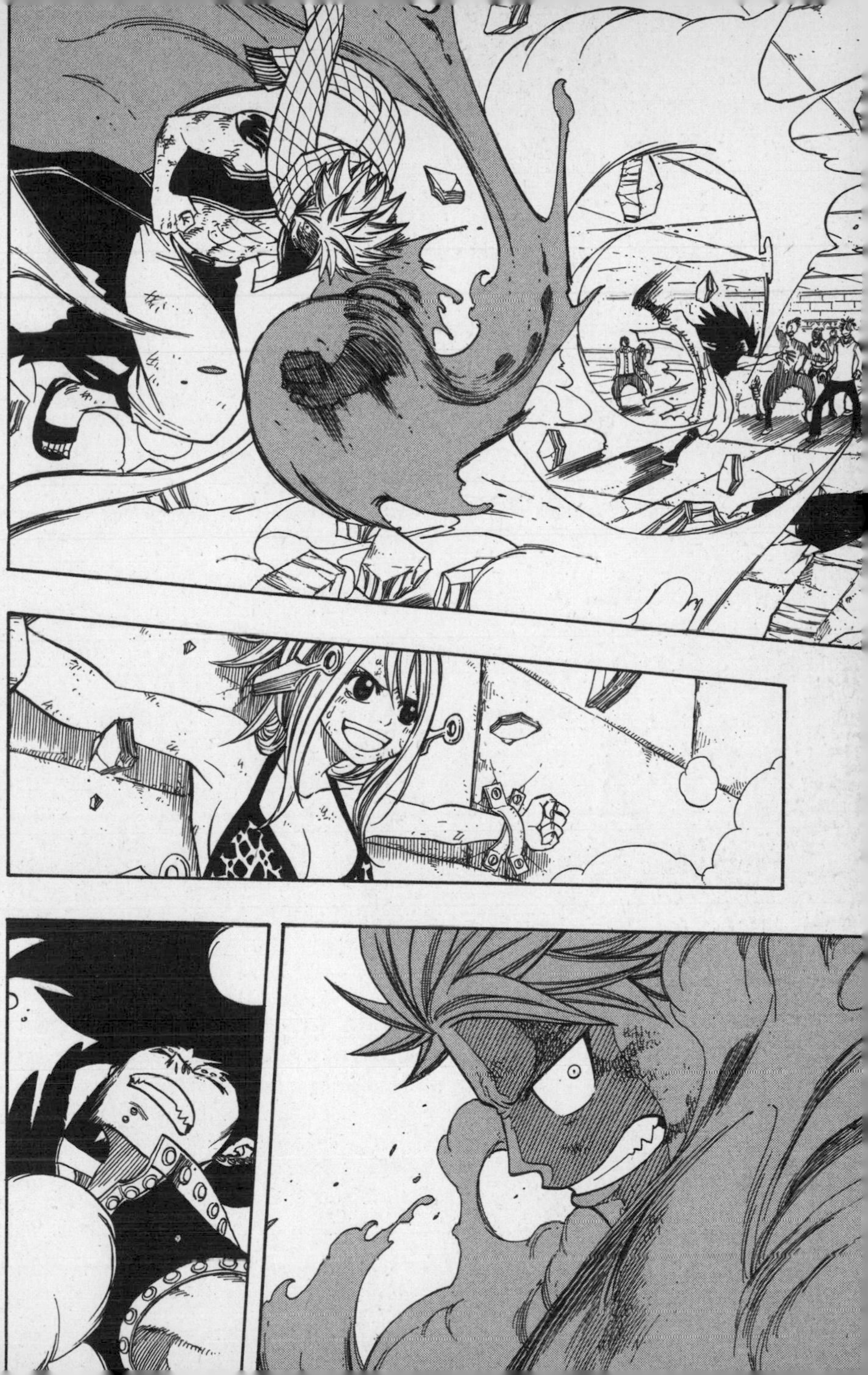

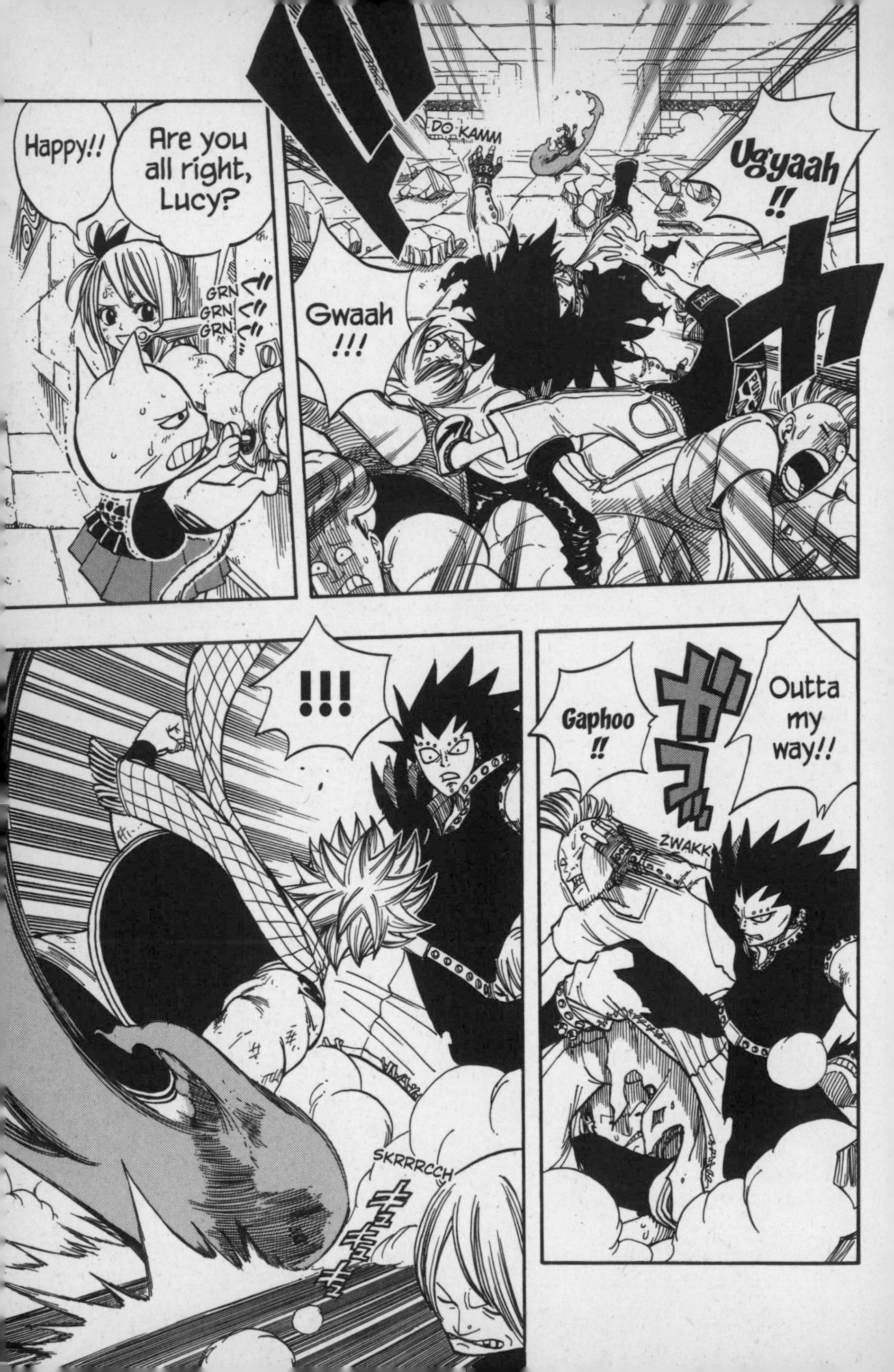
DO-KAMM
Ugyaah!!
Gwaah!!!
Are you all right, Lucy?
Happy!!
GRN GRN GRN
Outta my way!!
Gaphoo!!
ZWAKK
!!!
SKRRRCH

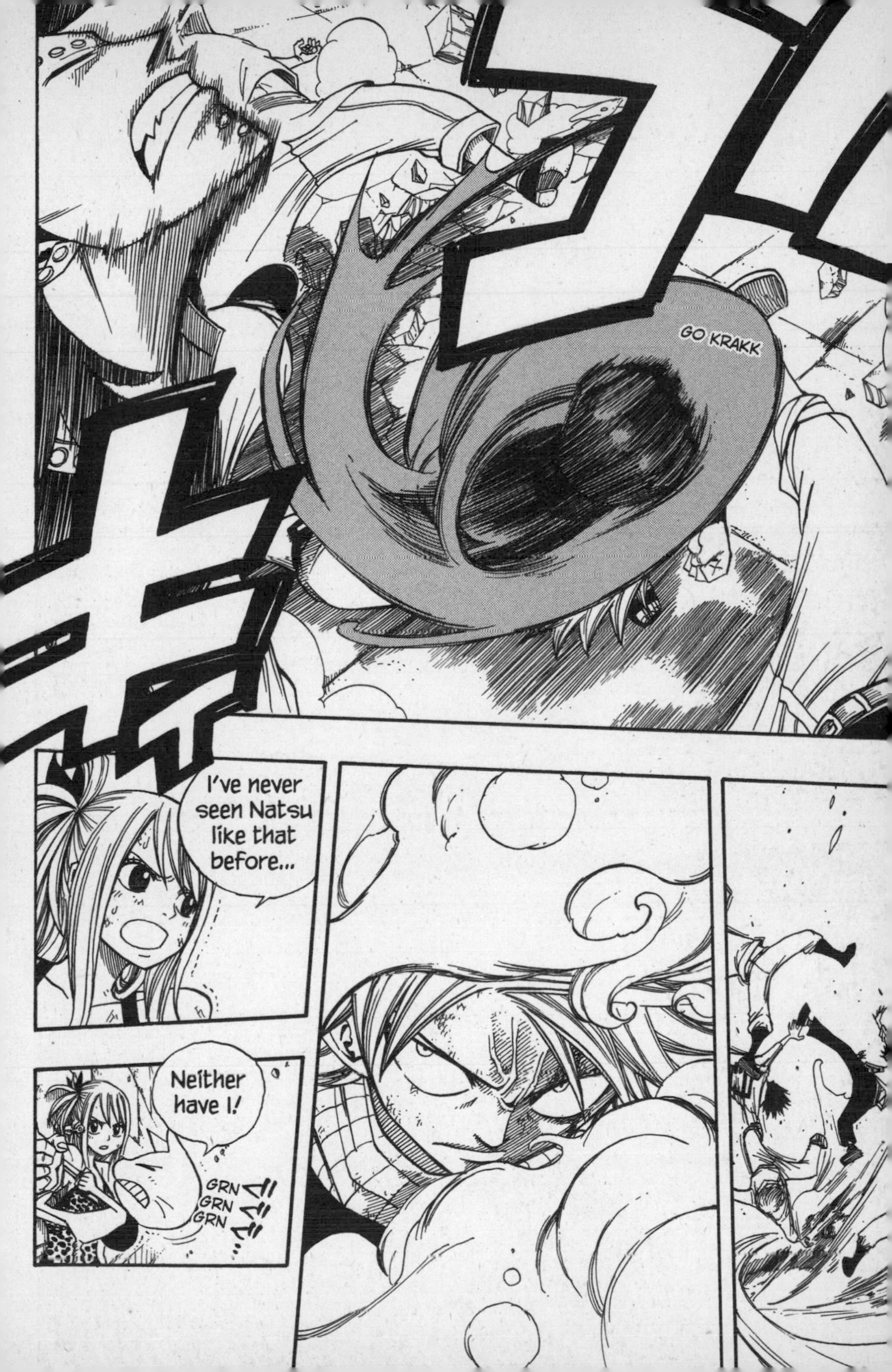
GO KRAKK
I've never seen Natsu like that before...
Neither have I!
GRN GRN GRN

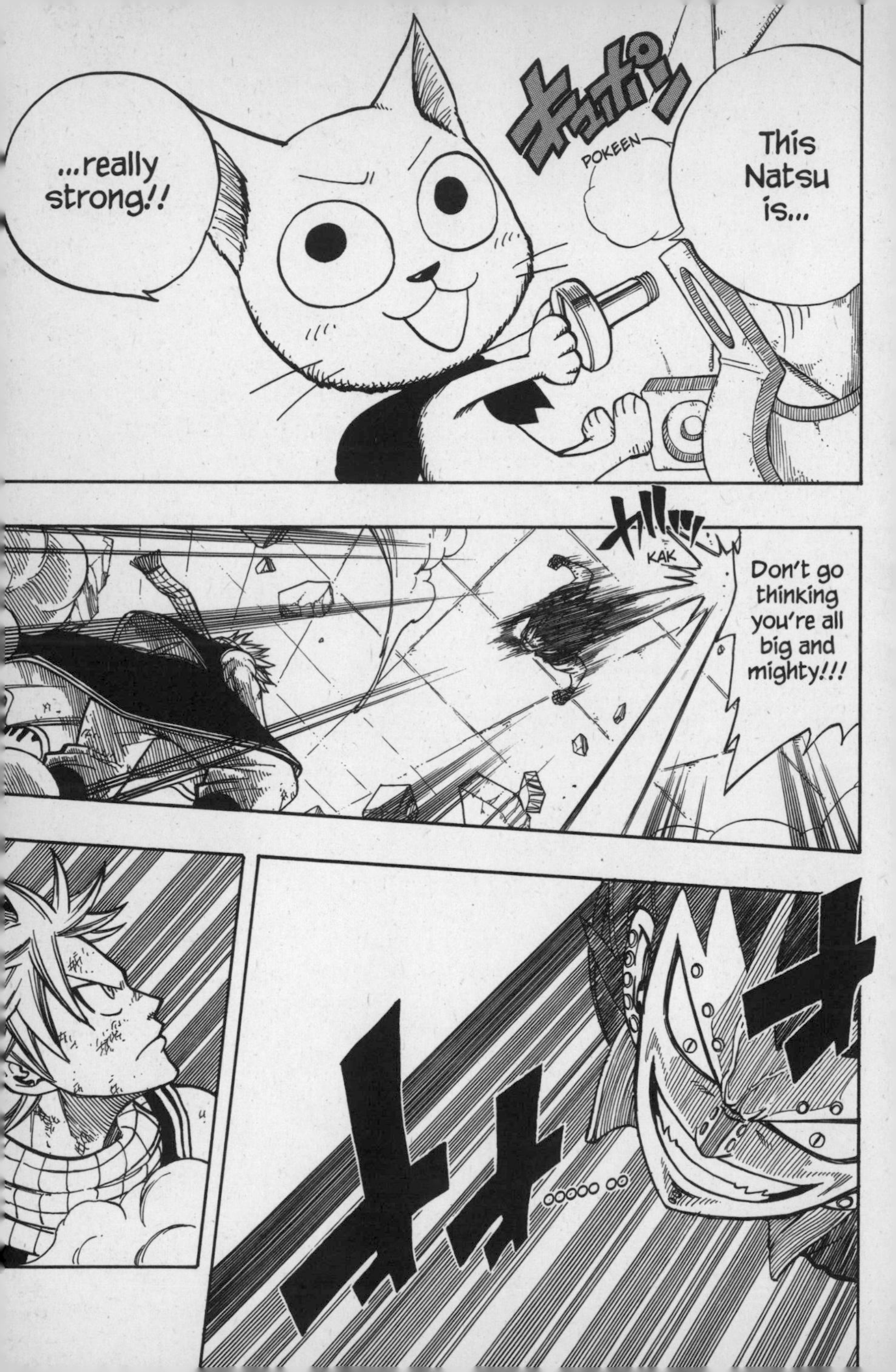
This Natsu is...
POKEEN
...really strong!!
KAK
Don't go thinking you're all big and mighty!!!
ooooo oo

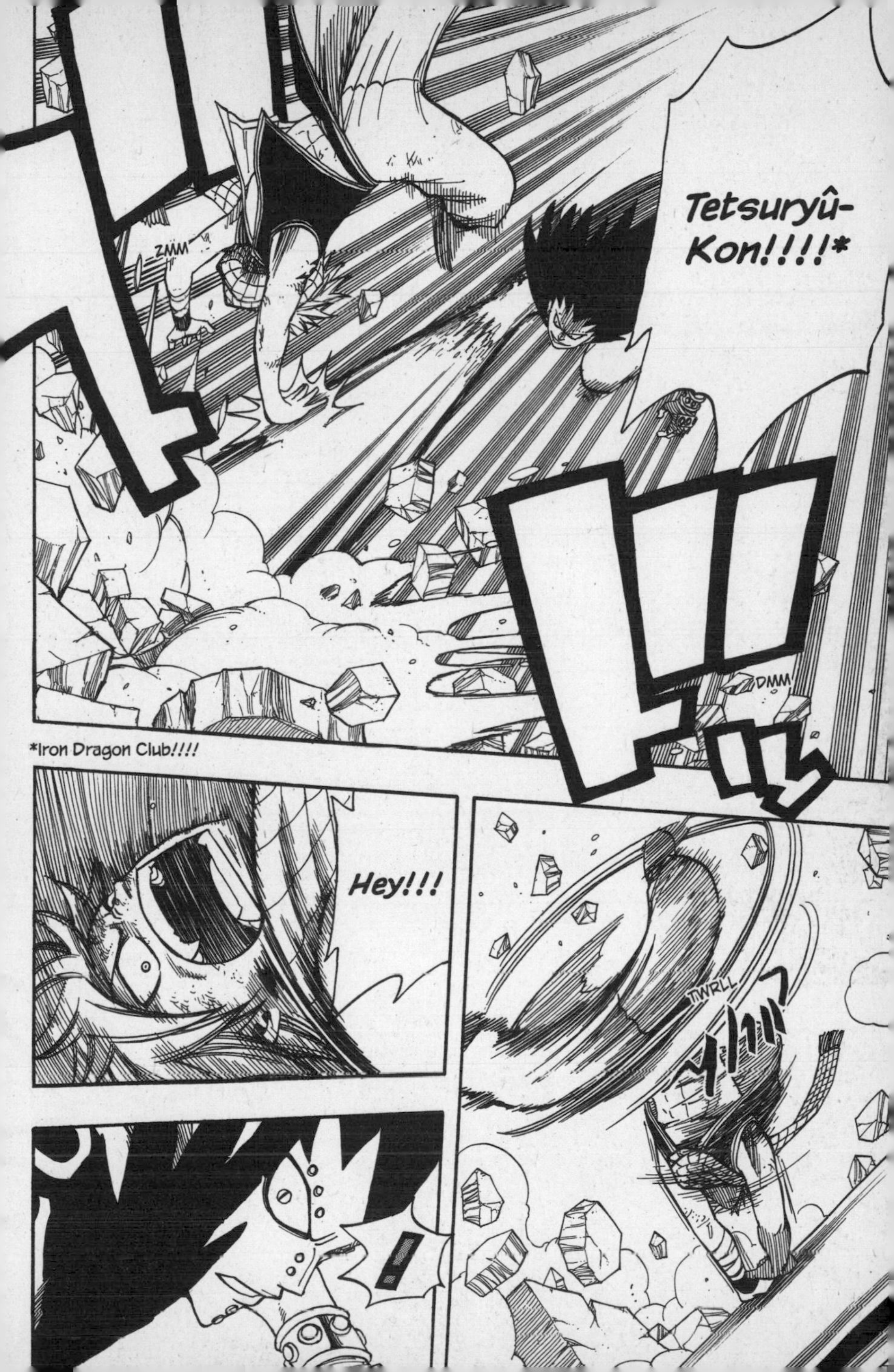
Tetsuryû-
Kon!!!!*
ZMM
DMM
*Iron Dragon Club!!!!
Hey!!!
TWRLL

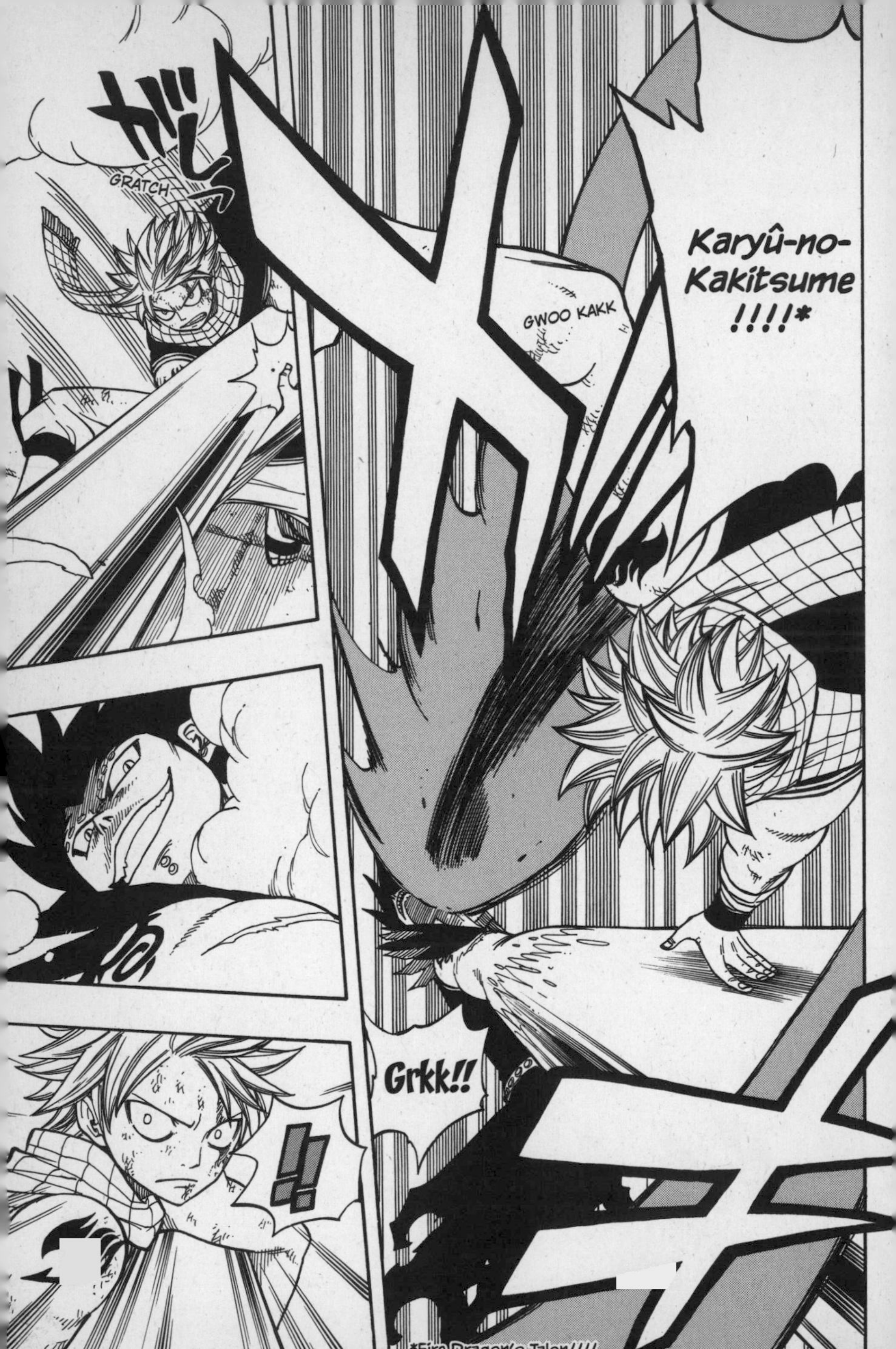
Karyû-no-Kakitsume !!!!*
GWOO KAKK
Grkk!!
GRATCH

*Fire Dragon's Talon!!!!

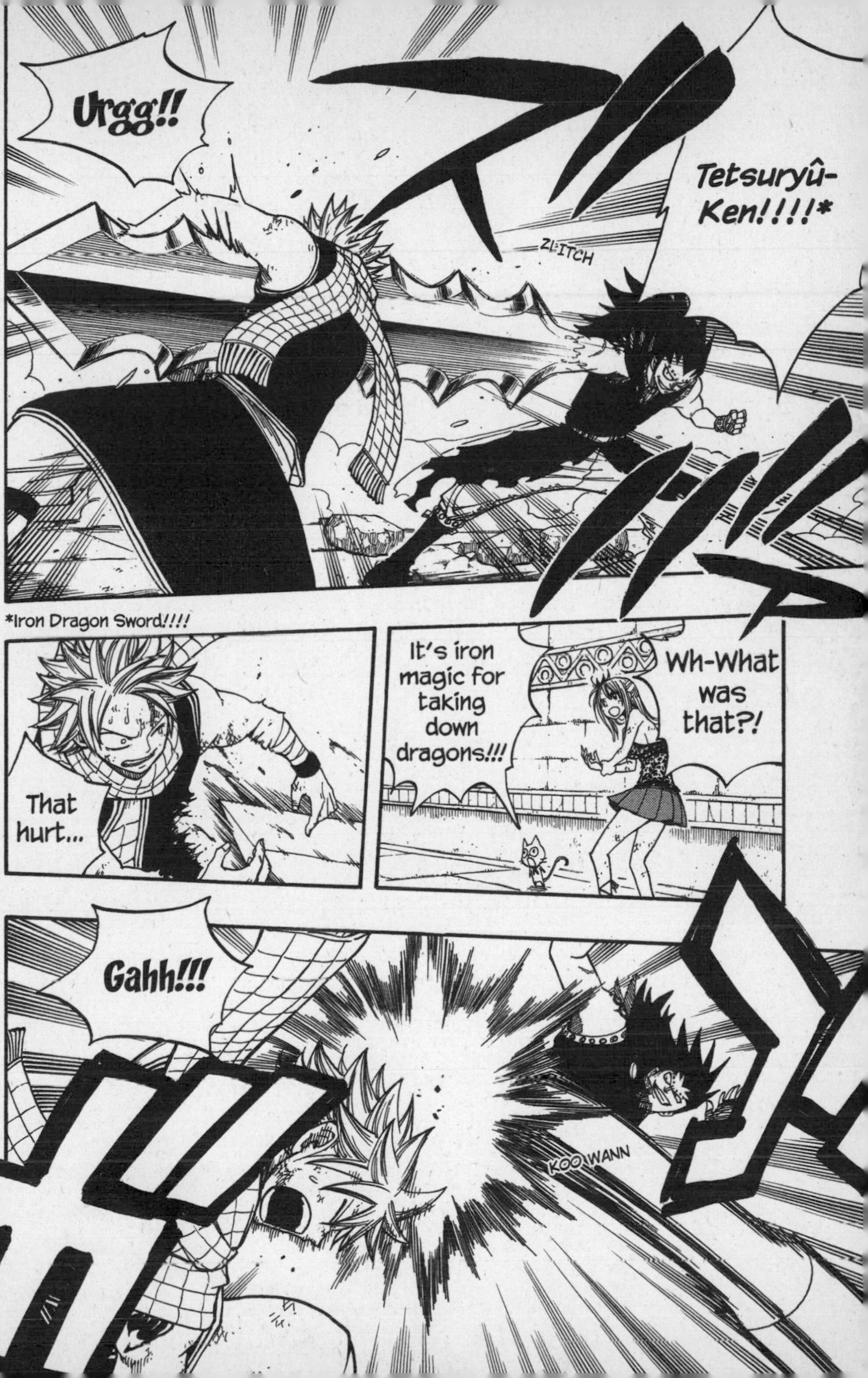
Tetsuryû-Ken!!!!*
ZLITCH
Urgg!!
Wh-What was that?!
It's iron magic for taking down dragons!!!
That hurt...
KOO WANN
Gahh!!!

*Iron Dragon Sword!!!!

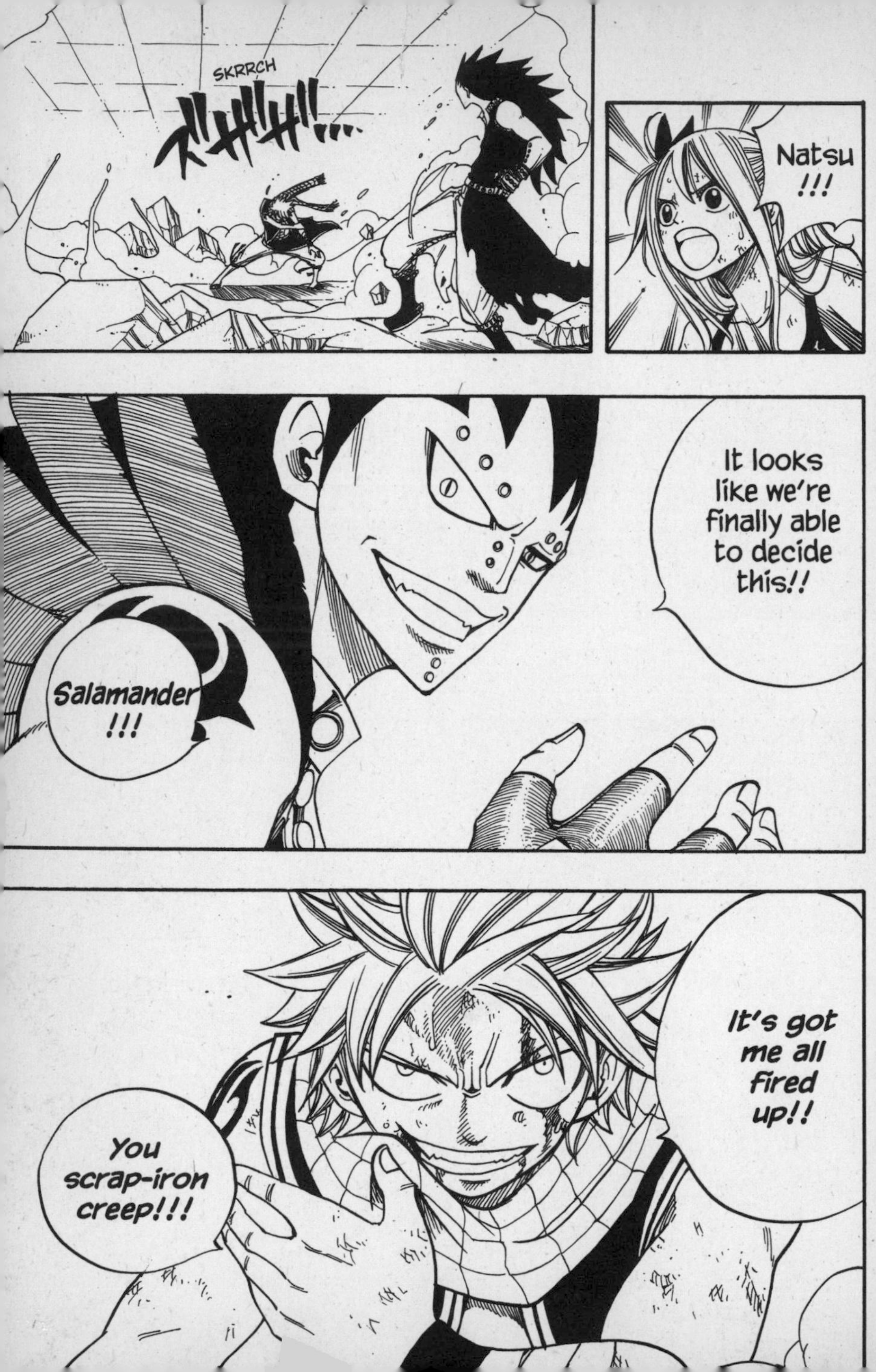
Natsu !!!
SKRRCH
It looks like we're finally able to decide this!!
Salamander !!!
It's got me all fired up!!
You scrap-iron creep!!!

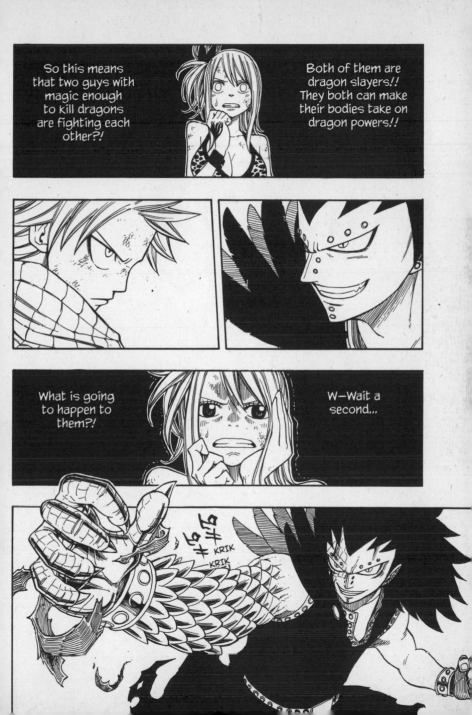

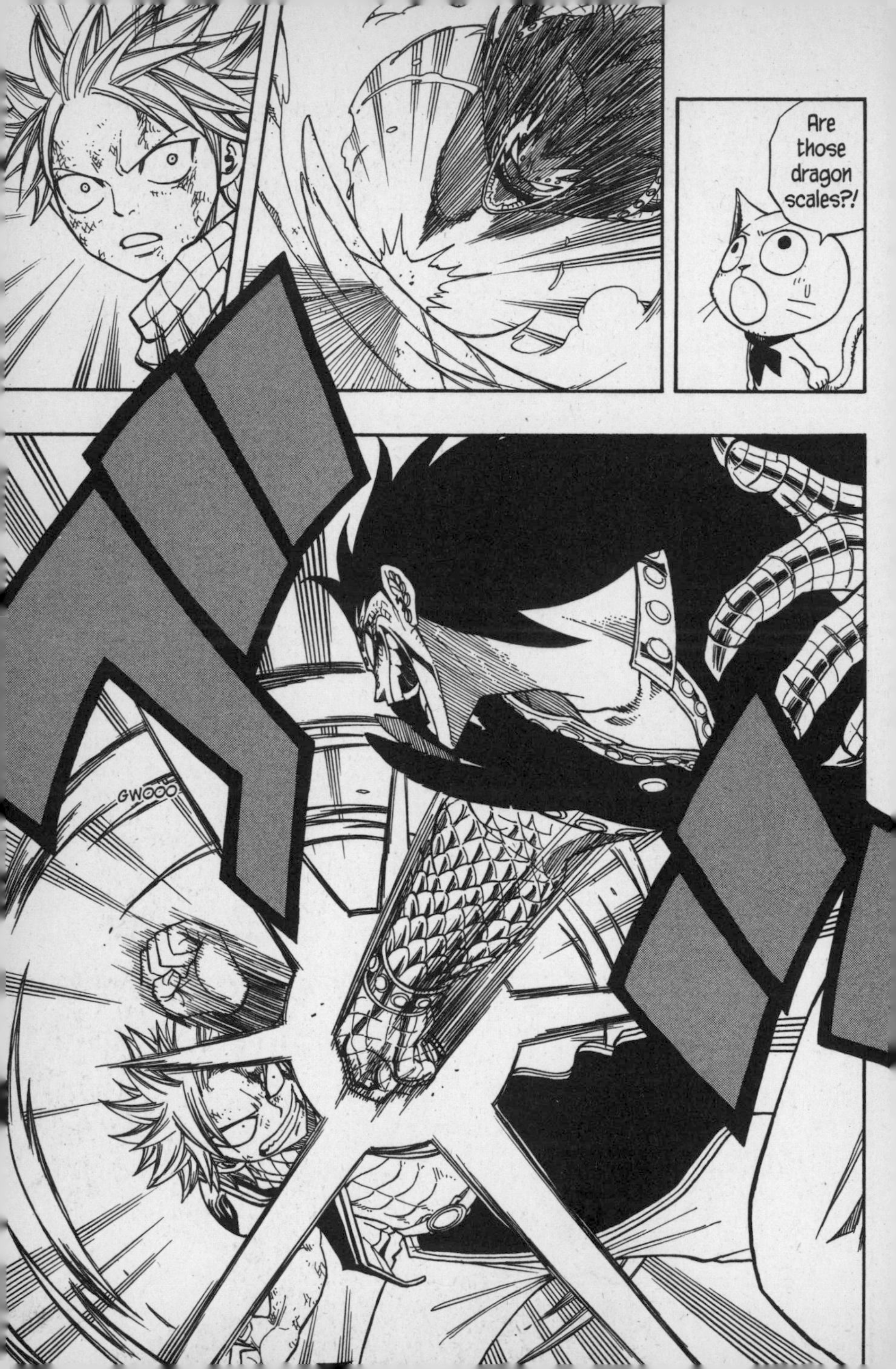
Are those dragon scales?!
GWOOO

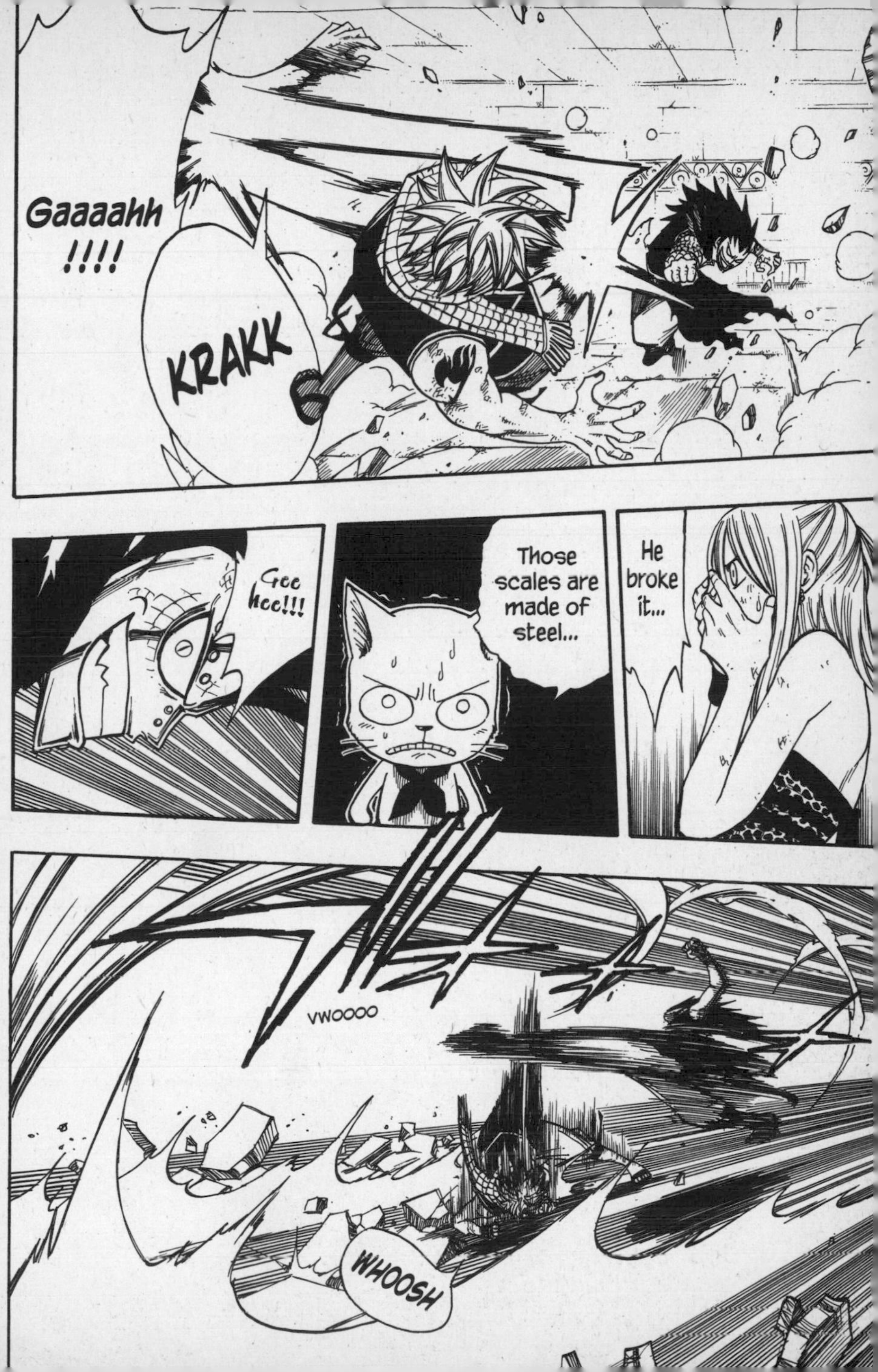
Gaaaahh !!!!
KRAKK
He broke it...
Those scales are made of steel...
Gee hee!!!
VWOOOO
WHOOSH

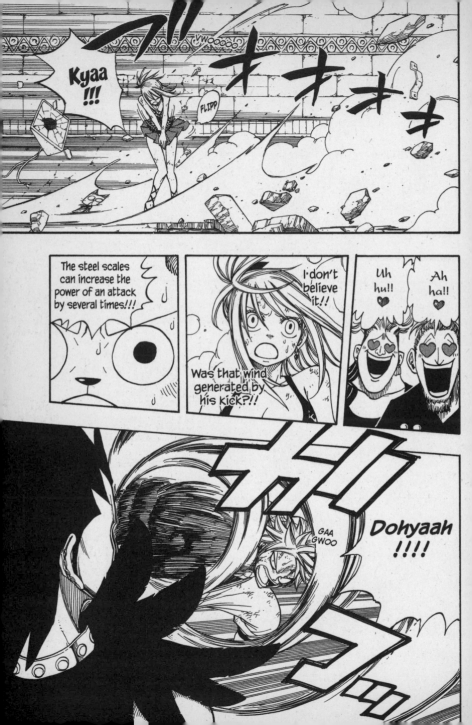

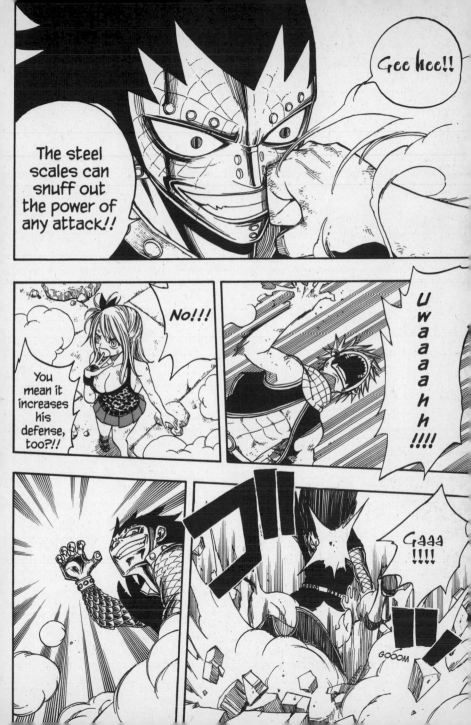

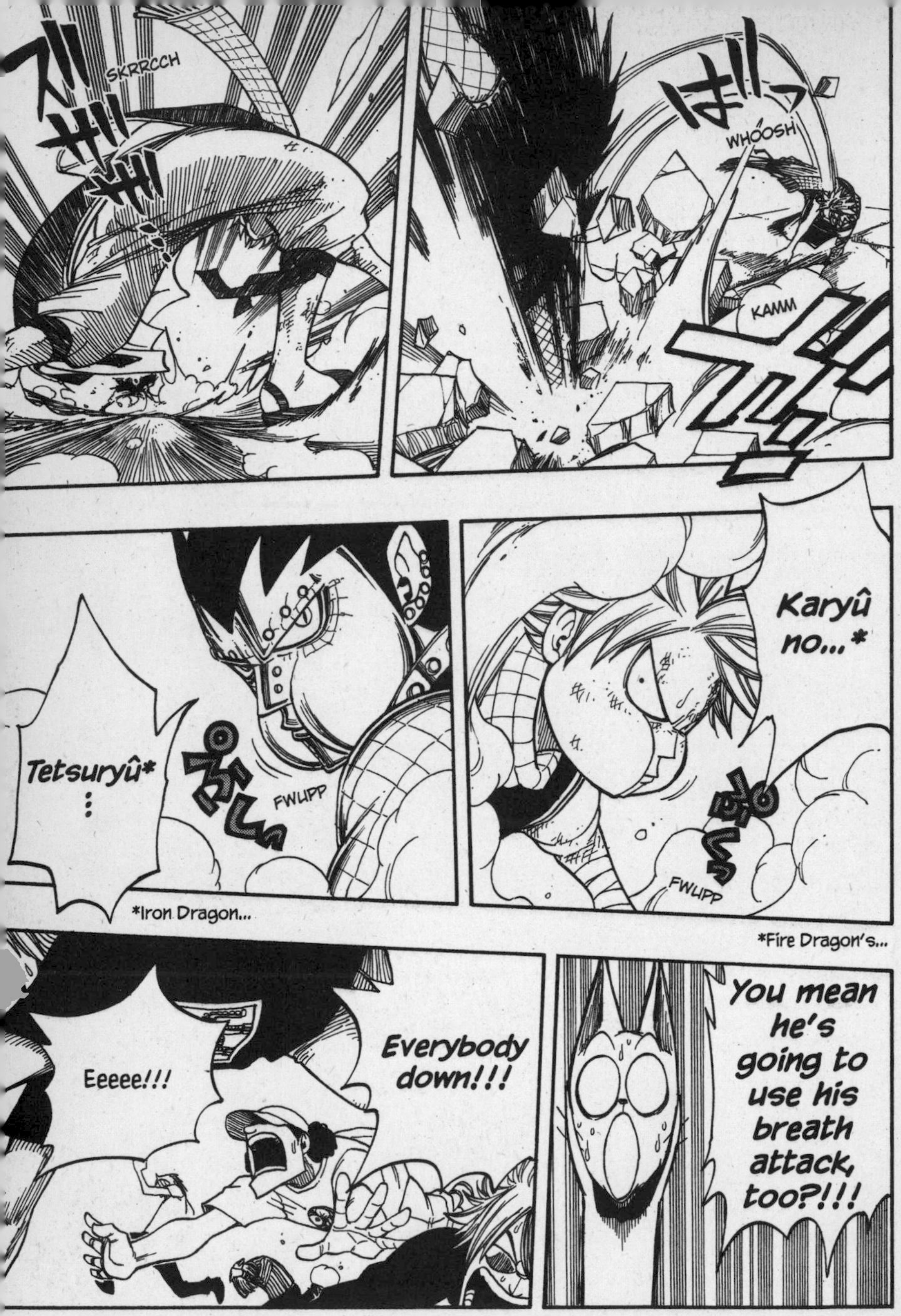
WHOOSH
KAMM
SKRRCCH
Karyû no...*
FWUPP
Tetsuryû* ...
FWUPP
You mean he's going to use his breath attack, too?!!!
Everybody down!!!
Eeeee!!!

*Iron Dragon...

*Fire Dragon's...

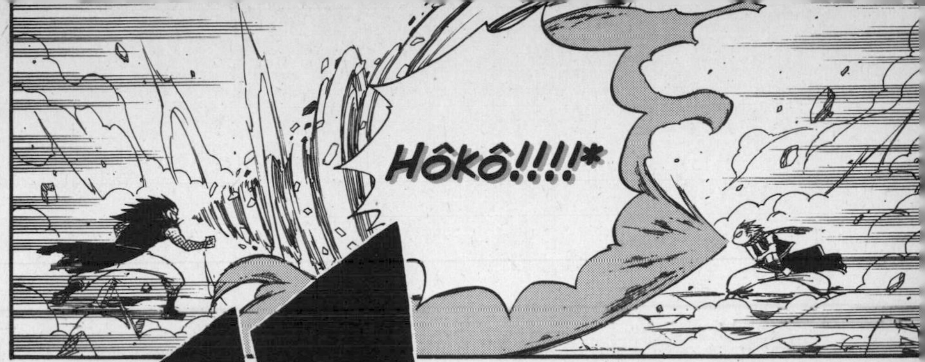
Hôkô!!!!*
DOO OOM

*Roar!!!!

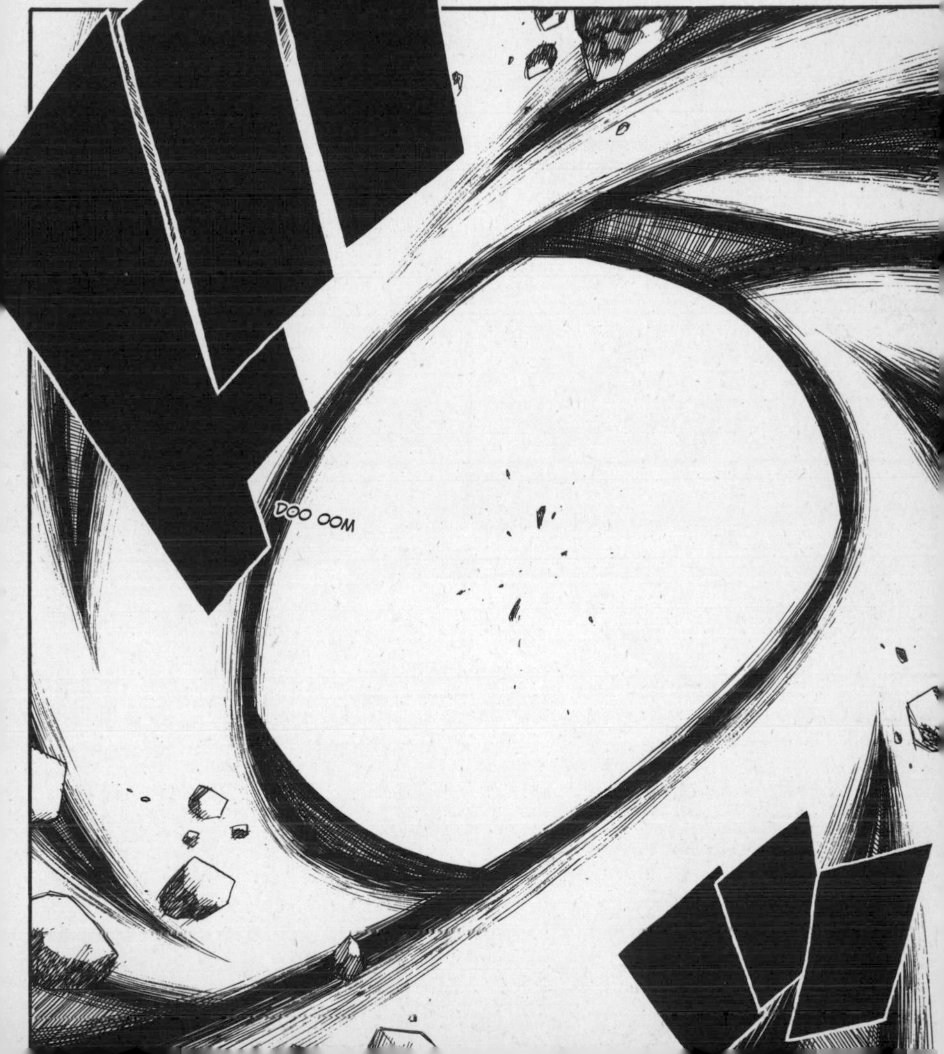

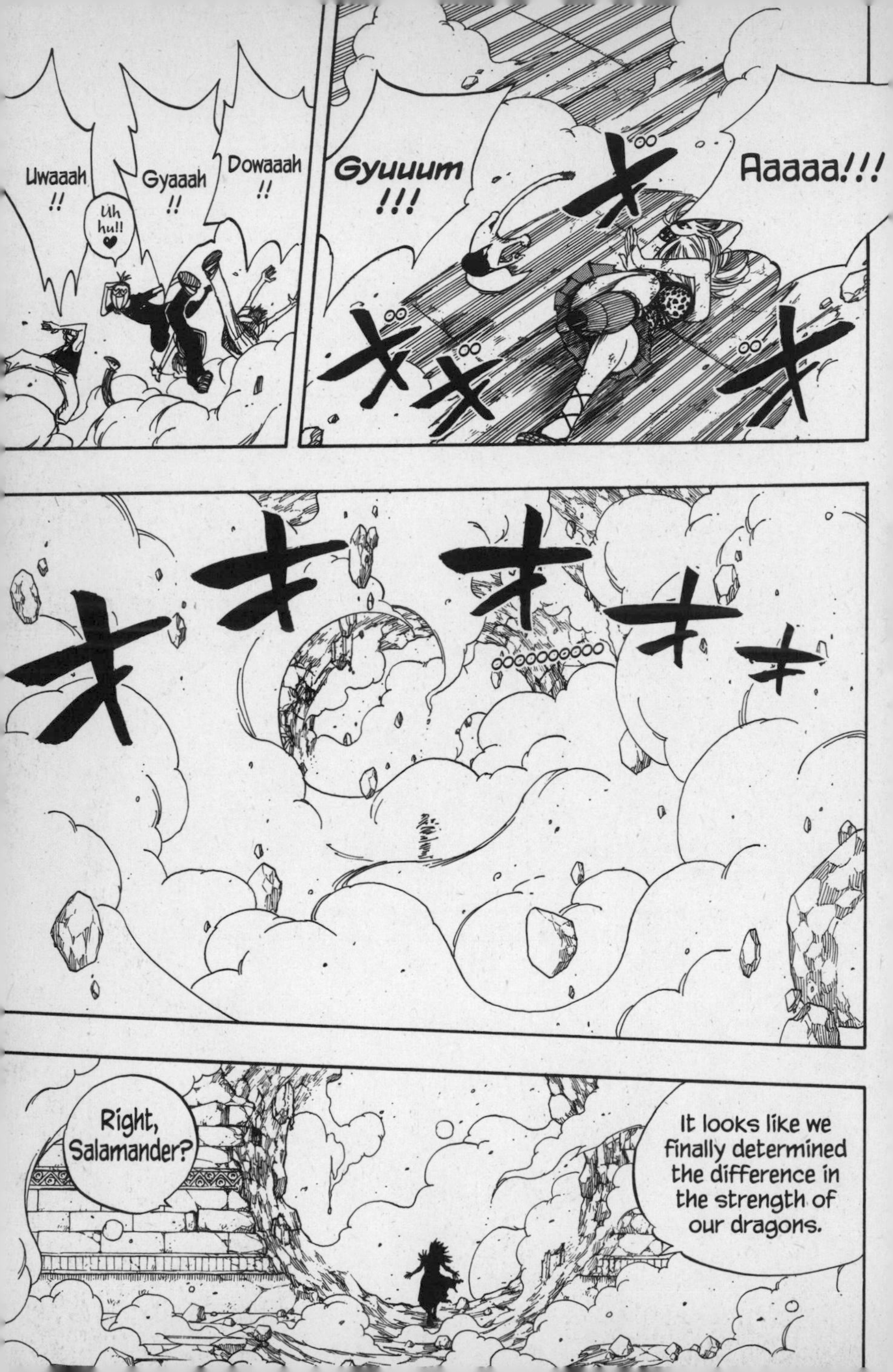
Aaaaa!!!
Gyuuum !!!
Dowaaah !!
Gyaaah !!
Uh hu!! ♥
Uwaaah !!
It looks like we finally determined the difference in the strength of our dragons.
Right, Salamander?

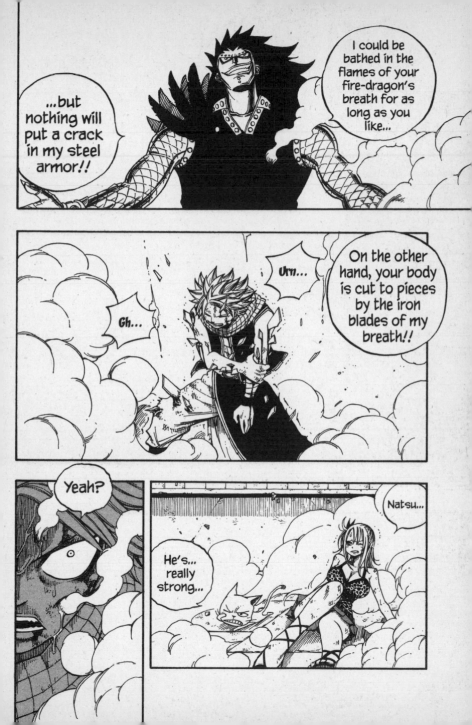

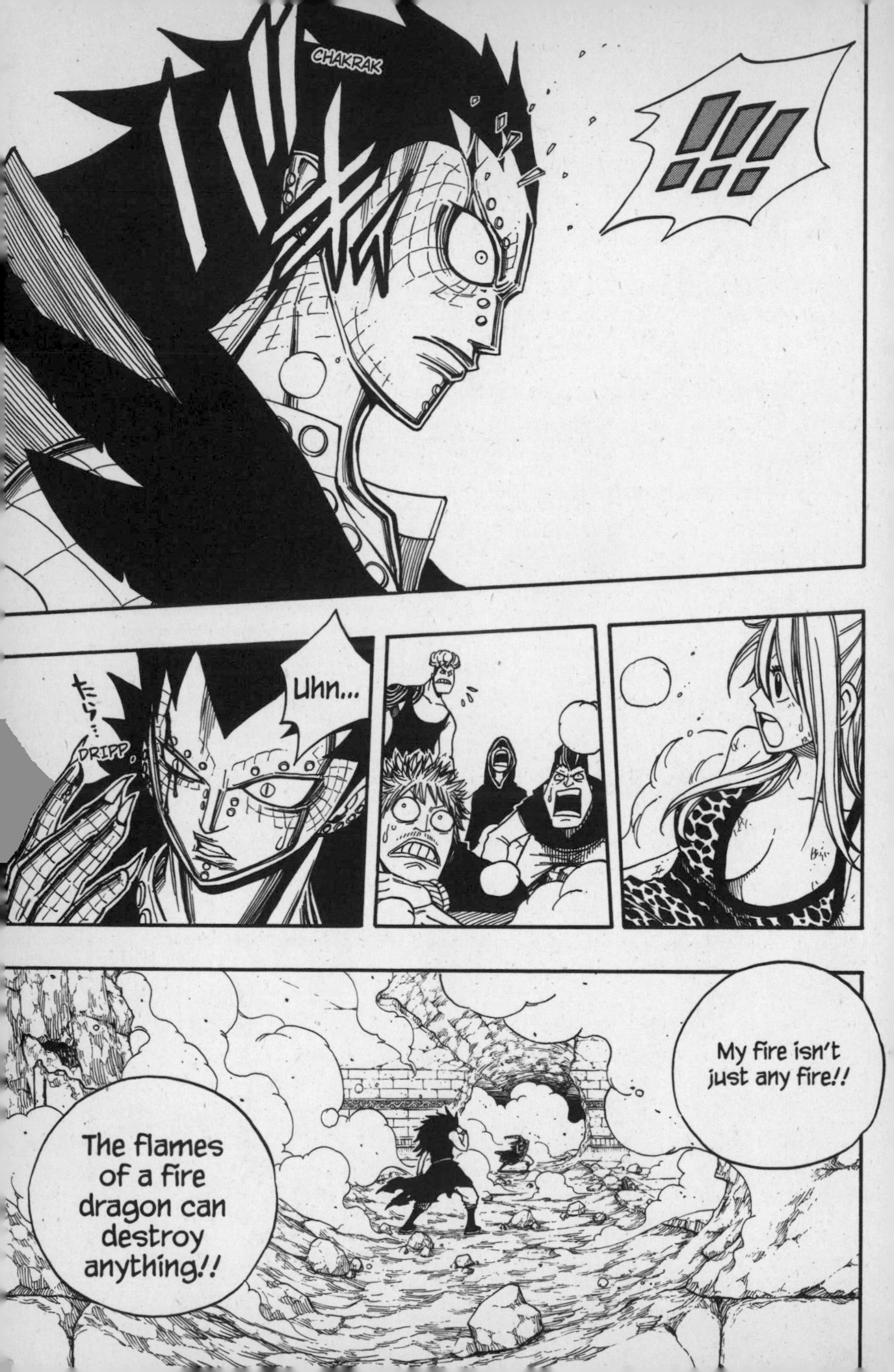
!!!
CHAKRAK
Uhn...
DRIPP
My fire isn't just any fire!!
The flames of a fire dragon can destroy anything!!

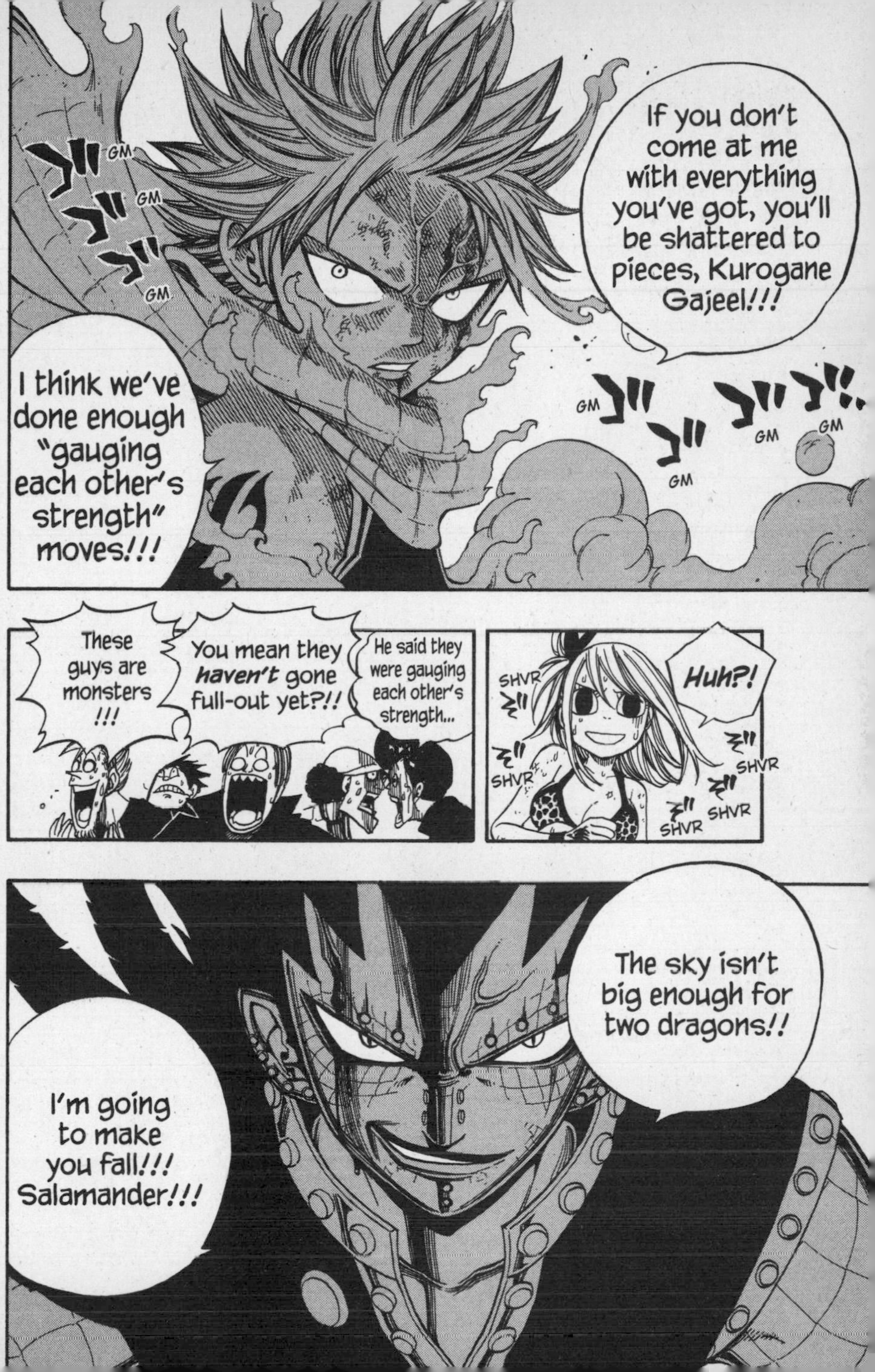
If you don't come at me with everything you've got, you'll be shattered to pieces, Kurogane Gajeel!!!
GM GM GM GM GM
GM GM GM
I think we've done enough "gauging each other's strength" moves!!!
Huh?!
SHVR SHVR SHVR SHVR SHVR
He said they were gauging each other's strength...
You mean they *haven't* gone full-out yet?!!
These guys are monsters!!!
The sky isn't big enough for two dragons!!
I'm going to make you fall!!! Salamander!!!

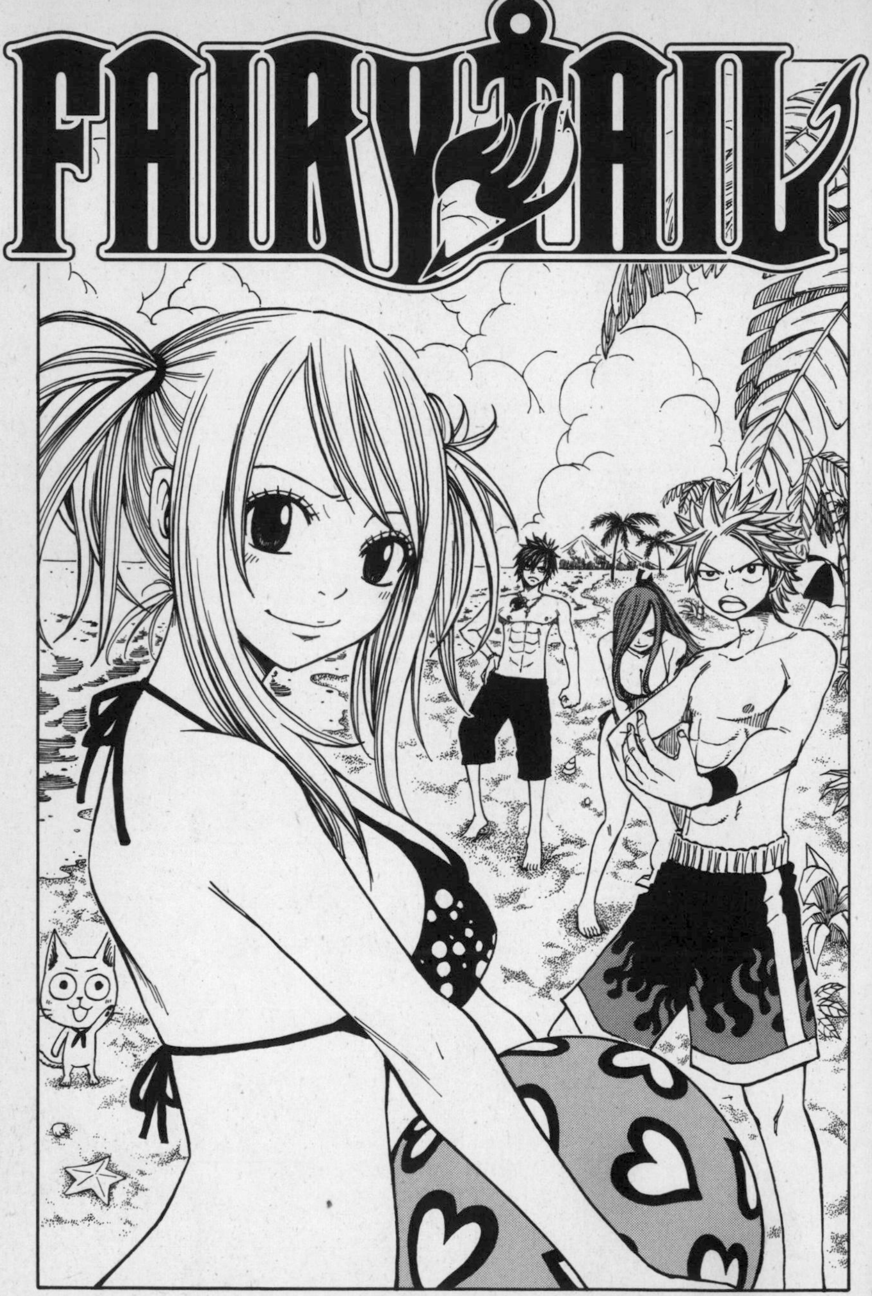
FAIRY TAIL

Chapter 62: When the Fairy Fell

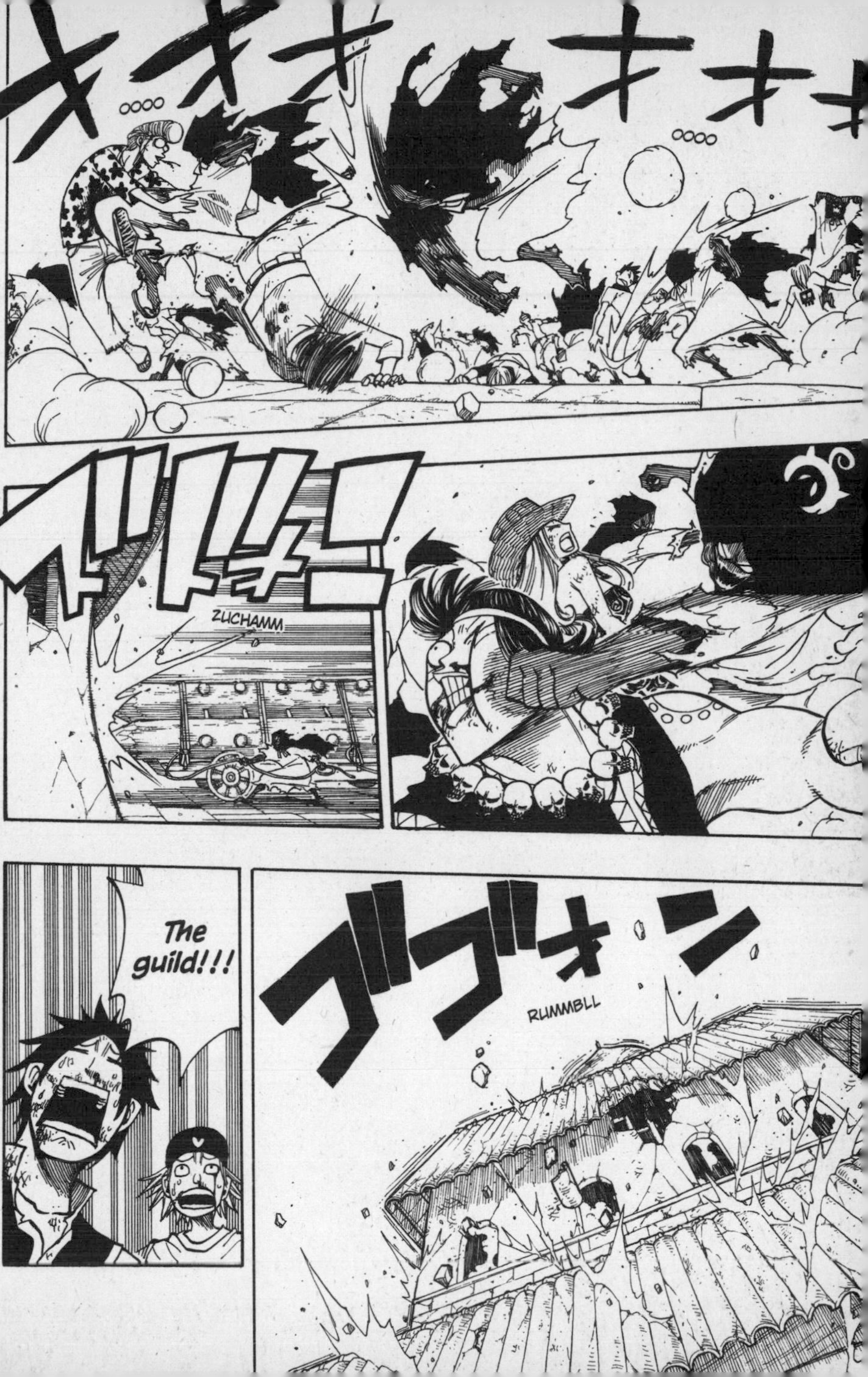

ZUCHAMM
The guild!!!
RUMMBLL

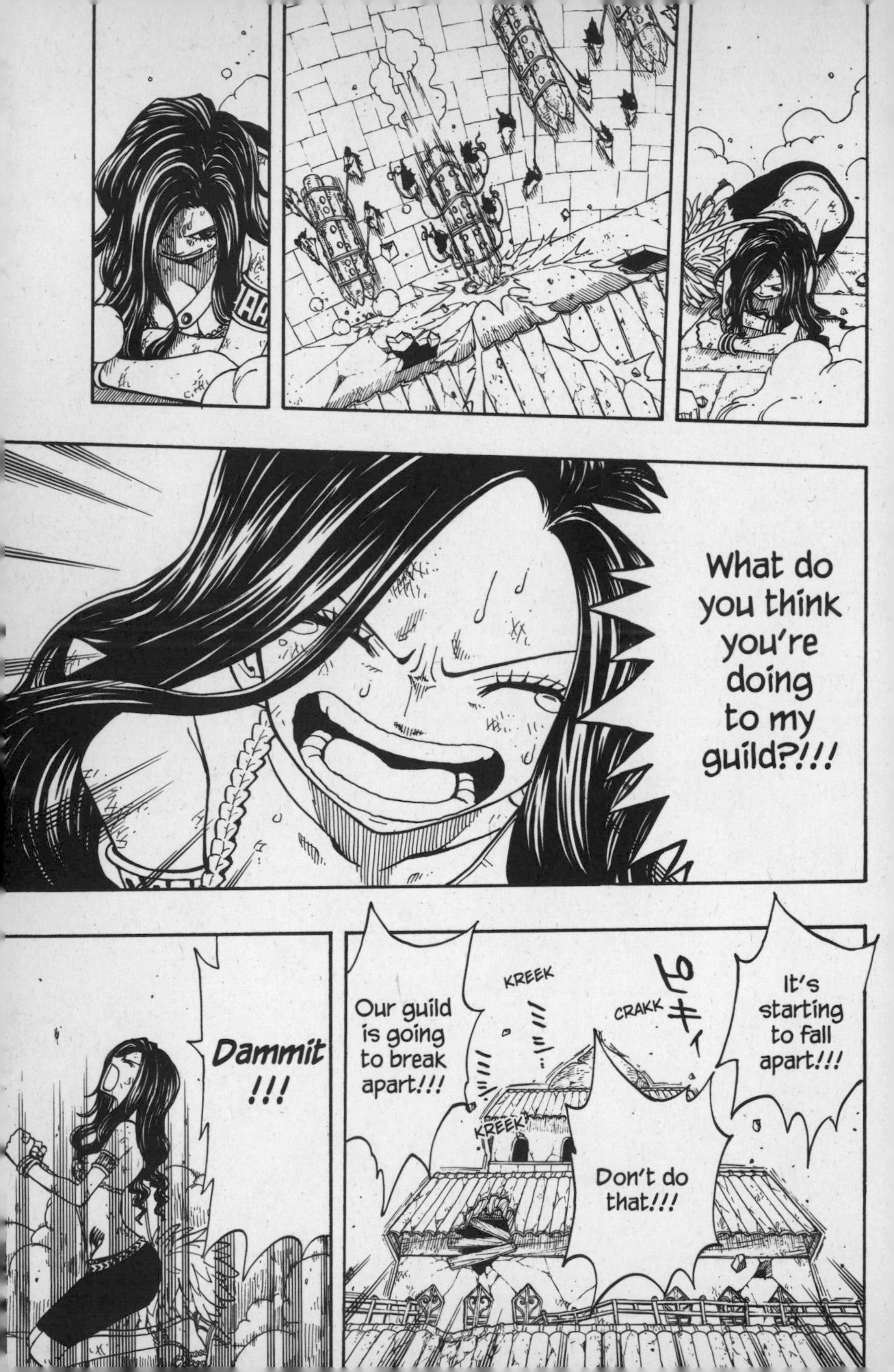
What do you think you're doing to my guild?!!!
It's starting to fall apart!!!
CRAKK
KREEK
Our guild is going to break apart!!!
KREEK
Don't do that!!!
Dammit!!!

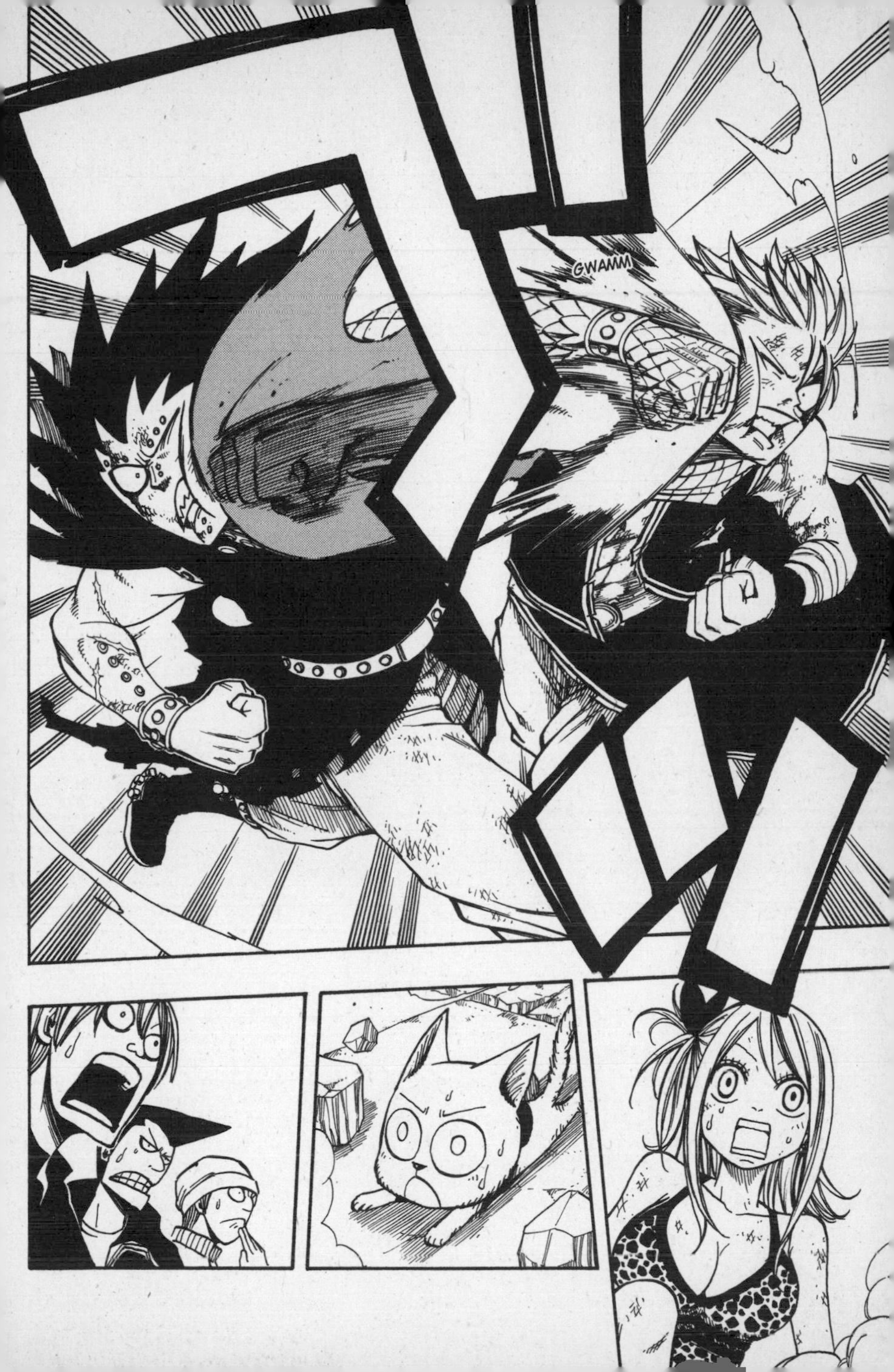
GWAMM

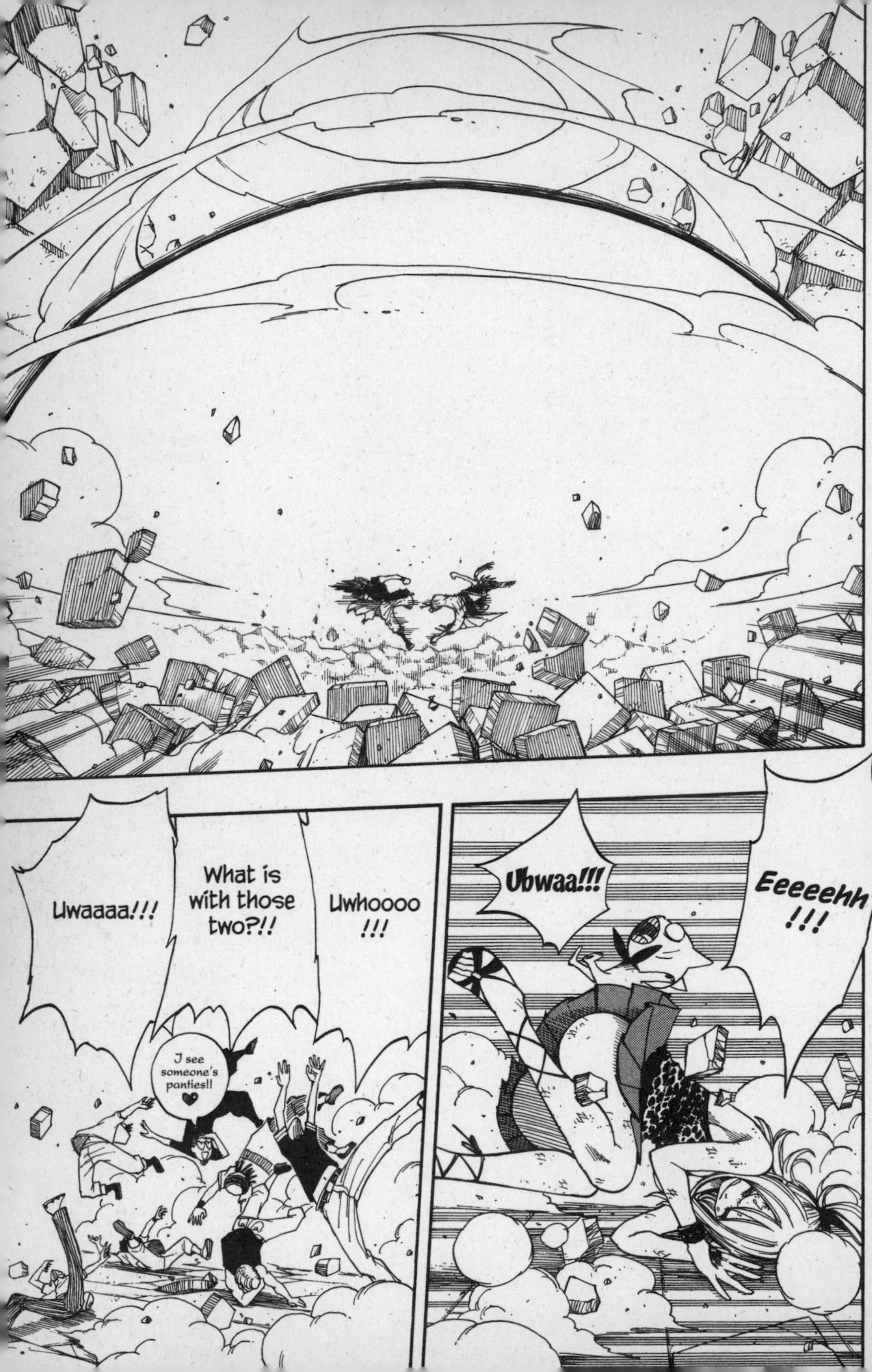
Eeeeehh !!!
Ubwaa!!!
Uwhoooo !!!
What is with those two?!!
Uwaaaa!!!
I see someone's panties!! ♥

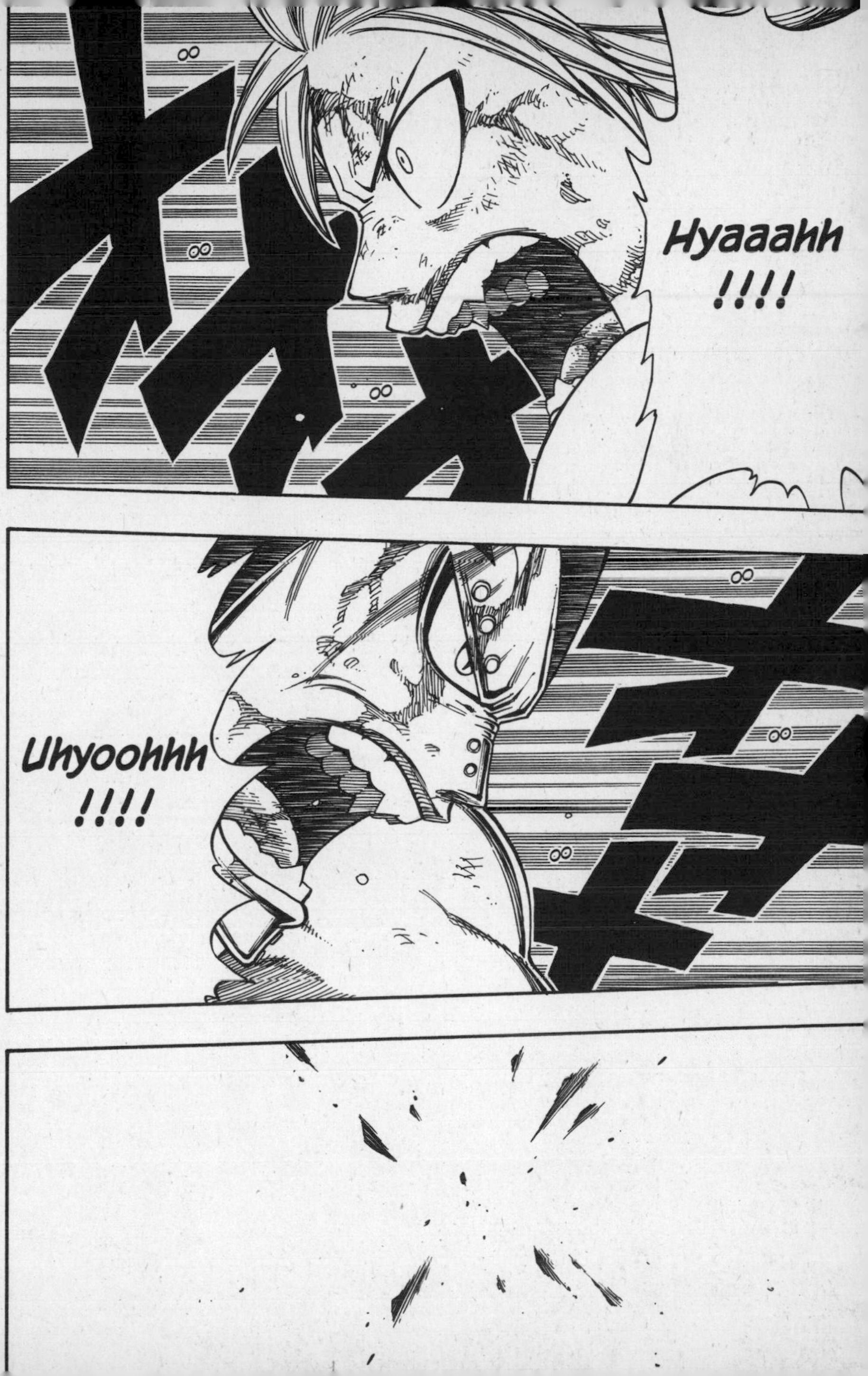
Hyaaahh !!!!
Uhyoohhh !!!!

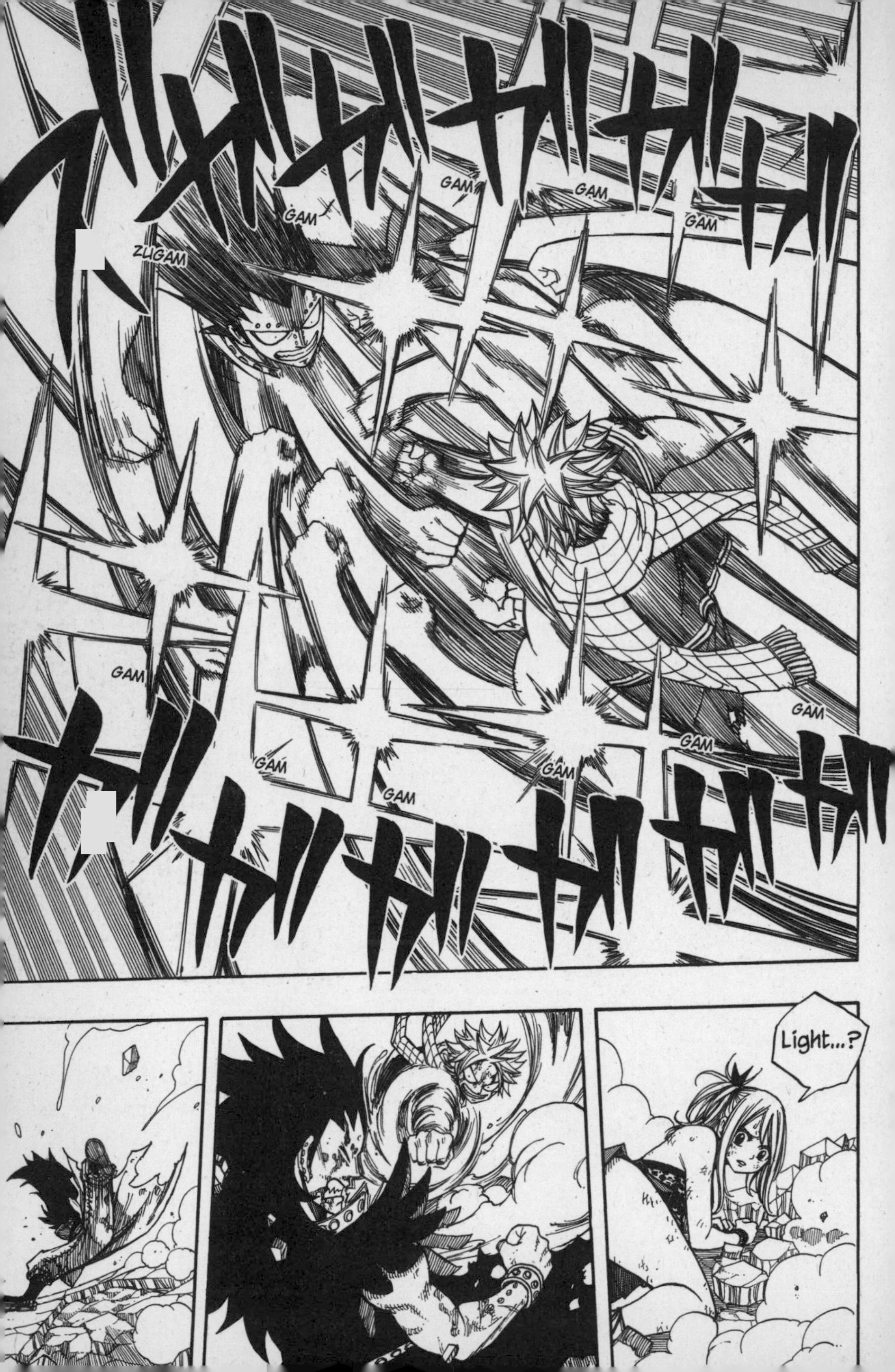
GAM
GAM
GAM
GAM
ZUGAM
GAM
GAM
GAM
GAM
GAM
GAM
Light...?

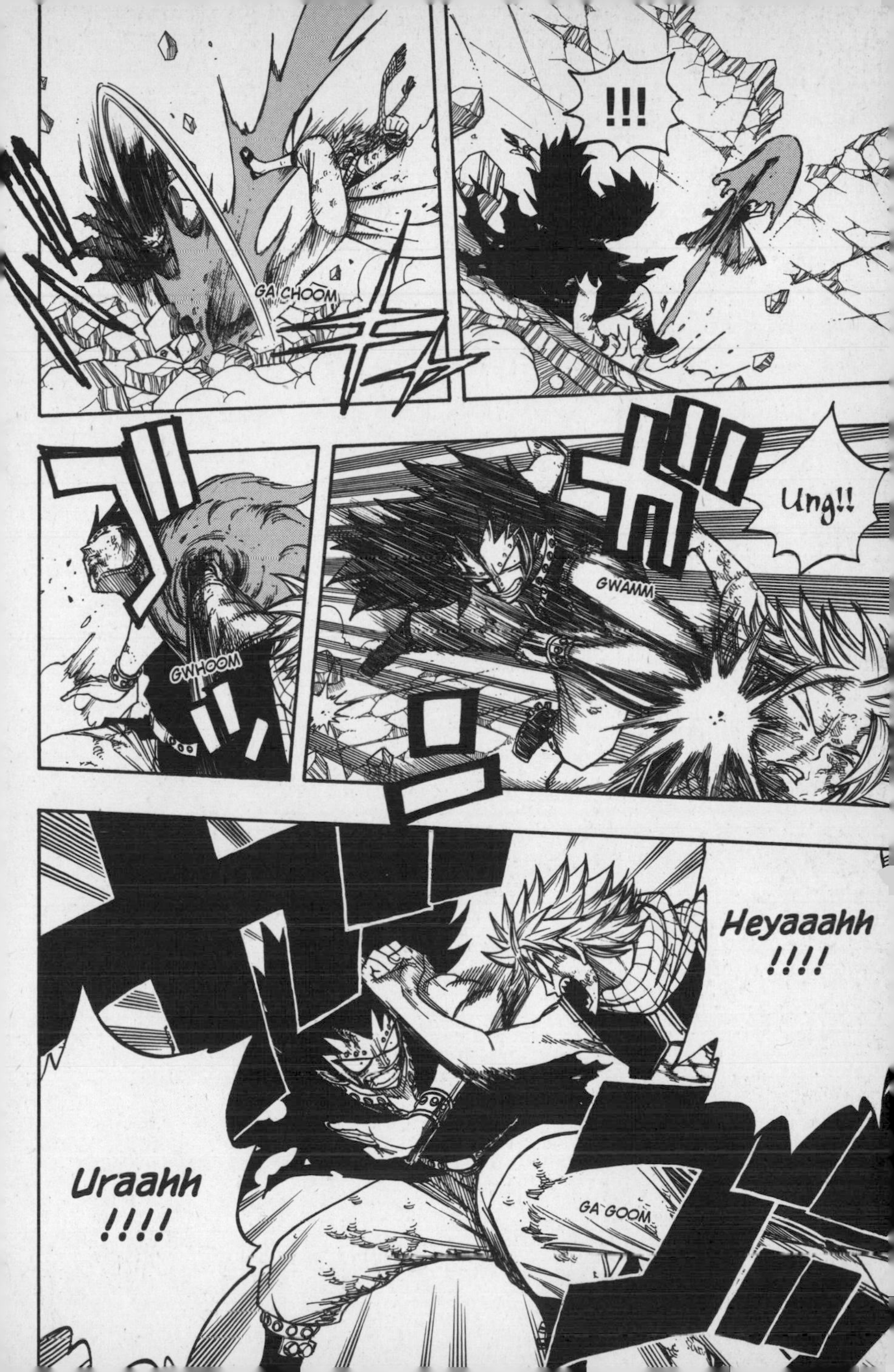
!!!
GA CHOOM
Ung!!
GWAMM
GWHOOM
Heyaaahh !!!!
Uraahh !!!!
GA GOOM

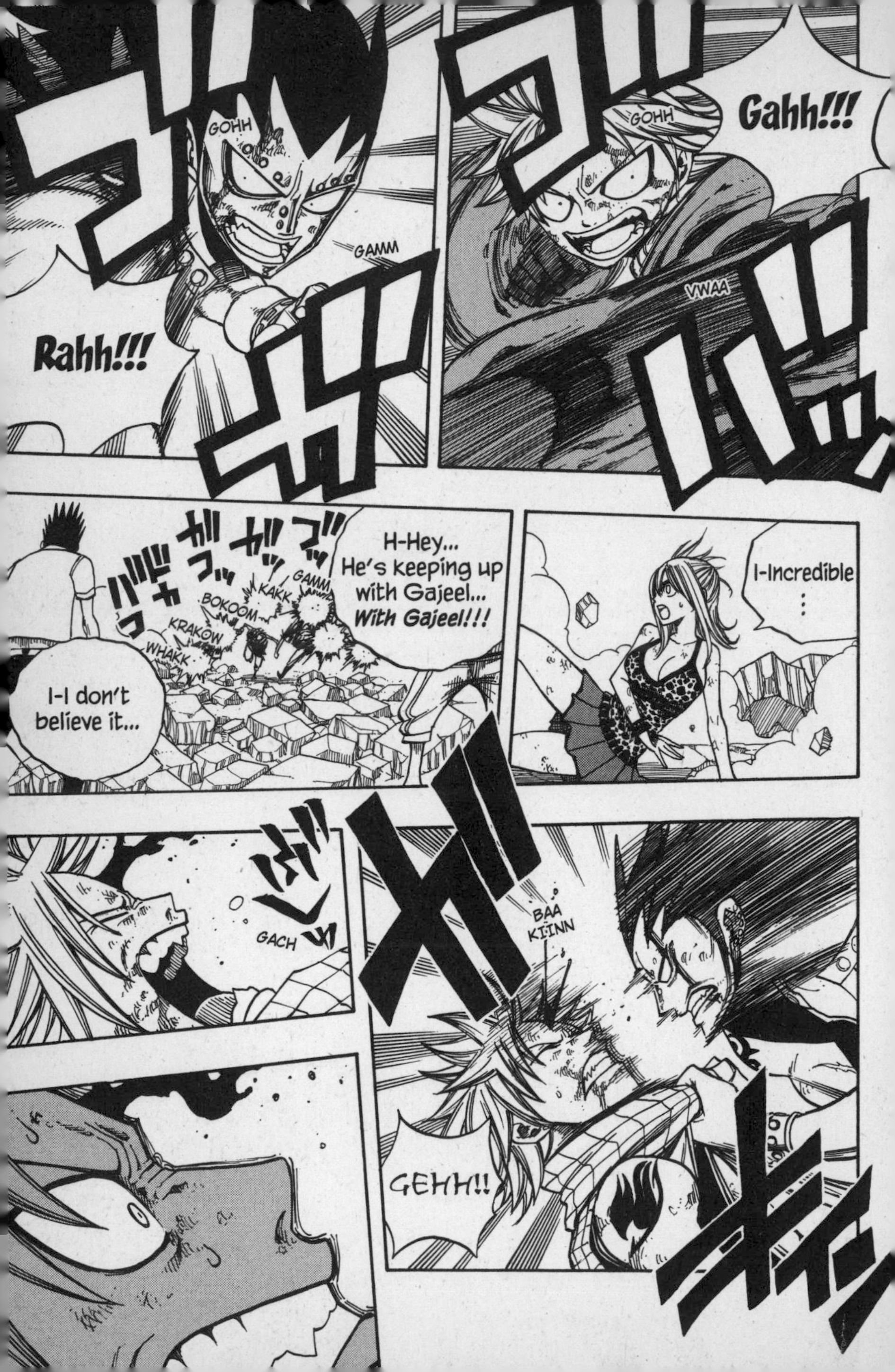
GOHH
Gahh!!!
VWAA
GOHH
GAMM
Rahh!!!
I-Incredible
...
H-Hey...
He's keeping up
with Gajeel...
With Gajeel!!!
GAMM
KAKK
BOKOOM
KRAKOW
WHAKK
I-I don't
believe it...
BAA
KIINN
GEHH!!
GACH

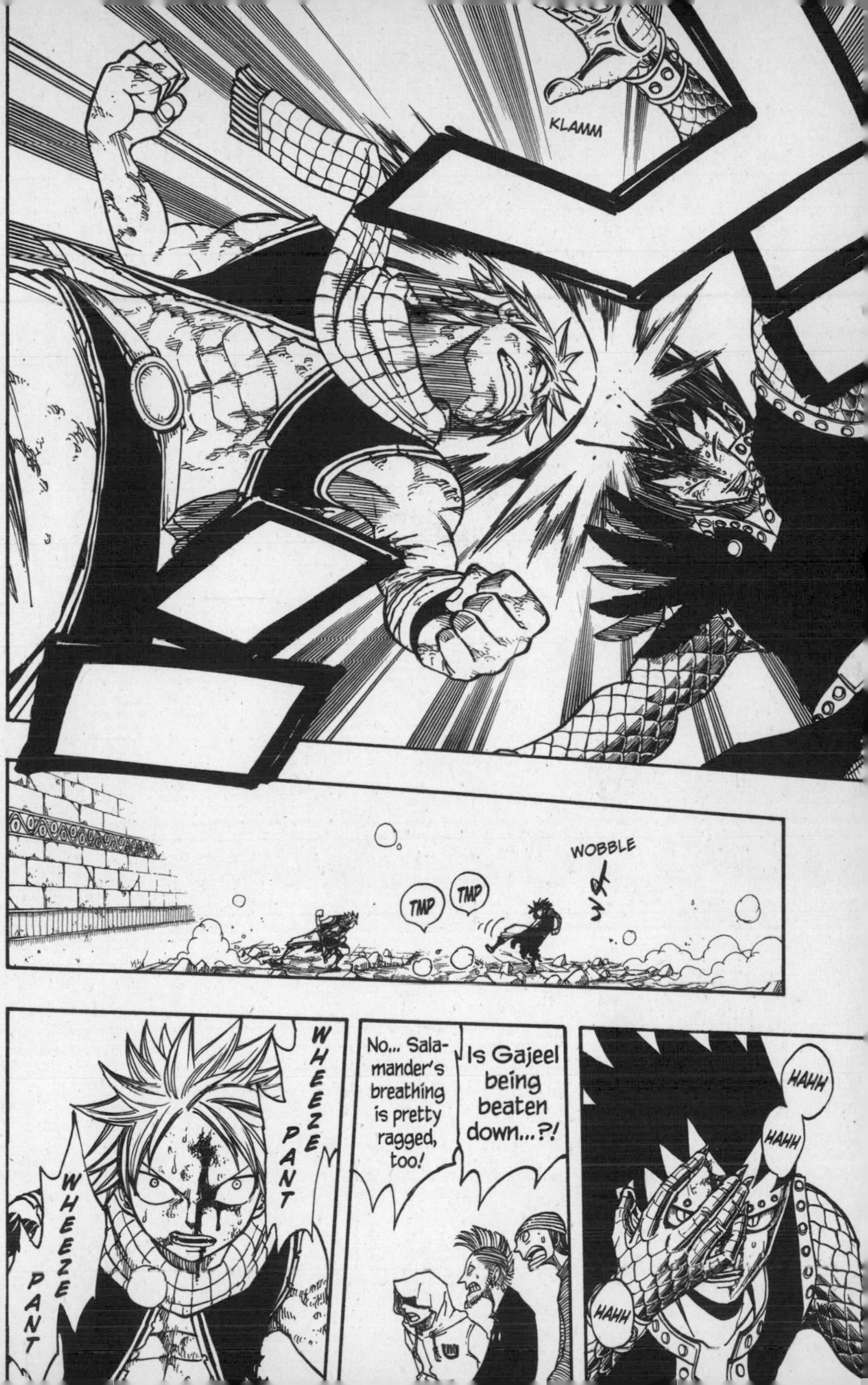

KLAMM
WOBBLE
TMP
TMP
HAHH
HAHH
HAHH
Is Gajeel being beaten down...?!
No... Salamander's breathing is pretty ragged, too!
WHEEZE
PANT
WHEEZE
PANT

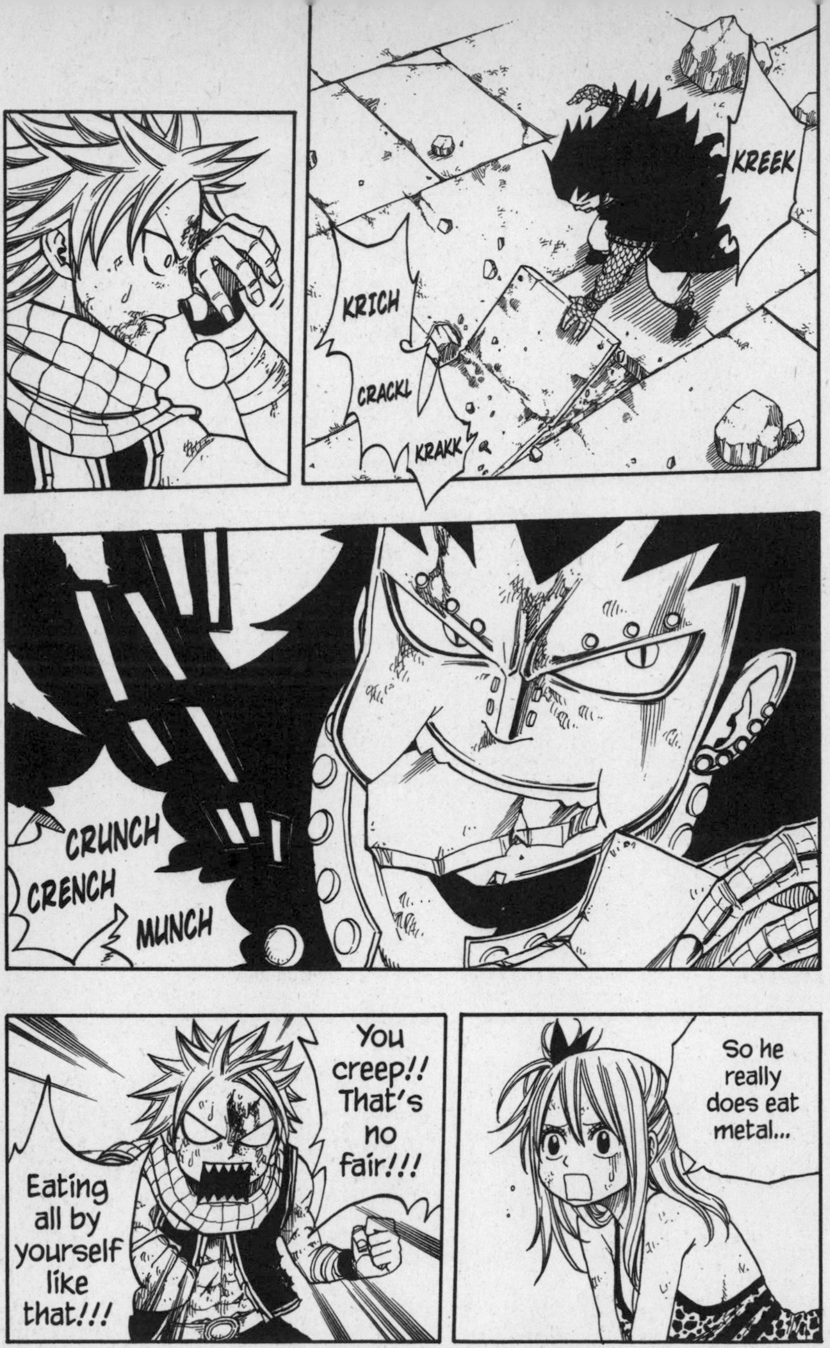
KREEK
KRICH
CRACKL
KRAKK
CRUNCH
CRENCH
MUNCH
So he really does eat metal...
You creep!! That's no fair!!!
Eating all by yourself like that!!!

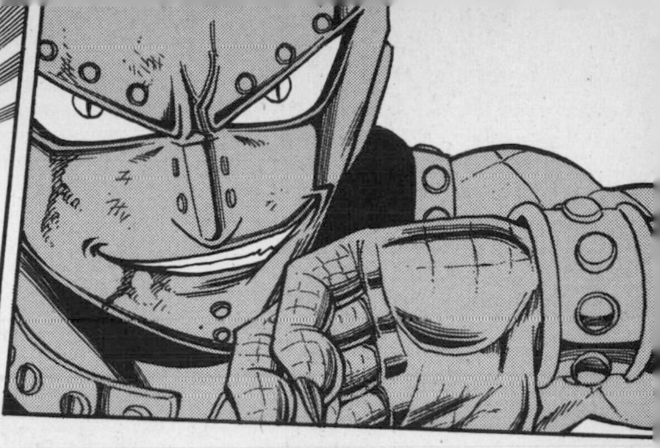

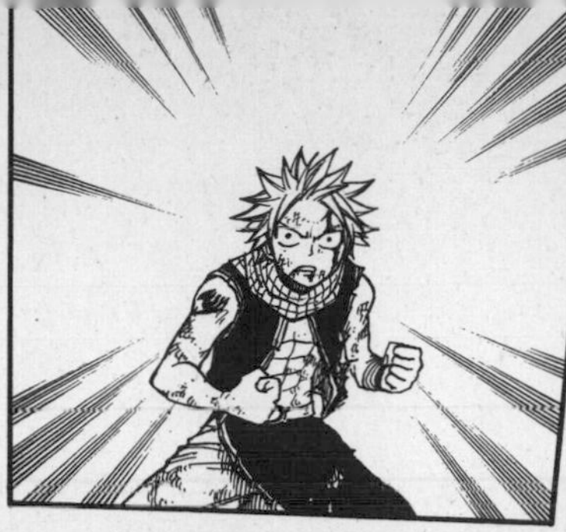

*Iron Dragon Lance: Demon Logs!!!!!

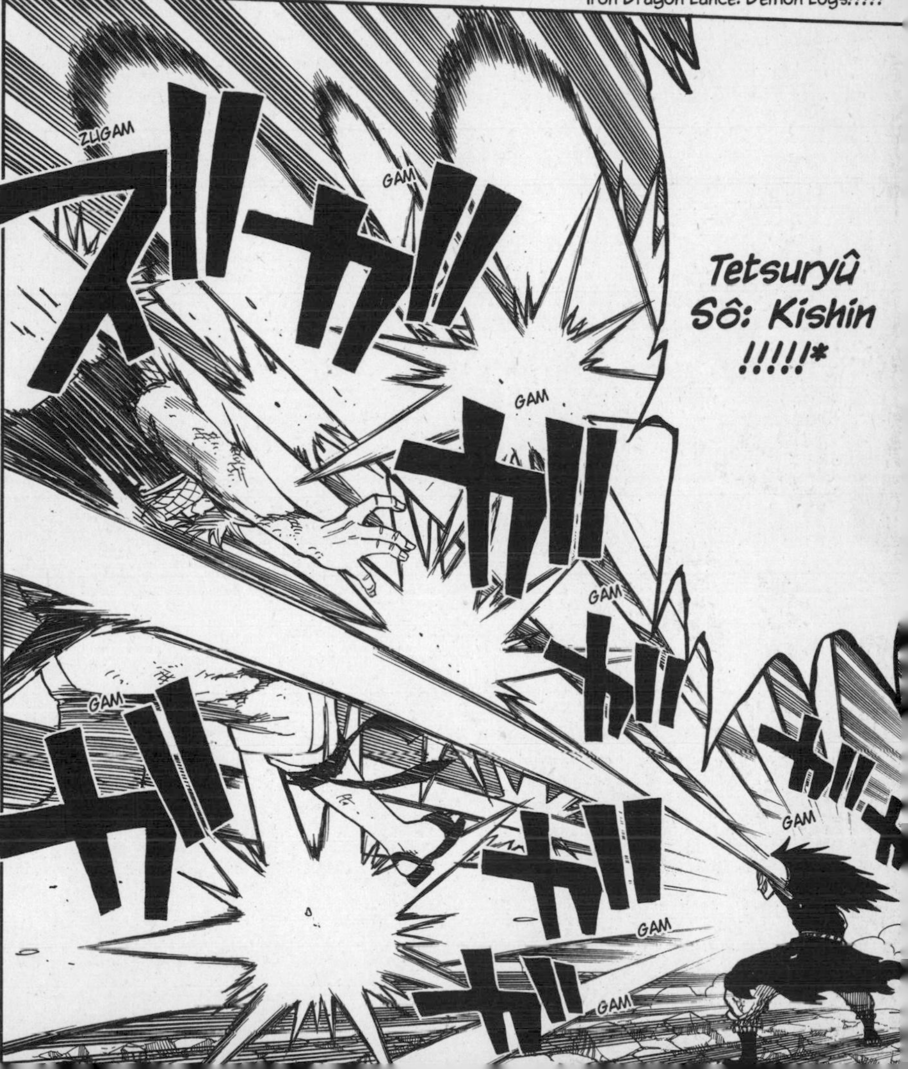
Tetsuryû Sô: Kishin !!!!!*
ZUGAM
GAM
GAM
GAM
GAM
GAM
GAM
GAM

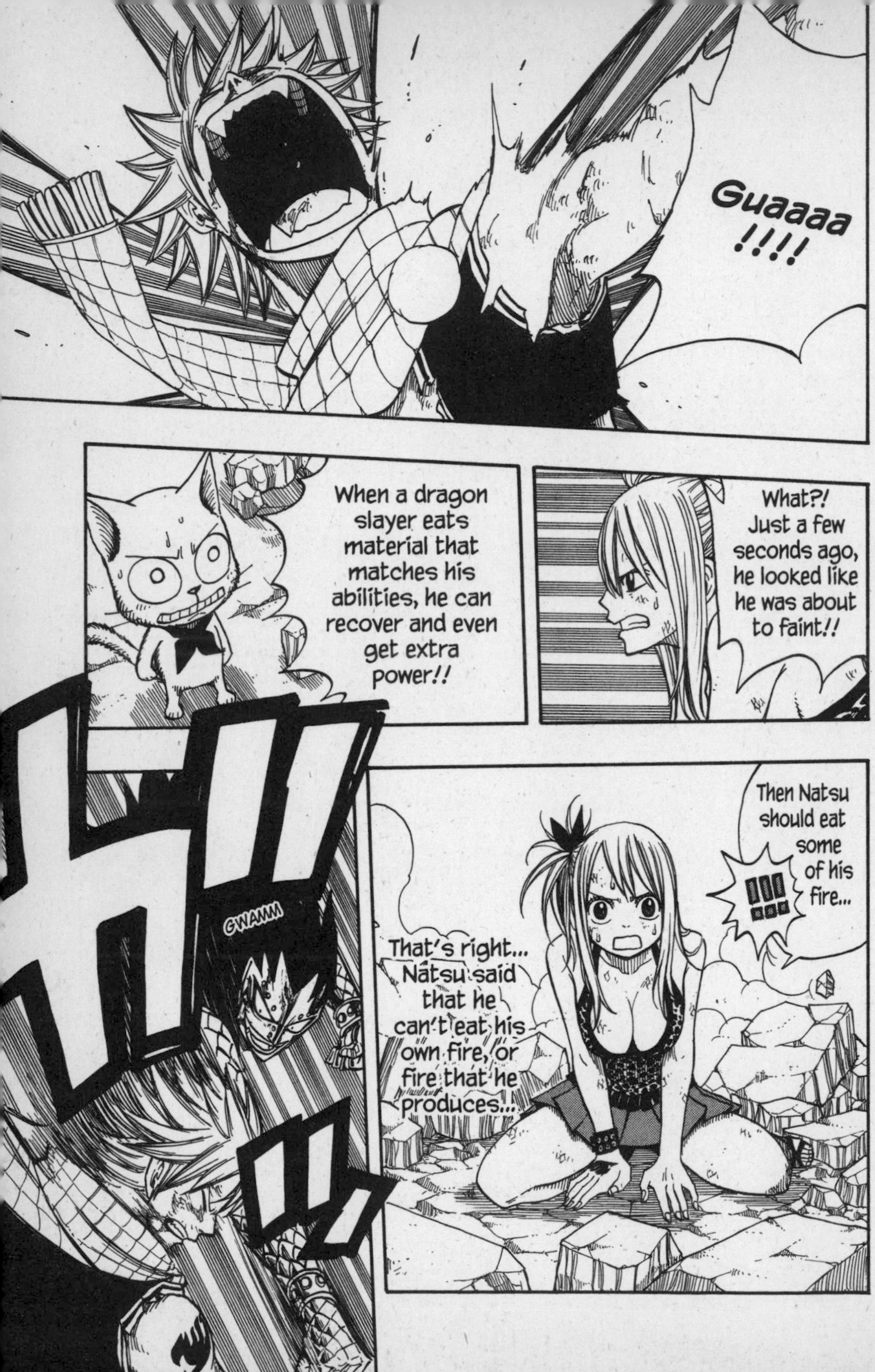
Guaaaa !!!!
What?! Just a few seconds ago, he looked like he was about to faint!!
When a dragon slayer eats material that matches his abilities, he can recover and even get extra power!!
Then Natsu should eat some of his fire...
!!!
That's right... Natsu said that he can't eat his own fire, or fire that he produces...
GWAMM

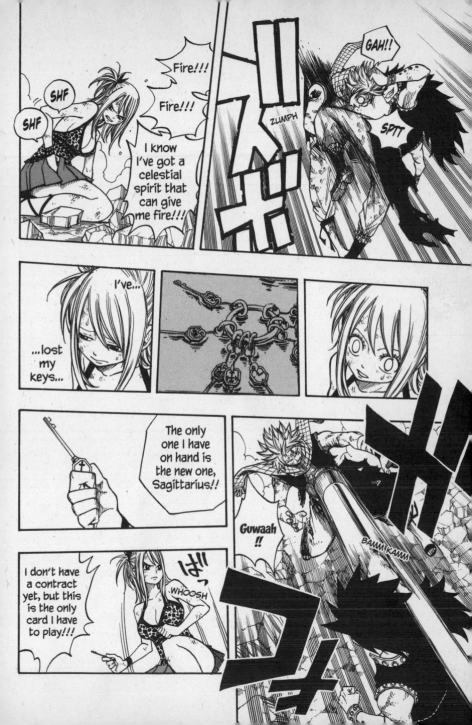

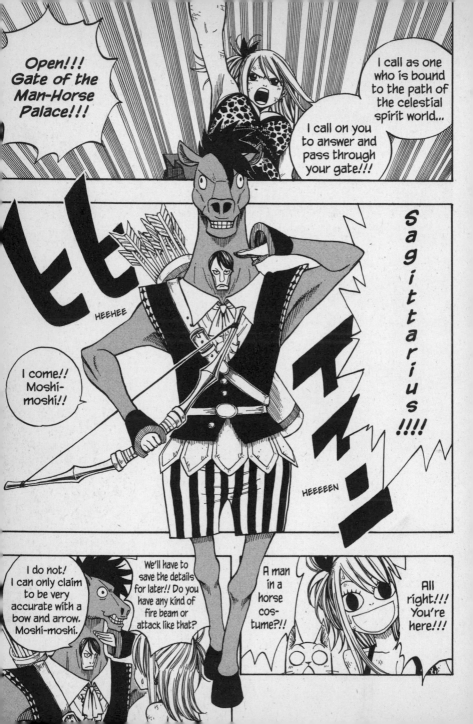

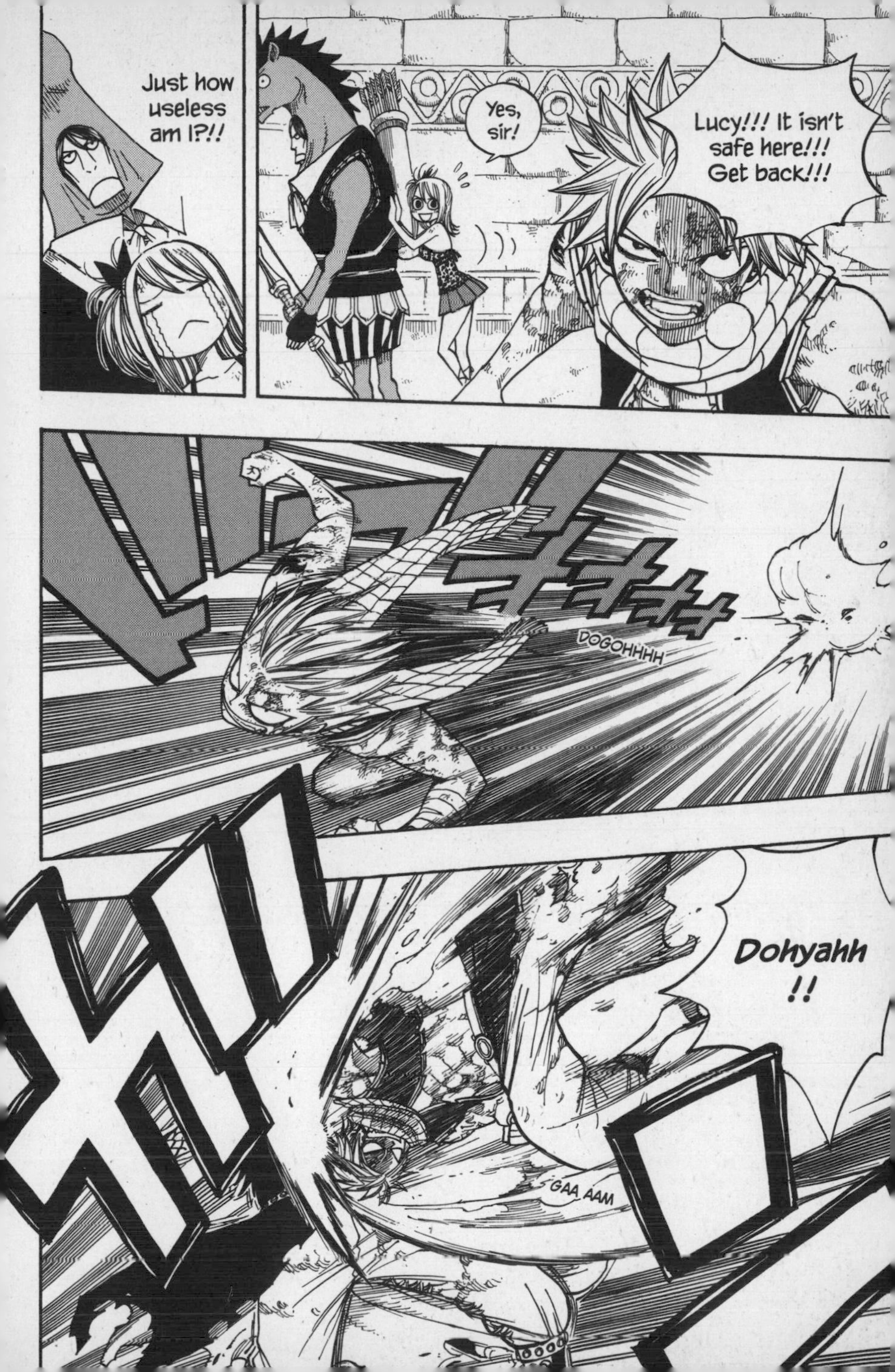
Lucy!!! It isn't safe here!!! Get back!!!
Yes, sir!
Just how useless am I?!!
DOGOHHHH
Dohyahh !!
GAA AAM

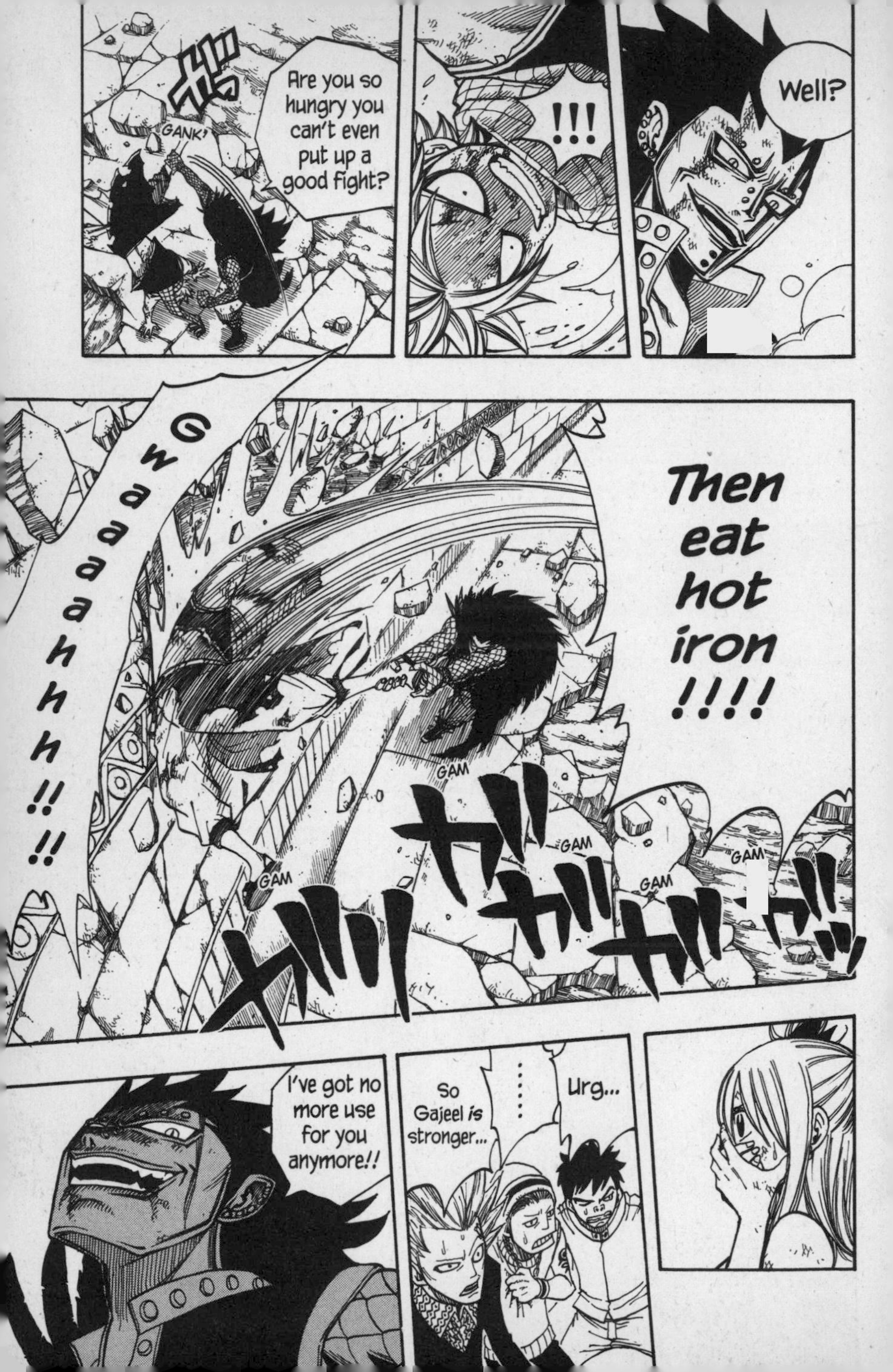
Well?
!!!
Are you so hungry you can't even put up a good fight?
GANK
Then eat hot iron!!!!
Gwaaaaaahhhh!!!!
GAM
GAM
GAM
GAM
GAM
Urg...
.....
So Gajeel is stronger...
I've got no more use for you anymore!!

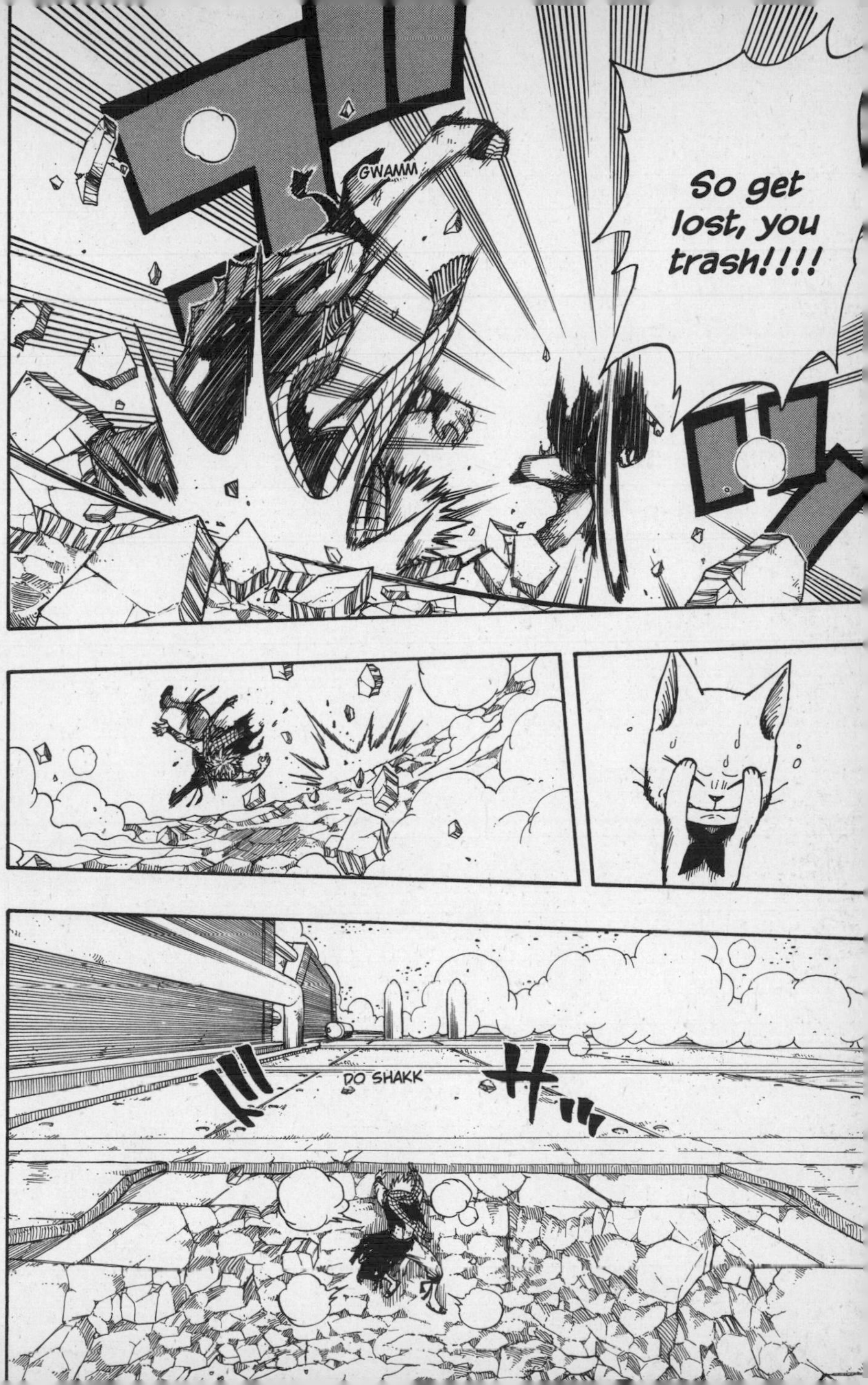
So get lost, you trash!!!!
GWAMM
DO SHAKK

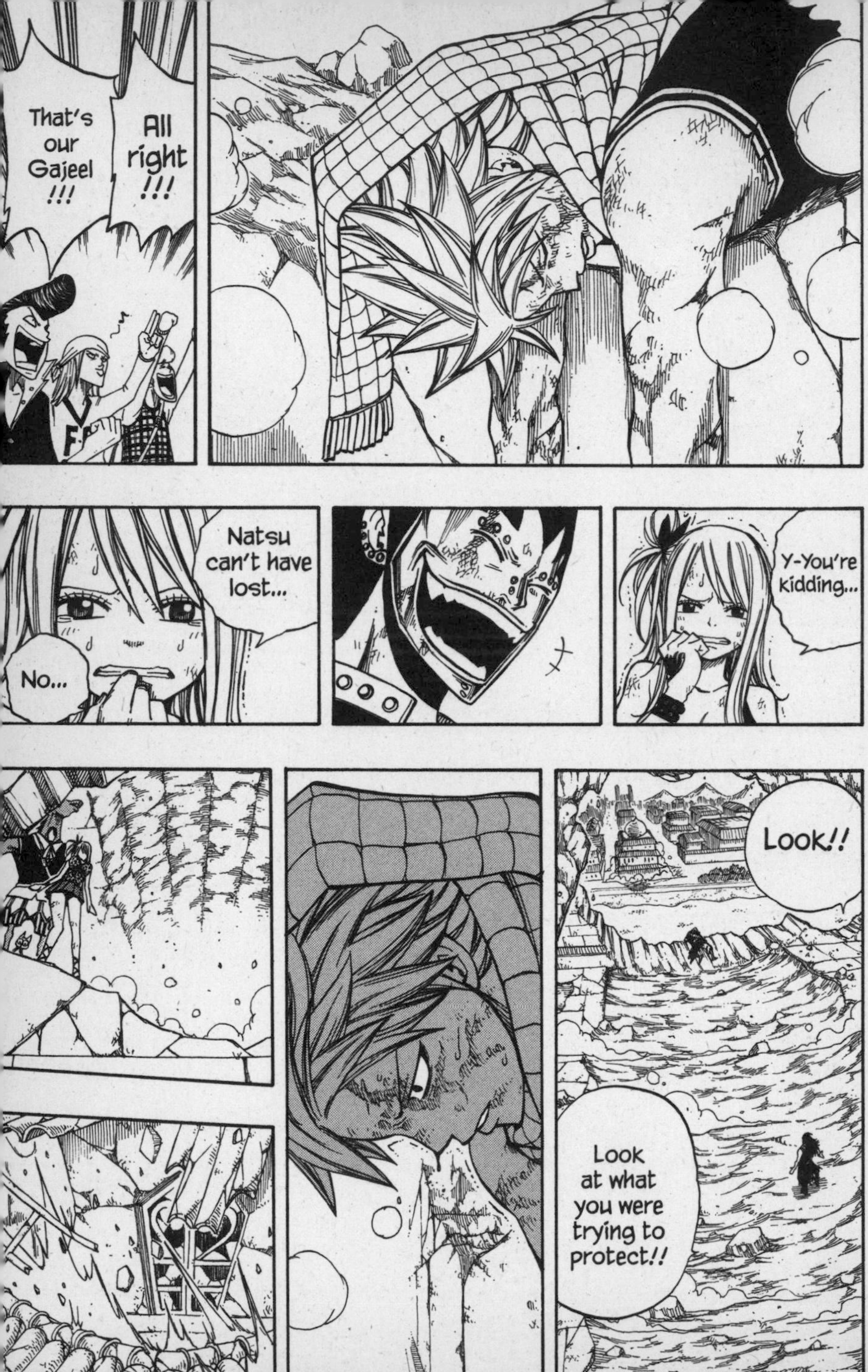
All right!!!
That's our Gajeel!!!
Y-You're kidding...
Natsu can't have lost...
No...
Look!!
Look at what you were trying to protect!!

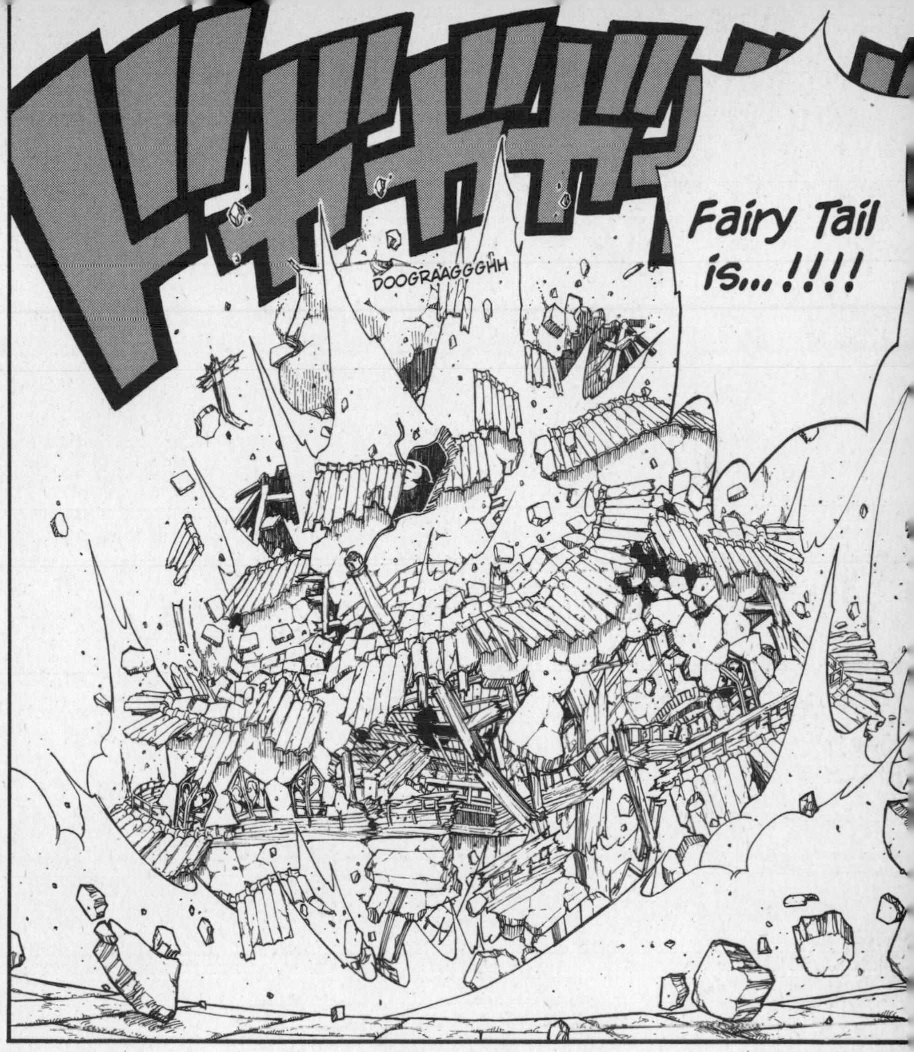
DOOGRAAGGGHH
Fairy Tail is...!!!!

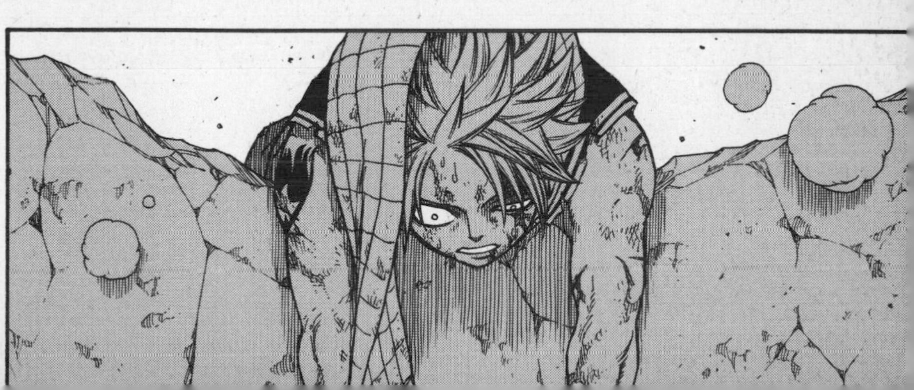

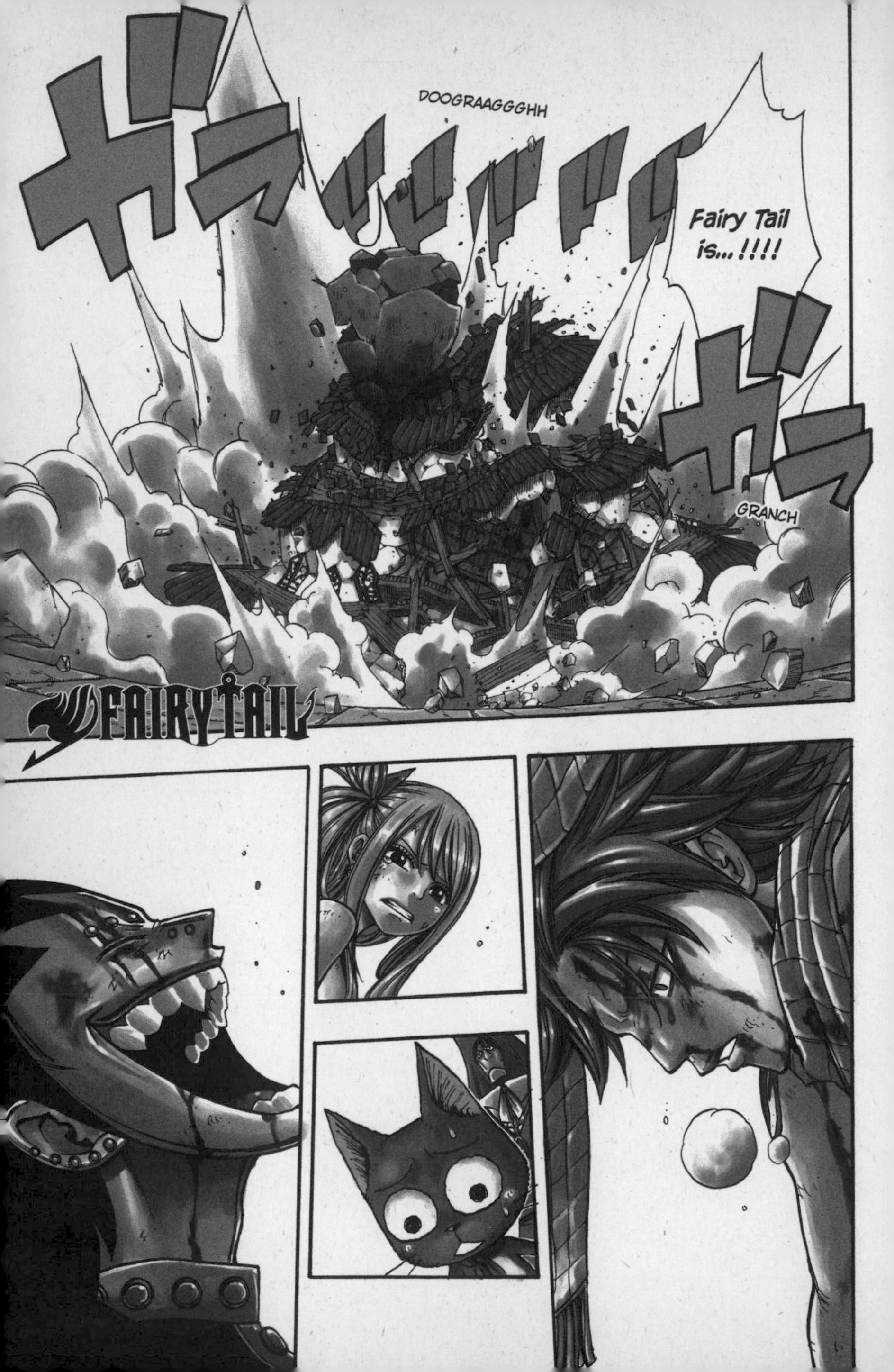
Fairy Tail is...!!!!
DOOGRAAGGGHH
GRANCH
FAIRY TAIL

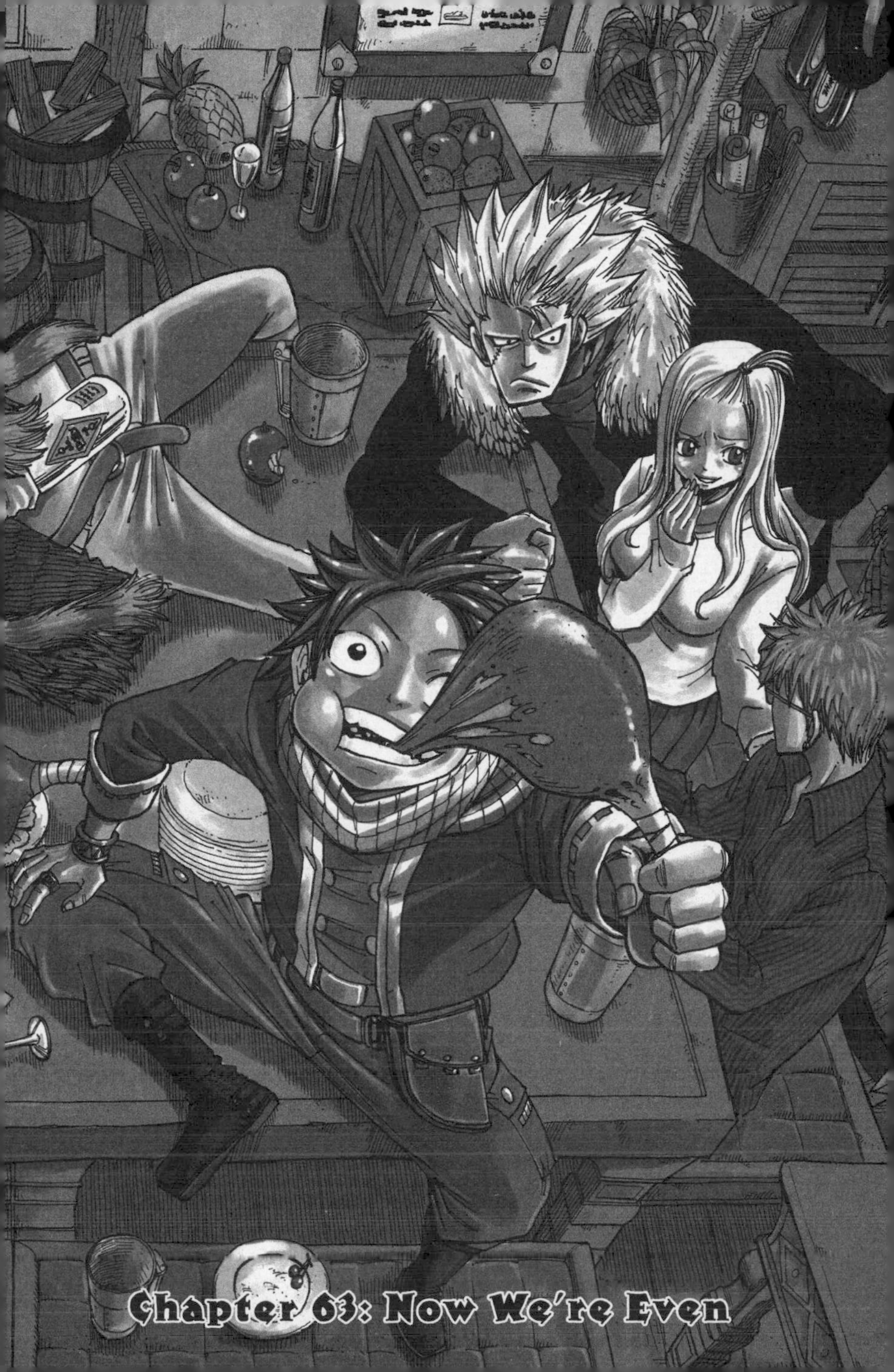
Chapter 63: Now We're Even

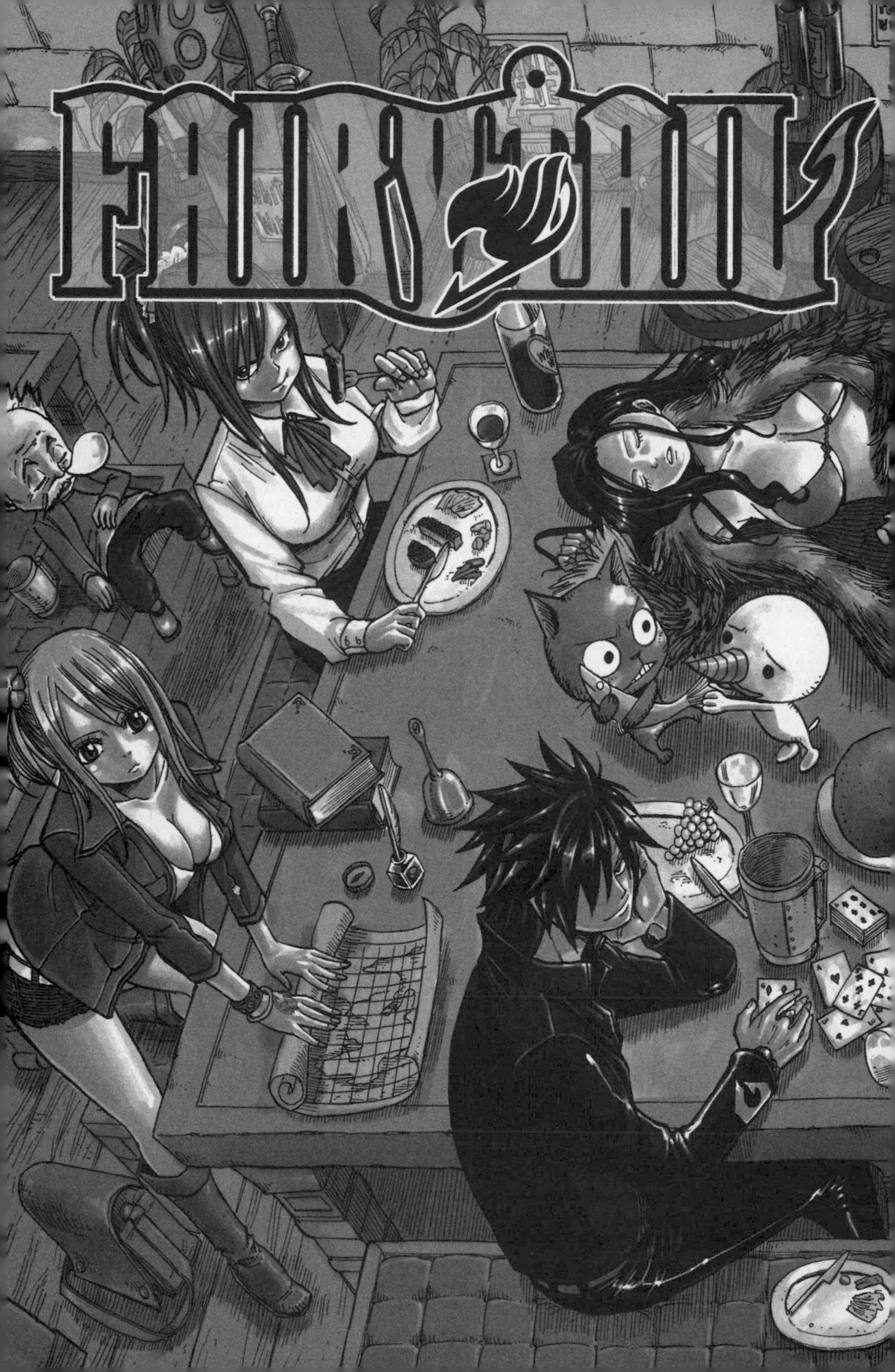
FAIRY TAIL

FAIRY TAIL

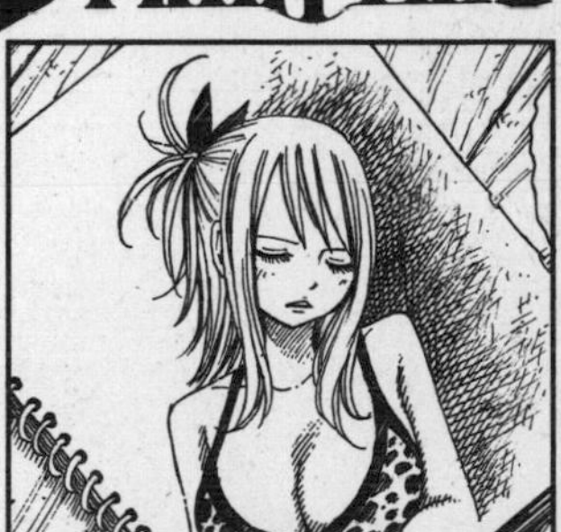

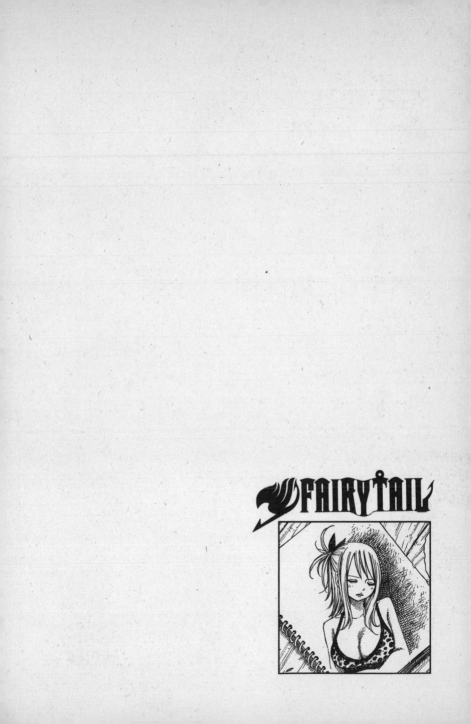

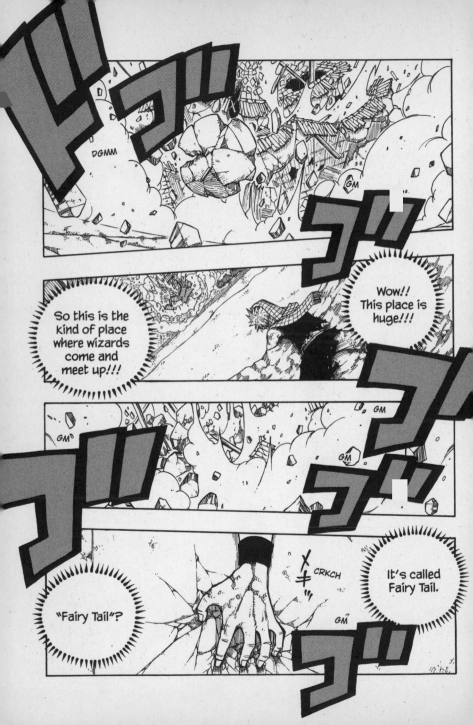

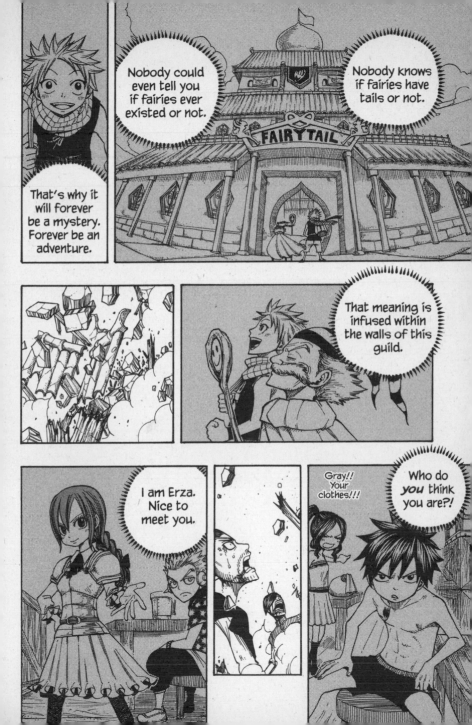

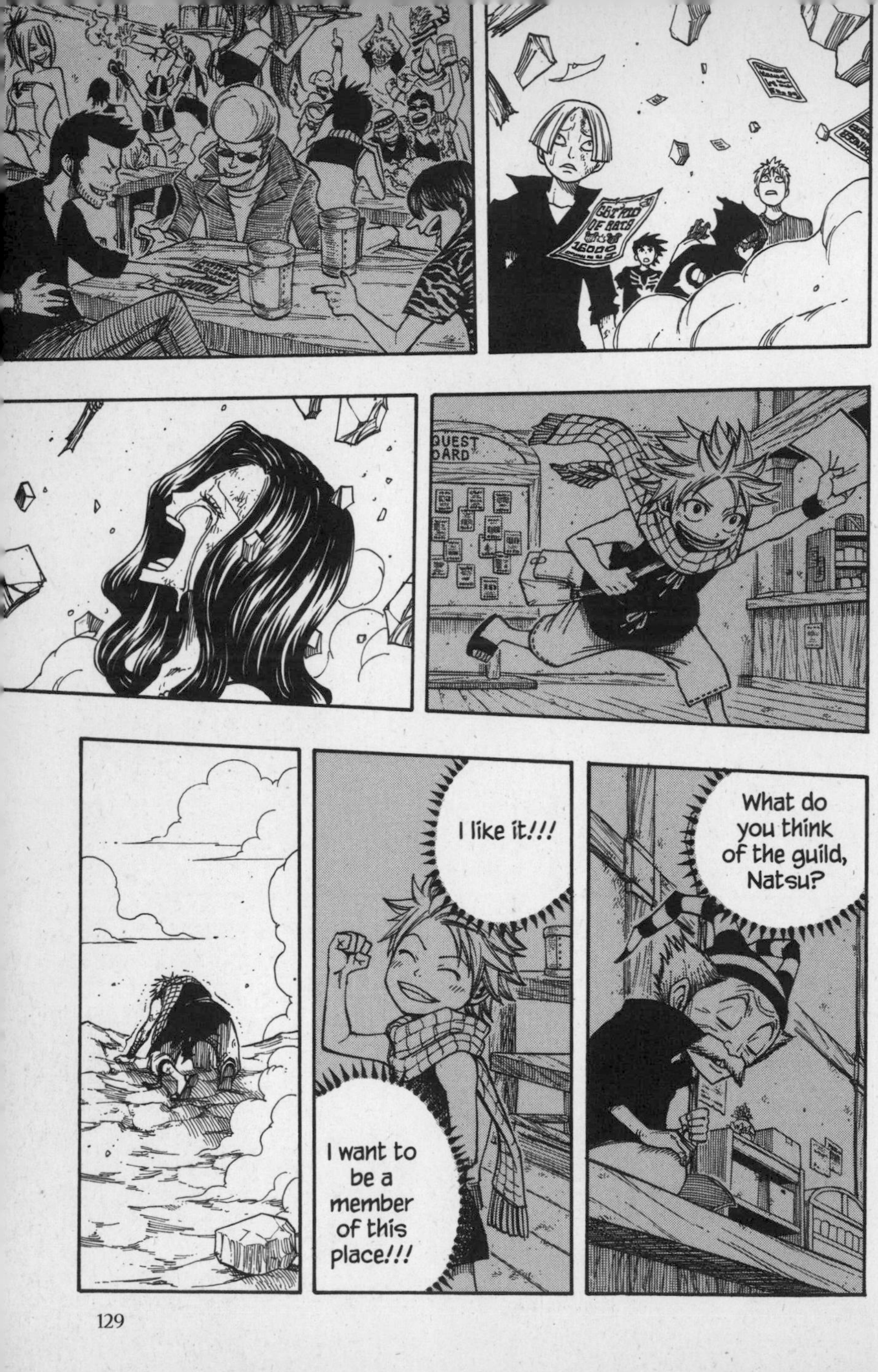
What do you think of the guild, Natsu?
I like it!!!
I want to be a member of this place!!!

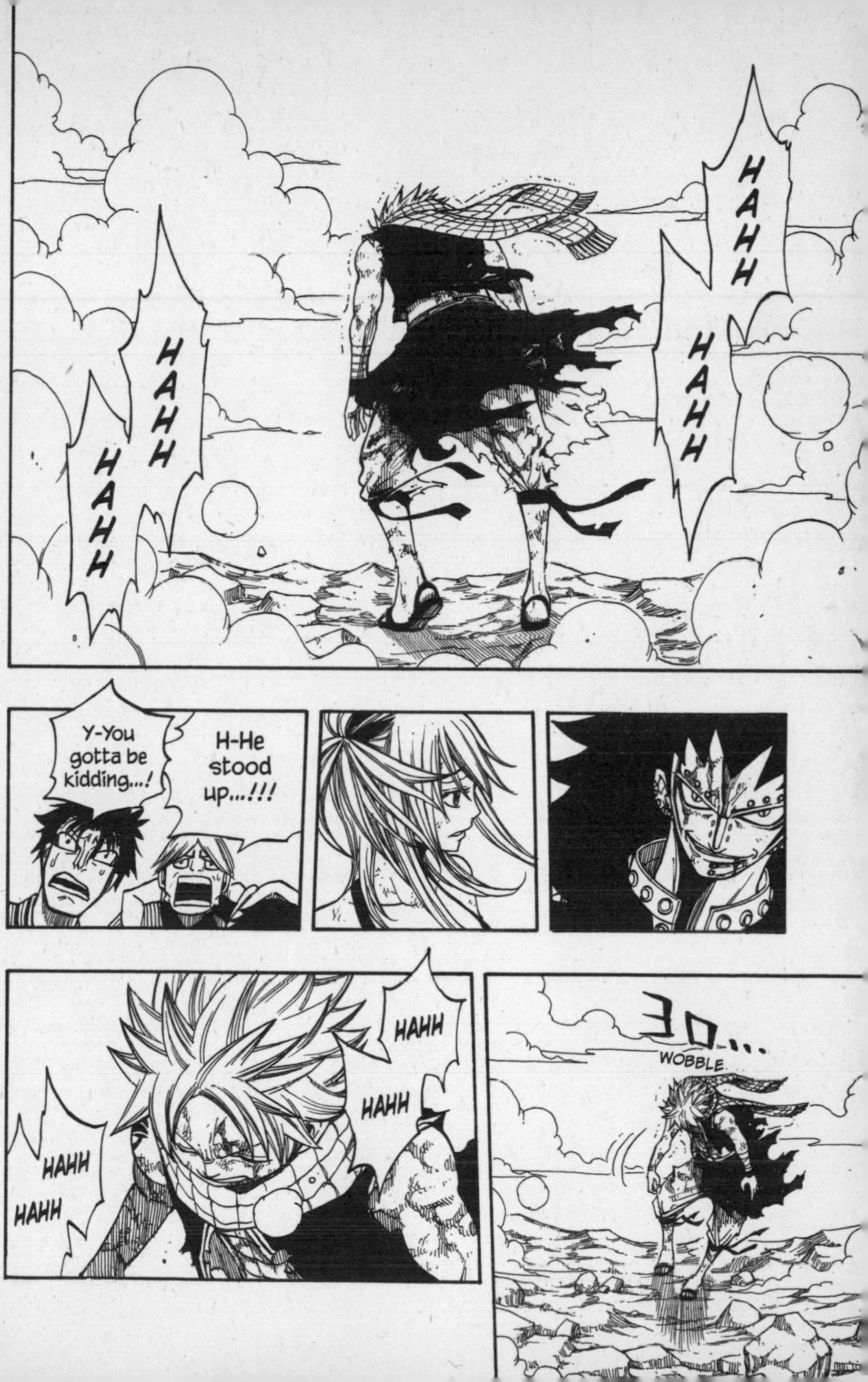
HAHH
HAHH
HAHH
HAHH
H-He stood up...!!!
Y-You gotta be kidding...!
ヨロ...
WOBBLE
HAHH
HAHH
HAHH
HAHH

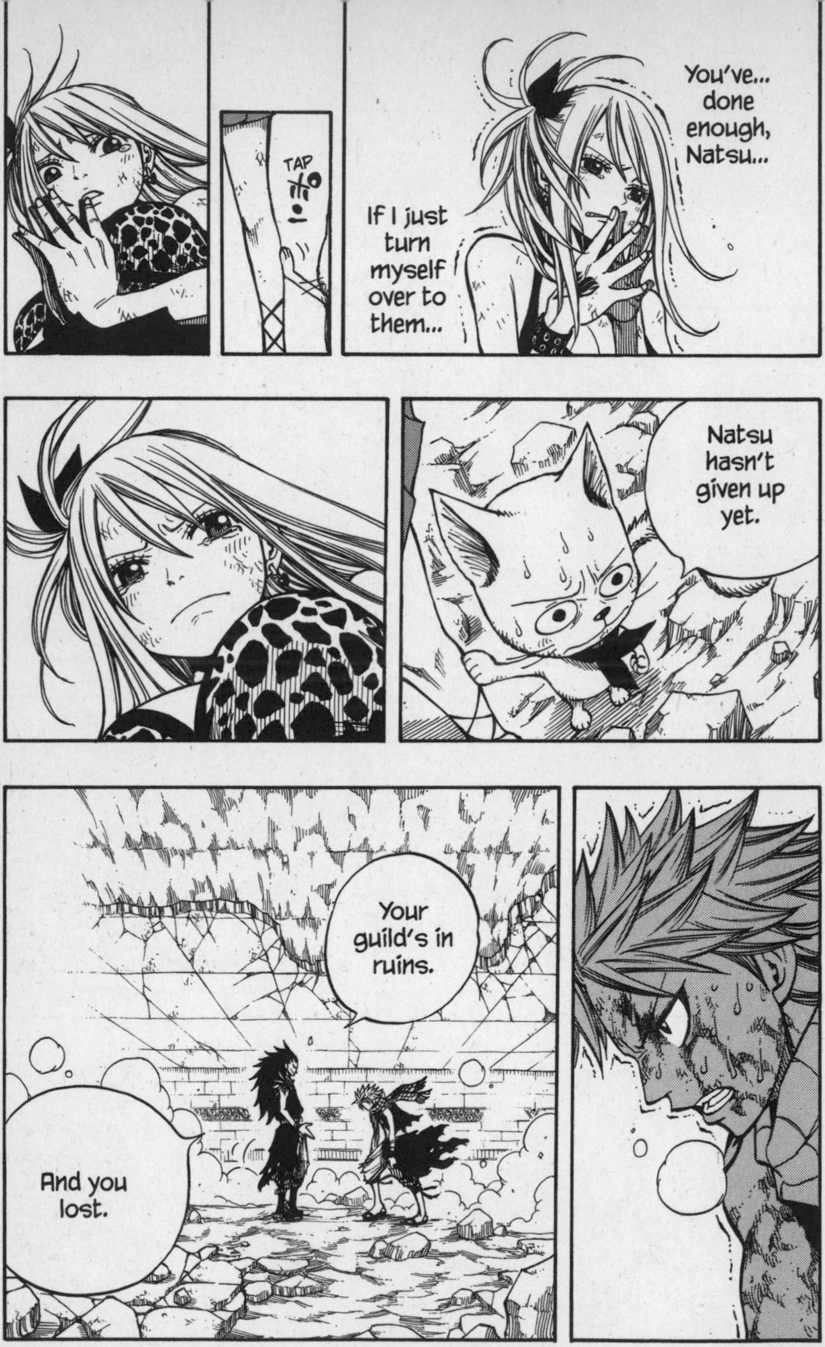
You've... done enough, Natsu...
If I just turn myself over to them...
TAP
Natsu hasn't given up yet.
Your guild's in ruins.
And you lost.

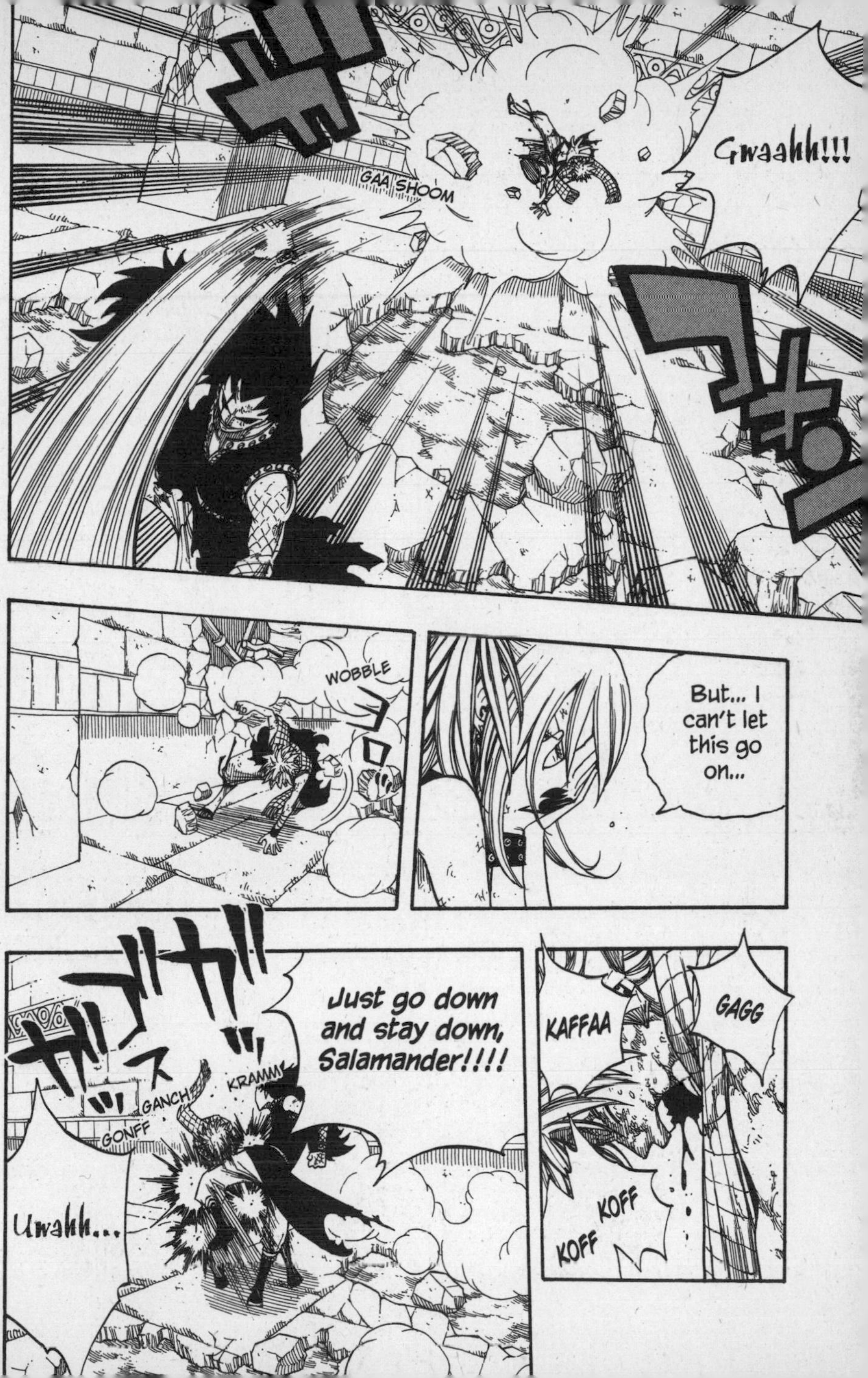
Gwaahh!!!
GAA SHOOM
But... I can't let this go on...
WOBBLE
GAGG
KAFFAA
KOFF
KOFF
Just go down and stay down, Salamander!!!!
KRAMM
GANCH
GONFF
Uwahh...

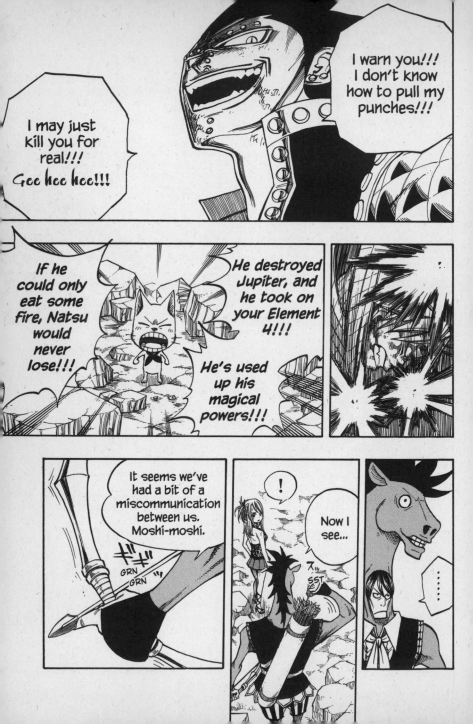

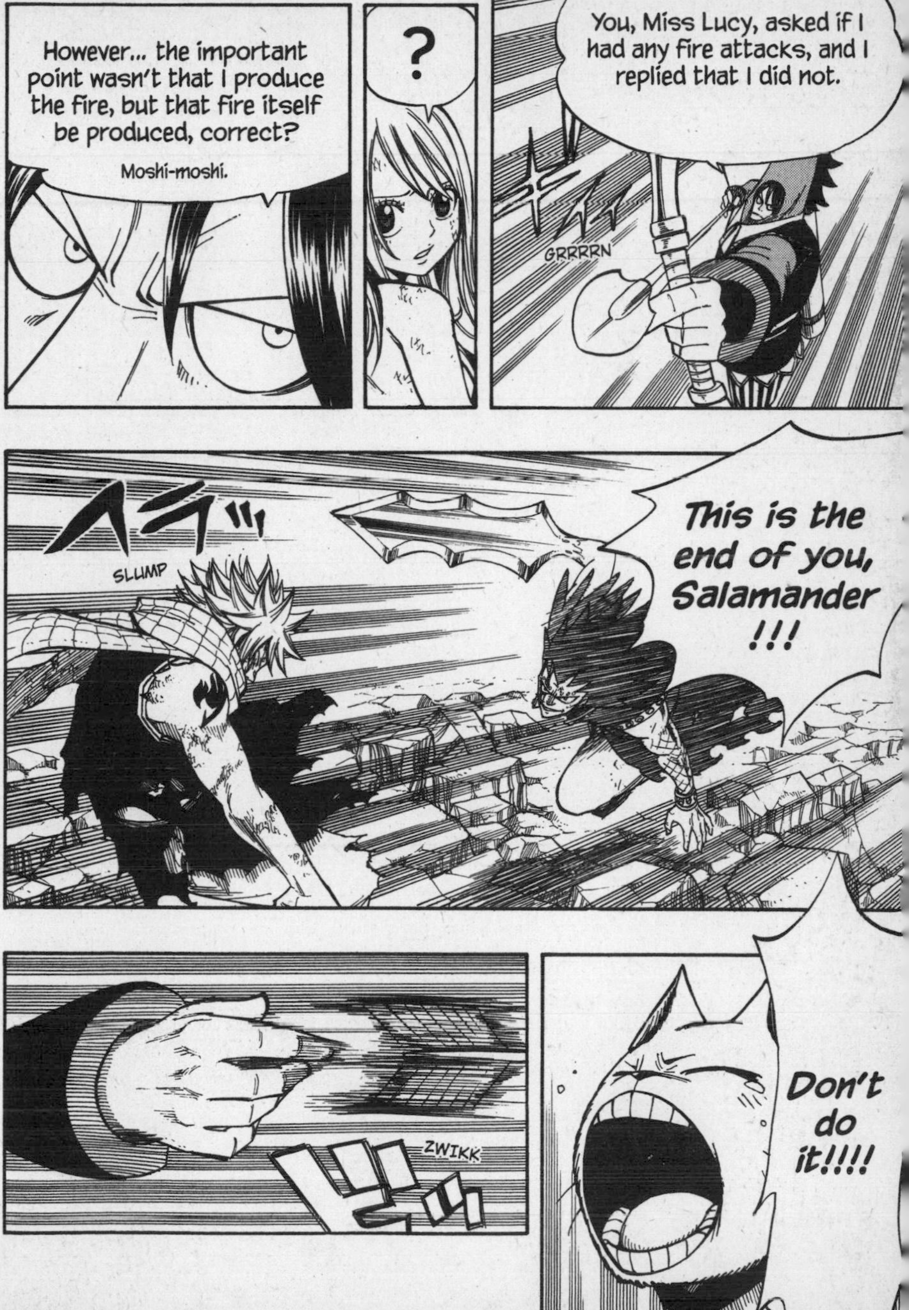
You, Miss Lucy, asked if I had any fire attacks, and I replied that I did not.
GRRRRN
?
However... the important point wasn't that I produce the fire, but that fire itself be produced, correct?
Moshi-moshi.
This is the end of you, Salamander !!!
SLUMP
Don't do it!!!!
ZWIKK

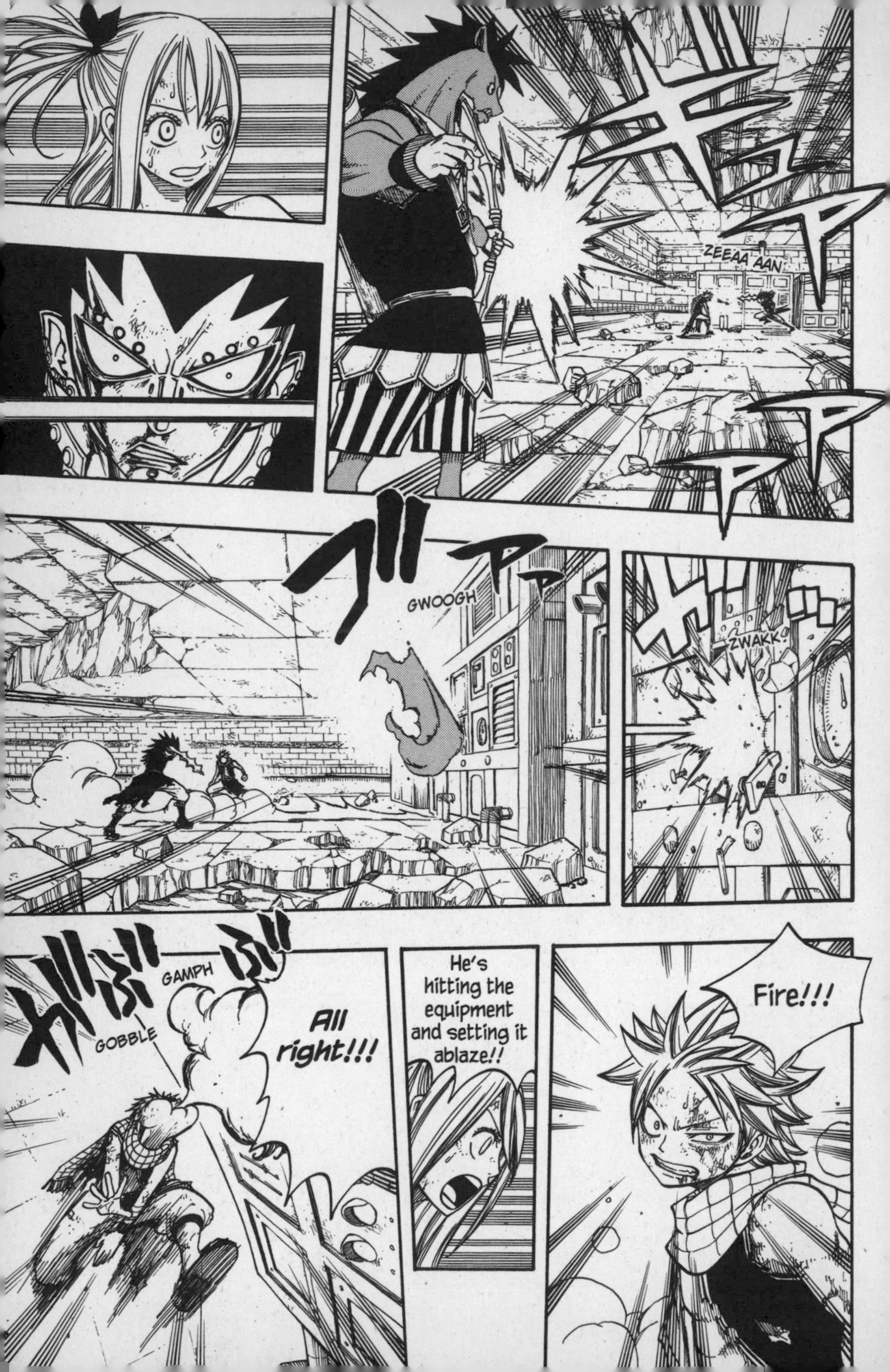
ZEEAA AAN
ZWAKK!
GWOOGH
Fire!!!
He's hitting the equipment and setting it ablaze!!
All right!!!
GAMPH
GOBBLE

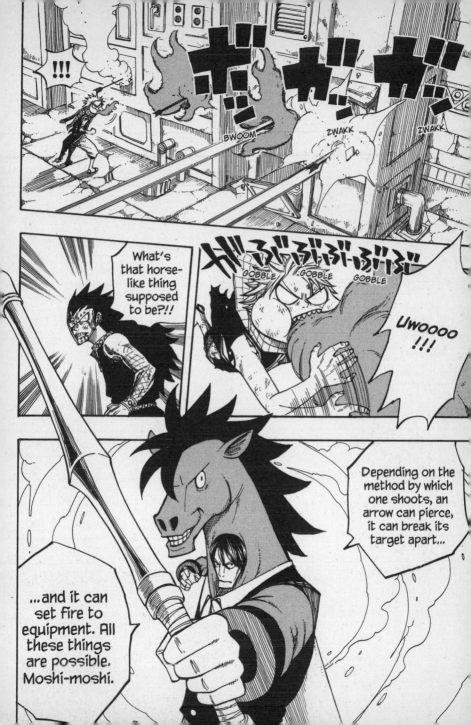

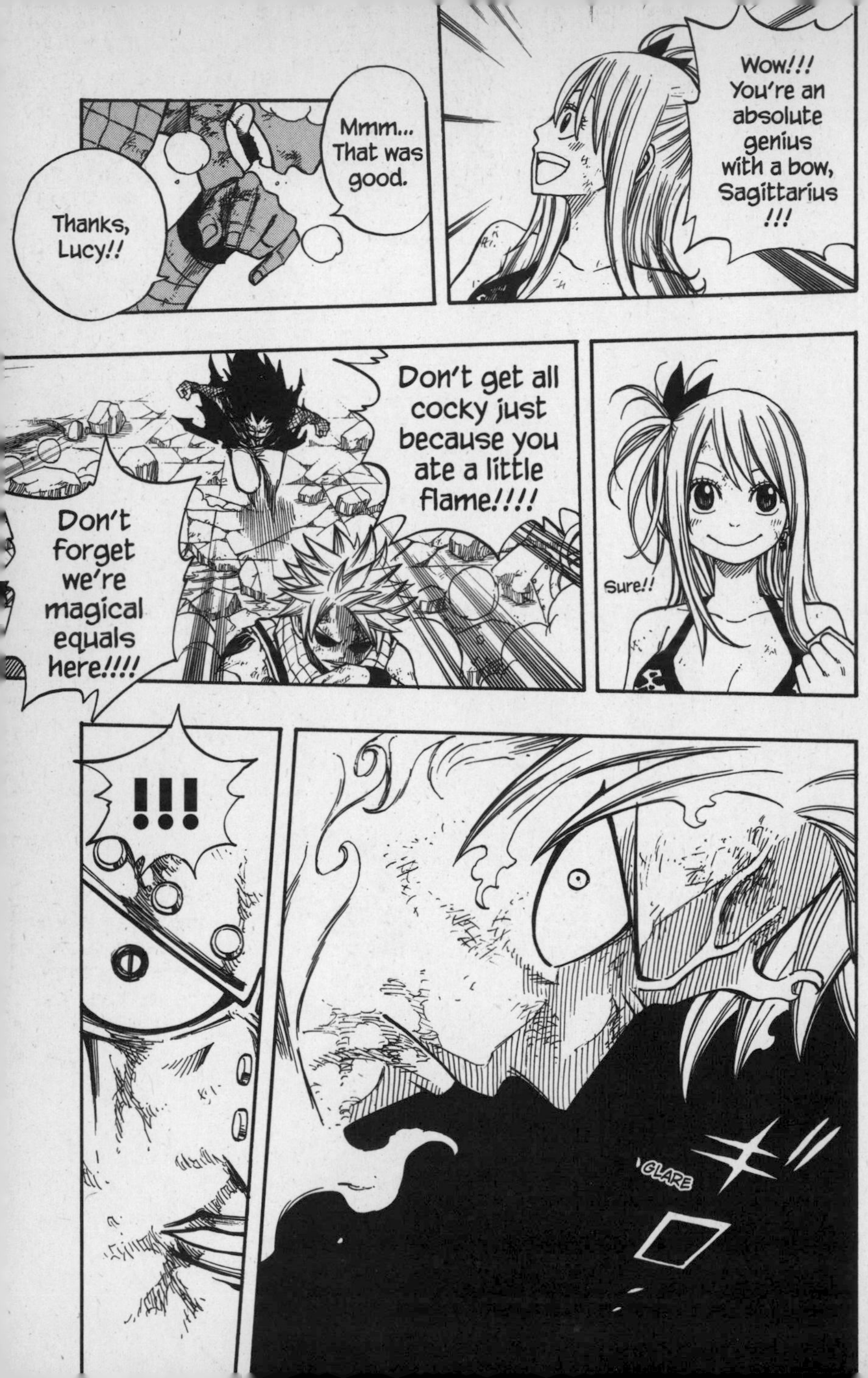
Wow!!! You're an absolute genius with a bow, Sagittarius !!!
Mmm... That was good.
Thanks, Lucy!!
Sure!!
Don't get all cocky just because you ate a little flame!!!!
Don't forget we're magical equals here!!!!
GLARE
!!!

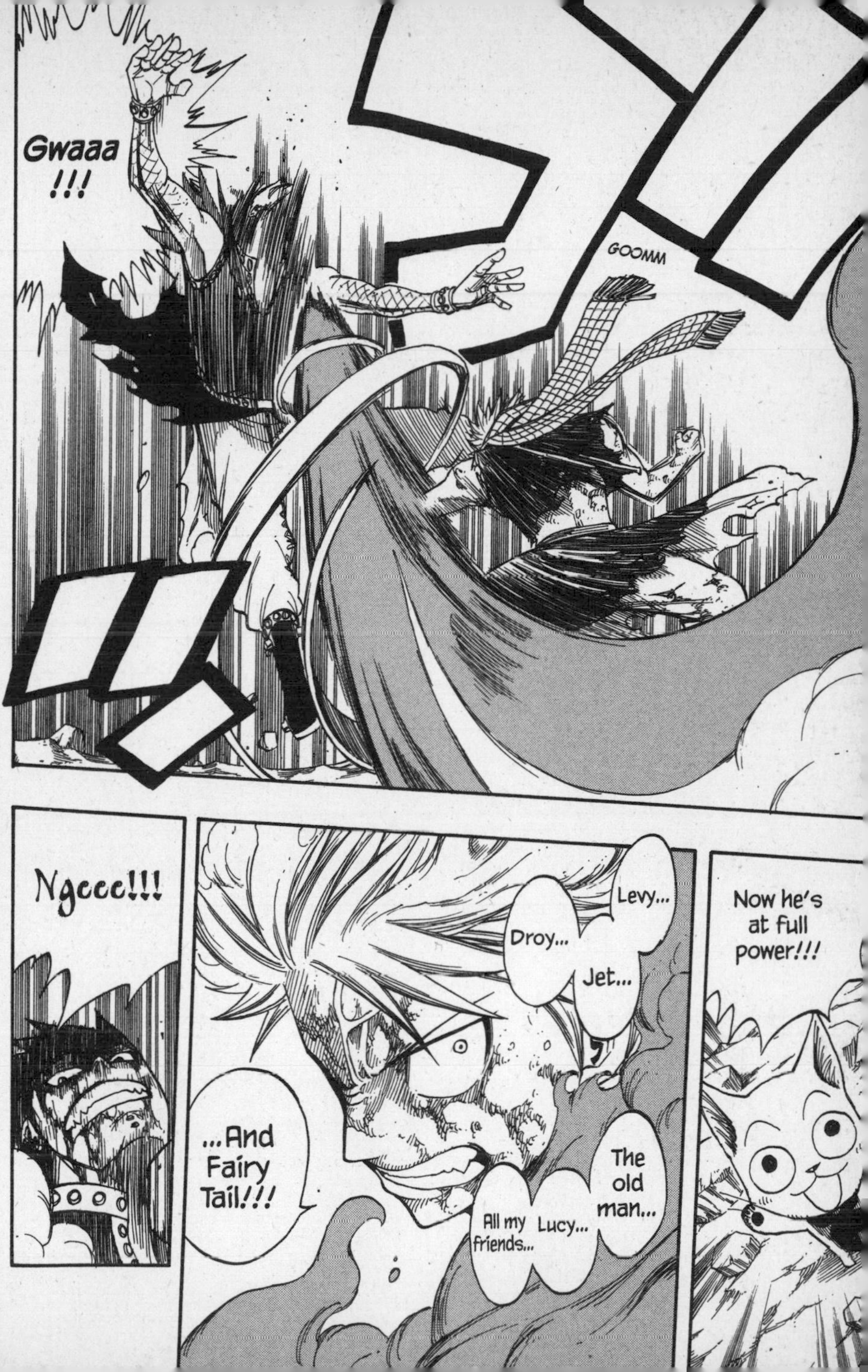
GOOMM
Gwaaa!!!
Now he's at full power!!!
Levy...
Droy...
Jet...
The old man...
Lucy...
All my friends...
...And Fairy Tail!!!
Ngccc!!!

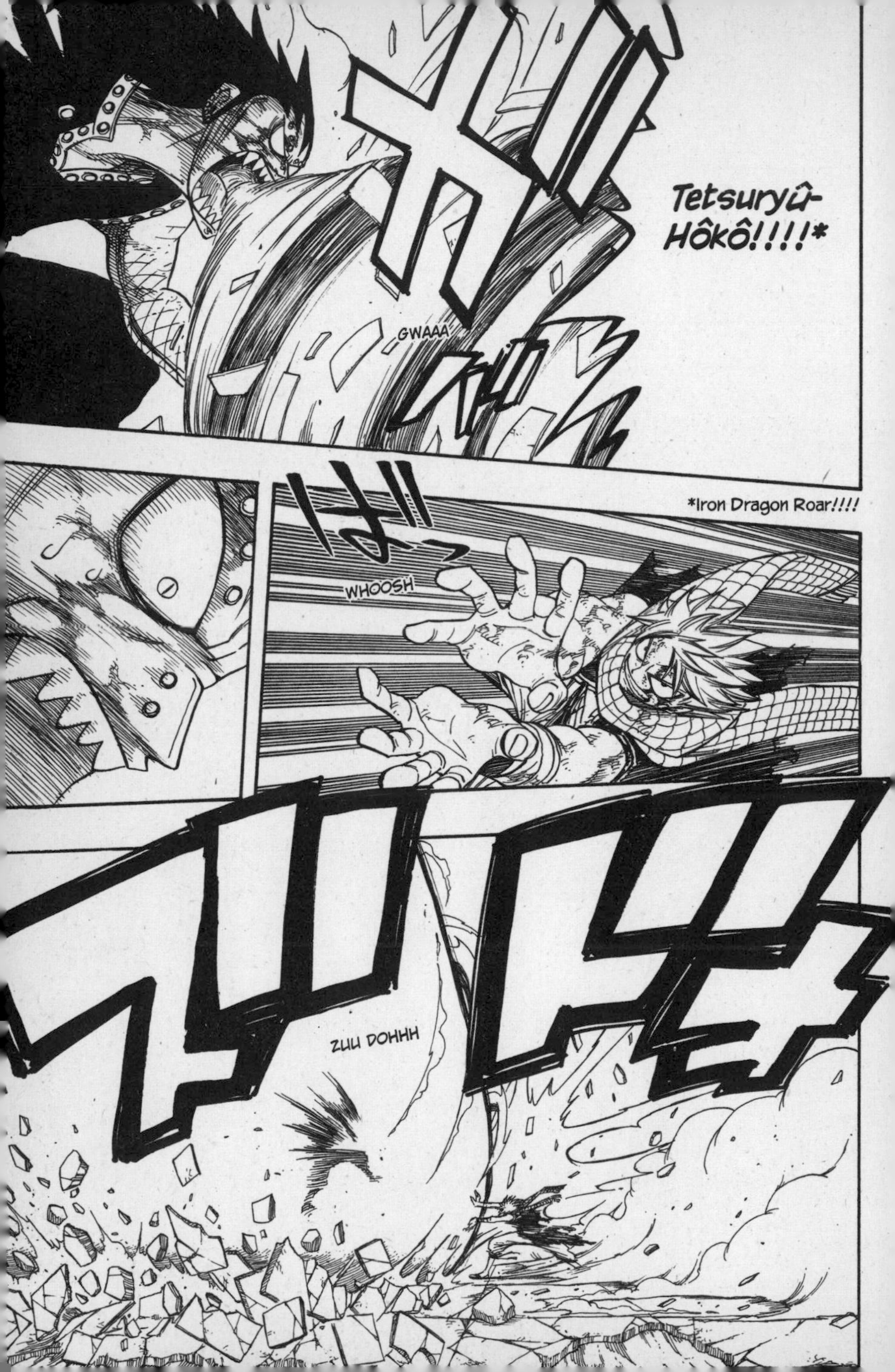
Tetsuryû-Hôkô!!!!*
GWAAA
*Iron Dragon Roar!!!!
WHOOSH
ZUU DOHHH

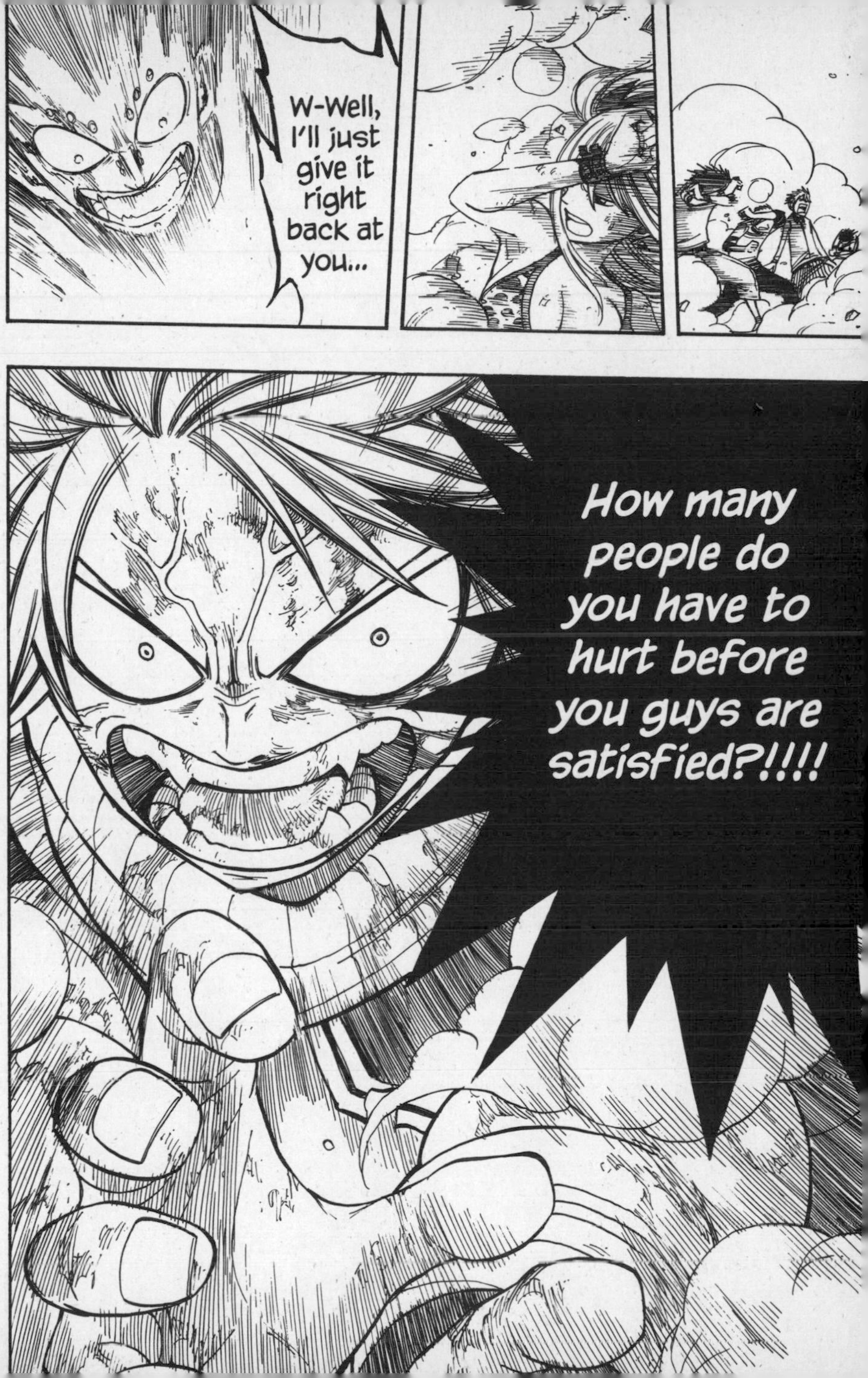
W-Well, I'll just give it right back at you...
How many people do you have to hurt before you guys are satisfied?!!!!

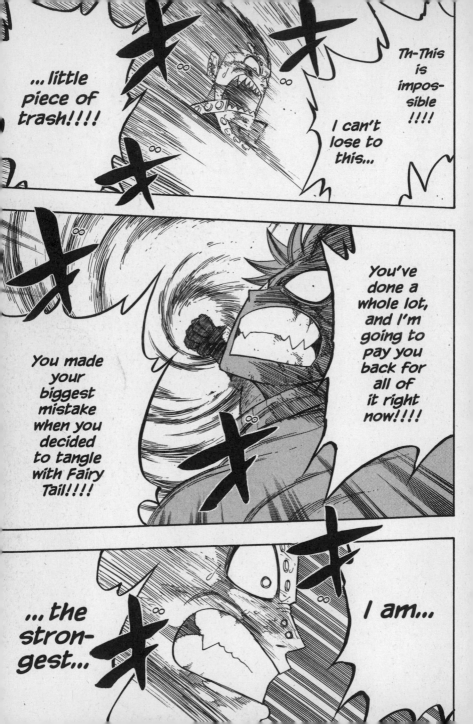

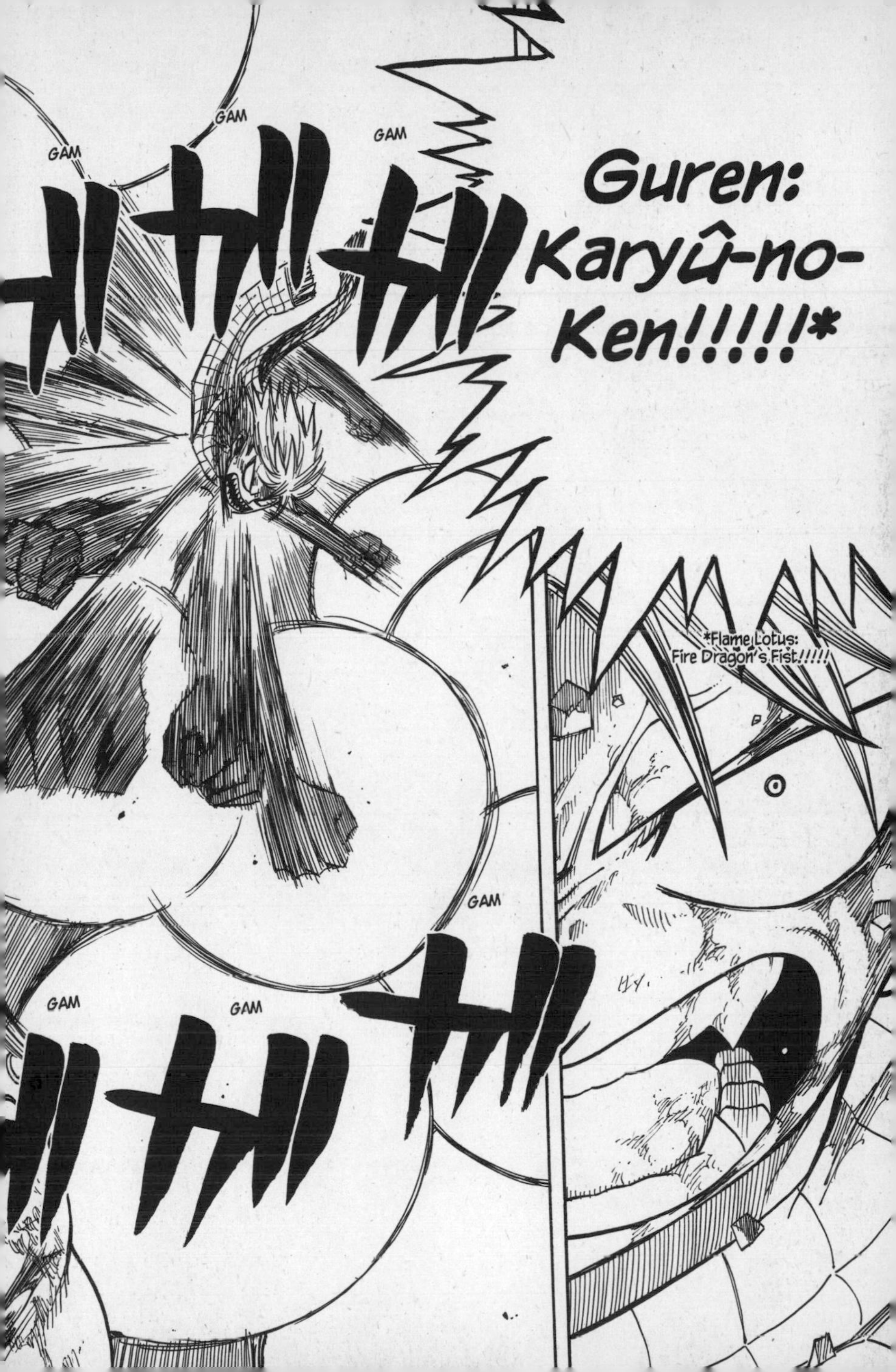
Guren: Karyû-no-Ken!!!!!*
*Flame Lotus: Fire Dragon's Fist!!!!!
GAM
GAM
GAM
GAM
GAM
GAM

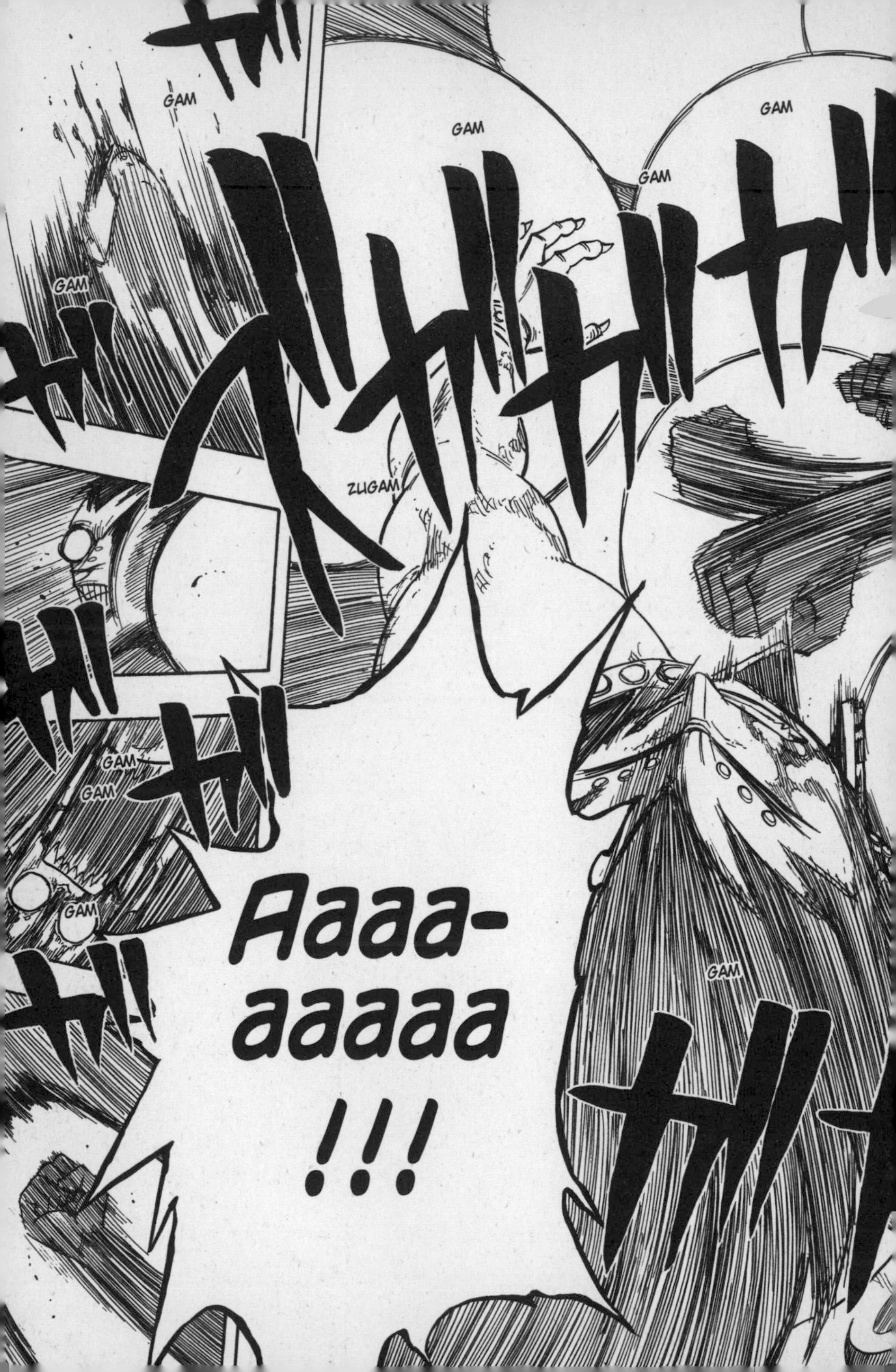
GAM
GAM
GAM
GAM
GAM
ZUGAM
GAM
GAM
GAM
GAM
Aaaa-aaaaa!!!

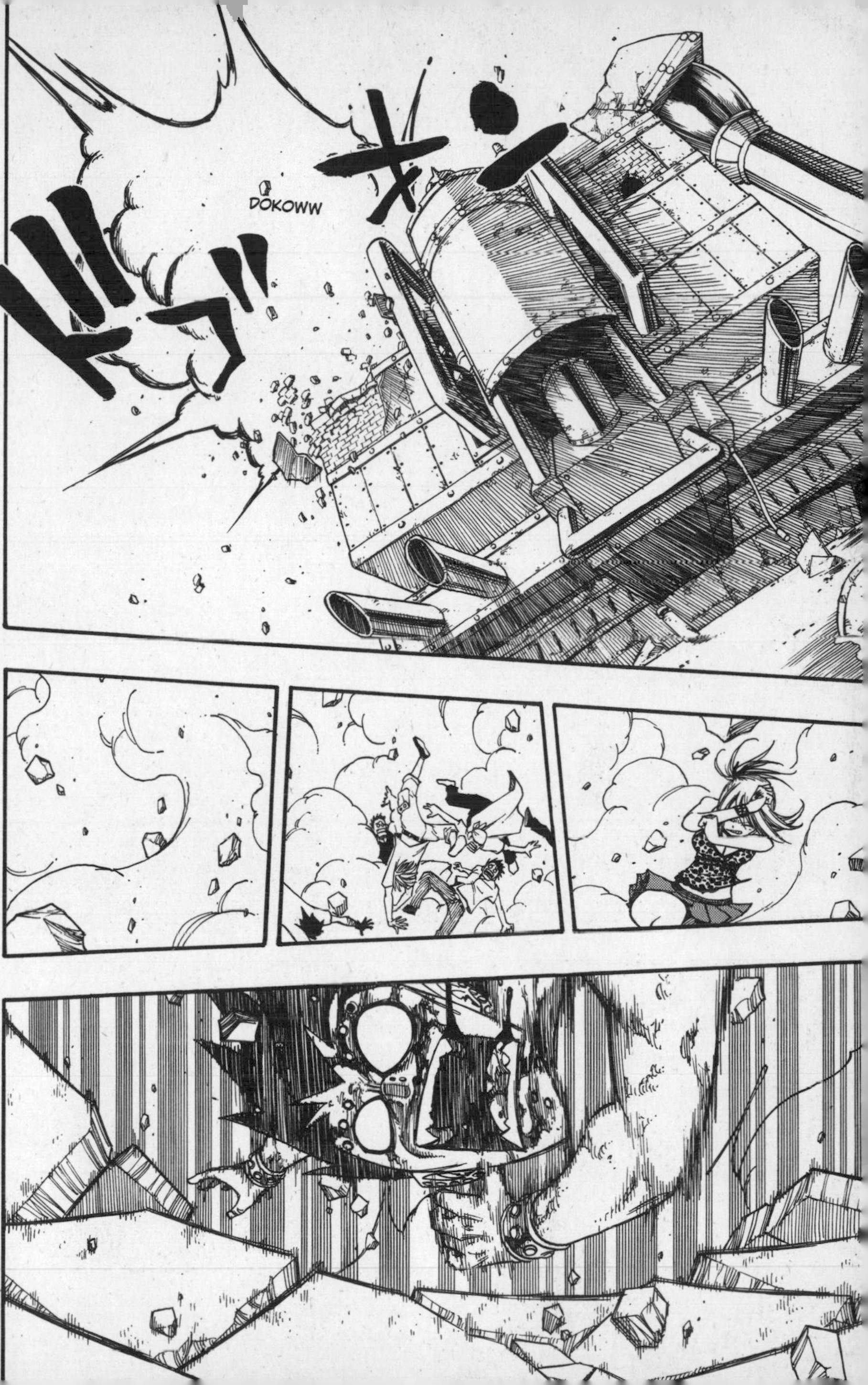
DOKOWW

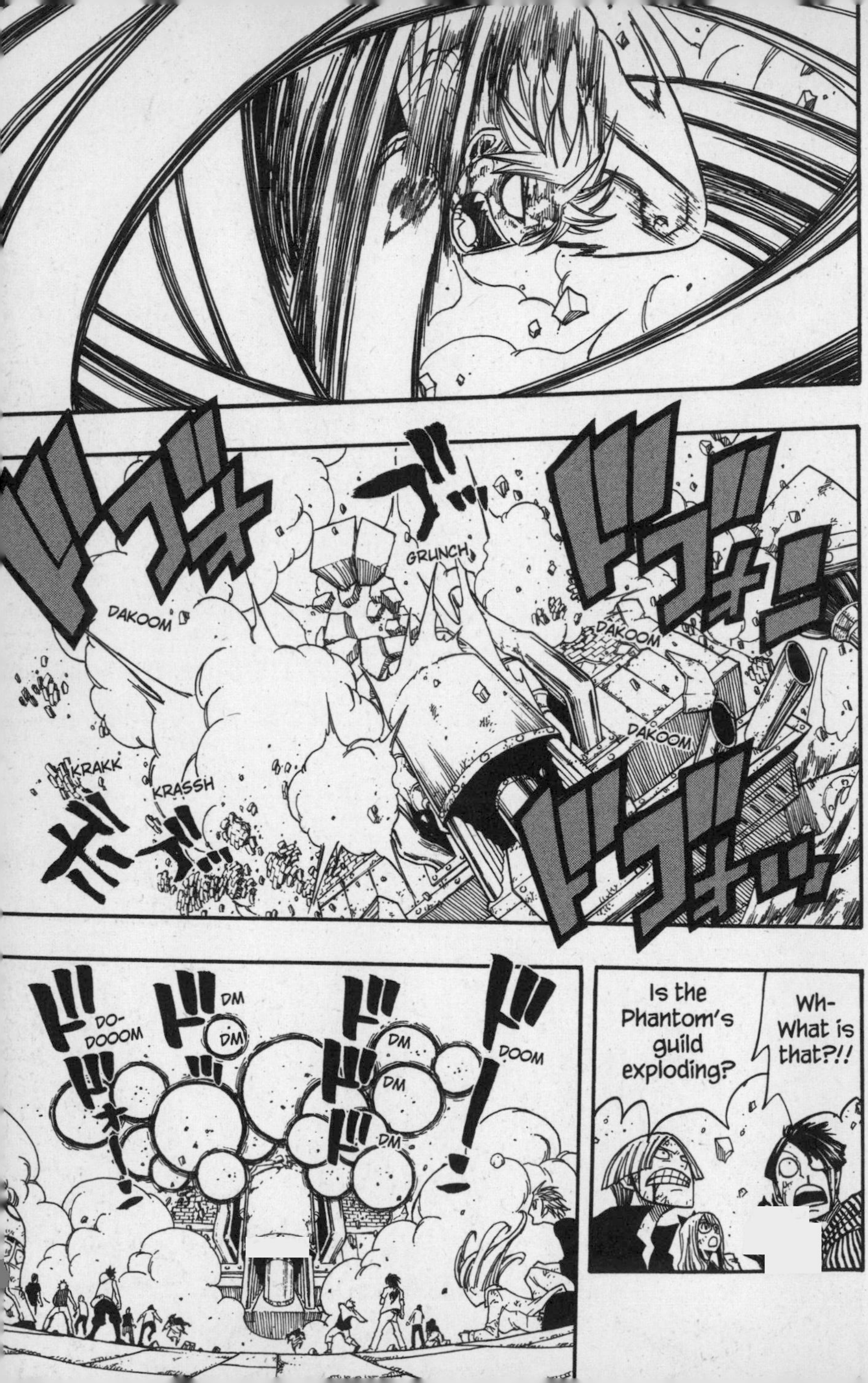
DAKOOM
DAKOOM
GRUNCH
DAKOOM
KRASSH
KRAKK
Wh- What is that?!!
Is the Phantom's guild exploding?
DOOM
DM
DM
DM
DM
DM
DO-DOOOM

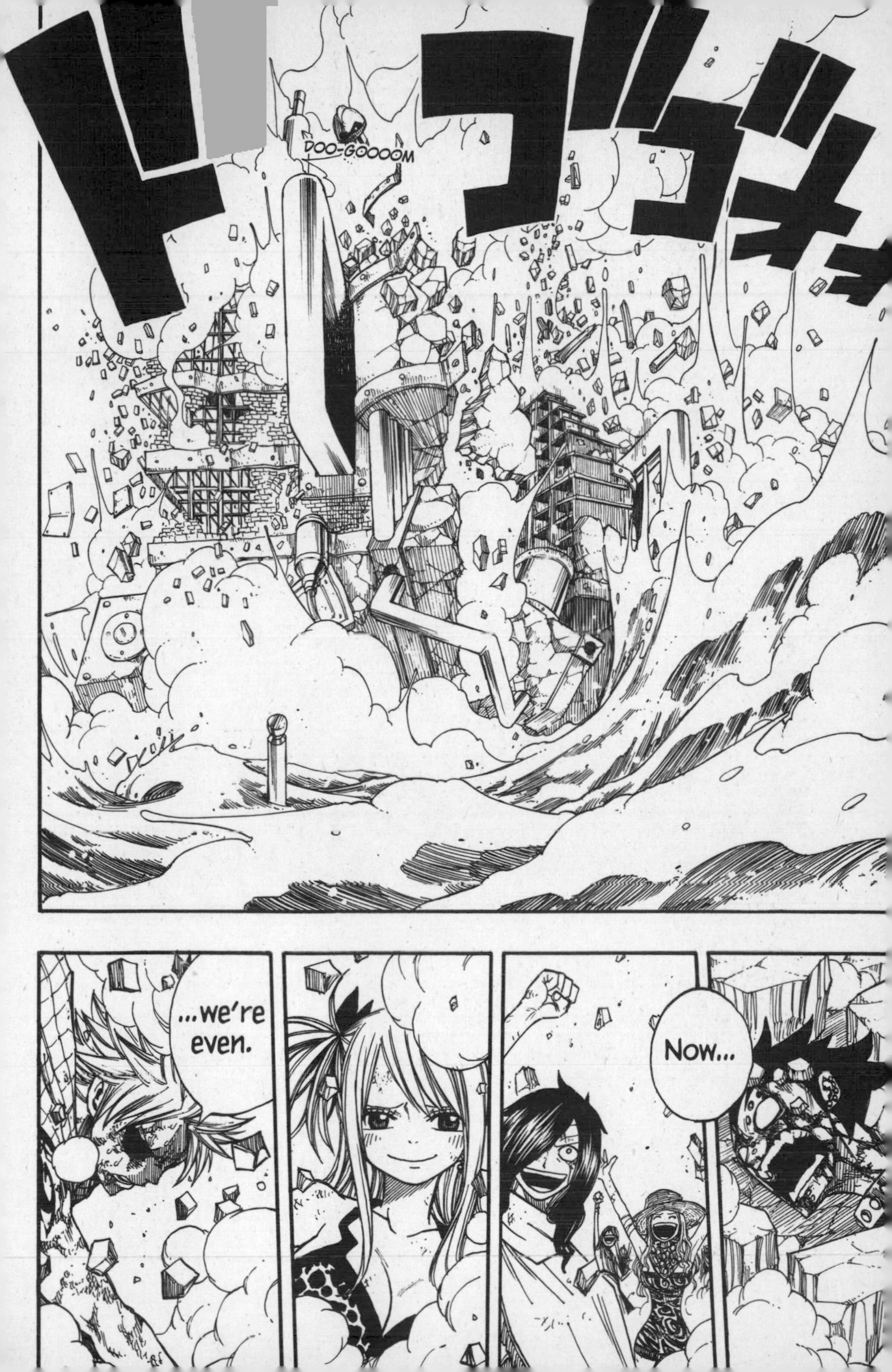
DOO-GOOOOM
Now...
...we're even.

FAIRY TAIL

Chapter 64: The Best Guild

M.test
1000
M.test

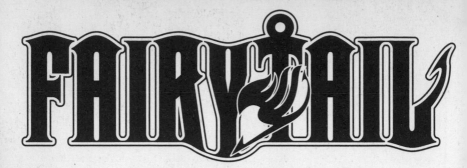

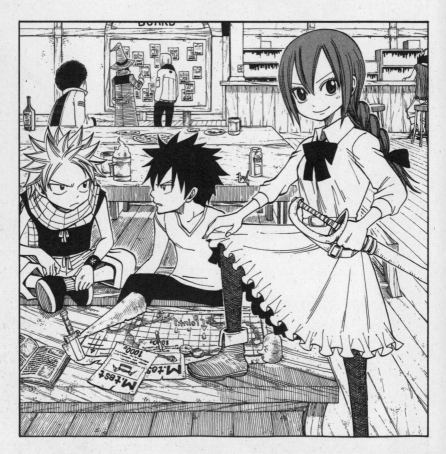

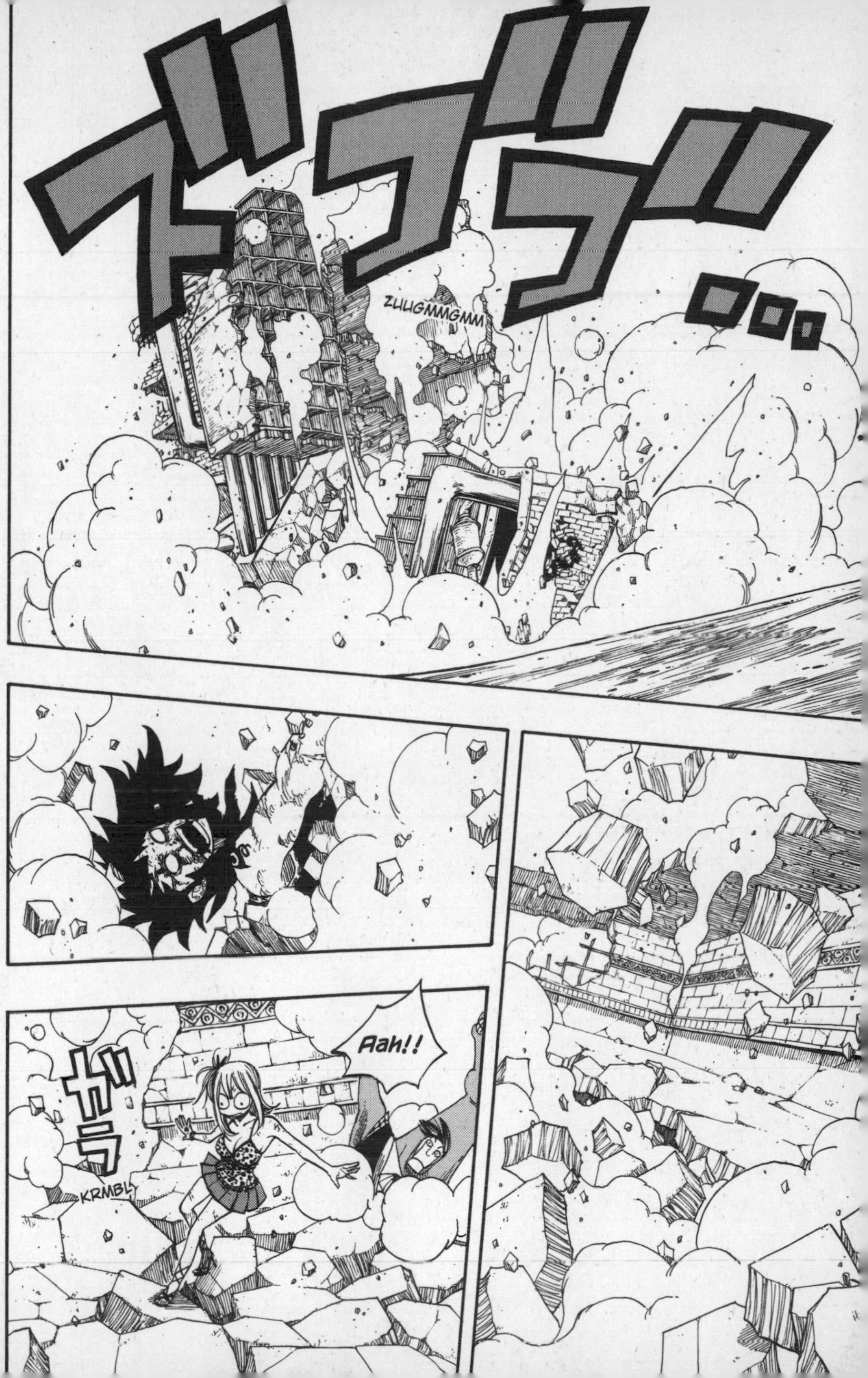
ZUUGMMGMM
Aah!!
KRMBL

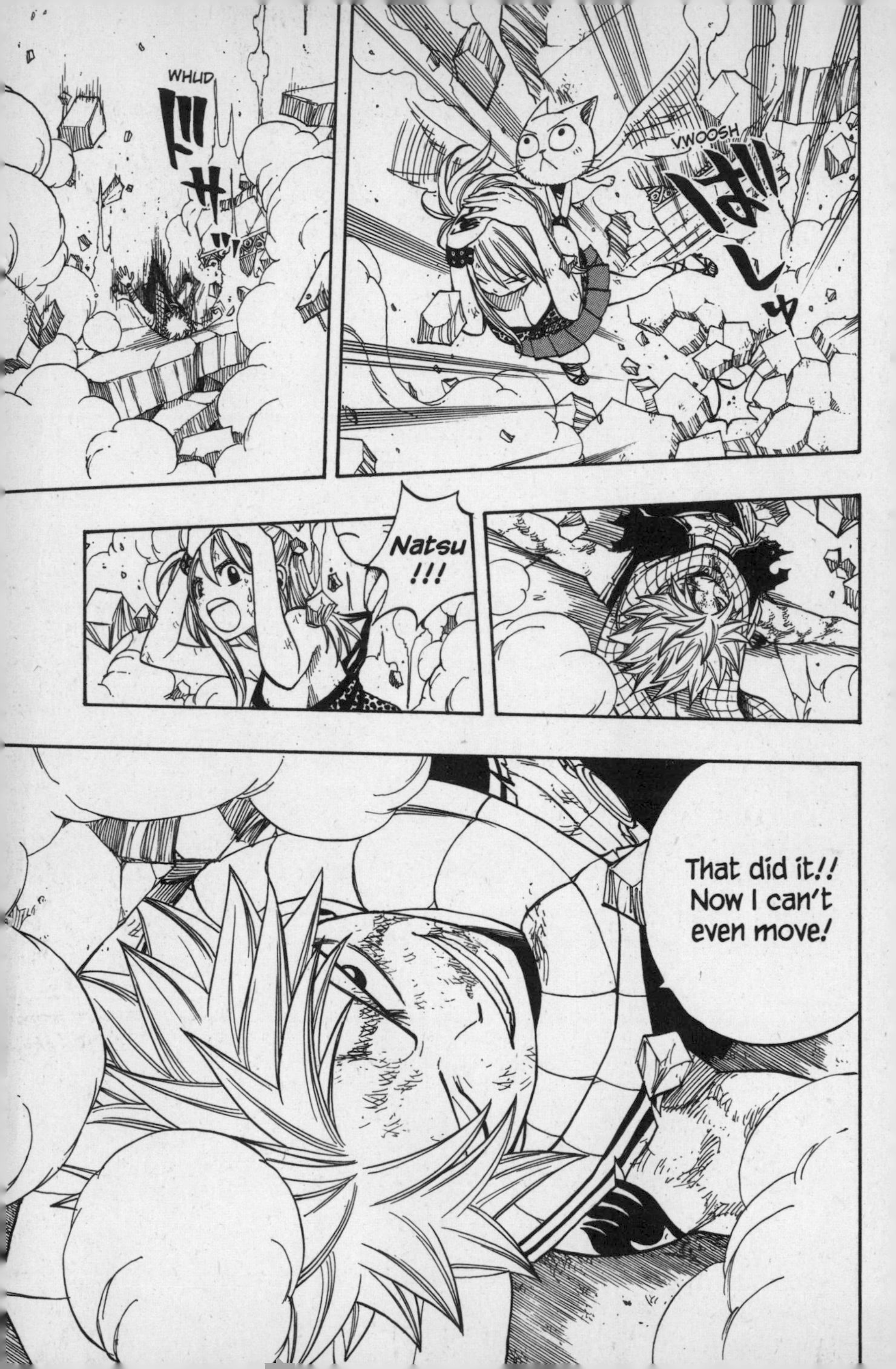
VWOOSH
ばしゅ
WHUD
ドサッ
Natsu!!!
That did it!! Now I can't even move!

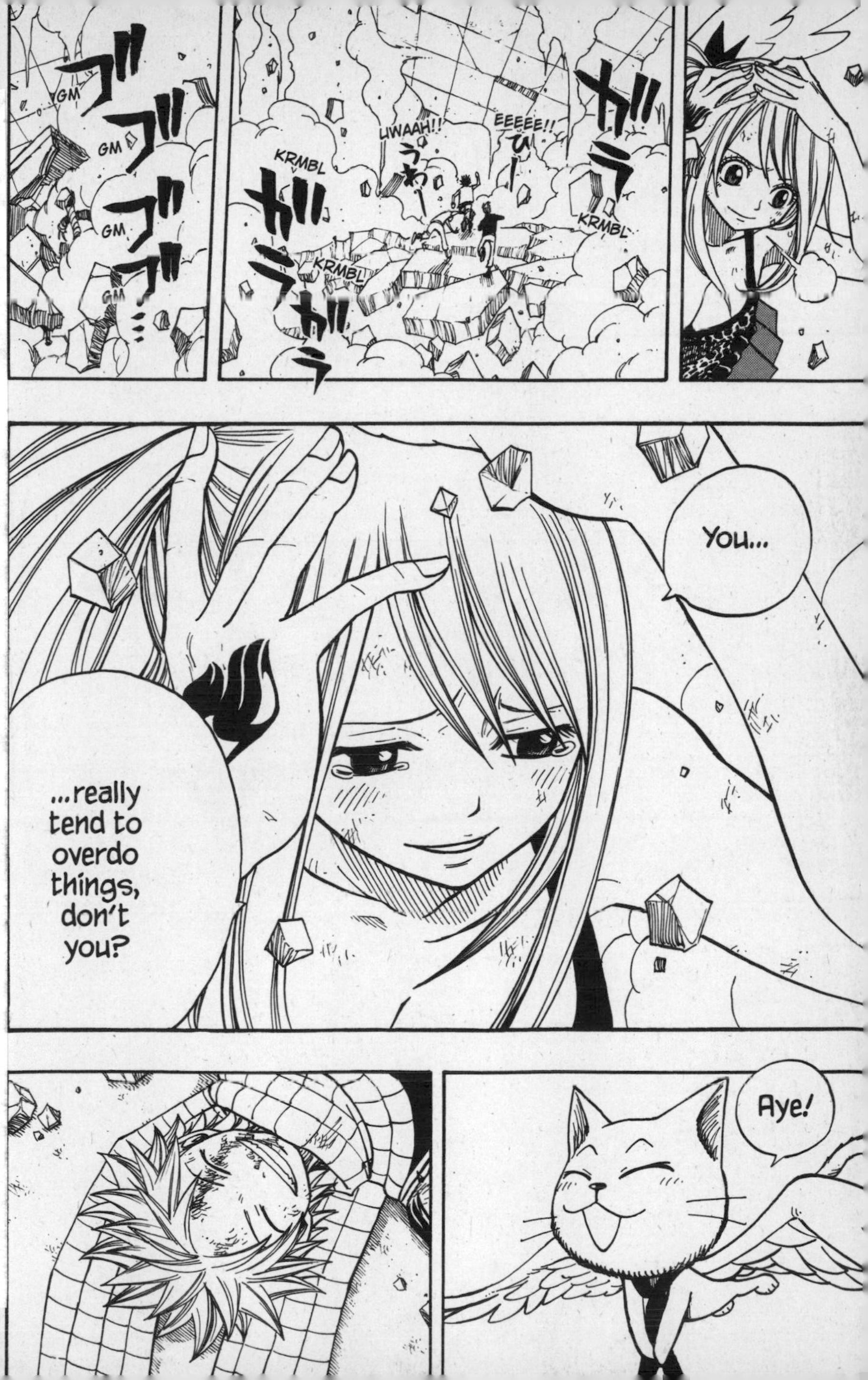
ガラ
KRMBL
EEEEE!!
ひー
UWAAH!!
うわっ
KRMBL
ガラ
KRMBL
ガラ
GM
ゴゴゴゴ
GM
GM
GM
You...
...really tend to overdo things, don't you?
Aye!

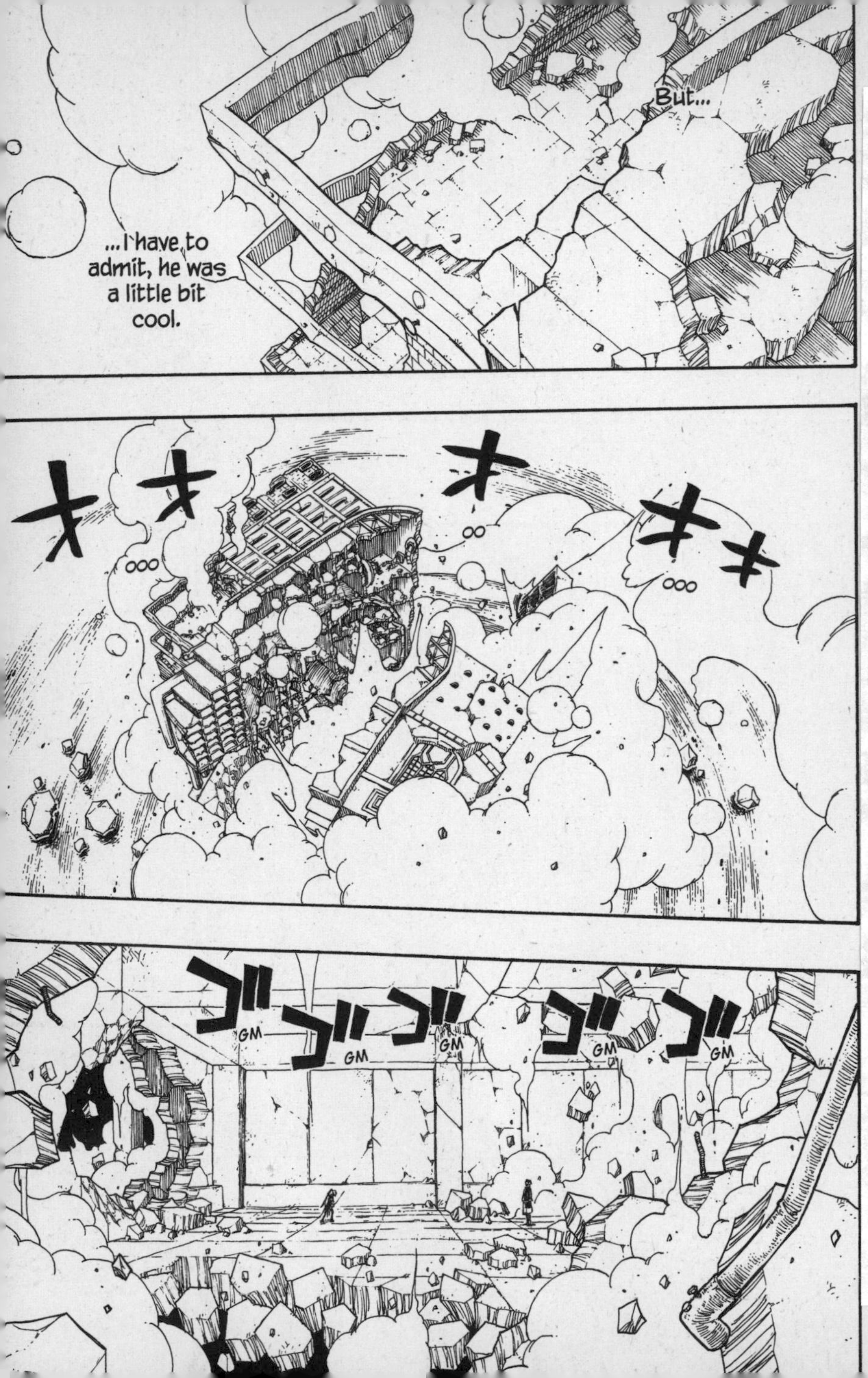

But...
...I have to admit, he was a little bit cool.
GM GM GM GM GM

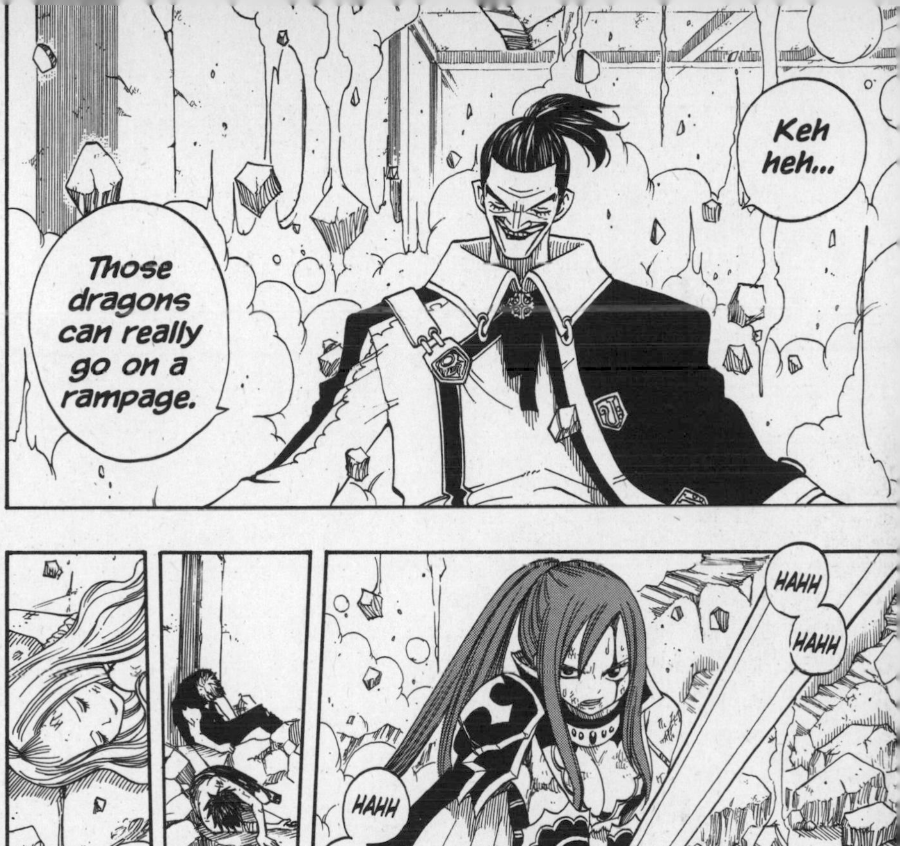
Keh heh...
Those dragons can really go on a rampage.
HAHH
HAHH
HAHH
HAHH
I see you weren't able to figure Natsu's battle strength into your calculations.
KRESH
H-He's probably on a par with me. It's possible that he is even more powerful...

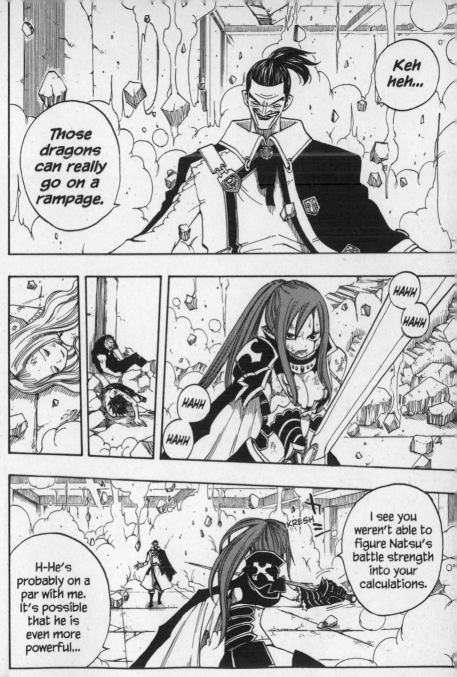

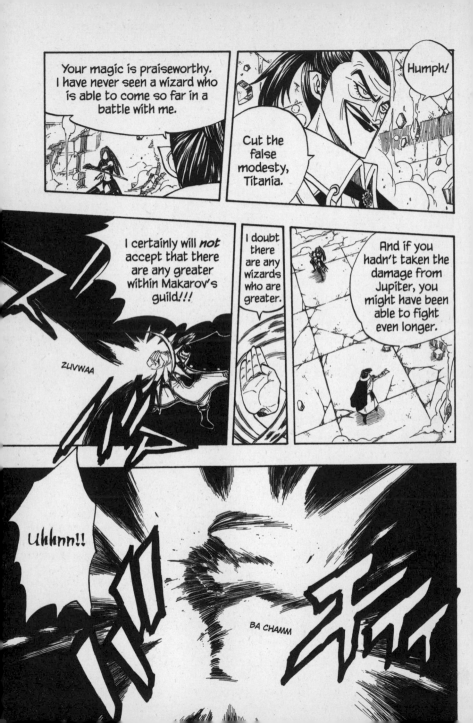

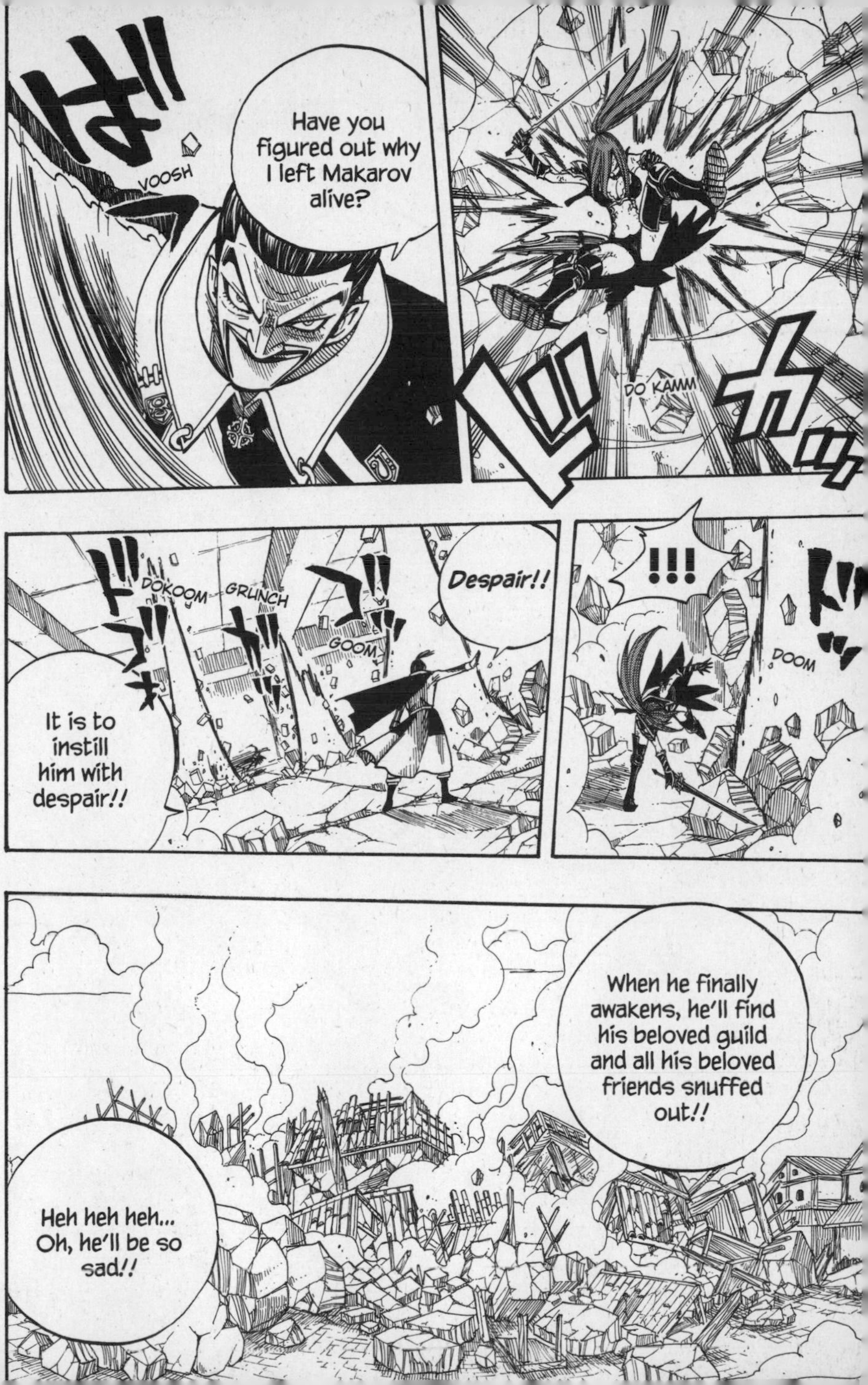
DO KAMM
VOOSH
Have you figured out why I left Makarov alive?
!!!
DOOM
Despair!!
GOOM
GRUNCH
DOKOOM
It is to instill him with despair!!
When he finally awakens, he'll find his beloved guild and all his beloved friends snuffed out!!
Heh heh heh... Oh, he'll be so sad!!

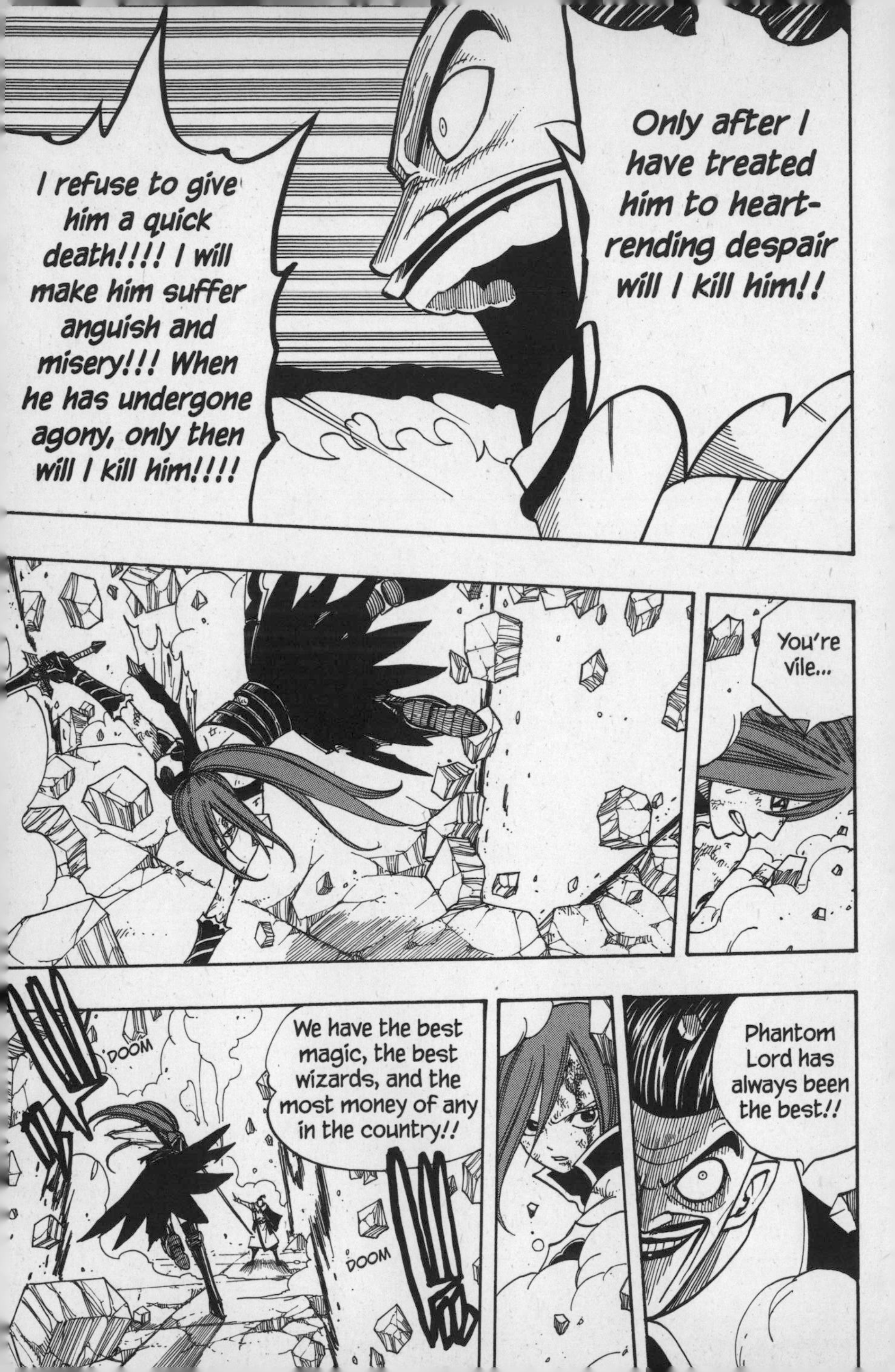
Only after I have treated him to heart-rending despair will I kill him!!
I refuse to give him a quick death!!!! I will make him suffer anguish and misery!!! When he has undergone agony, only then will I kill him!!!!
You're vile...
Phantom Lord has always been the best!!
We have the best magic, the best wizards, and the most money of any in the country!!
DOOM
DOOM

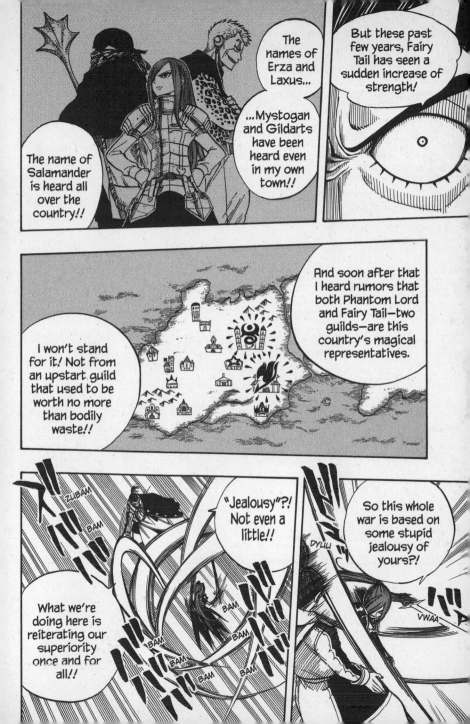

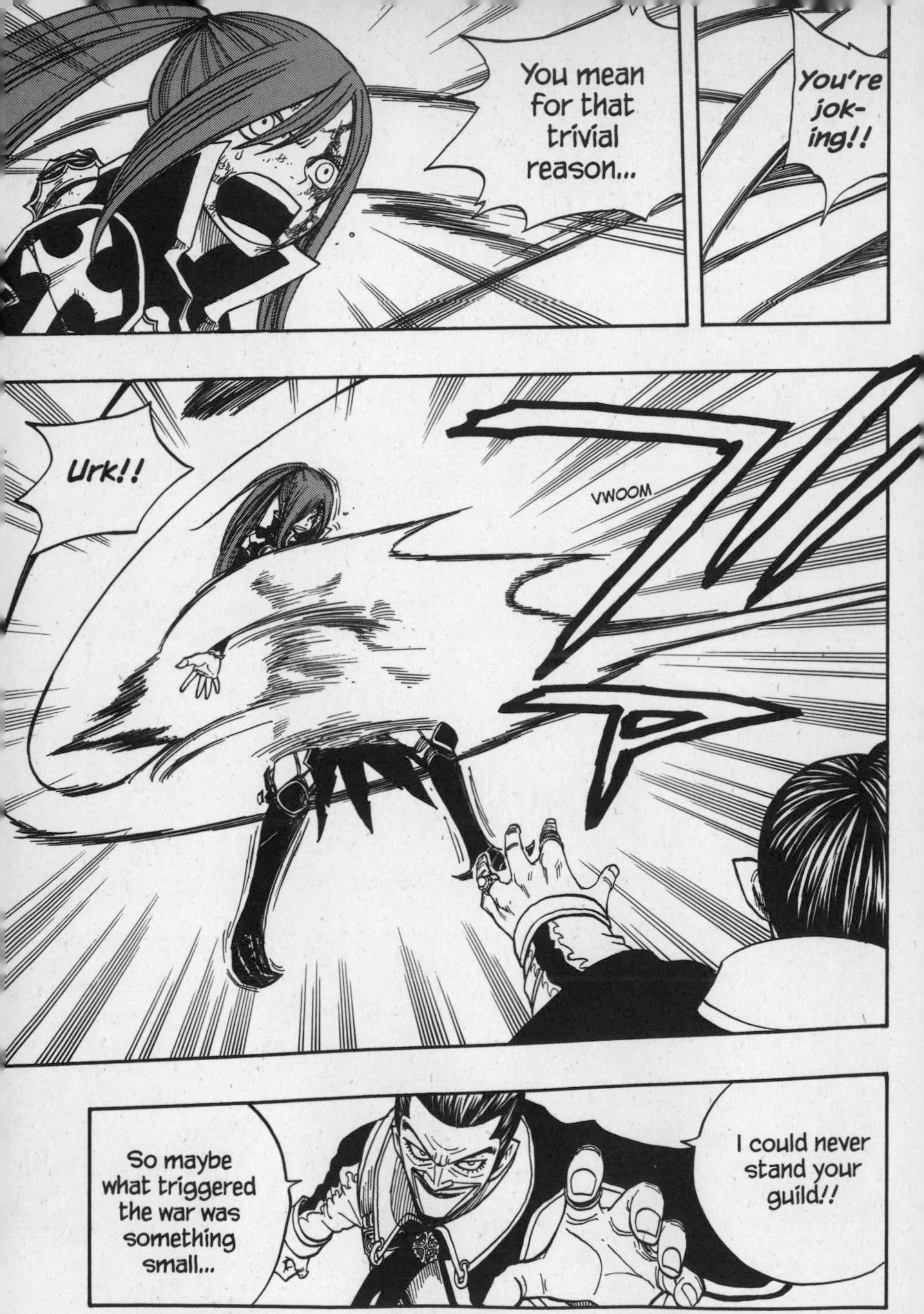
You're jok-ing!!
You mean for that trivial reason...
VWOOM
Urk!!
I could never stand your guild!!
So maybe what triggered the war was something small...

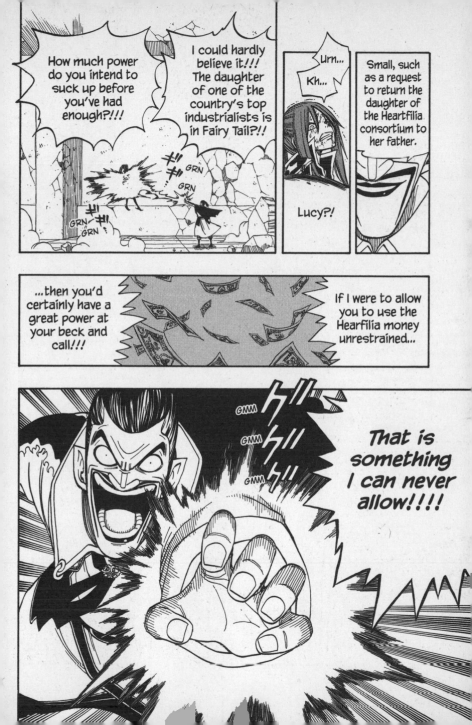

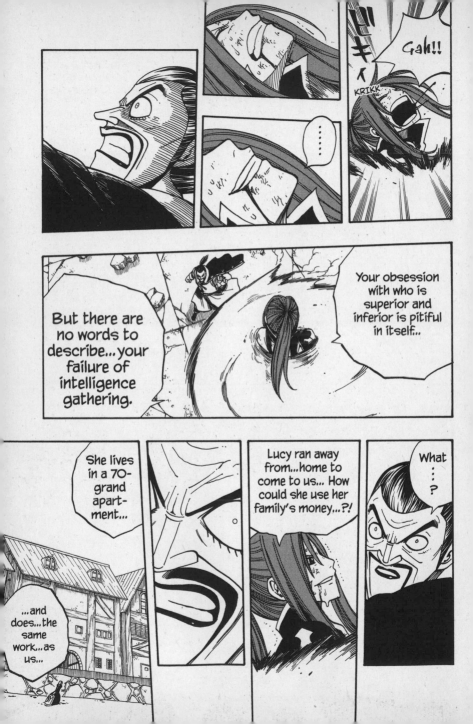

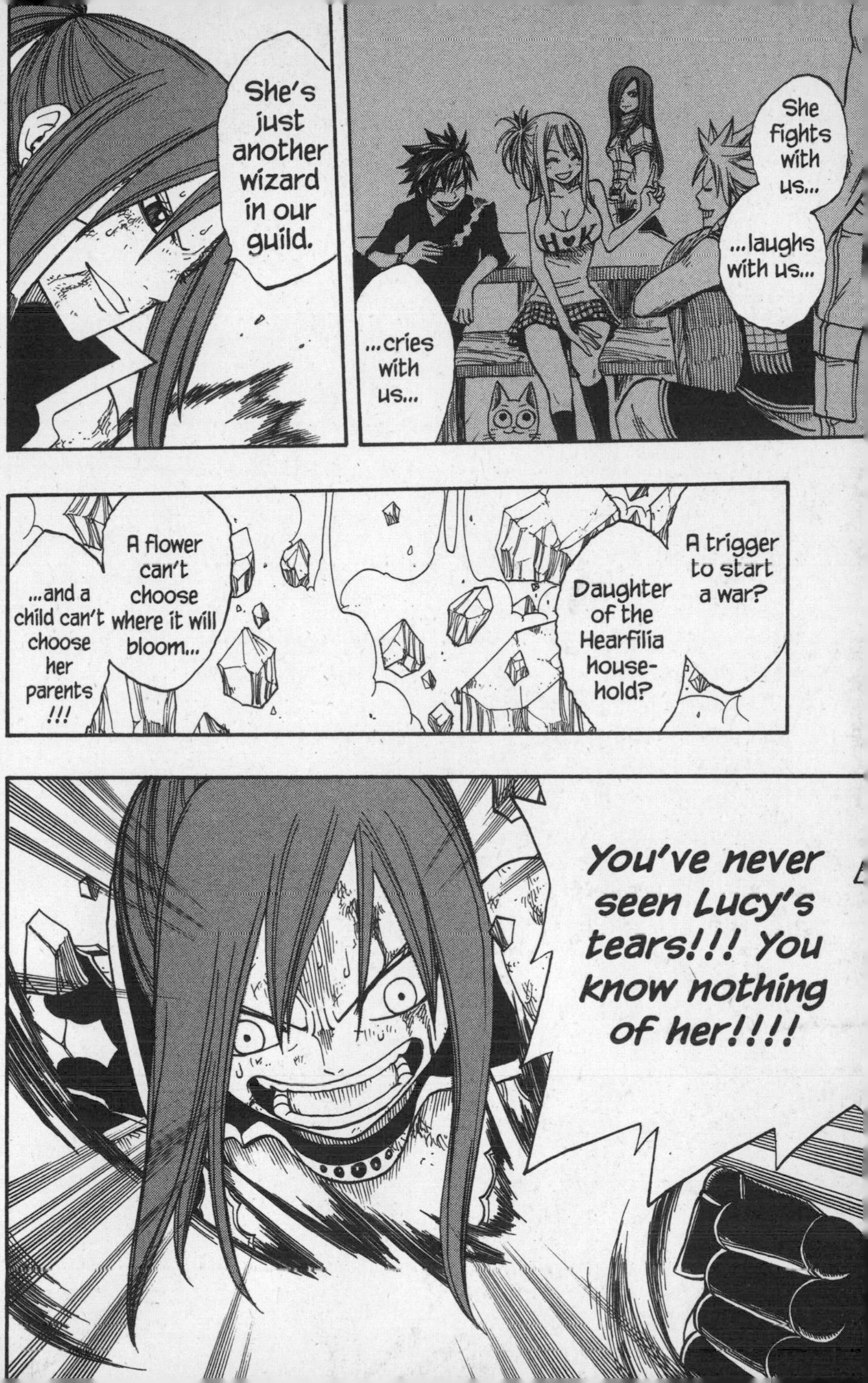
She fights with us...
...laughs with us...
...cries with us...
She's just another wizard in our guild.
A trigger to start a war?
Daughter of the Hearfilia house-hold?
A flower can't choose where it will bloom...
...and a child can't choose her parents!!!
You've never seen Lucy's tears!!! You know nothing of her!!!!

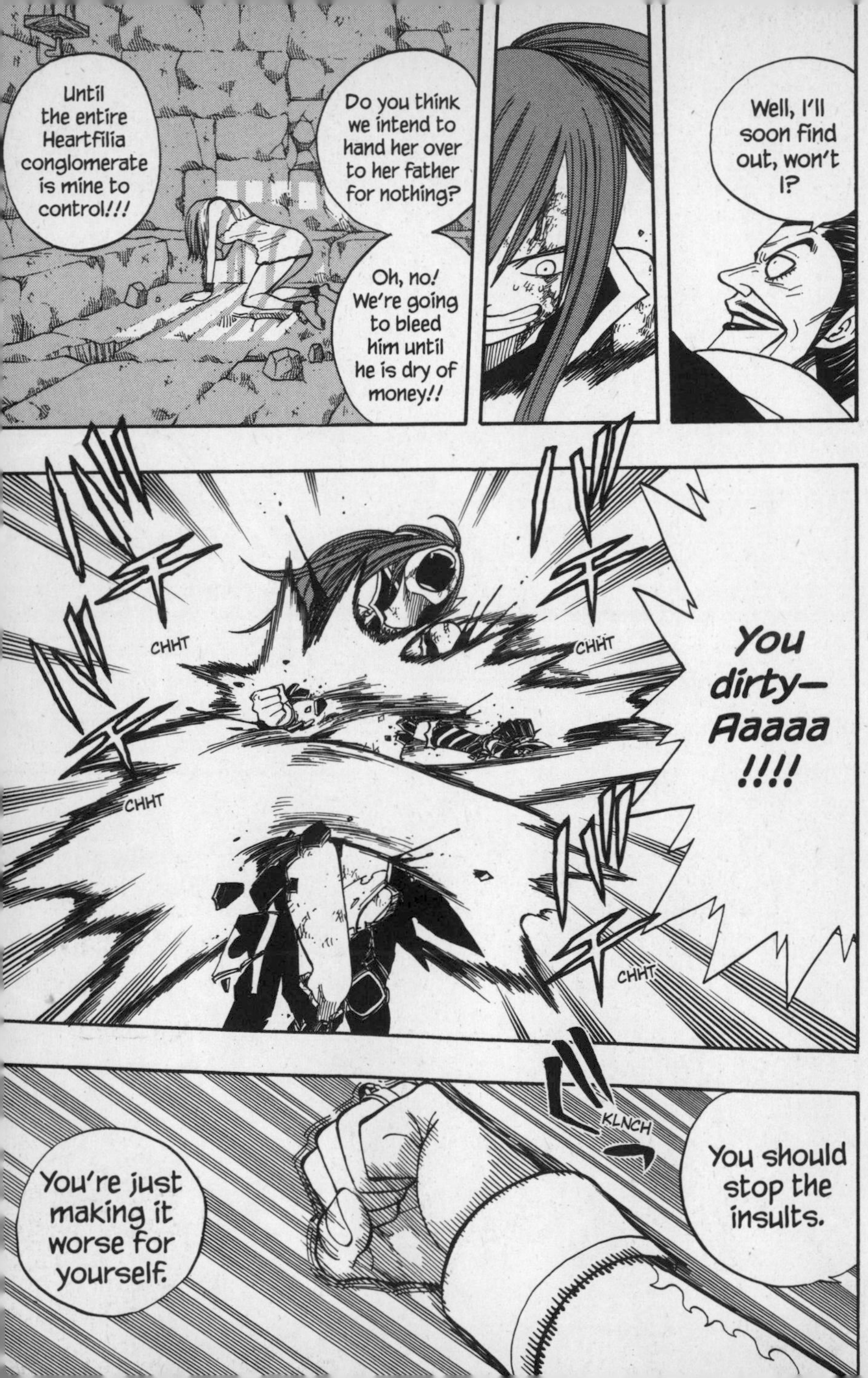
Well, I'll soon find out, won't I?
Do you think we intend to hand her over to her father for nothing?
Oh, no! We're going to bleed him until he is dry of money!!
Until the entire Heartfilia conglomerate is mine to control!!!
CHHT
You dirty— Aaaaa !!!!
CHHT
CHHT
CHHT
You should stop the insults.
KLNCH
You're just making it worse for yourself.

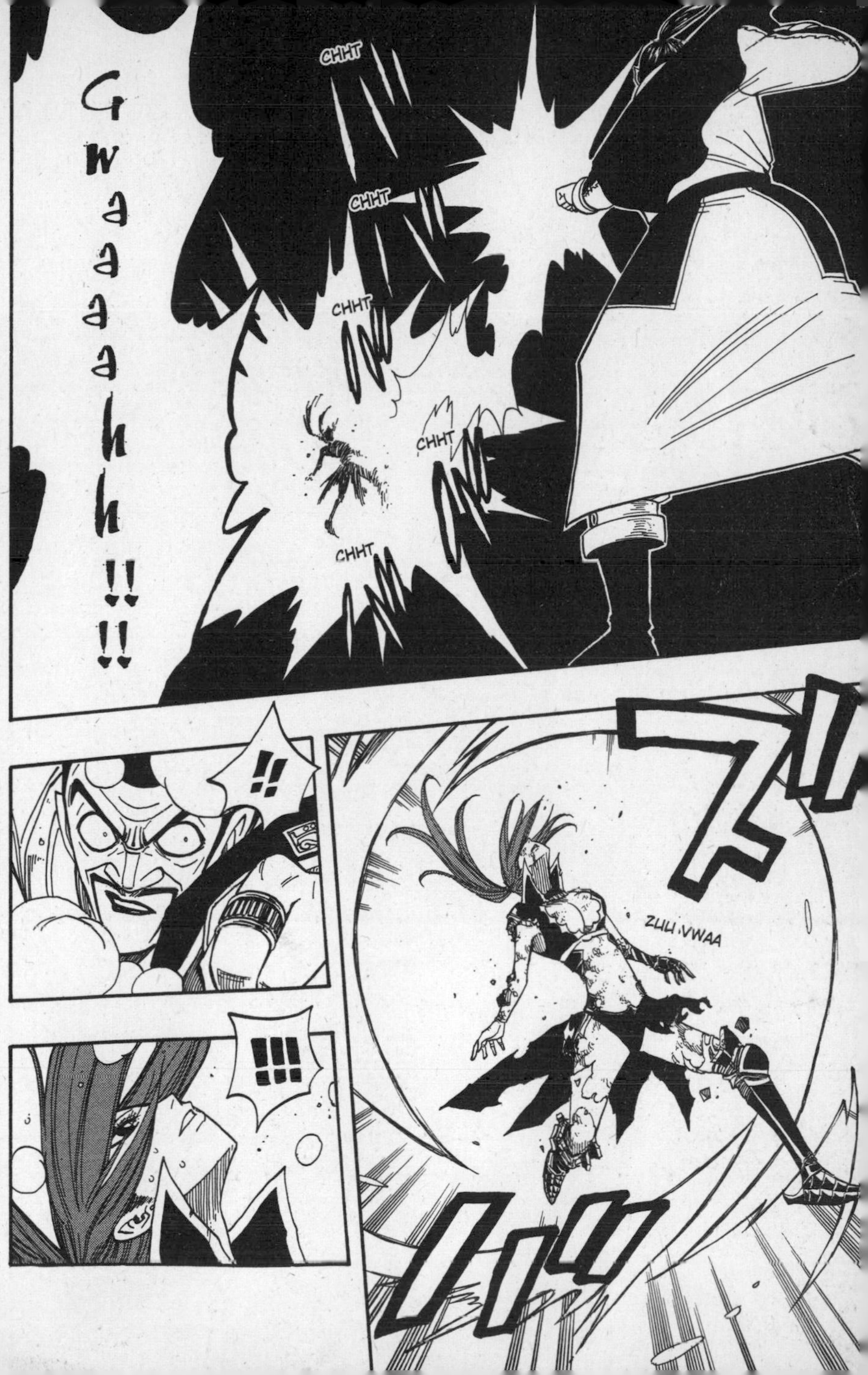
CHHT
CHHT
CHHT
CHHT
CHHT
Gwaaaahh!!!!
ZUUUVWAA
!!
!!!!

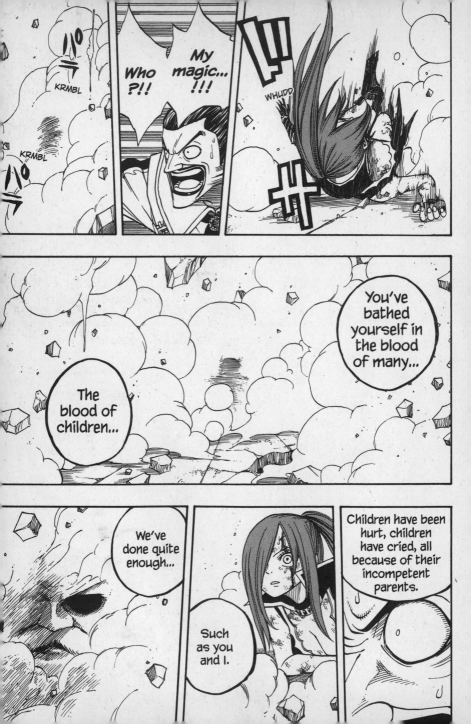

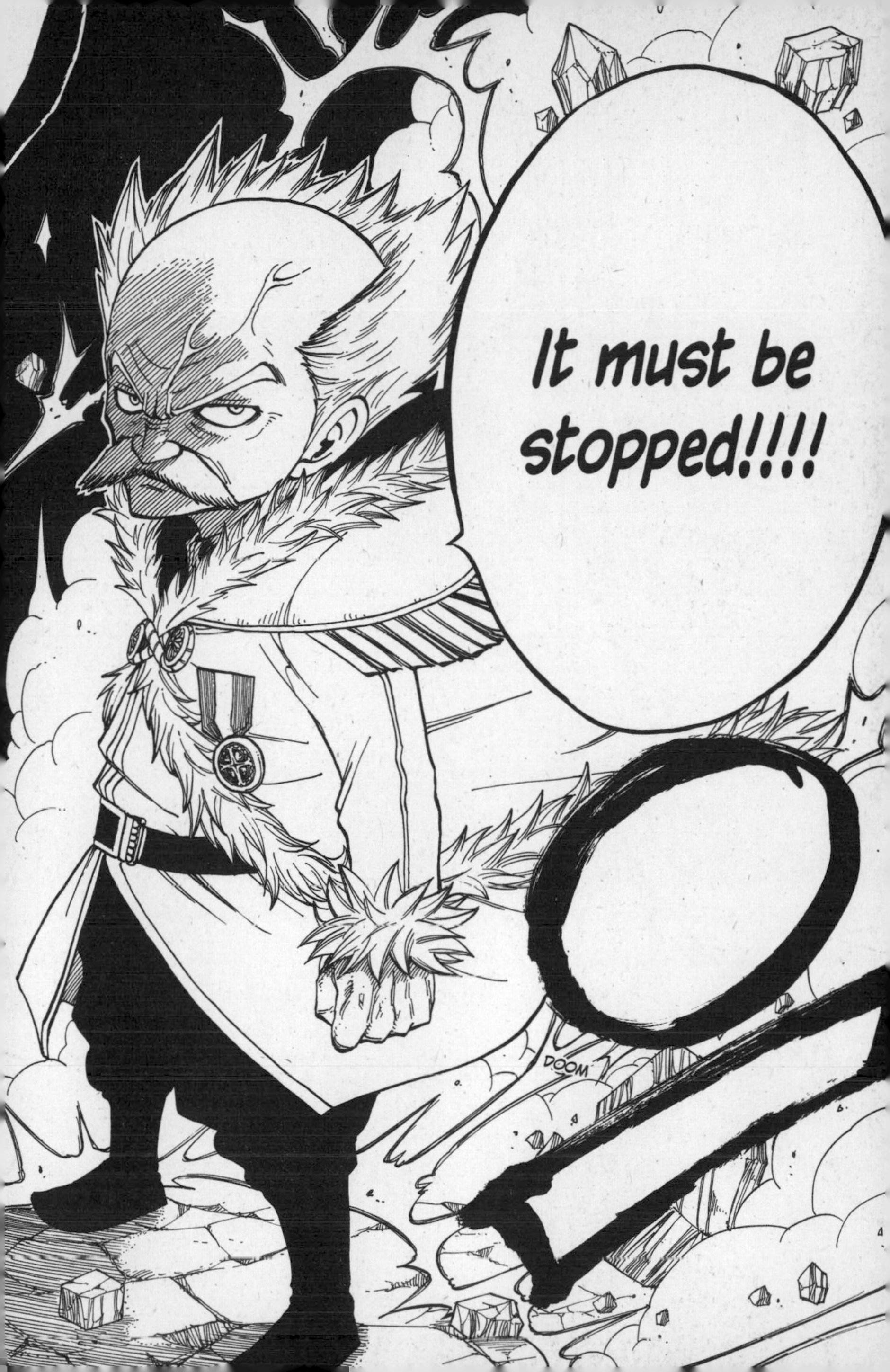
It must be stopped!!!!
DOOM

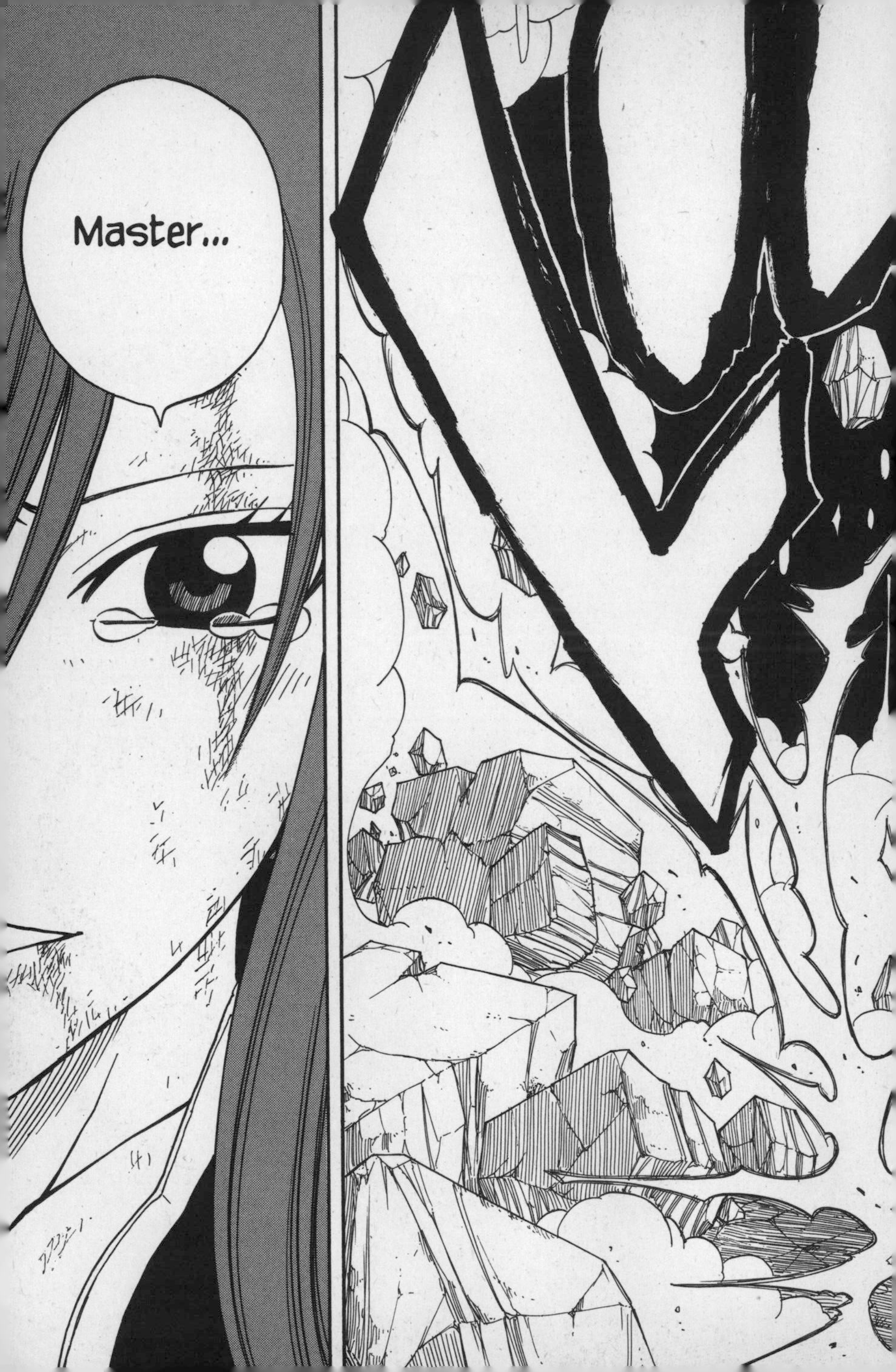
Master...

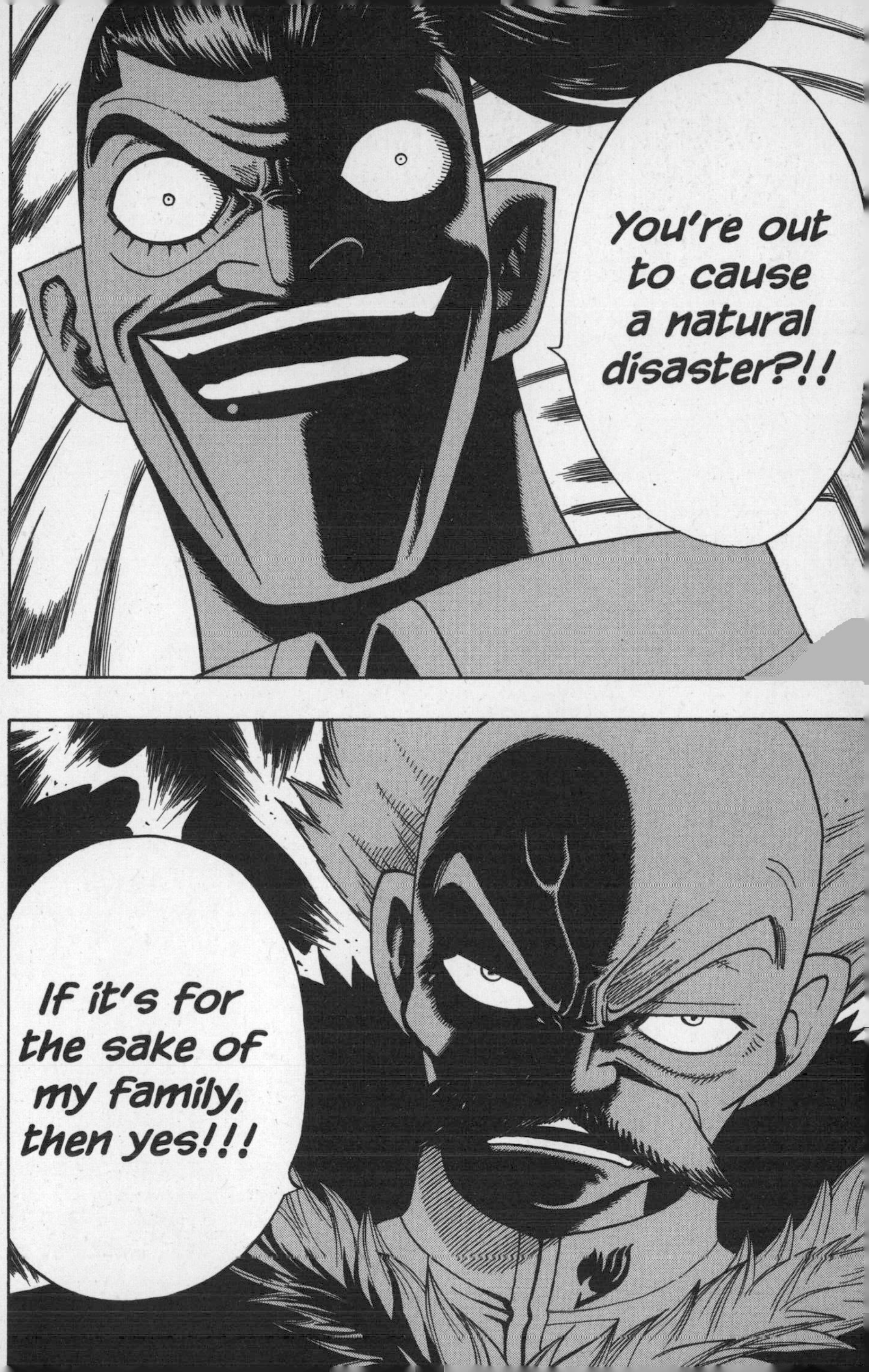
You're out to cause a natural disaster?!!
If it's for the sake of my family, then yes!!!

FAIRY TAIL

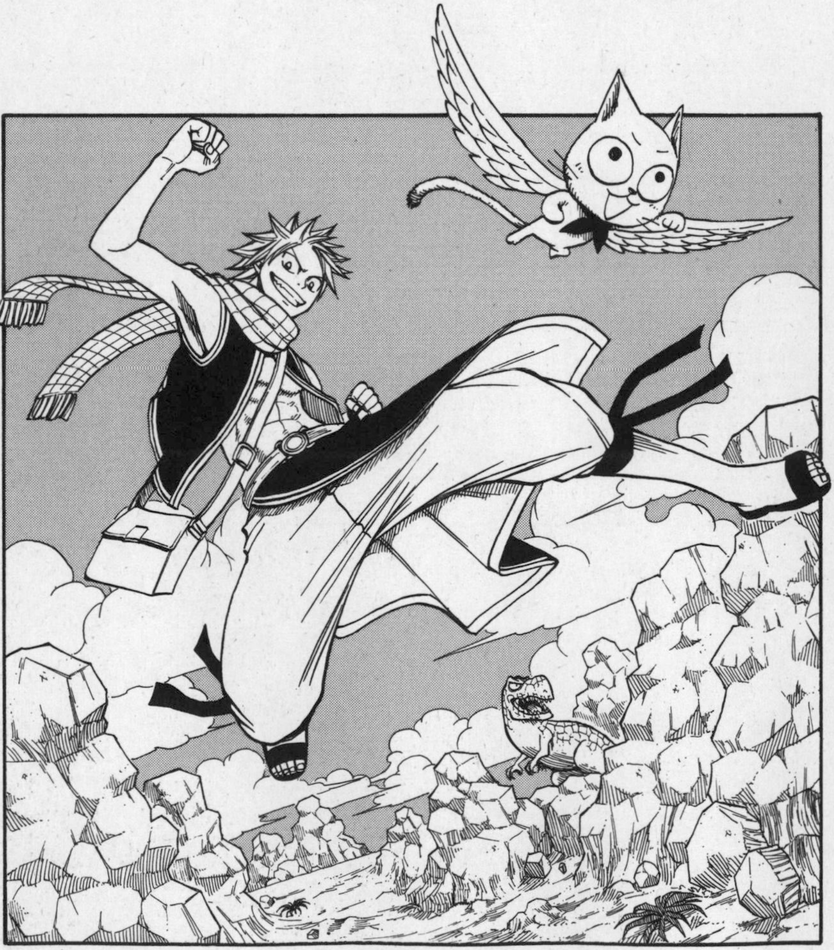

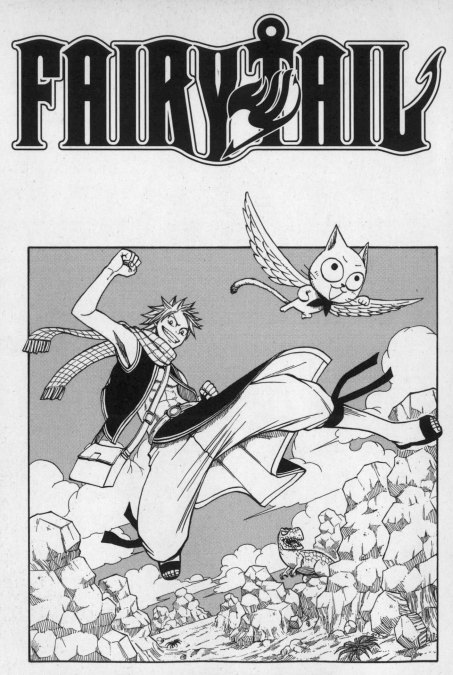

Chapter 65: Fairy Law

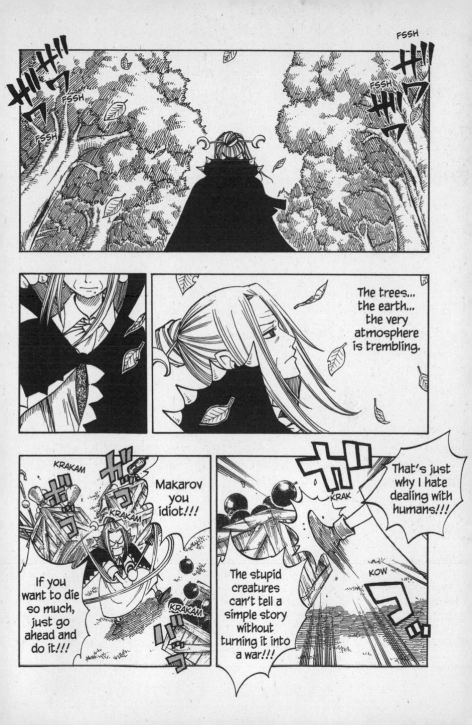

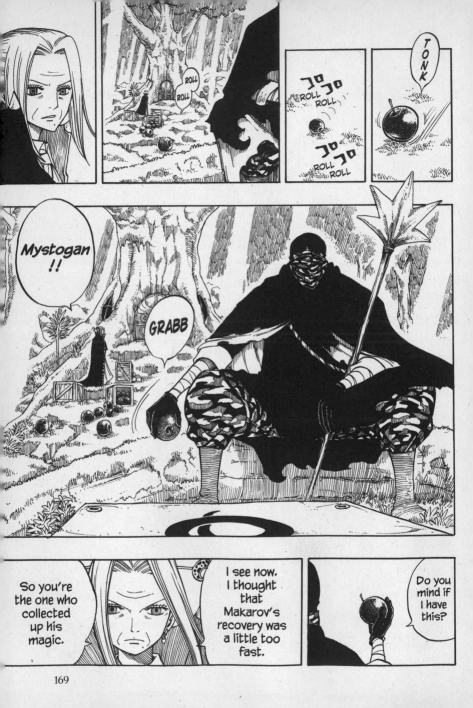

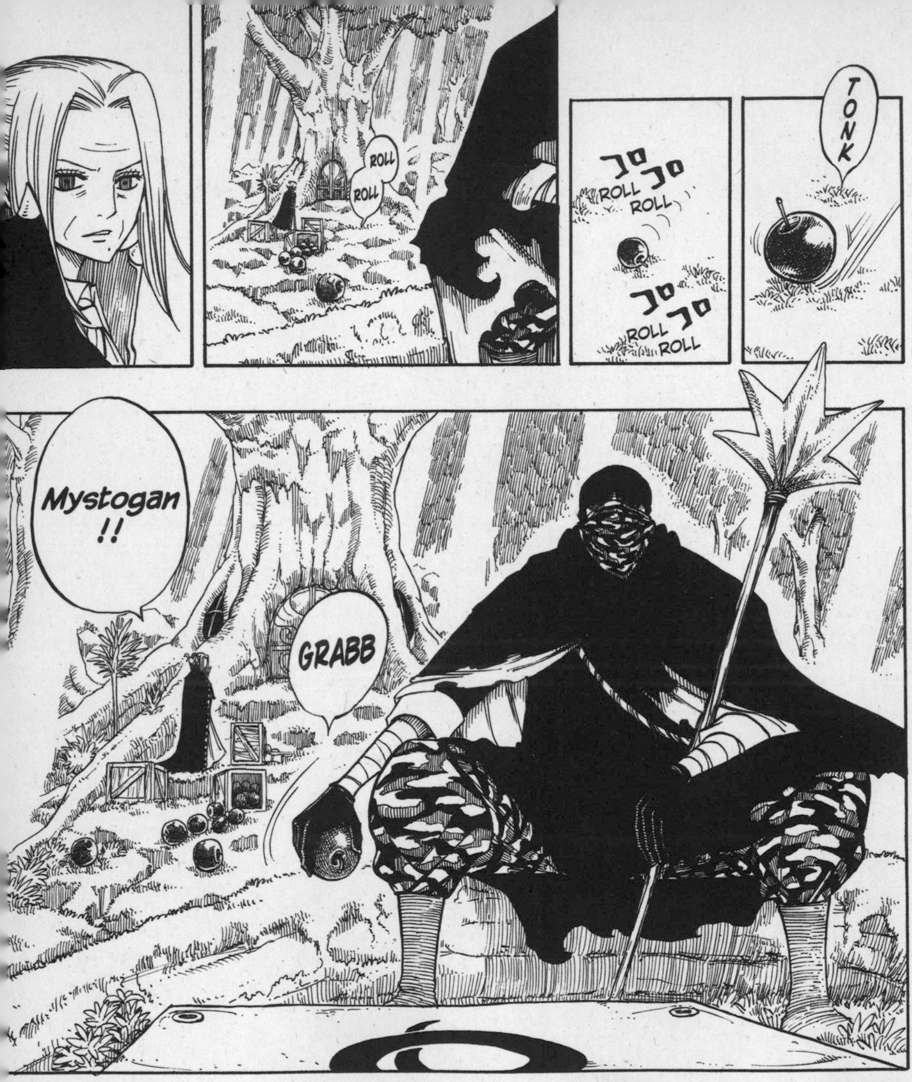
TONK
コロ コロ
ROLL ROLL
コロ コロ
ROLL ROLL
ROLL
ROLL
GRABB
Mystogan !!
Do you mind if I have this?
I see now. I thought that Makarov's recovery was a little too fast.
So you're the one who collected up his magic.

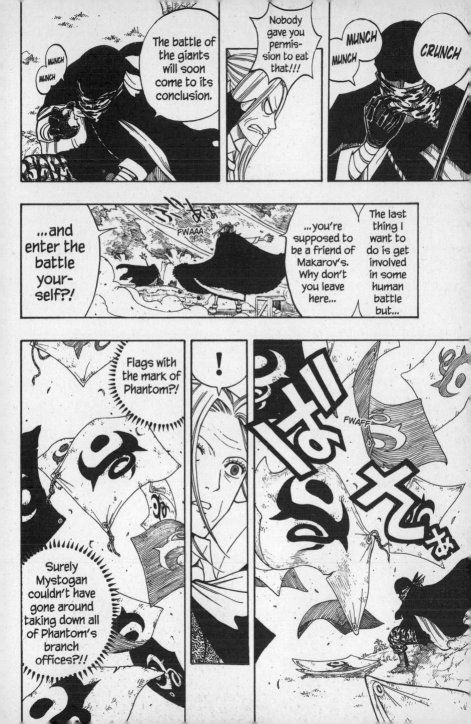

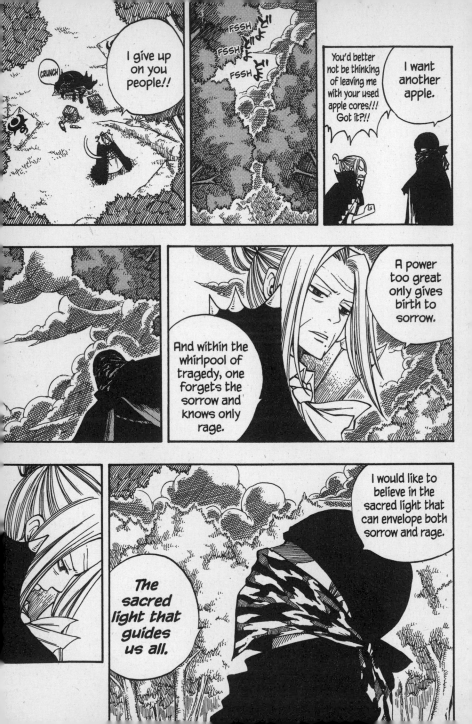

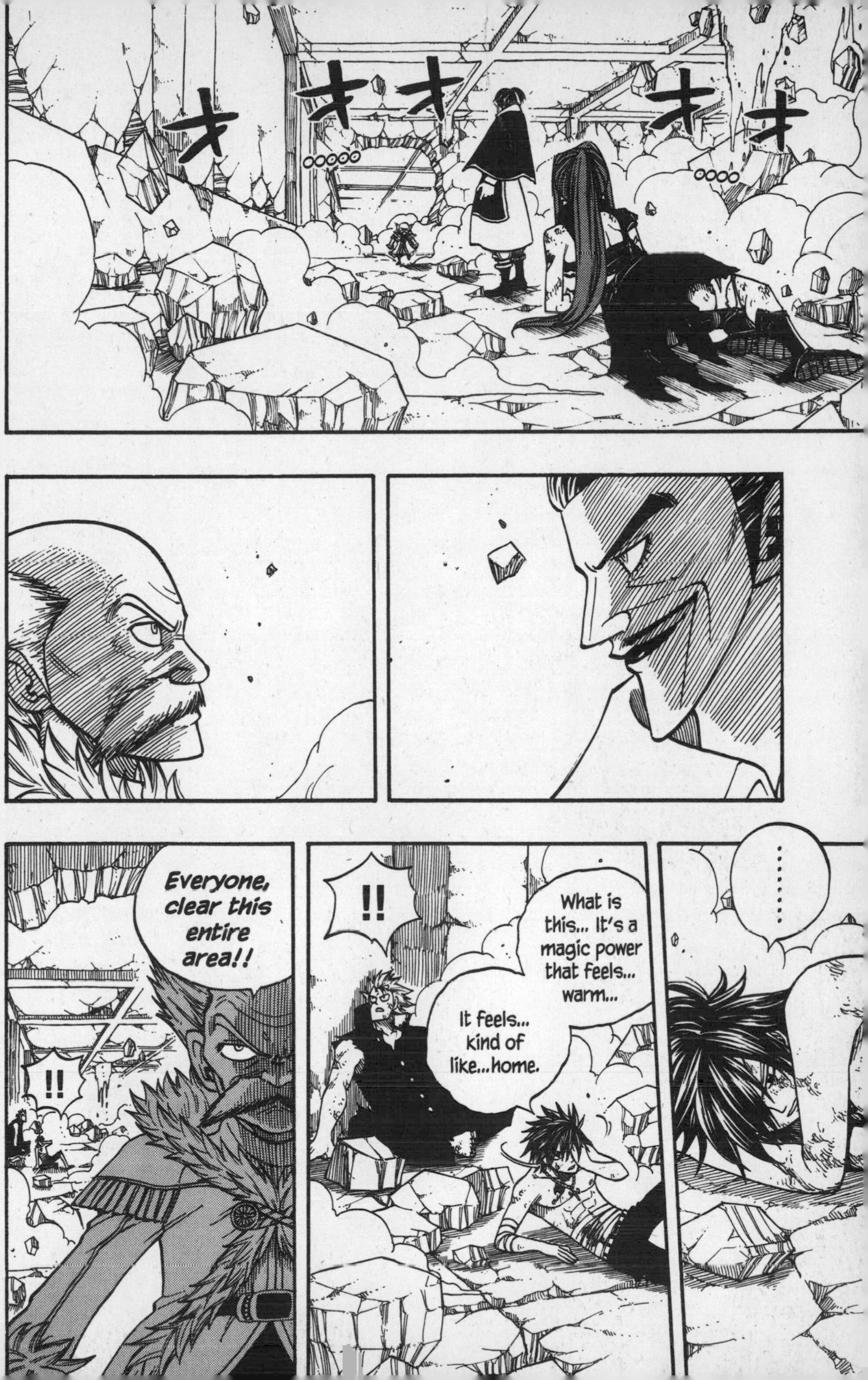
オオ
オオオ
……
!!
What is this... It's a magic power that feels... warm...
It feels... kind of like...home.
Everyone, clear this entire area!!
!!

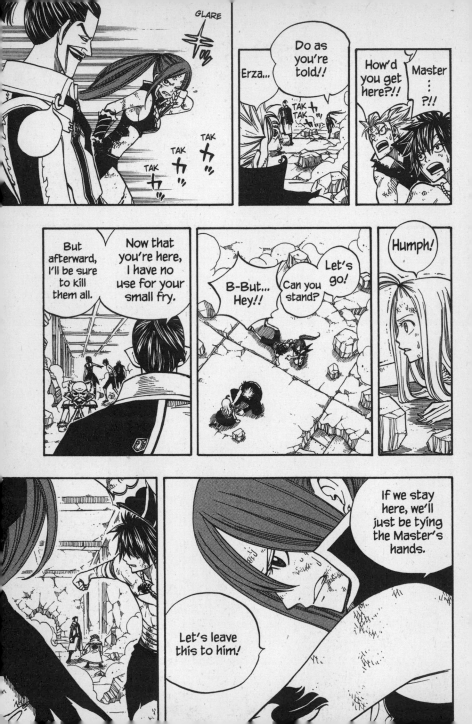

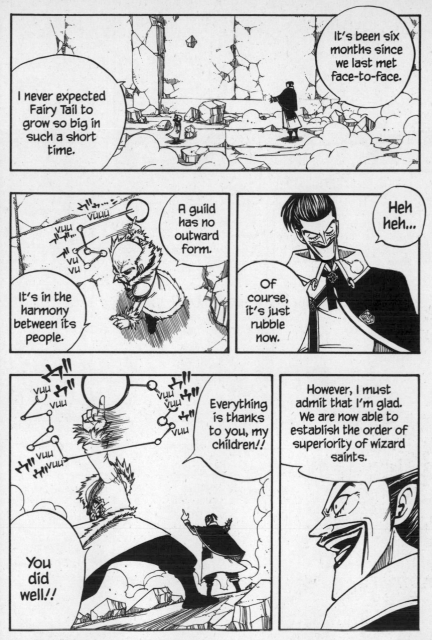

It's been six months since we last met face-to-face.

I never expected Fairy Tail to grow so big in such a short time.

A guild has no outward form.

It's in the harmony between its people.

Heh heh...

Of course, it's just rubble now.

Everything is thanks to you, my children!!

You did well!!

However, I must admit that I'm glad. We are now able to establish the order of superiority of wizard saints.

174

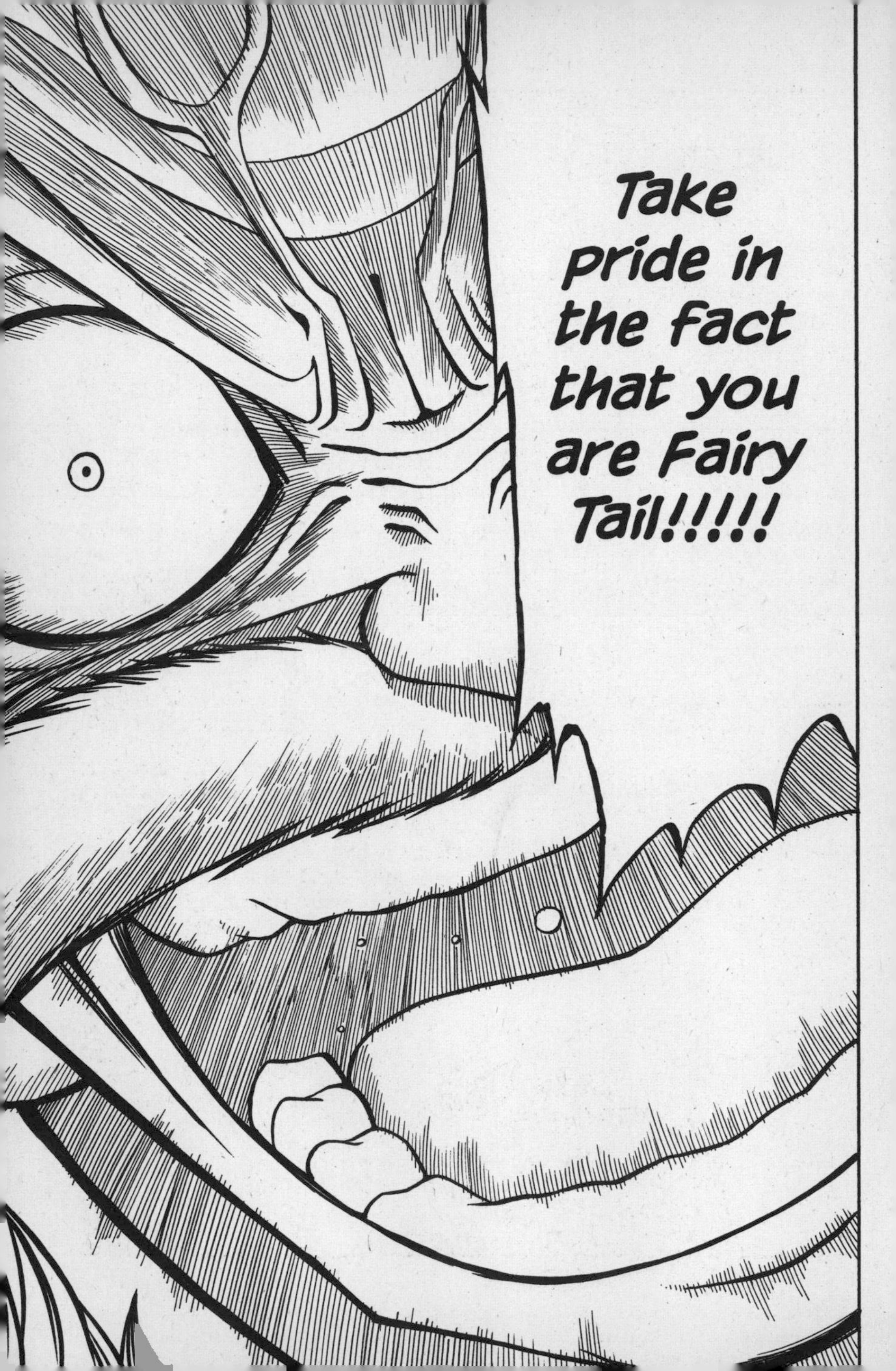
Take pride in the fact that you are Fairy Tail!!!!!

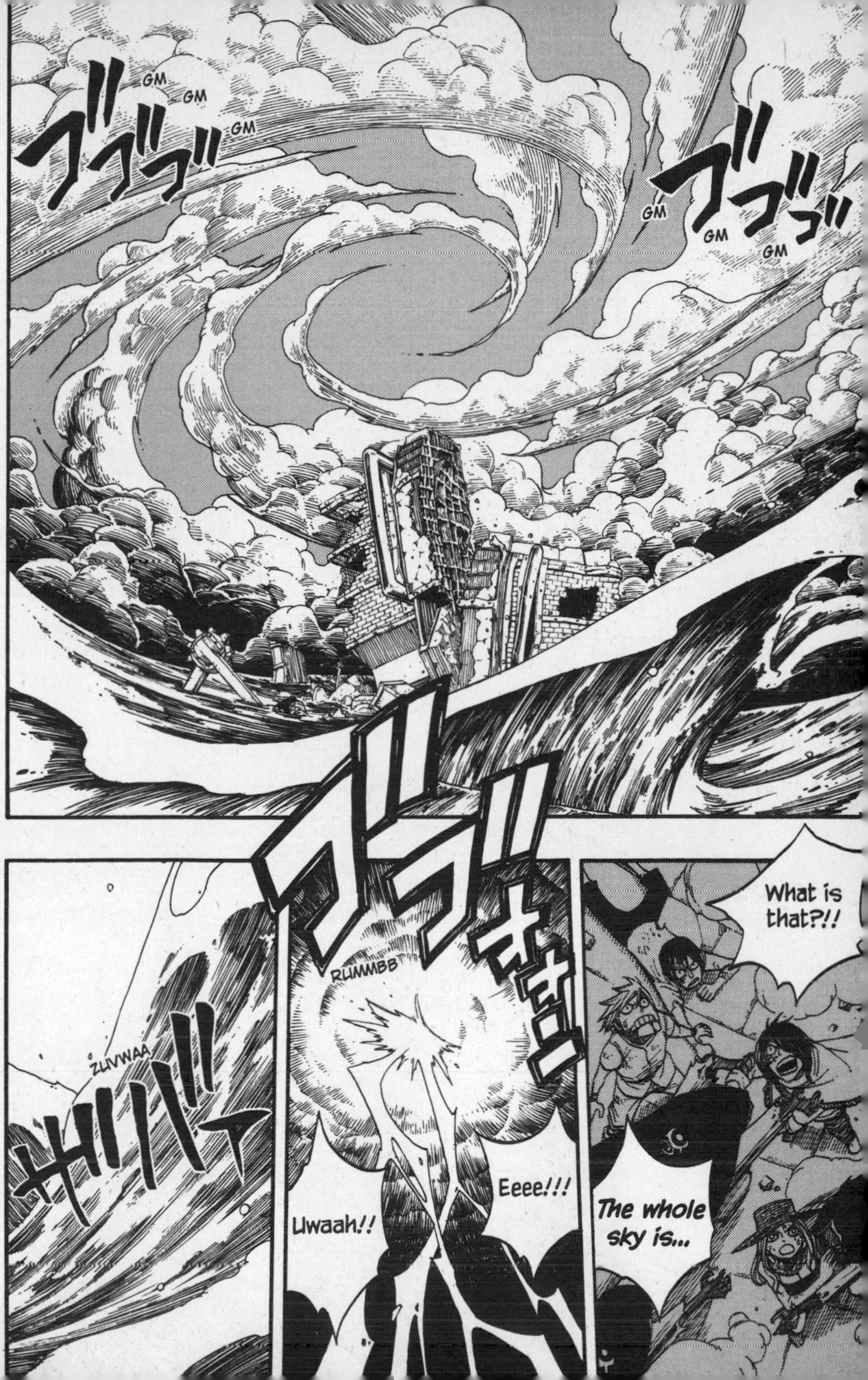
GM GM GM
GM GM GM
RUMMBB
What is that?!!
The whole sky is...
Eeee!!!
Uwaah!!
ZUVWAA

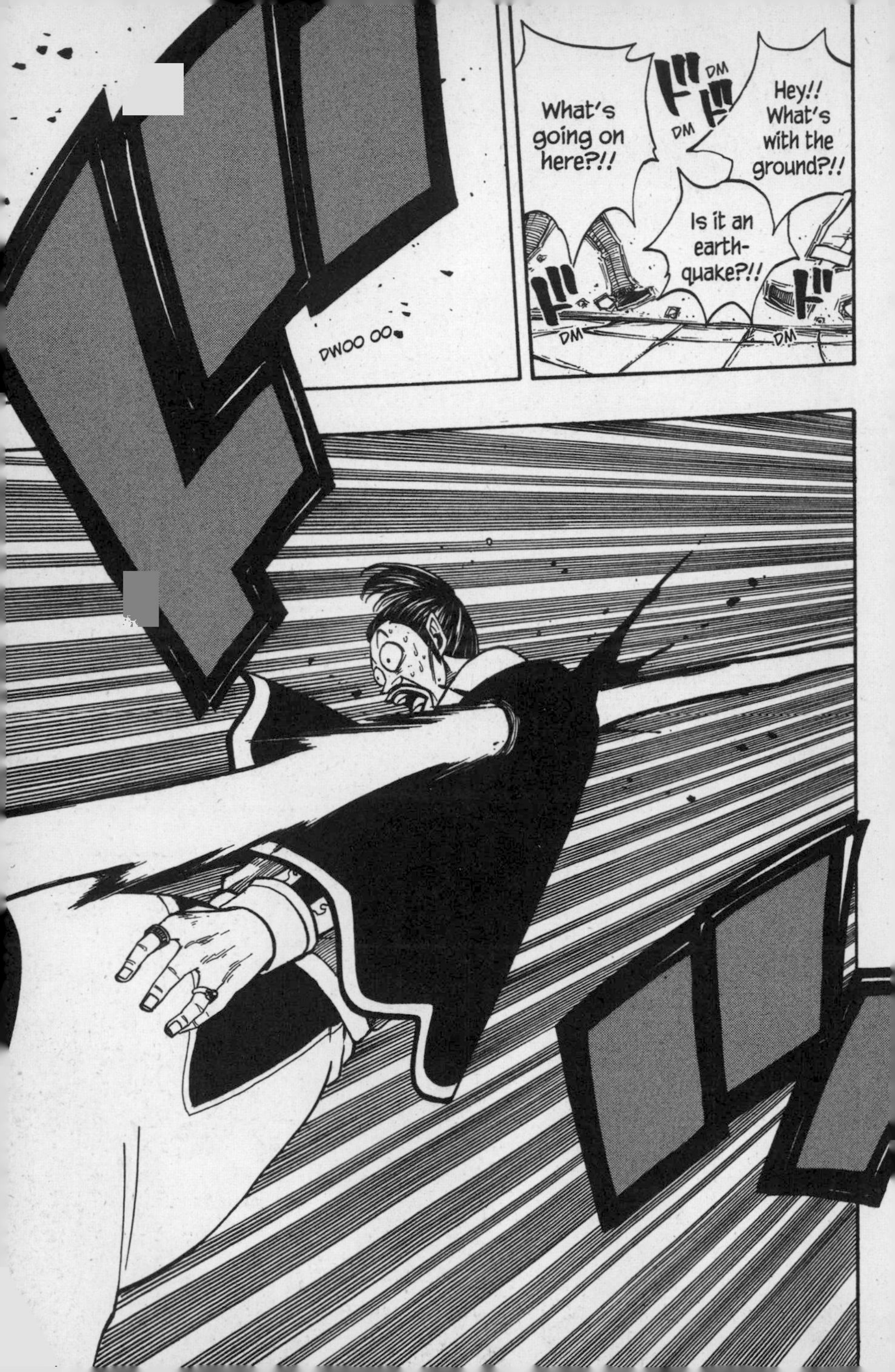
Hey!! What's with the ground?!!
DM
DM
What's going on here?!!
Is it an earth-quake?!!
DM
DM
DWOO OO

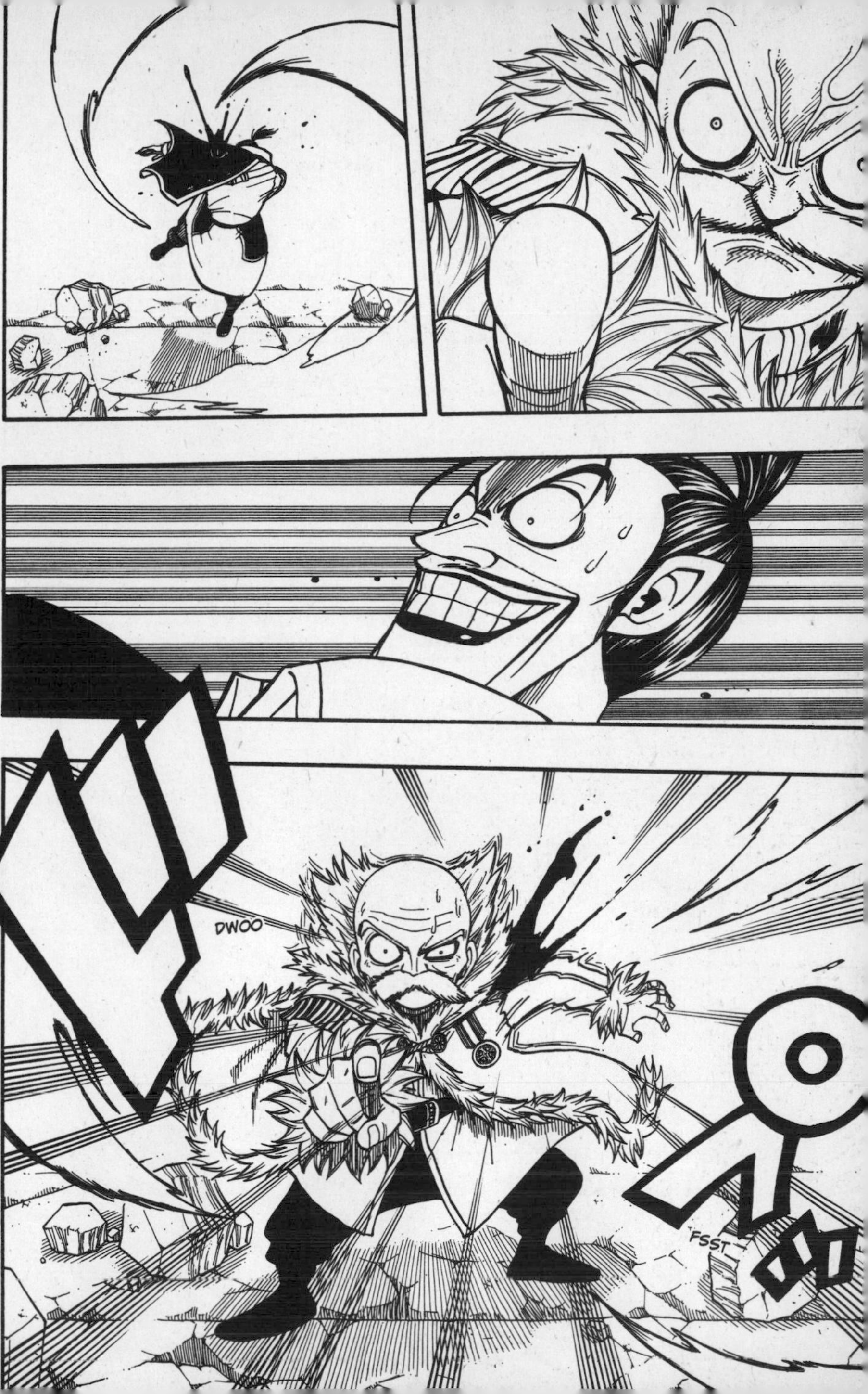
FSST
DWOO

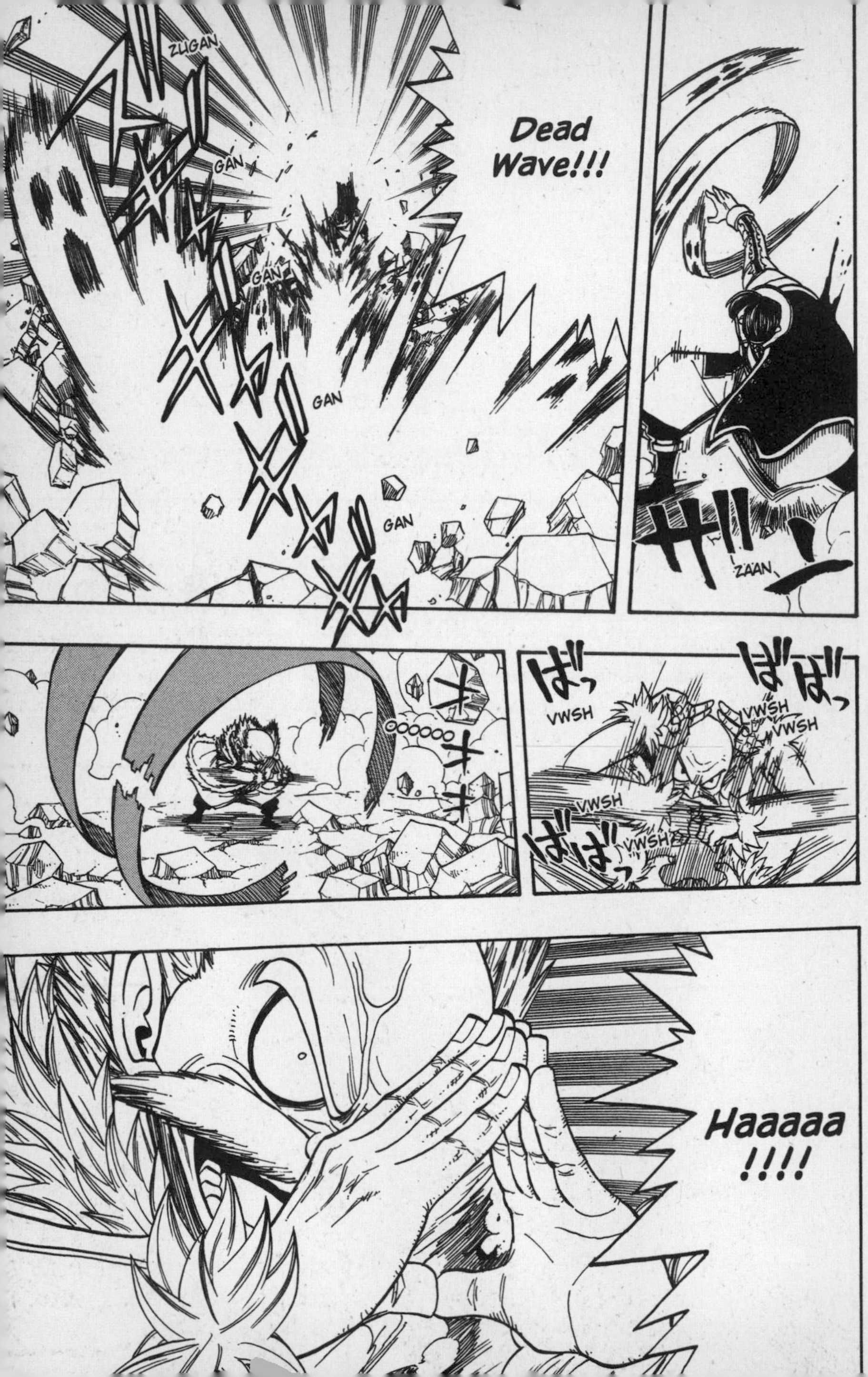
ZAAN
Dead Wave!!!
ZUGAN
GAN
GAN
GAN
GAN
VWSH
VWSH
VWSH
VWSH
VWSH
OOOOOOO
Haaaaa
!!!!

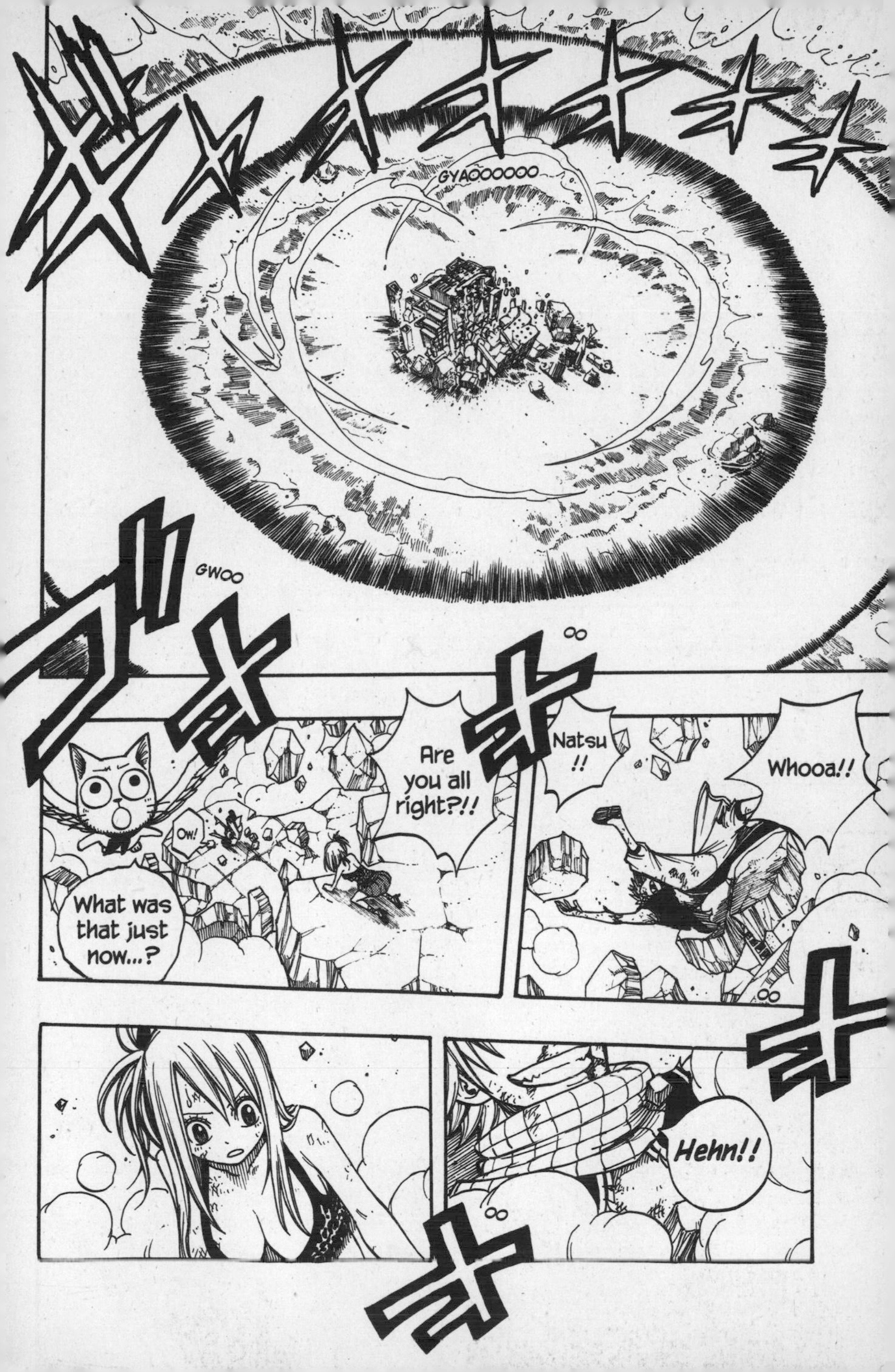
GYAOOOOOO
GWOO
Whooa!!
Natsu !!
Are you all right?!!
Ow!
What was that just now...?
Hehn!!

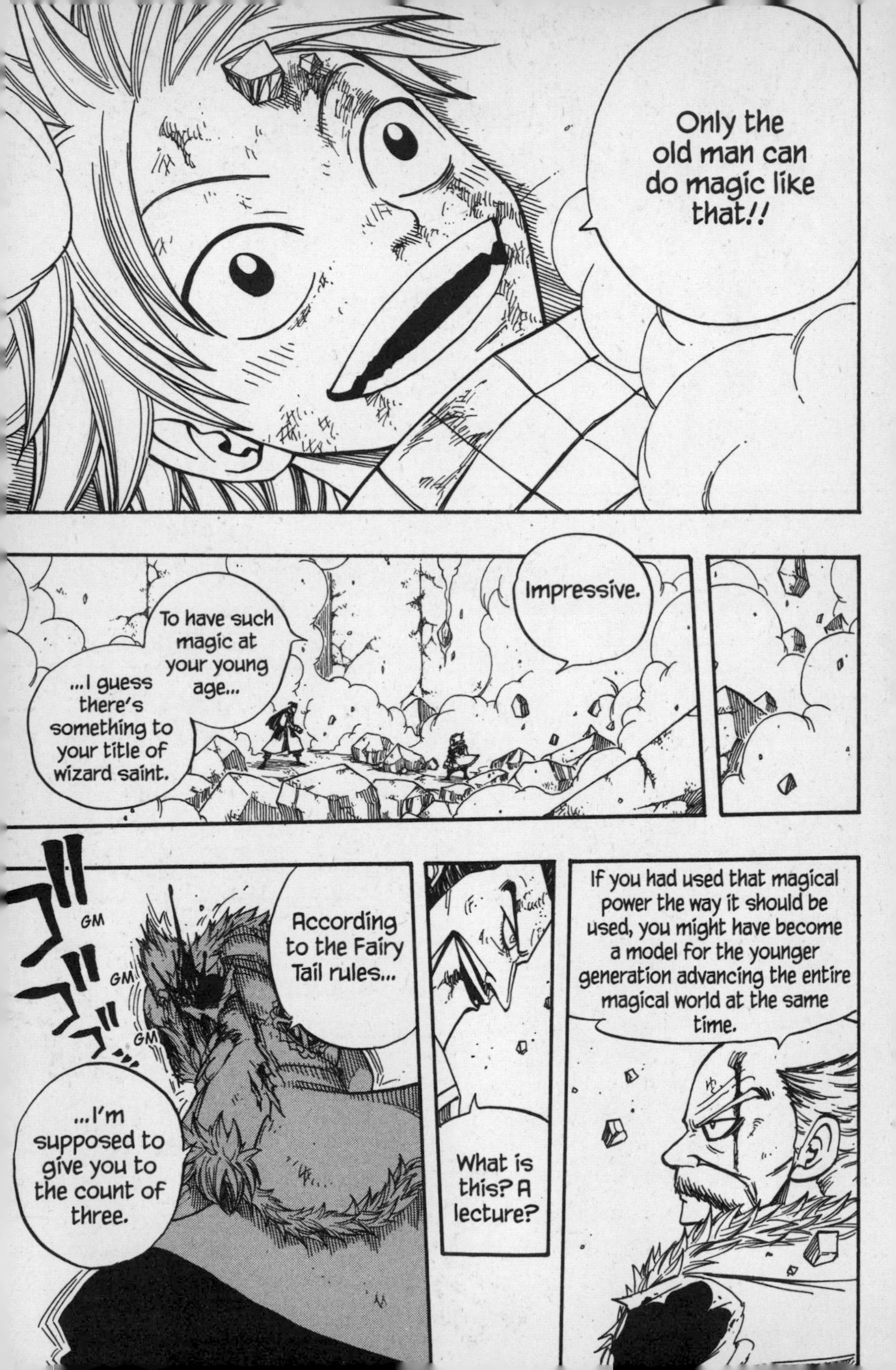

Only the old man can do magic like that!!
Impressive.
To have such magic at your young age...
...I guess there's something to your title of wizard saint.
If you had used that magical power the way it should be used, you might have become a model for the younger generation advancing the entire magical world at the same time.
What is this? A lecture?
According to the Fairy Tail rules...
GM
GM
GM
...I'm supposed to give you to the count of three.

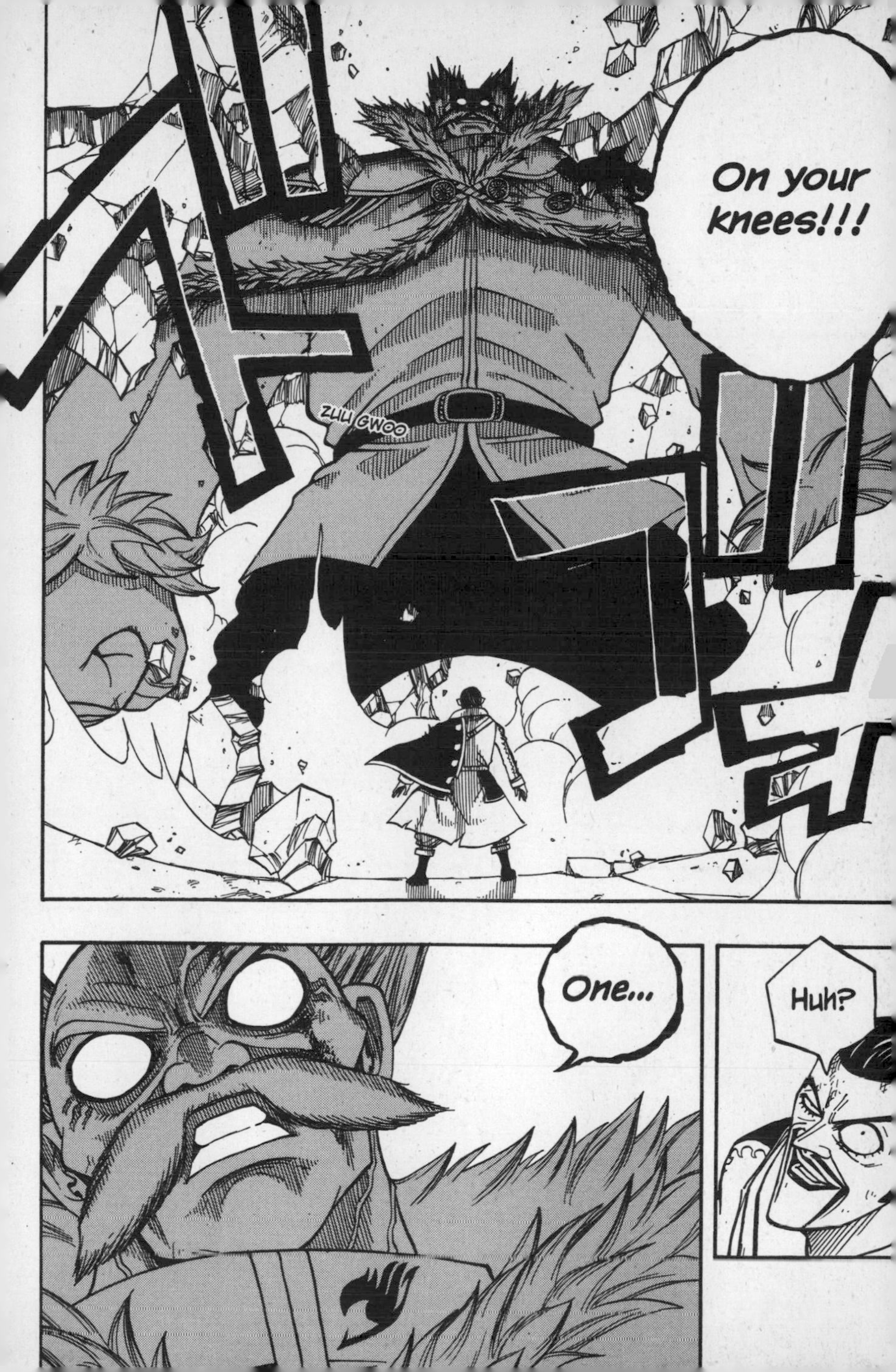
On your knees!!!
ZUU GWOO
Huh?
One...

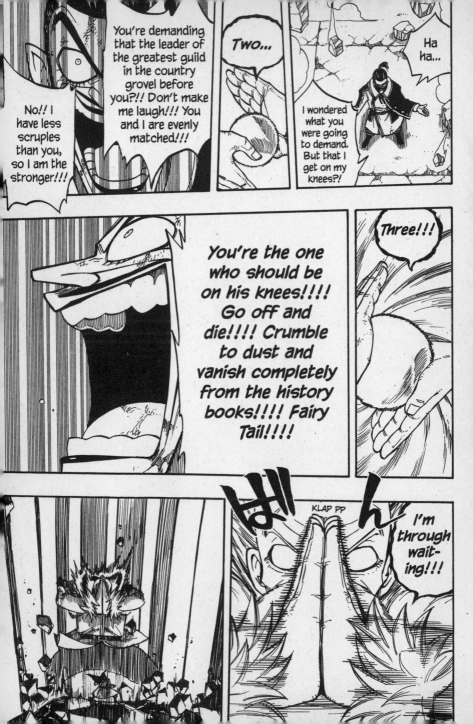

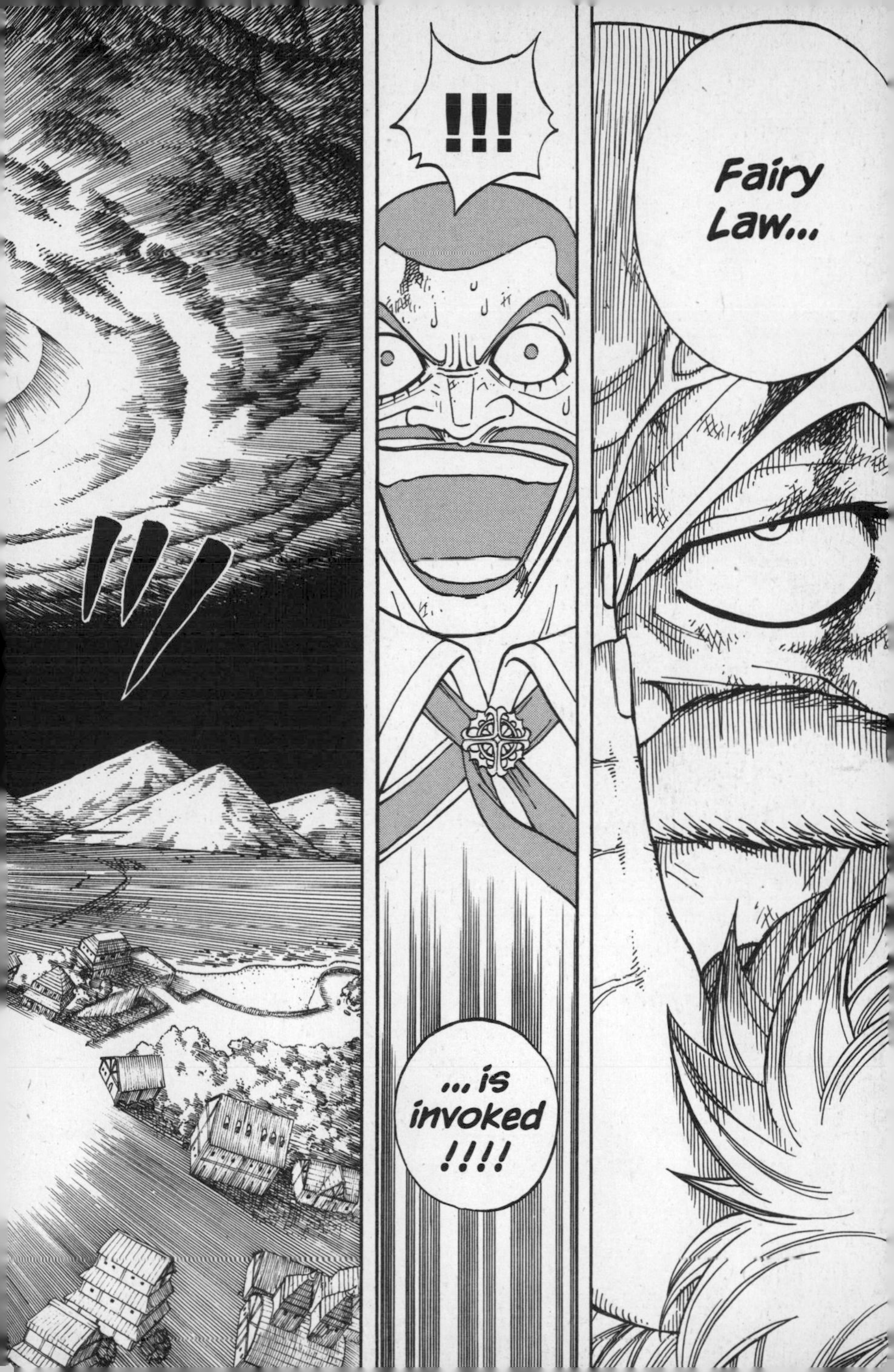
Fairy Law...
!!!
...is invoked !!!!

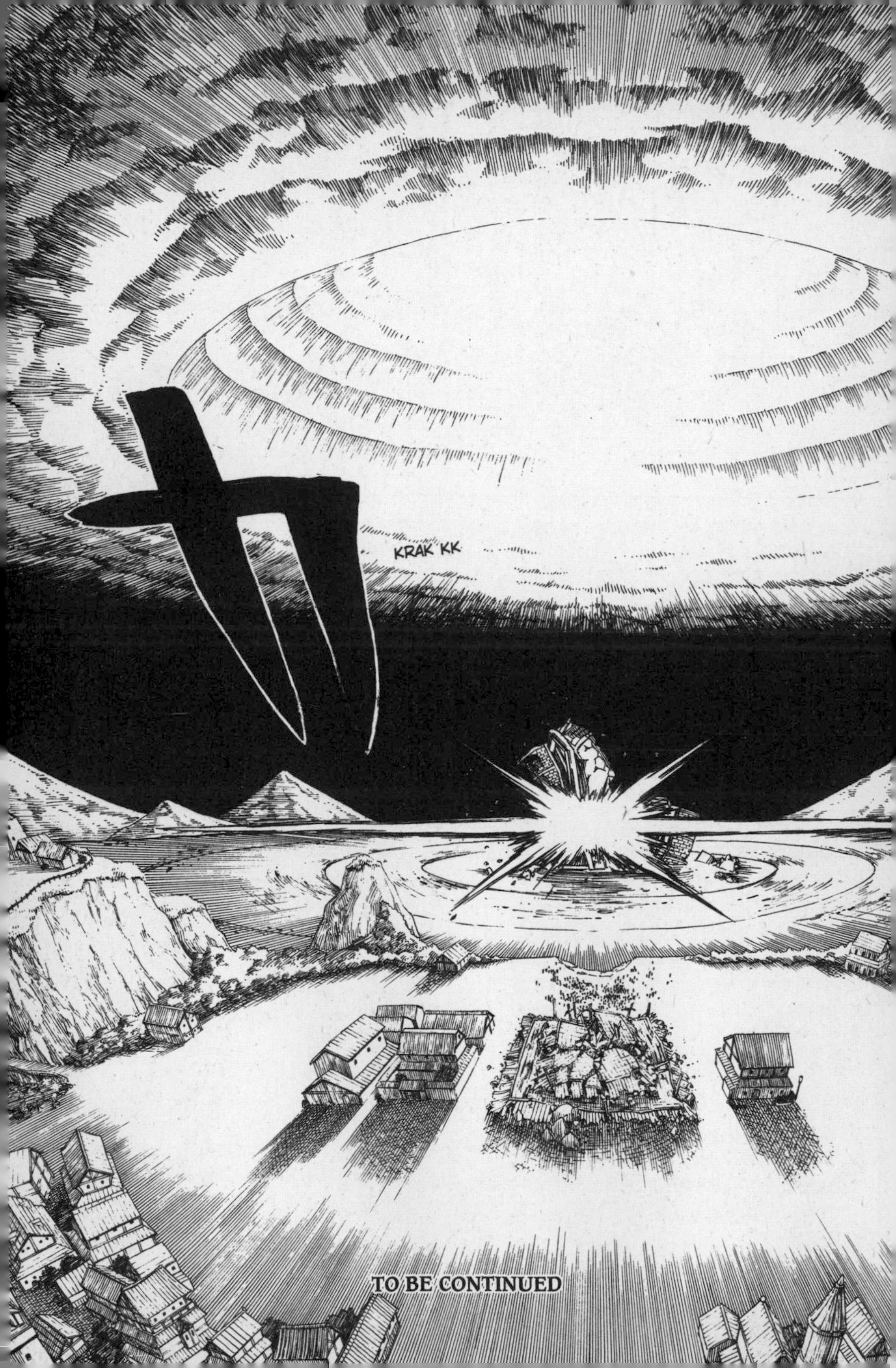
KRAK KK
TO BE CONTINUED

Continued from the left-hand page ⬇

Mira: Shall we read the next question?

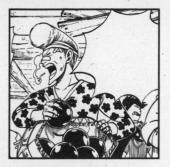

What's a lacrima?

Lucy: It's a magical crystal. A magic item that even normal humans can use.
Mira: That's right. I think for people living in the world these questions are coming from, you should picture a lighter in your minds. Even if you can't do magic, you can make fire with a lighter, right? In the same way, there are magical items in our world that have made their way into people's everyday lives.
Lucy: "Lacrima"...that means "a tear," right?
Mira: Yep! But if lacrima are distributed too widely, then our work as wizards might dry up! I think that's why the creator gave it such a masochistic-sounding name.

 : Is...that...right...?

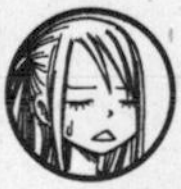

Mira: And now, our final question.
Lucy: All right!! Now we hit the sea!!
Mira: It's a question about the sea.
Lucy: Eh?

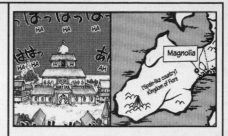

Magnolia
[Spain-like country] Kingdom of Fiore
HA HA HA
HA HA
AH
FAIRY TAIL

In some scenes, the Fairy Tail guild is shown right in front of a huge sea, but on the map, the guild seems to be pretty far inland...?

Mira: ....
Lucy: ....

 :Why don't we go swimming, Lucy?

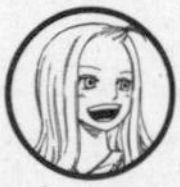

Lucy: Sure! ♥ But what is the meaning of this?!
Mira: You've got to give the reader credit. He's pretty sharp.
Lucy: I'm sure the author is putting on a face that says, "Oops!" right now.
Mira: Actually, that's a lake.
Lucy: Don't you think it might be a little too big for a lake?

 : Let's just say it's a lake and let it go at that, okay?

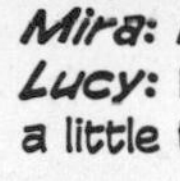

Lucy: I-I...guess...it's okay...
Mira: Fine! Now, let's go swimming.

 : With a lake that close, I don't have any idea why we came all the way to the seaside to swim, though.

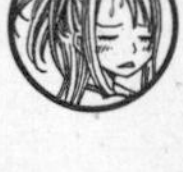

Special Request
Explain the Mysteries of Fairy Tail!

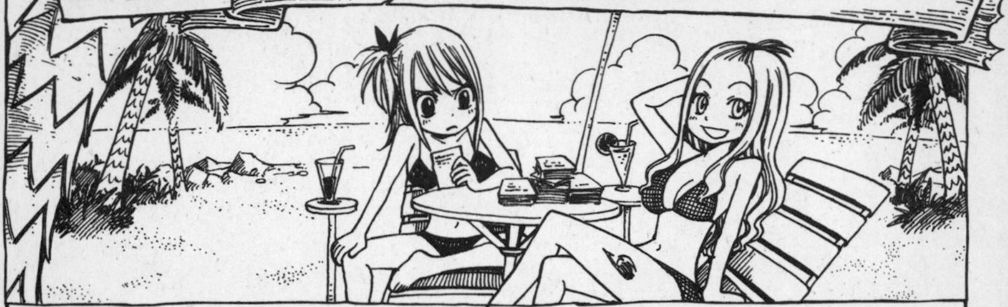

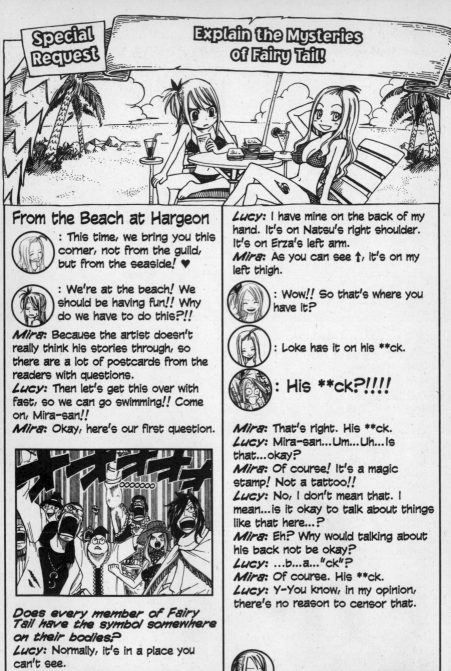

From the Beach at Hargeon

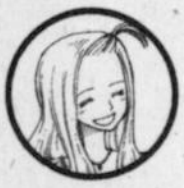 : This time, we bring you this corner, not from the guild, but from the seaside! ♥

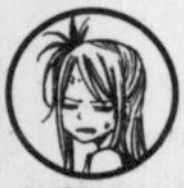 : We're at the beach! We should be having fun!! Why do we have to do this?!!

Mira: Because the artist doesn't really think his stories through, so there are a lot of postcards from the readers with questions.
Lucy: Then let's get this over with fast, so we can go swimming!! Come on, Mira-san!!
Mira: Okay, here's our first question.

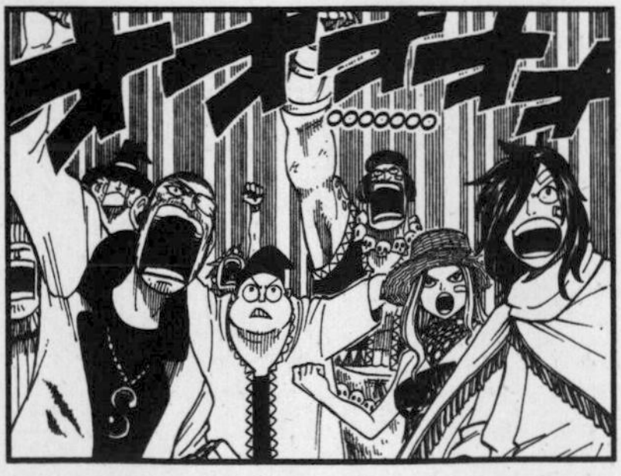
OOOOOOO

Does every member of Fairy Tail have the symbol somewhere on their bodies?
Lucy: Normally, it's in a place you can't see.
Mira: Yes, of course everybody does.
Lucy: I have mine on the back of my hand. It's on Natsu's right shoulder. It's on Erza's left arm.
Mira: As you can see ↑, it's on my left thigh.

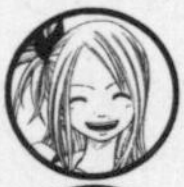 : Wow!! So that's where you have it?

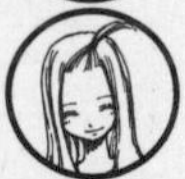 : Loke has it on his **ck.

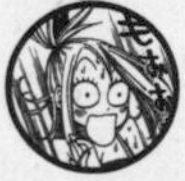 : His **ck?!!!!

Mira: That's right. His **ck.
Lucy: Mira-san...Um...Uh...Is that...okay?
Mira: Of course! It's a magic stamp! Not a tattoo!!
Lucy: No, I don't mean that. I mean...is it okay to talk about things like that here...?
Mira: Eh? Why would talking about his back not be okay?
Lucy: ...b...a..."ck"?
Mira: Of course. His **ck.
Lucy: Y-You know, in my opinion, there's no reason to censor that.

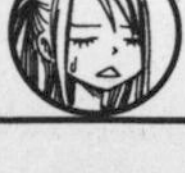

Continued on the right-hand page ↗

TAIL D'ART

The *Fairy Tail* Guild d'Art is an explosion of fan art! Please send in your black-and-white art on large postcard stock!! Those chosen to be published will get a signed mini poster!♪ Make sure you write your real name and address on the back of your postcard!

FAIRY TAIL

Kagawa Prefecture, Tôjûrô

▼Whoa! He's cool!! It looks like Gray's popularity isn't slipping in the slightest! (How does a guy that shy and retiring do it?)

FAIRY
TAIL
Natsu
Gray
Erza
Lucy

Akita Prefecture, Mikan-bako

▼I especially like Erza and the odd way that she shines.

Gray
Natsu
Lucy
Erza
FAIRY TAIL

Shizuoka Prefecture, Chawanmushi

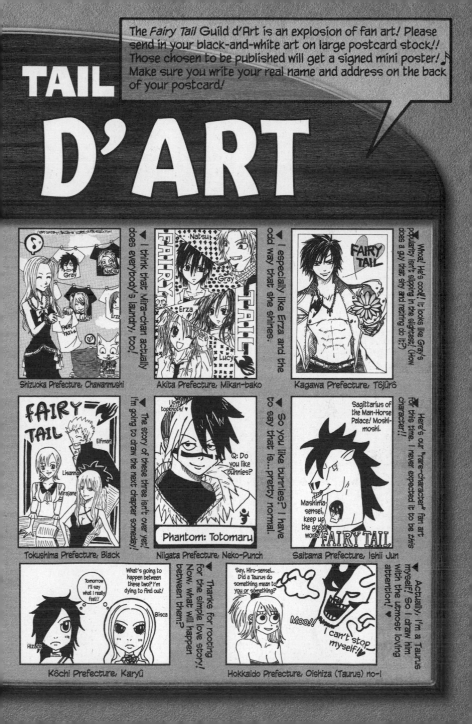

▼I think that Mira-chan actually does everybody's laundry, too!

Sagittarius of the Man-Horse Palace! Moshi-moshi.
Mashima-sensei, keep up the great work!
FAIRY TAIL

Saitama Prefecture, Ishii Jun

▼Here's our "rare-character" fan art for this time. I never expected it to be *this* character!!

I love topknots! ♥
Q: Do you like bunnies?
Phantom: Totomaru

Niigata Prefecture, Neko-Punch

▼So you like bunnies? I have to say that is...pretty normal.

FAIRY TAIL
Elfman
Lisanna
Mirajane

Tokushima Prefecture, Black

▼The story of these three isn't over yet! I'm going to draw the next chapter someday!

Say, Hiro-sensei... Did a Taurus do something mean to you or something?
Moo!!
I can't stop myself!♥

Hokkaido Prefecture, Oishiza (Taurus) no-i

▼Actually, I'm a Taurus myself! So I draw him with the utmost loving attention! ♥

What's going to happen between these two? I'm dying to find out!
Tomorrow I'll say what I really feel!!
Bisca
Alzack

Kôchi Prefecture, Karyû

▼Thanks for rooting for the simple love story! Now, what will happen between them?

Send to DEL REY MANGA, Hiro Mashima, 1745 Broadway, New York, NY 10019, delreymanga@randomhouse.com*

*Del Rey Manga will make every effort to send your letters to Mashima, but cannot guarantee a response.

FAIRY GUILD

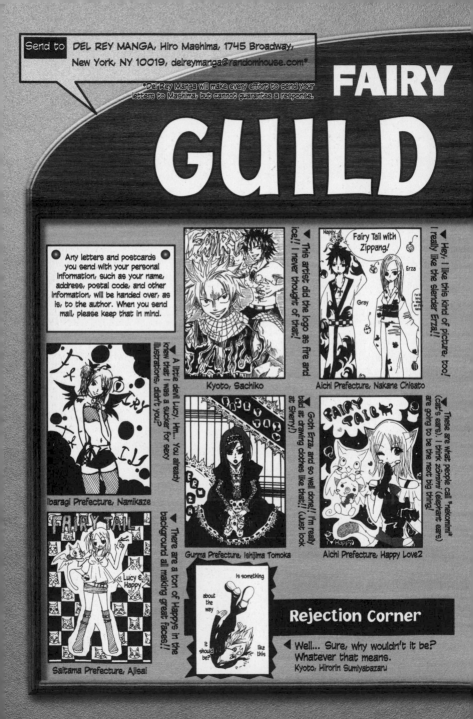

Any letters and postcards you send with your personal information, such as your name, address, postal code, and other information, will be handed over, as is, to the author. When you send mail, please keep that in mind.

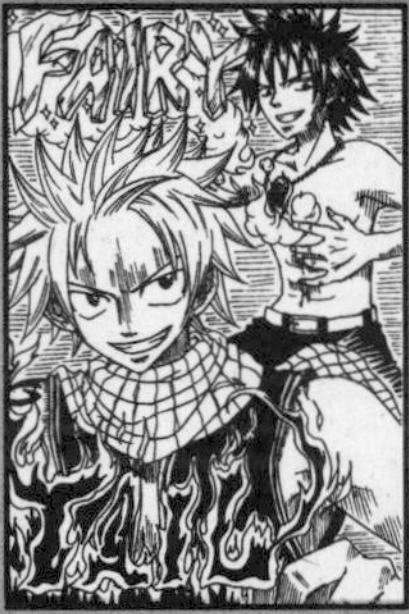
FAIRY

Kyoto, Sachiko

▼ This artist did the logo as fire and ice!! I never thought of that!

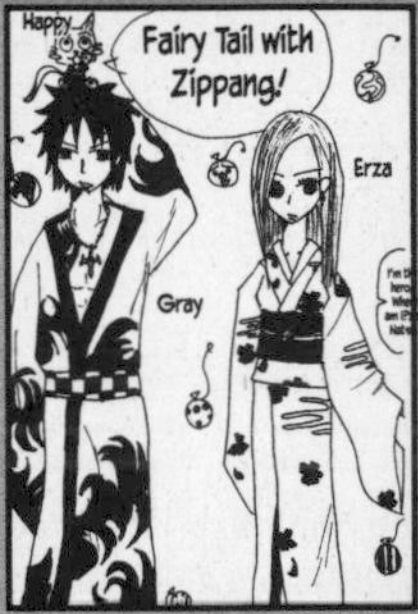
Happy
Fairy Tail with Zippang!
Erza
Gray

Aichi Prefecture, Nakane Chisato

▼ Hey, I like this kind of picture, too! I really like the slender Erza!!

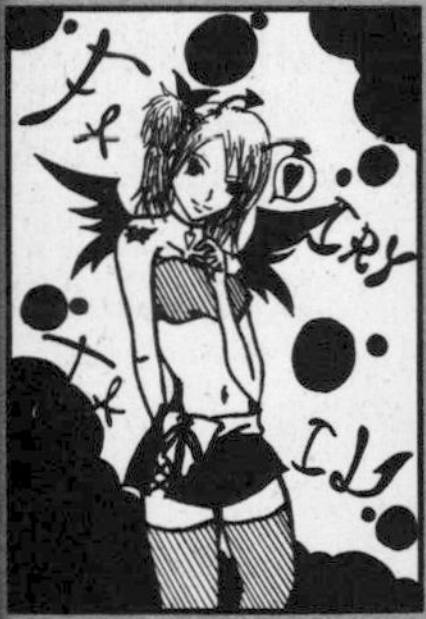

Ibaragi Prefecture, Namikaze

▼ A little devil Lucy. Hm... You already knew that I was a sucker for sexy illustrations, didn't you!?

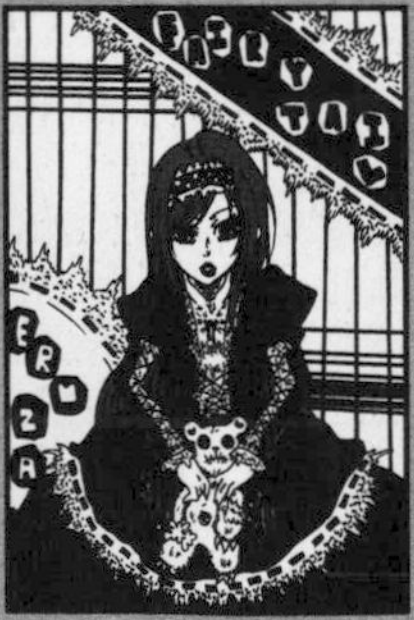

Gunma Prefecture, Ishijima Tomoka

▼ Goth Erza, and so well done!! I'm really bad at drawing clothes like that!! (Just look at Sherry!)

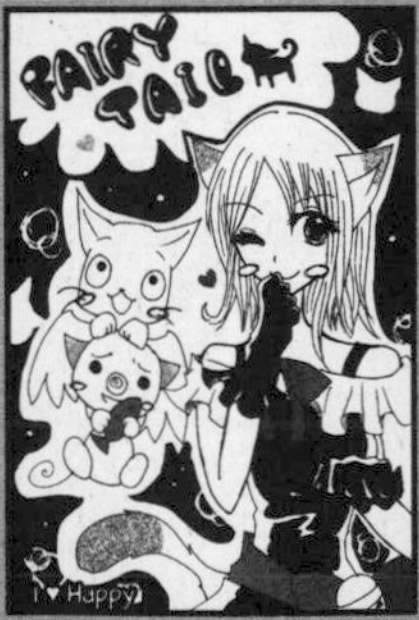
FAIRY TAIL
I ♥ Happy

Aichi Prefecture, Happy Love2

▼ These are what people call "nekomimi" (cat's ears). I think *zōmimi* (elephant ears) are going to be the next big thing!

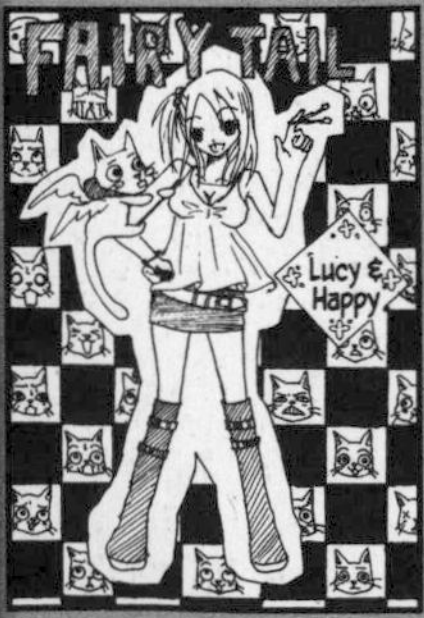
FAIRY TAIL
Lucy & Happy

Saitama Prefecture, Ajisai

▼ There are a ton of Happys in the background all making great faces!!

Rejection Corner

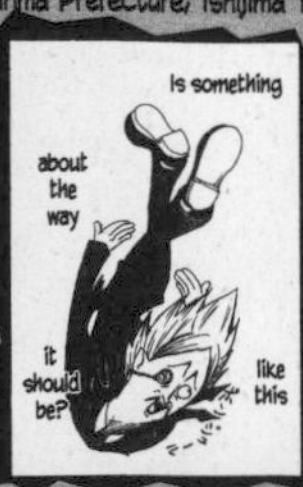
Is something
about the way
it should be?
like this

◀ Well... Sure, why wouldn't it be? Whatever that means.

Kyoto, Hirorin Sumiyabazaru

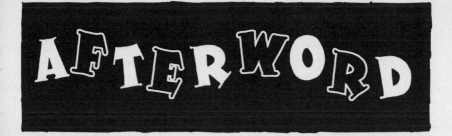

AFTERWORD

Once I set on the idea of doing a dragon slayer, I knew that other dragon slayers would show up. And after a long wait, the one who showed up was Gajeel-kun (at work, we all call him Gajeel-kun (♠♠)). As Natsu's rival, he was extremely scary right from the start. Actually, there was a fight scene planned between Gajeel-kun on one side and Loke (guy with glasses) and Reedus (big guy) on the other, but with the way the episode shaped up, it had to be cut. Still, instead we got a pretty hot fight between him and Natsu, so we'll call it a good thing. Right at the very beginning, some characters called the dragon-slaying magic "Dragon Slayer," but in point of fact, dragon slayers are the people who use dragon-slaying magic. Sorry for all the confusion. This wasn't a mistake. It's just such an old form of magic that the characters don't understand the term anymore. As time went on, people had trouble differentiating between the magic and the users of that magic. But I didn't get that across to the readers very well, huh?(♠)

By the way, there are even more dragon slayers in this world. They may appear over the course of the story, but then again, they may not. The dragon, Igneel, passed on the techniques for slaying dragons and then disappeared. Hmm…A weird story. But I have my reasons for it, and those reasons may become key information later on. But then again, they may not. Hmm…I sort of forgot what I was trying to say, so I'm just going to end this here.

About the Creator

HIRO MASHIMA was born May 3, 1977, in the Nagano prefecture. His series *Rave Master* has made him one of the most popular manga artists in America. *Fairy Tail*, currently being serialized in *Weekly Shonen Magazine*, is his latest creation.

Translation Notes

Japanese is a tricky language for most Westerners, and translation is often more art than science. For your edification and reading pleasure, here are notes on some of the places where we could have gone in a different direction in our translation of the work, or where a Japanese cultural reference is used.

General Notes:
Wizard

In the original Japanese version of *Fairy Tail*, you'll find panels in which the English word "wizard" is part of the original illustration. So this translation has taken that as its inspiration and translated the word *madôshi* as "wizard." But *madôshi*'s meaning is similar to certain Japanese words that have been borrowed by the English language, such as judo (the soft way) and kendo (the way of the sword). *Madô* is the way of magic, and *madôshi* are those who follow the way of magic. So although the word "wizard" is used in the original dialogue, a Japanese reader would be likely to think not of traditional Western wizards such as Merlin or Gandalf, but of martial artists.

Names

Hiro Mashima has graciously agreed to provide official English spellings for just about all of the characters in *Fairy Tail*. Because this version of *Fairy Tail* is the first publication of most of these spellings, there will inevitably be differences between these spellings and some of the fan interpretations that may have spread throughout the Web or in other fan circles. Rest assured that the spellings contained in this book are the spellings that Mashima-sensei wanted for *Fairy Tail*.

Fair-Weather Charm, page 3

The Japanese have a popular charm that is supposed to avert rain: the *teru-teru bôzu*, where *teru* means "to shine" as in sunshine, and *bôzu* means a Buddhist priest or monk. To make one, a white tissue, napkin, or cloth is wrapped around a ball and tied off at the "neck" making a head with the rest of the cloth or paper trailing off as robes. Usually a smiley face is drawn on it (see page 15 for a slightly clumsy example). It is called a "*bôzu*" because it has a round, bald head much like Buddhist monks or priests do. Once the charm is made, it is usually hung under the roof's rafters as a charm to stop the rain. If it is hung upside down, it is supposed to encourage the rain to fall.

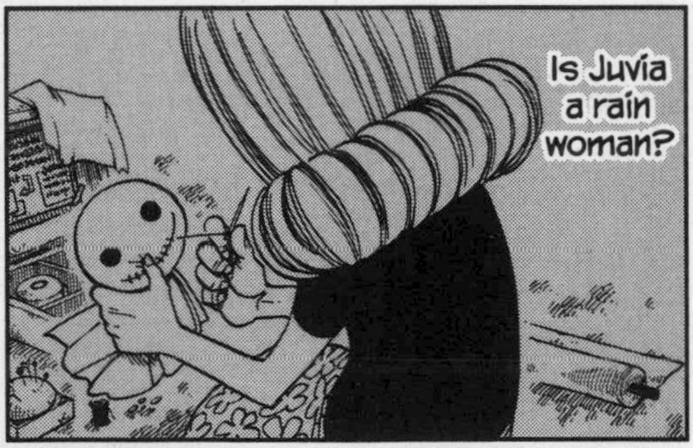
Is Juvia a rain woman?

Rain Woman, page 15

Rain Women (*Ame onna* in Japanese) are a recurrent theme in Japanese folklore, and later, much used in manga and anime. In ancient Japan's agrarian culture, the rain women were called upon to help rain fall on the crops, and some worshipped *Ame onna* as deities. In more recent depictions they tend to be tragic figures who bring nonstop rain wherever they go, shunned and ostracized for something they cannot control.

Nattô, page 63

There are foods in nearly every culture that are generally loved by those within the culture and abhorred by almost anyone coming to the culture from the outside. Hawaii has *poi,* the Inuit have *muqtuq* blubber, and the Japanese have *nattô. Nattô* is a strong-smelling fermented soybean dish in which beans are connected by a viscous, stringy, slimy fluid. The dish is very nutritious, containing *nattokinase,* a fibrinolytic enzyme that is said to prevent clotting in the arteries. However, despite the benefits, most non-Japanese can't palate it. Of course, there are some Western lovers of *nattô,* and a large number of Japanese who do not eat it—in other words, there are always exceptions—but the rule is, Japanese love *nattô* and foreigners can't stand the stuff.

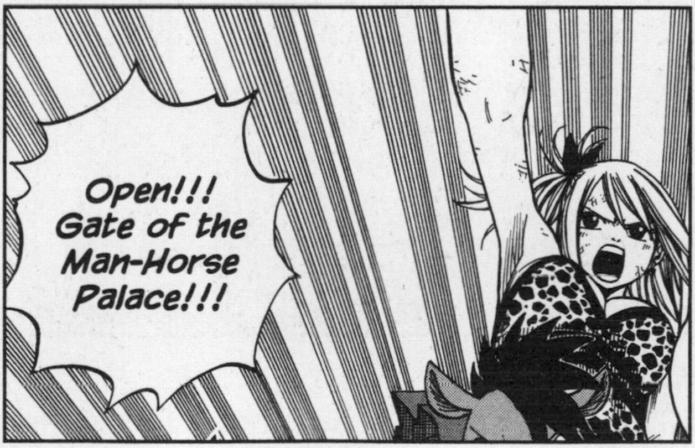
Open!!! Gate of the Man-Horse Palace!!!

Man-Horse Palace, page 117

Sagittarius is Latin for "Archer," and that is how it is referred to in astrology, but in Greek mythology, Sagittarius is Chiron, the Centaur. Chiron was unlike the other, bestial centaurs, and instead was a wise and learned hunter and healer. In this version, Mashima-sensei makes a joke of the man-horse by presenting it in an unusual way. However, if I had translated the palace as the "Centaur Palace," Mashima's version of the man-horse wouldn't follow logically as it does with the more literal translation of "Man-Horse Palace."

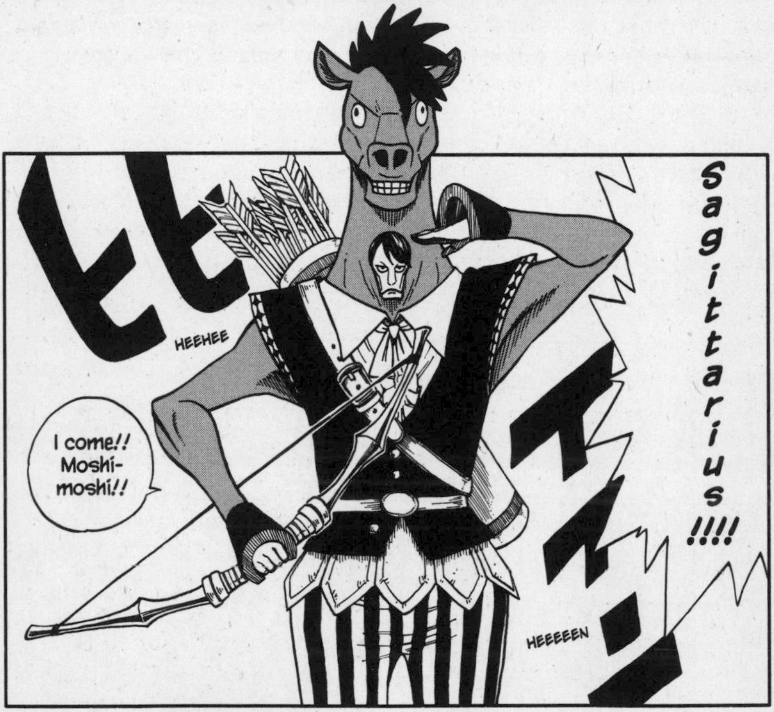
Sagittarius!!!!
HEEHEE
I come!! Moshi-moshi!!
HEEEEEN

Moshi-moshi, page 117

At first, I thought Sagittarius's "moshi-moshi," was a Japanese horse sound, but I could find no incidents of horses using that sound in my research. (If you know of examples, let me know!) I just have to assume that it is a cute sentence-ending sound much like Cancer's "-ebi" at the end of his sentences (see the note in volume 2). By the way, the phrase, "moshi-moshi" is generally used as the English "hello" is used when answering the phone or when tentatively trying to get someone's attention. That doesn't seem to be Sagittarius's meaning when using the phrase here, though.

Topknots, page 188

Most samurai-movie fans recognize the classic samurai hairstyle of a shaved forehead and a topknot (an oiled ponytail that comes forward over the top of the head). It is called in Japanese a *chonmage*. Totomaru doesn't have the samurai style of topknot, but he does have a rather punk-style topknot.

Preview of Volume 9

We're pleased to present you with a preview from volume 9. Please
check our website (www.delreymanga.com) to see when this volume will
be available in English. For now you'll have to make do with Japanese!

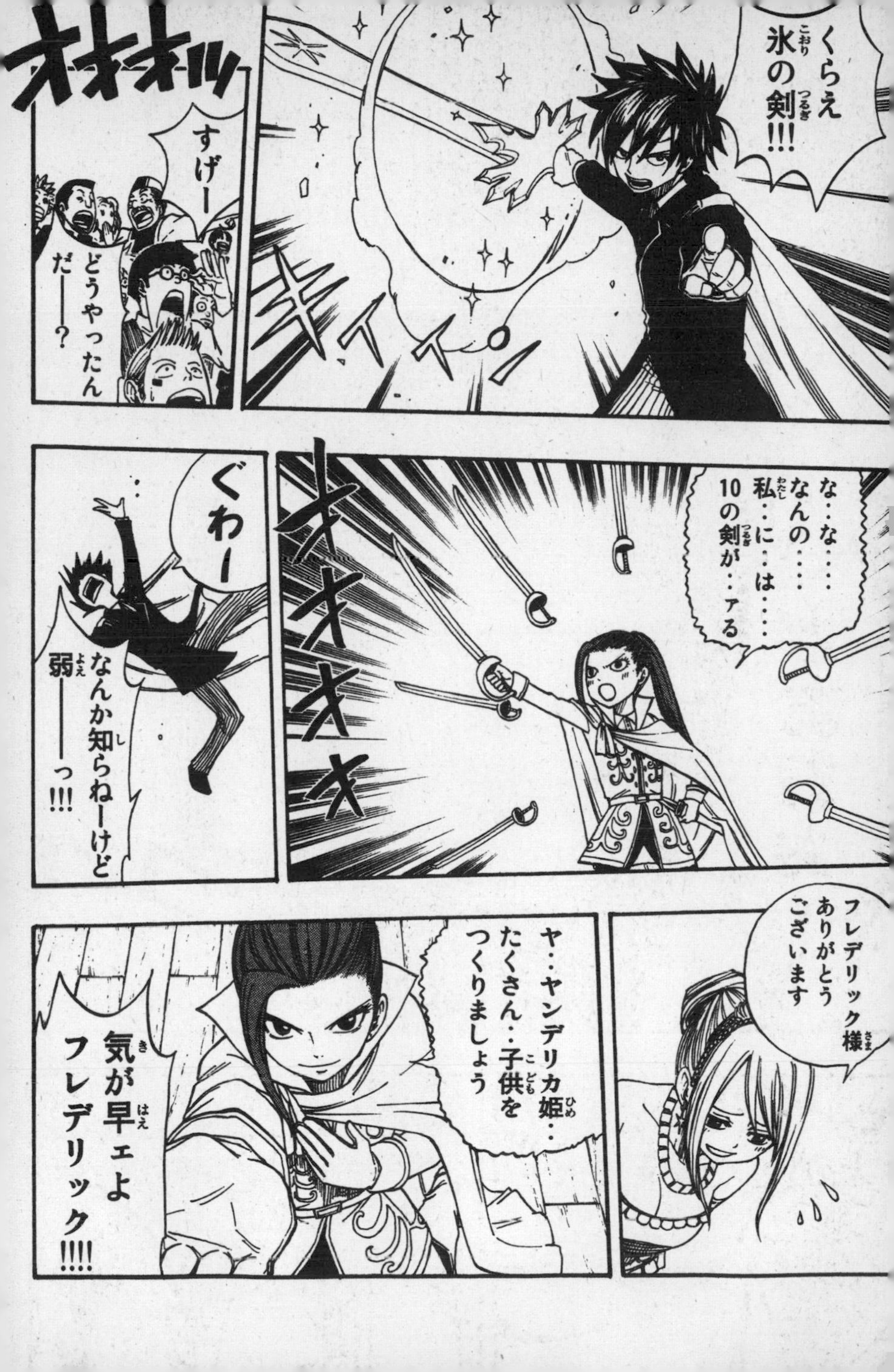

くらえ氷の剣!!!
キイイィン
オオオオッ
すげー
どうやったんだ――?
な…な…… なんの…… 私…に…は…… 10の剣が…ァる
オオオオオ
ぐわー
なんか知らねーけど弱――っ!!!
フレデリック様ありがとうございます
ヤ…ヤンデリカ姫… たくさん…子供を つくりましょう
気が早ェよフレデリック!!!!

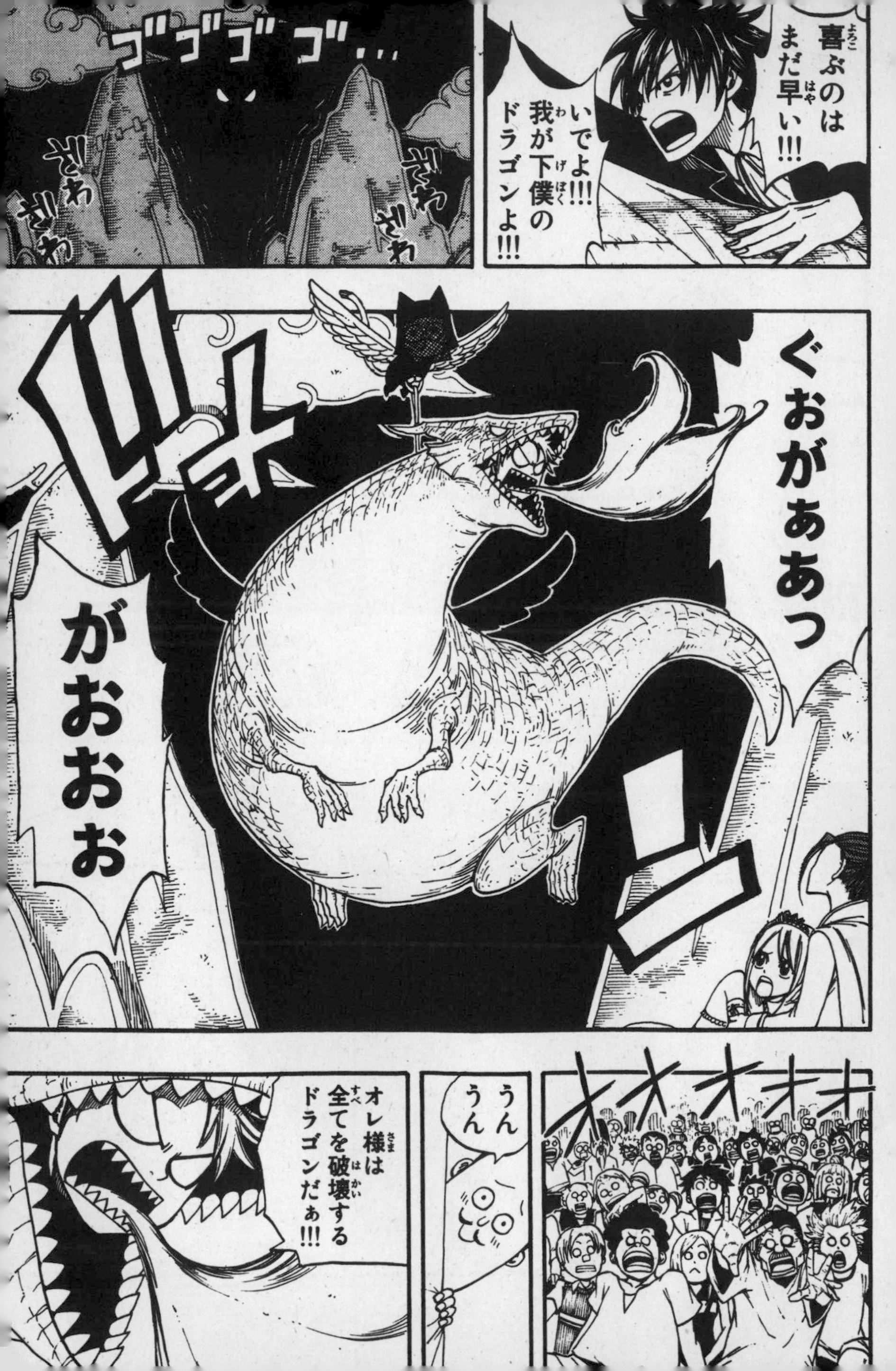
喜ぶのはまだ早い!!!
いでよ!!! 我が下僕のドラゴンよ!!!
ゴゴゴゴ…
ざわざわ
ざわざわ
ぐおがああっ
がおおお
オオオオ
うんうん
オレ様は全てを破壊するドラゴンだぁ!!!

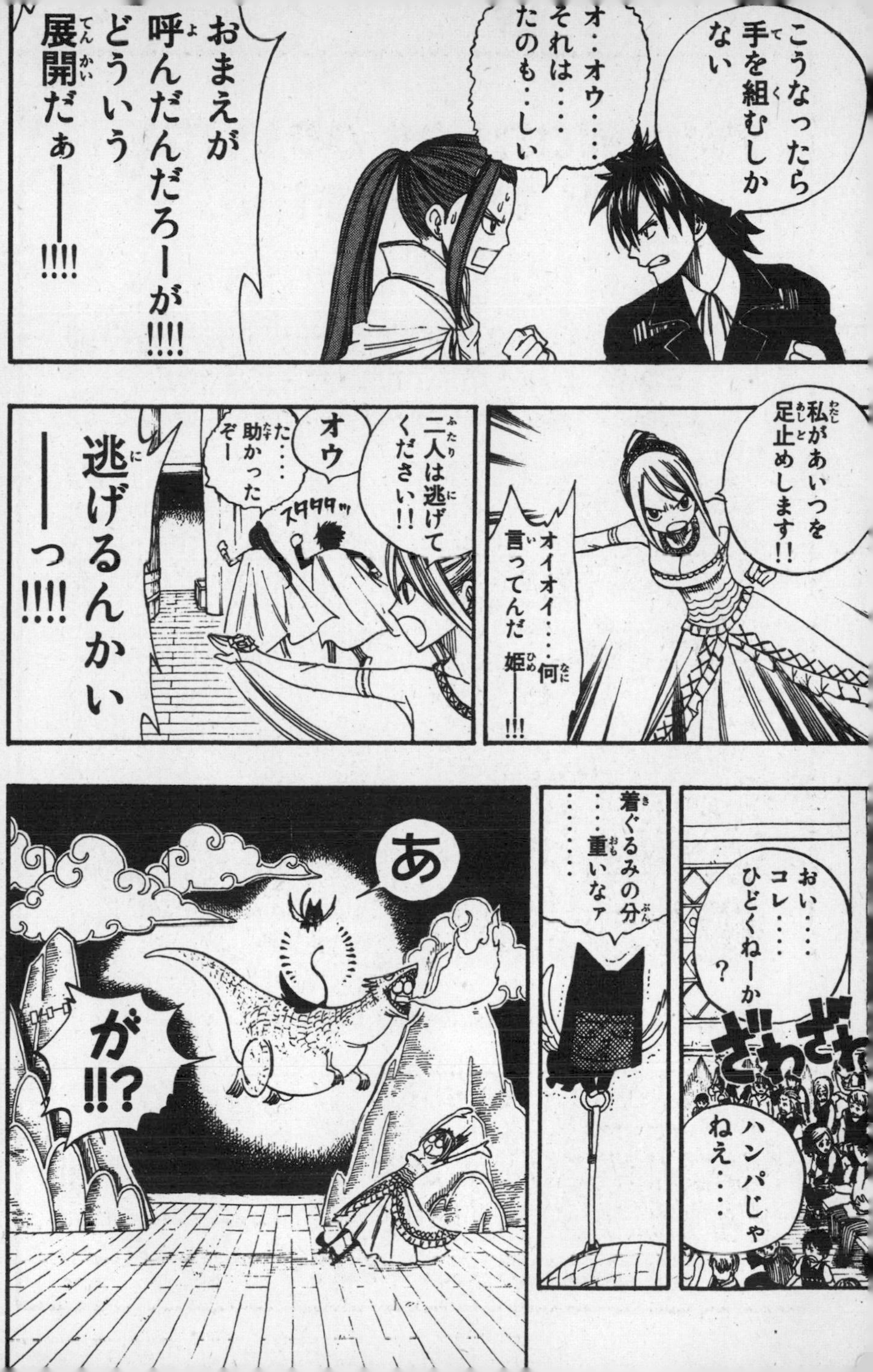
こうなったら手を組むしかない
オ…オウ……それは……たのも…しい
おまえが呼んだんだろーが!!!!
どういう展開だぁ―――!!!!
私があいつを足止めします!!
オイオイ……何言ってんだ姫―――!!!
二人は逃げてください!!
オウ
た……助かったぞー
スタタタッ
逃げるんかい―――っ!!!!
おい……コレ……ひどくねーか?
ざわざわ
ハンパじゃねえ……
着ぐるみの分……重いなァ……
あ
が!!?

Contents

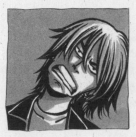

It happened so fast! My original goal of ten volumes is already in sight. Before I started, I thought that my previous work was so long (thirty-five volumes) that this time, I'd limit it to only about ten volumes. But it turned out to be much more fun drawing *FT* than I originally thought it would be. It looks like I can make this story a lot longer than planned! So root for me as I continue on...at least to volume 11!!

—Hiro Mashima

Honorifics Explained

Throughout the Del Rey Manga books, you will find Japanese honorifics left intact in the translations. For those not familiar with how the Japanese use honorifics and, more important, how they differ from American honorifics, we present this brief overview.

Politeness has always been a critical facet of Japanese culture. Ever since the feudal era, when Japan was a highly stratified society, use of honorifics—which can be defined as polite speech that indicates relationship or status—has played an essential role in the Japanese language. When addressing someone in Japanese, an honorific usually takes the form of a suffix attached to one's name (example: "Asuna-san"), is used as a title at the end of one's name, or appears in place of the name itself (example: "Negi-sensei," or simply "Sensei").

Honorifics can be expressions of respect or endearment. In the context of manga and anime, honorifics give insight into the nature of the relationship between characters. Many English translations leave out these important honorifics and therefore distort the feel of the original Japanese. Because Japanese honorifics contain nuances that English honorifics lack, it is our policy at Del Rey not to translate them. Here, instead, is a guide to some of the honorifics you may encounter in Del Rey Manga.

-**san:**   This is the most common honorific and is equivalent to Mr., Miss, Ms., or Mrs. It is the all-purpose honorific and can be used in any situation where politeness is required.

-**sama:**   This is one level higher than "-san" and is used to confer great respect.

-**dono:**   This comes from the word "tono," which means "lord." It is an even higher level than "-sama" and confers utmost respect.

-kun: This suffix is used at the end of boys' names to express familiarity or endearment. It is also sometimes used by men among friends, or when addressing someone younger or of a lower station.

-chan: This is used to express endearment, mostly toward girls. It is also used for little boys, pets, and even between lovers. It gives a sense of childish cuteness.

Bozu: This is an informal way to refer to a boy, similar to the English terms "kid" and "squirt."

**Sempai/
Senpai:** This title suggests that the addressee is one's senior in a group or organization. It is most often used in a school setting, where underclassmen refer to their upperclassmen as "sempai." It can also be used in the workplace, such as when a newer employee addresses an employee who has seniority in the company.

Kohai: This is the opposite of "sempai" and is used toward underclassmen in school or newcomers in the workplace. It connotes that the addressee is of a lower station.

Sensei: Literally meaning "one who has come before," this title is used for teachers, doctors, or masters of any profession or art.

-[blank]: This is usually forgotten in these lists, but it is perhaps the most significant difference between Japanese and English. The lack of honorific means that the speaker has permission to address the person in a very intimate way. Usually, only family, spouses, or very close friends have this kind of permission. Known as *yobisute*, it can be gratifying when someone who has earned the intimacy starts to call one by one's name without an honorific. But when that intimacy hasn't been earned, it can be very insulting.

PAL

8

Hiro Mashima

Translated and adapted by William Flanagan
Lettered by North Market Street Graphics

Ballantine Books · New York

Fairy Tail volume 8 is a work of fiction. Na
and incidents are the products of the authors imagination or
are used fictitiously. Any resemblance to actual events, locales, or
persons, living or dead, is entirely coincidental.

A Del Rey Manga/Kodansha Trade Paperback Original

Published in the United States by Del Rey, an imprint of The Random House Publishing Group, a division of Random House, Inc., New York.

DEL REY is a registered trademark and the Del Rey colophon is a trademark of Random House, Inc.

Publication rights arranged through Kodansha Ltd.

First published in Japan in 2008 by Kodansha Ltd., Tokyo

ISBN 978-0-345-51040-2

Printed in the United States of America

www.delreymanga.com

9 8 7 6 5 4 3 2 1

Translator/Adapter: William Flanagan
Lettering: North Market Street Graphics